Fourth Edition

The Career Tool Kit

Skills for Success

Carol Carter

Gary Izumo

PEARSON

Boston • Columbus • Indianapolis • New York • San Francisco • Upper Saddle River
Amsterdam • Cape Town • Dubai • London • Madrid • Milan • Munich • Paris • Montréal • Toronto
Delhi • Mexico City • São Paulo • Sydney • Hong Kong • Seoul • Singapore • Taipei • Tokyo

Editor-in-Chief: Jodi McPherson

Acquisitions Editor: Katie Mahan

Editorial Assistant: Erin Carreiro

Senior Managing Editor: Karen Wernholm

Associate Managing Editor: Tamela Ambush

Senior Production Project Manager: Sheila Spinney

Digital Assets Manager: Marianne Groth

Executive Marketing Manager: Amy Judd

Marketing Assistant: Sophia M. Rester

Senior Author Support/Technology Specialist: Joe Vetere

Rights and Permissions Advisor: Cheryl Besenjak

Procurement Manager/Boston: Evelyn Beaton

Procurement Specialist: Megan Cochran

Senior Art Director: Heather Scott

Text Design and Production Coordination: Electronic Publishing Services Inc.

Composition and Illustrations: Jouve

Cover Design: Studio Montage

Cover photos: Shutterstock

Photo credits: Throughout: Headphones icon: Kellis/Fotolia, Post-it icon: Lucio/Fotolia, Red toolbox icon: Fotolia, Construction tools icon: Fotolia, Tape measure icon: Fotolia, Hardhat, blueprint and rulers icon: Maksym Yemelyanov/Fotolia; 1: Kurhan/Fotolia; p. 2: Rob/Fotolia; p. 3: Fotolia; p. 4: Fotolia; p. 7: Auremar/Fotolia; p. 10: Tatagatta/Fotolia; p. 12: Fotolia; p. 14: Lev Dolgatsjov/Fotolia; p. 18: Fotolia; p. 21: Fotolia; p. 22: Fotolia; p. 28: Fotolia; p. 29: Sanjay Deva/Fotolia; p. 30: Auremar/Fotolia; p. 34: Gina Sanders/Fotolia; p. 36: Fotolia; p. 40: Val Thoermer/Fotolia; p. 42: Fotolia; p. 46: Paulus Nugroho R/Fotolia; p. 48: Somenski/Fotolia; p. 52: Mr.Markin/Fotolia; p. 50: Andy Dean/Fotolia; p. 65: Mario Beauregard/Fotolia; p. 66: Ieva Geneviciene/Fotolia; p. 69 (top): Fotolia; p. 69 (bottom): Raphael Daniaud/Fotolia; p. 70: Fotolia; p. 71: Fedels/Fotolia; p. 74: Fotolia; p. 77: Rangizzz/Fotolia; p. 80 (top left): Andy Dean/Fotolia; p. 80 (bottom left): Fotolia; p. 75: Fotolia; p. 90: Fotolia; p. 91: Yuri Arcurs/Fotolia; p. 92: Sanjay Deva/Fotolia; p. 93: Fotolia; p. 96: Fotolia; p. 99: Fotolia; p. 102: Paulus Nugroho R/Fotolia; p. 113: Fotolia; p. 115: Fotolia; p. 118: Yuri Arcurs/Fotolia; p. 105: Suprijono Suharjoto/Fotolia; p. 131: FotolEdhar/Fotolia; p. 132: Tyler Olson/Fotolia; p. 133: Nyul/Fotolia; p. 134: Fotolia; p. 138: Edie Layland/Fotolia; p. 140: Sergej Khackimullin/Fotolia; p. 141 (top): Sergey Melnikov/Fotolia; p. 141 (bottom): Fotolia; p. 147: Andres Rodriguez/Fotolia; p. 147: Fotolia; p. 148: Fotolia; p. 155: Auremar/Fotolia; p. 157: Andres Rodriguez/Fotolia; p. 159: Deklofenak/Fotolia; p. 161: Fotolia; p. 162 (middle left): Fotolia; p. 162 (bottom left): Fotolia; p. 158: Fotolia; p. 173: Yuri Arcurs/Fotolia; p. 174: Fotolia; p. 176: Fotolia; p. 178 (top): Fotolia; p. 178 (bottom): Fotolia; p. 180: Fotolia; p. 183: Fotolia; p. 187: Guido Vrola/Fotolia; p. 188: Fotolia; p. 196: Paul Hill/Fotolia; p. 206: Pressmaster/Fotolia; p. 207: Fotolia; p. 210: Maximino gomes/Fotolia; p. 215 (top right): Fotolia; p. 215 (bottom right): Sergey Galushko/Fotolia; p. 216: Diego Cervo/Fotolia; p. 218 (top left): Yuri Arcurs/Fotolia; p. 218 (bottom left): Fotolia; p. 228: Doris Oberfrank/Fotolia; p. 229: Kzenon/Fotolia; p. 232: Fotolia; p. 241: Fotolia; p. 242: Anandkrish/Fotolia; p. 244: Fotolia; p. 248: Sebastian Duda/Fotolia; p. 249: Fotolia; p. 255: Taramara/Fotolia; p. 258: Fotolia; p. 259: Auremar/Fotolia; p. 260: Fotolia; p. 250: Akeeris/Fotolia; p. 266: Fotolia; p. 267: Fotolia; p. 270: Kzenon/Fotolia; p. 272: Tyler Olson/Fotolia; p. 277: Fotoli; p. 279: Tommaso Lizzul/Fotolia; p. 287: Fotolia; p. 288: Fotolia; p. 294: Scott Griessel/Fotolia; p. 283: Senkaya/Fotolia; p. 292: Fotolia; p. 293 (top left): Mrgarry/Fotolia; p. 293 (middle left): Marco Rullkötter/Fotolia; p. 293 (middle right): Fotolia; p. 293 (bottom right): Maksim Samasiuk/Fotolia; p. 301: Elenathewise/Fotolia; p. 302: Fotolia; p. 304: Fotolia; p. 307: Fotolia; p. 312: Tyler Olson/Fotolia; p. 315: Viorel Sima/Fotolia; p. 317: Auremar/Fotolia; p. 321 (middle left): Kzenon/Fotolia; p. 321 (bottom left): Fotolia; p. 313: Fotolia

Library of Congress Cataloging-in-Publication Data

Carter, Carol.
Career tool kit: the skills for success / Carol Carter, Gary Izumo.—Fourth edition.
    pages cm
ISBN 978-0-13-218053-5
1. Vocational guidance.   2. Career development.   3. Students—Employment.   I. Title.
HF5381.C366 2014
650.14—dc23

2012033071

10 9 8 7 6 5 4 3 2—V0UD—18 17 16 15 14

ISBN-13: 978-0-13-218053-5
ISBN-10: 0-13-218053-7

Dedication

We dedicate this book to displaced workers finding a new career, homemakers going back to get the skills they need for their next phase in life, and all the rest of you who seek to fulfill your potential, both personally and professionally. We hope you find success and happiness as you develop your skills, define your careers, and strive to achieve your goals. Learning is a lifelong endeavor and we hope this book will be one of your tools for life. This book is for you. Enjoy!

About the Authors

Carol Carter was a C student in high school. During her senior year, she got a wake-up call when her brother told her that she had intelligence, but she wouldn't go far in life unless she believed in herself enough to work hard. She began college knowing she was "behind the eight ball" in terms of her skills. What she lacked in experience, she made up for with elbow grease and persistence. She maximized her strength as an interpersonal and intrapersonal learner. The work paid off and she graduated college with honors and a desire to help other students.

Carol is committed to helping students of all ages turn on their brains, get motivated, and discover their abilities. As President of her own company, LifeBound, she teaches study, interpersonal, and career skills to middle school, high school students and college students to help them become competitive in today's global world. She trains and certifies coaches in academic coaching skills, and focuses on at-risk students with her volunteer teaching at the federal prison and her LifeBound work in the Denver housing projects. "All students are at-risk for something, whether it is academic, emotional, social, or economic," says Carol. "If each of us is allowed to be human and accept our flaws, we can overcome our limitations and be the best for ourselves and others."

Carol also speaks on educational topics nationally and internationally.

Her first book, *Majoring in the Rest of Your Life*, launched her writing career and opened the door to her work on the *Keys to Success* series and *The Career Tool Kit*.

Gary Izumo is an educator and consultant for the University of California, Davis—The Center for Human Services, where he has been honored for excellence in teaching and outstanding service. Gary conducts workshops and executive coaching focusing on Leadership and Organizational Effectiveness and has worked as a consultant for both major corporations and entrepreneurial firms in the private sector.

In addition, Gary has authored a number of books, including *Keys to Career Success, The Career Tool Kit, Keys to Workplace Effectiveness,* and *Stop Parenting—Start Coaching: How to Motivate, Inspire, and Connect with Your Teenager* and has written a business column for the *Los Angeles Times,* Ventura County Edition and CareerBuilder. He is a former consultant with McKinsey & Company, Practice Leader of Strategic Management Consulting for PricewaterhouseCoopers, and has been a full-time business professor at both two and four-year colleges.

In his consulting work, Gary has coached individuals on a diverse set of issues—from tactical challenges such as effective communication and resolving workplace conflict to more strategic ones like vision, leadership and efficiency versus effectiveness. The following are selected examples of topics he has coached and written on.

- Difficult Talk May Also Be the Most Important
- Learning In a Demanding World
- Keeping Promises
- Knowing How to Disagree
- Sustaining Success

- Re-Building Trust
- Risk-Taking
- Tough Decisions
- Next Steps
- Networking
- Personal and Professional Balance

Gary is an enthusiastic swimmer and reader, but most of all he enjoys spending time with his family and friends. He believes in contributing to the community and he is an active volunteer to local schools on curriculum and technology matters as well as working with human service organizations in areas such as welfare to work and children and family services. Gary is a graduate of Occidental College with a degree in economics and received his MBA from the University of California at Los Angeles.

Contents

Part III   Moving Forward

We Wrote This With You In Mind

There are many useful books written about achieving success in school and life. This book is special because it focuses on the skills necessary to successfully transition from school to work, and is tailored for your particular experience and needs as a student in a community college or vocational school. We know you have already made the important choice to build a solid foundation for a successful career and a better life—that's what brought you to this educational experience. Now we want to help you develop a set of essential success skills we call "tools."

This book is entitled *The Career Tool Kit* because it contains information about the tools you need to build a long, happy, and successful working life, just as a tool box might contain the essential tools for a carpenter to build a house. The tools in this book will also help you to successfully finish your educational program and shift into your career. In addition, just as a tool kit keeps your tools together so you can carry them around, this book holds the information you need in one convenient place. The skills described in this book will easily fit into your routine of daily activities.

This Book Has Three Major Benefits

FIRST, it will assist you while you are in school. You can apply several of the skills mentioned in this book to your working life and your student life: reading, writing, studying, listening, and so forth. Tools such as a positive attitude and self-image will fuel your success both inside and outside of school. Budgeting knowledge will help you organize your finances to help you juggle your school tuition and other expenses. In addition, we describe many useful resources available to you at your school. You are spending your hard-earned money on your education—to get your money's worth, take advantage of everything you can from your educational experience. This includes your diploma or certificate. Much of the advice in these pages will help you stay in school and succeed at the tasks you will embark on.

SECOND, it will help you search for, find, and land the job that you want. This book helps you get to know yourself better so you can understand what types of jobs will best suit your unique talents, skills, and qualities. It provides information on the job search—how to network, where to find job listings, who can help you locate opportunities, and how to apply. It guides you through the application process and shows you how to present yourself in the best possible light in a cover letter, on a resume, and in an interview. Furthermore, it assists you to handle both failure and success.

THIRD, it will continue to help you throughout your career. These pages contain valuable information about managing your time and money. There is important information on workplace communication with bosses, co-workers, clients, and customers. Additionally, this book provides a discussion of the qualities and skills employers look for in their employees, information concerning your rights on the job, and a section on critical thinking at work (decision making and problem solving). We know career success is affected by your physical and mental health as you seek to manage and balance the stresses of your working and personal lives. That is why we provide tips on improving and maintaining your mental and physical well-being throughout the chapters. Advice about motivation, patience, active listening, and other useful subjects will serve you in the coming years.

The book's special features will assist you in making the most of your reading. We have organized the material into sections that break down the information. If you skim through the book before reading, you will see these elements in each chapter.

QUOTATIONS. At the beginning of each chapter, you will find an inspirational and thought-provoking quote to help you start each chapter with the right mind set.

LEARNING OBJECTIVES. This section lists questions you will be able to answer as you work through the chapter's readings and activities.

LEARNING FROM EXPERIENCE. Interviews and quotes from people who have made choices similar to yours—current students, as well as graduates already in the workplace—appear throughout. These people are "in the trenches" and can give you an accurate, personal picture of what to expect as you transition into the work force.

Name	Profession	Chapter/Insight
Ray Golding	Machinist and mechanical engineering student	*Chapter 1* Find the Right Mindset: Choose Your Equipment
Andrea Selena	FedEx service rep and real estate agent	*Chapter 2* Unlock Your Personal Power: Keys to the Tool Kit
Eton Jackson	GIS software project manager and officer in the U.S. Army Reserves	*Chapter 3* Manage Your Time and Money: Make the Most of Key Resources
Amy Lee	Part-time Apple sales associate and graphic arts student	*Chapter 4* Your Basic Skills: Sharpen Your Tools
Marilyn Roberts	Freelance writer and usability specialist	*Chapter 5* Explore the Job Market: Find a Fit
Dolores Nero	Boutique owner and culinary student	*Chapter 6* Get the Hang of Networking: Tools that Create Opportunity
Estaben Chavez	Hairdresser	*Chapter 7* Build Your Personal Brand: Put Your Tools to Good Use
Krayton Walker	Technical assistant and electronic engineering student	*Chapter 8* Select Your Tools for the Interview: Winning Strategies to Seal the Deal
Chai Boonmee	Nail technician and cosmetology student	*Chapter 9* Diversity in the Workplace: Today's World
Kai Mahaulu	Security officer	*Chapter 10* Get the Job Done with Communication: Stay Ahead of the Curve
Shilah Hunt	Emergency medical technician	*Chapter 11* Stand Out on the Job: Pack Up Your Tool Kit

TECHNOLOGY AT WORK. These brief topics describe the many ways that new technologies shape our world, challenging you to learn more about the advancing technologies relevant to your life, school, and career.

NOW YOU TRY IT. This section allows you to stop and evaluate what you are learning in the chapter. It gives you an opportunity to take the information provided and connect it to your own life experiences.

YOUR TOOL KIT AT WORK. This section contains an assortment of hands-on activities that let you apply what you have just learned to specific questions and situations. You will strengthen your knowledge as you complete the activities.

For those who have used *The Career Tool Kit* in previous editions, you will be pleased to see the following list of NEW and REVISED content in this revision.

`NEW` **Discussion of the skills needed to meet the demands of the 21st century workplace incorporated throughout every chapter** to provide you with a realistic expectation of what will be required to compete in today's competitive job market.

`NEW` **Real-life scenarios about individuals getting started out in the job world or re-entering the workforce begin every chapter** and their stories are carried throughout, providing you with conceptual context.

`NEW` **Important topics** are covered, such as developing and maintaining a positive self-image, managing time, budgeting and organizing finances, avoiding or reducing credit debt, tracking down the resources available at school, and working in a business environment in a world built around social networking.

`NEW` **Self-awareness** coverage helps you to get to know yourself better and shows you how to search for and win the job that you want, and the *Now You Try It* activities within the chapters encourage you to practice concepts as they are discussed,

`NEW` **Expanded technology coverage** throughout, particularly in the *Learning From Experience, Technology at Work,* and *Your Tool Kit at Work* features, shows you the ever-increasing importance of technology in today's workplace.

`NEW` **Additional topics include** in-person and online networking skills; workplace communication with bosses, co-workers, clients, and customers; qualities and skills that employers look for in their employees; rights on the job; critical thinking at work (decision making and problem solving); improving and maintaining your mental health, social intelligence, motivation, patience, and listening skills.

`REVISED` **Workplace *myths* versus *realities*** ensures you have an accurate sense of the modern workplace.

`REVISED` *Real People, Real Stories* **has evolved into** *Learning From Experience* and features interview and quotes from people *in the trenches*—current students and professionals already in the workplace who have made choices similar to those you are facing.

`NEW` **Chapter 5: Explore the Job Market: Find a Fit** is a brand new chapter that focuses on researching possible careers and jobs that are a fit for your talents, abilities, values, and needs. It also introduces the *hidden* job market, and how it is created.

`REVISED` **Chapter 6: Get the Hang of Networking: Tools that Create Opportunity** is a completely revised chapter that now explores the art of networking, both in person and online. It focuses on how to track down the right jobs, investigate them, and conduct informational interviews, and includes social media topics.

`REVISED` **Chapter 7: Build Your Personal Brand: Put Your Tools to Good Use** is a completely revised chapter that digs into the details of every part of a modern resume, shows you how to craft attention-getting cover letters, and helps you build a winning portfolio.

`NEW` **Chapter 8: Select Your Tools for the Interview: Winning Strategies to Seal the Deal** is a new chapter that expands on strategies that help you get the job you want—from the clothing you wear, to voice and mannerisms, to handling objections and salary negotiations, to dealing with both failure and success.

Your education is what you make of it. Your school, teachers, class work, and reading give you endless opportunities to learn and improve yourself in preparation for career success. These are the tools that you will use to build your future. However, you are responsible for picking up those tools and actually using them. When you use what you read in this book, you are taking advantage of the chance to clear your way to success.

The strength of the future you construct with your tools is up to you. But we feel confident that by pursing further knowledge, you have put yourself on the right path. Refer to *The Career Tool Kit* for help as you make your way to the job and career you want, from school to work, and keep it with you as you continue down the path, using your tools to mold your experiences into a long and successful life as a working citizen.

Acknowledgments

This book is a labor of love. We have been mission-driven about this book since day one because it helps career changers, certificate degree earners and academic searchers find their skills and abilities for life outside of college. With the economic challenges we've faced recently, being able to have specific skills—whether you are welder, a certified nursing assistant or someone with your own heating and cooling business—is essential for you and for those who hire you to work for them.

We need to thank many people who have helped bring this book to life. Their advice, hard work, and information have been invaluable to us. We extend our heartfelt thanks to Jodi McPherson, our editor-in-chief, Katie Mahan, our editor, Amy Judd, our executive marketing manager, and Erin Carreiro, our editorial assistant. Special thanks to Carol Trueheart, a talented manager of both people and content, who heads up the development team.

In the first edition, Priscilla McGeehon, Eileen O'Sullivan, Stephen Hartner, Mary Carnis, Denise Brown, Marianne Frasco, Laura Ierardi, Fred Hamden, Jackie Fitzgerald, Melissa Carrigan, Hal Balmer, Elizabeth Kaster, and Julie Hildebrand of Prentice Hall launched this book. Sarah Kravits was involved in the first edition and made numerous contributions along with our publishing team. We thank all of you today.

In this edition, we worked with a wonderful production team under Karen Wernholm. We thank Sheila Spinney, our production project manager, and Diana Neatrour and the team at Electronic Publishing Services Inc., who helped develop the beautiful design and make the difficult decisions about content and visuals for a concise and pointed read.

On our team, Martha Roden was our developmental editor. She kept us on schedule and made strong judgments to improve and update each and every example. Her optimism, can-do attitude, and ability to keep a process on schedule, made her an invaluable member of our team. My assistants, Brittany Havey and Megan Adams, were instrumental in reading the chapters and sharing their insights as young professionals. Angelica Jestrovich was helpful in guiding our process and connecting our web efforts with our revisions. Thuyanh Astbury, our editorial intern, was very helpful as she weighed in on photo selections, in-chapter exercises, and each chapter's content. Thanks to each and every one of you for your dedication and hard work.

We are grateful to our teacher reviewers for their insights and their suggestions: Barbara H. Carter, Pasco-Hernando Community College; GeorgeAnn Drennan, University of New Mexico; Edye Garner, University of Wisconsin-Madison; Pamela Hoffman, Appalachian State University; Gary L. Kramer, Brigham Young University; Bob Nelson, Rutgers University; Robert C. Speirs, Jr., Hartnell College; Carolyn Curtis, Naugatuck Valley Community-Technical College; Linda Hjorth, DeVry Institute of Technology; Ziad Mubaslet, Advanced Career Training; John Schlenker, University of Maine; Phillip Sell, Highline Community College; Earl Wilkie, Pennsylvania Institute of Technology; and Monica Zeigler, Pace University. Specials thanks to Pete Affeld, Dave Baker, and Dick Dormuth at Computer Learning Centers, Melissa Carrigan, for connecting us with TCI, Elaine Carroll at Katherine Gibbs, for help in tracking down interviewees, Judy Northrup, for financial advice, Ward Deutschman, for review and advice.

Interviewees who filled us in on the real world picture: Beverly Andre, Lisa Durden, Wray Gould, Lois Griffin, Catherine Hartlove, Daniel Hernandez, Alicia Jackson, Delores Lay, Noel Lee, Susan Lugay, Lisa Mercado, Karen Mitchell, Finus A. Rascoe, Jr., Aretha Thompson, and Jay Wade.

Fleet students who tested applications: John Isiah Allen, Lisa Bailey, Della Bankert, Levell Herbert, William Maurice Holland Jr., Jessica J. Lambert, Sean Miller, Jennifer Waters, Kevin Yearick, and Carolyn Elizabeth Zylka. Bob Giudice at Technology Career Institute (TCI), Scott Carter, for thinking of our name, Patricia Cuff and Patricia Spencer Vaughan for their contributions to the first edition that helped created a foundation for this edition.

Barbara Rudy Foti and Suzanne Weissinger for classroom suggestions.

Cynthia Nordberg and Kathleen Cole, for research and support.

Thank you, too, to all the others who have contributed their valuable energies to make this book a reality.

Finally, we'd like to thank teachers everywhere who continue to help students learn, grow, and improve their lives and the world. From working with returning vets, to displaced workers, to those who are summoning the courage to graduate and start their own business, your dedication, energy, and commitment to excel provide a model of leadership for all of us at all ages and stages of life. We salute your inspired work and encourage you to be the engine of progress, jobs and quality for our new economy.

Please contact us with any feedback or ways we might improve this learning experience for you. Websites where you can learn, read blogs from young and seasoned professionals, and submit your own experiences include:

- www.lifebound.com
- www.lifeboundcoaching.com
- www.caroljcarter.com

Carol Carter
President, LifeBound
Caroljcarter@lifebound.com

Gary Izumo
Gary Izumo and Associates
gizumo@yahoo.com

Pearson Course Redesign

Did You Know?
Course Redesign is the process of restructuring the way course content is delivered with the goal of increasing both student achievement and institutional productivity. Pearson has successfully partnered with colleges and universities engaged in Course Redesign for over ten years through workshops, Faculty Advisor programs, and online conferences.

Take Action!
Get involved by attending a Pearson-hosted Course Redesign event. Hear from Faculty Advisors already involved in course redesign at various stages and in a variety of disciplines. Our Faculty Advisors are experienced in implementing MyLab/Mastering for redesign. They are ready to share what they have learned and offer advice.

Learn More
Learn more about Pearson Course Redesign resources and events at www.pearsoncourseredesign.com

Pearson MyStudentSuccessLab
Faculty Advisor Network

What is F.A.N.?

The Faculty Advisor Network is Pearson's peer-to-peer mentoring program in which we ask experienced MyStudentSuccessLab users to share their best practices and expertise with current and potential customers.

How do they help?

Our Faculty Advisors are experienced in supporting new and potential MyStudentSuccessLab users in a variety of ways such as:

• One-on-one phone and email coaching

• Webinars and presentations

• Live workshops and training sessions

Learn More

Contact your Pearson representative to connect with a Faculty Advisor or learn more about the FacultyAdvisory Network.

MyStudentSuccessLab™

PEARSON

MyStudentSuccessLab is an online solution designed to help students acquire the skills they need to succeed for ongoing personal and professional development. They will have access to peer-led video interviews and develop core skills through interactive practice exercises and activities that provide academic, life, and professionalism skills that will transfer to ANY course.

How can "skills" be measured – and what can you do with the data?

Measurement Matters – and is ongoing in nature. No one is ever an "expert" in 'soft skills' – something students learn once and never think about again. They take these skills with them for life.

Learning Path Diagnostic

- For the course, 65 Pre-Course questions (Levels I & II Bloom's) and 65 Post-Course questions (Levels III & IV Bloom's) that link to key learning objectives in each topic.

- For each topic, 20 Pre-Test questions (Levels I & II Bloom's) and 20 Post-Test questions (Levels III & IV Bloom's) that link to all learning objectives in the topic.

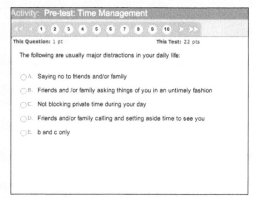

What gets your attention?

It's about engagement. Everyone likes videos.
Good videos, conveniently organized by topic.

FinishStrong247 YouTube channel

- Best of 'how to' for use as a practical reference
  (i.e. — manage your priorities using a smart phone)

- Save time finding good video.

- All videos have been approved by members of our student advisory board and peer reviewed.

How can everyone get trained?

We all want a 'shortcut to implementation.'
Instructors want to save time on course prep.
Students want to know how to register, log in, and know 'what's due, and when.'
We can make it easy.

Implementation Guide

- Organized by topic, provides time on task, grading rubrics, suggestions for video use, and more.

- Additional videos and user guides, registration and log in guides, and technical support for instructors and students at www.mystudentsuccesslab.com

MyStudentSuccessLab Feature set:

Learning Path provides:
- 65 Pre-Course (Levels I & II Bloom's) and 65 Post-Course (Levels III & IV Bloom's)
- 20 Pre-Test (Levels I & II Bloom's) and 20 Post-Test (Levels III & IV Bloom's)
- Overview (i.e. – Learning Outcomes)
- Student Video Interviews (with Reflection questions)
- Practices and Activities Tied to Learning Path
- FinishStronger247 YouTube channel with student-vetted supporting videos

Student Inventories:

1. **Golden Personality**—Similar to Meyers Briggs—it offers a personality assessment and robust reporting for students to get actionable insights on personal style. www. talentlens.com/en/employee-assessments/golden.php

2. **ACES (Academic Competence Evaluation Scales)**—Strength inventory that identifies and screens students to help educators prioritize skills and provides an overview of how students see themselves as learners. Identifies at-risk students. www.pearsonassessments.com/HAIWEB/Cultures/en-us/ Productdetail.htm?Pid=015-8005-805

3. **(Watson-Glaser) Thinking Styles**—Helps students understand their thought process and how they tend to approach situations. Shows how you make decisions. www.thinkwatson.com/mythinkingstyles

Student Resources:
Pearson Students Facebook page, FinishStrong247 YouTube channel, MySearchLab, Online Dictionary, Plagiarism Guide, Student Planner, MyProfessionalismKit resources including video cases. GPA, Savings, Budgeting, and Retirement Calculators.

Instructor Resources:
Instructor Implementation Guide supports course prep with Overview, Time on Task, Grading rubric, etc.

MyStudentSuccessLab Topic List:

A First Step: Goal Setting	Memory and Studying
Communication	Problem Solving
Critical Thinking	Reading and Annotating
Financial Literacy	Stress Management
Information Literacy	Teamwork
Interviewing	Test Taking
Job Search Strategies	Time Management
Learning Preferences	Workplace Communication (formerly 'Professionalism')
Listening and Taking Notes in Class	Workplace Etiquette
Majors/Careers and Resumes	

MyLabsPlus Available upon request for MyStudentSuccessLab

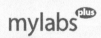

MyLabsPlus service is a dynamic online teaching and learning environment designed to support online instruction programs with rich, engaging customized content. With powerful administrator tools and dedicated support, MyLabsPlus is designed to support growing online instruction programs with an advanced suite of management tools. Working in conjunction with MyLabs and Mastering content and technology, schools can quickly and easily integrate MyLabsPlus into their curriculum.

Student Success CourseConnect

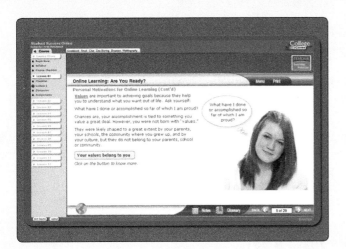 

Student Success CourseConnect (http://www.pearsonlearningsolutions.com/courseconnect) is one of many award-winning CourseConnect customizable online courses designed by subject matter experts and credentialed instructional designers, and helps students 'Start strong, Finish stronger' by building skills for ongoing personal and professional development.

Topic-based interactive modules follow a consistent learning path, from Introduction, to Presentation, to Activity, then Review. Student Success CourseConnect is available in your school's learning management system (LMS) and includes relevant video, audio, and activities. Syllabi, discussion forum topics and questions, assignments, and quizzes are easily accessible and it accommodates various term lengths as well as self-paced study.

Course Outline (i.e. 'Lesson Plans')

1. Goal setting, Values, and Motivation
2. Time Management
3. Financial Literacy
4. Creative Thinking, Critical Thinking, and Problem Solving
5. Learning Preferences
6. Listening and Note-Taking in Class
7. Reading and Annotating
8. Studying, Memory, and Test-Taking
9. Communicating and Teamwork
10. Information Literacy
11. Staying Balanced: Stress Management
12. Career Exploration

"What makes my CourseConnect course so successful is all the engagement that is built-in for students. My students really benefit from the videos, and all the interactivity that goes along with the classes that I've designed for them."

—Kelly Kirk, Director of Distance Education, Randolph Community College

"It's truly great that Pearson is invested in using the latest technologies to reach me in ways beside the traditional educational model. This innovative approach is one of the best ways to facilitate the education of students of my generation."

—Zach Gonzales, Student, University of Denver

ALWAYS LEARNING

PEARSON

Resources for Online Learning or Hybrid

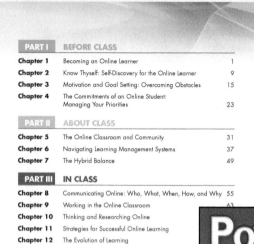

Power Up: A Practical Student's Guide to Online Learning, 2/e

Barrett / Poe / Spagnola-Doyle

© 2012 • ISBN-10: 0132788195 • ISBN-13: 9780132788199

Serves as a textbook for students of all backgrounds who are new to online learning and as a reference book for instructors who are also novices in the area, or who need insight into the perspective of such students. Provides readers with the knowledge and practice they need to be successful online learners.

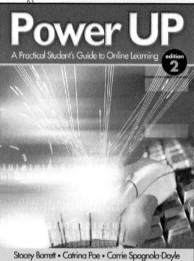

"We have used this excellent text with all cohorts of the last two years, as the text is an integral part of the first course in our graduate online program. Students love that it's user-friendly and practical. Instructors see this text as a powerful learning tool that is concise yet is able to be comprehensive in its coverage of critical skills and knowledge that support online student success."

—Dr. William Prado
Associate Professor & Director,
Business Program, Green Mountain College

CourseSmart is the Smarter Way

To learn for yourself, visit www.coursesmart.com

Introducing CourseSmart, The world's largest online marketplace for digital texts and course materials.

A Smarter Way for Students

CourseSmart is convenient. Students have instant access to exactly the materials their instructor assigns.

CourseSmart offers choice. With CourseSmart, students have a high-quality alternative to the print textbook.

CourseSmart saves money. CourseSmart digital solutions can be purchased for up to 50% less than traditional print textbooks.

CourseSmart offers education value. Students receive the same content offered in the print textbook enhanced by the search, note-taking, and printing tools of a web application.

Resources

Online Instructor's Manual – This manual is intended to give instructors a framework or blueprint of ideas and suggestions that may assist them in providing their students with activities, journal writing, thought-provoking situations, and group activities.

Online PowerPoint Presentation – A comprehensive set of PowerPoint slides that can be used by instructors for class presentations and also by students for lecture preview or review. The PowerPoint Presentation includes bullet point slides with overview information for each chapter. These slides help students understand and review concepts within each chapter.

Assessment via MyStudentSuccessLab – It is an online solution—*and powerful assessment tool*—designed to help students build the skills they need to succeed for ongoing personal and professional development at www.mystudentsuccesslab.com

Create tests using a secure testing engine within MyStudentSuccessLab (similar to Pearson MyTest) to print or deliver online. The high quality and volume of test questions allows for data comparison and measurement, which is highly sought after and frequently required from institutions.

- Quickly create a test within MyStudentSuccessLab for use online or to save to Word or PDF format and print

- Draws from a rich library of question test banks that complement course learning outcomes

- Like the option in former test managers (MyTest and TestGen), test questions in MyStudentSuccessLab are organized by learning outcome

- On National average, Student Success materials are customized by 78% of instructors—in both sequence and depth of materials, so organizing by learning outcomes (as opposed to 'chapter') saves customers' time

- Questions that test specific learning outcomes in a text chapter are easy to find by using the ACTIVITIES/ASSESSMENTS MANAGER in MyStudentSuccessLab

- MyStudentSuccessLab allows for personalization with the ability to edit individual questions or entire tests to accommodate specific teaching needs

- Because MyStudentSuccessLab is written to learning outcomes, this technology has breadth across any course where 'soft skills' are being addressed

LASSI – The LASSI is a 10-scale, 80-item assessment of students' awareness about and use of learning and study strategies. Addressing skill, will, and self-regulation, the focus is on both covert and overt thoughts, behaviors, attitudes and beliefs that relate to successful learning and that can be altered through educational interventions.

Noel Levitz/RMS – This retention tool measures Academic Motivation, General Coping Ability, Receptivity to Support Services, PLUS Social Motivation. It helps identify at-risk students, the areas with which they struggle, and their receptiveness to support.

Premier Annual Planner – This specially designed, annual 4-color collegiate planner includes an academic planning/ resources section, monthly planning section (2 pages/month), and weekly planning section (48 weeks; July start date). The Premier Annual Planner facilitates short-term as well as long-term planning. This text is spiral bound and convenient to carry with a 6 x 9 inch trim size.

PEARSON

IDentity Series—which will you choose?

Our consumer flavored "IDentity" Series booklets are written by national subject matter experts and offer strategies and activities for immediate application. These essential supplements can be packaged with any text or purchased individually. Additional information is available at www.pearsonhighered.com/educator/series/IDentity-Series/12561.page

Now Featuring: IDentity Series: *Ownership*

Do you remember how you learned to ride a bike? It probably went something like, 'put on the training wheels, learn to brake/steer; remove training wheels, try to ride with a strong hand on the back to keep you balanced, try on your own as you wobbled along; then fell a few times before you...rode away and never looked back.'

If you teach students ownership of concepts in class, they are more likely to take responsibility for their successes and failures and "own" their learning. First, we offer a multimedia professional development course on Ownership in an easy-to-use online format that walks through teaching methods and includes ready-to-use activities, coaching tips, assessments, animations, and video on a topic. Second, we provide a short, affordable student booklet covering ownership essentials and the topic that can be used independently or as part of your course.

Instructors will learn how to use this groundbreaking four-step process to teach ownership to any student in any class. Students will learn how to take ownership over their education and ultimately their life path.

Complete list of current and forthcoming IDentity Series publications:

TOPIC	SKILLS	ISBN	TITLE	AUTHOR (S)
CAREER	Key Cognitive	0132819678	Now You're Thinking About Your Career	Chartrand et. al.
COLLEGE	Key Cognitive	0132825740	Now You're Thinking About College	Chartrand et. al.
CRITICAL THINKING	Key Cognitive	013286908X	Ownership: Critical Thinking	Stone
FINANCES (brief)	Contextual Skills & Awareness	0132819694	Financial Literacy	Torabi
FINANCES (comprehensive)	Contextual Skills & Awareness	0132819651	Financial Responsibility	Clearpoint Financial Solutions, Inc.
IDENTITY	Contextual Skills & Awareness	0321883330	Identity: Passport to Success	Graham
VETERANS / MILITARY	Contextual Skills & Awareness	0132886952	Finding Success as a Returning Veteran or Military Student	McNair/Stielow
GOAL SETTING	Academic Behaviors	0132868792	Ownership: Effective Planning	Stone
TEST TAKING	Academic Behaviors	0132869063	Ownership: Study Strategies	Stone
TIME MANAGEMENT	Academic Behaviors	0132869500	Ownership: Accountability	Stone

Pearson Success Tips
Which will you choose for your students?

Success Tips provides informational 1-page highlights on critical topics, available in three formats:

- *Success Tips* (6-panel laminate) includes MyStudentSuccessLab, Time Management, Resources All Around You, Now You're Thinking, Maintaining Your Financial Sanity, Building Your Professional Image

- *Success Tips for Professionalism* (6-panel laminate) includes Create Your Personal Brand, Civility Paves the Way Toward Success, Succeeding in Your Diverse World, Building Your Professional Image, Get Things Done with Virtual Teams, Get Ready for Workplace Success

- Choose pages from the list below to insert into a custom text via Pearson Custom Library.

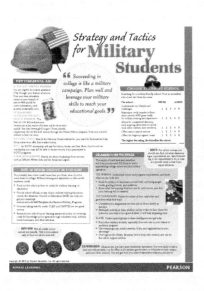

Blackboard	0132853159	Success Tips: Welcome to Blackboard!
Brand U	0132850788	Success Tips: Create Your Personal Brand
Campus Resources	0132850605	Success Tips: Resources All Around You
Civility	0132853140	Success Tips: Civility Paves the Way Toward Success
Critical Thinking	0132850729	Success Tips: Now You're Thinking
Diversity	0132850753	Success Tips: Succeeding in Your Diverse World
eCollege	0132850664	Success Tips: Welcome to eCollege!
Finances	0132850710	Success Tips: Maintaining Your Financial Sanity
Goal Setting	0132850702	Success Tips: Set and Achieve Your Goals
Information Literacy	0132850613	Success Tips: Information Literacy Is Essential to Success
Moodle	013285077X	Success Tips: Welcome to Moodle!
MyStudentSuccessLab	0132850745	Success Tips: MyStudentSuccessLab
Note-Taking	0132850672	Success Tips: Good Notes Are Your Best Study Tool
Online Learning	013298153X	Success Tips: Power Up for Online Learning
Privacy	0132850796	Success Tips: Protect Your Personal Data
Professional Image	0132850826	Success Tips: Building Your Professional Image
Service Learning	0132886316	Success Tips: Service Learning What You Learn Helps Others
Stress Management	0132852071	Success Tips: Stay Well and Manage Stress
Test-Taking	0132850680	Success Tips: Prepare for Test Success
Time Management	0132850842	Success Tips: Time Management
Veterans	013285080X	Success Tips: Veterans/Military Returning Students
Virtual Teams	0132850761	Success Tips: Get Things Done with Virtual Teams
Workplace Success	0132850834	Success Tips: Get Ready for Workplace Success

PEARSON

Custom Publishing

As the industry leader in custom publishing, we are committed to meeting your instructional needs by offering flexible and creative choices for course materials that will maximize learning and engagement of students.

The Pearson Custom Library

Using our online book-building system, www.pearsoncustomlibrary.com, create a custom book by selecting content from our course-specific collections that consist of chapters from Pearson Student Success and Career Development titles and carefully selected, copyright cleared, third-party content, and pedagogy.
www.pearsonlearningsolutions.com/custom-library/pearson-custom-student-success-and-career-development

Custom Publications

In partnership with your Custom Field Editor, modify, adapt, and combine existing Pearson books by choosing content from across the curriculum and organize it around your learning outcomes. As an alternative, work with them to develop your original material and create a textbook that meets your course goals.
www.pearsonlearningsolutions.com/custom-publications

Custom Technology Solutions

Work with Pearson's trained professionals, in a truly consultative process, to create engaging learning solutions. From interactive learning tools to eTexts, to custom websites and portals, we'll help you simplify your life as an instructor.
www.pearsonlearningsolutions.com/higher-education/customizable-technology-resources.php

Online Education

Offers online course content for online learning classes, hybrid courses, and enhances the traditional classroom. Our award-winning product CourseConnect includes a fully developed syllabus, media-rich lecture presentations, audio lectures, a wide variety of assessments, discussion board questions, and a strong instructor resource package.
www.pearsonlearningsolutions.com/higher-education/customizable-online-courseware.php

For more information on how Pearson Custom Student Success can work for you, please visit www.pearsonlearningsolutions.com or call 800-777-6872

ALWAYS LEARNING

PEARSON

Find the Right Mindset

Choose Your Equipment

I am the people. . . . Do you know that all the great work of the world is done through me?

Carl Sandburg

 learning objectives

- How will this text help you with your career and life?
- What are the eight universal work skills that will help you at school, in your career, and in life?
- What is emotional intelligence and how can it help you?
- Why is a positive self-image important for your success?
- How can you stay motivated and committed throughout your life?
- How do you make or break a habit?
- How can patience help you in your career?
- Why are integrity and empathy such valuable skills and how do you develop them?
- What are some good ways to manage stress?

Cade graduated from college with a degree in mechanical engineering. He was recruited straight out of college by a national high-tech company, and worked for the company for eight years as a mechanical designer. Throughout that time, he used CAD systems to design controllers. Then the bottom fell out of the economy, Cade's division closed, and Cade was laid off. Luckily his wife worked as well, so the bills continued to be paid. However, after five months of fruitless searching and no job, Cade decided to re-enroll in school. He hopes to gain skills to become a manager, something he always wanted to do when he was a mechanical designer. He is looking forward to this course so he can learn more about the skills he needs to develop to become a good manager, as well as networking skills that will help him find another job.

As an engineer, he knows that he's more comfortable with computers than people, but he knows he needs to improve his people skills. In fact, he isn't sure if he's got what it takes to be a manager. In the past, he always had problems dealing with conflict and avoided situations in which people disagreed with him. But now he has no choice. He has only worked for one company and isn't sure what's out there in terms of jobs. He is going to have to meet other people, learn how to network and find out about companies and jobs, as well as improve his interpersonal skills. He really hopes this course will help him.

Like Cade, a lot of people are finding themselves in school again, taking another class and reading another book, in hopes of improving their chances in the job market. You have probably been through a few classes and more than a few books in your lifetime, so you deserve to know what is different about this text and this course.

The Career Tool Kit helps you develop the skills you need to succeed in your chosen career. Whether you are embarking on your first job, changing jobs, or just got laid off, these are the skills you need to be successful. Some of them are skills you have known about and used for years, whereas others may be new to you. This text puts them together in a way that places you on the cutting edge of today's job market.

Notice that the book title refers to a *tool kit.* We like the metaphor of a tool kit because it is portable and can carry a great number of tools for different purposes. The tools you stock in your tool kit are not the physical devices, but practical skills you will use throughout your career and your life. Using these tools, you will succeed in your current or future career, make the most of your talents, and make a difference, no matter where you work.

In this chapter, we talk about why you're here and introduce you to important universal work skills, as well as the concept of

myth

"My employer will train me so I will be successful."

reality

Your choice to go to school and take this class is the right one. With downsizing and "lean" organizations, managers and supervisors have little time to train new employees. New employees today cannot count on the employer to provide the training and coaching necessary for success. Instead, companies look for new employees with just the right mix of technical and career skills who won't require a lot of training.

myth

"I will get serious about how I get stuff done when I am done with school and start my career."

reality

Old habits die hard. Do you want to launch your career with a fast start or risk a bad first impression? The habits you formed at school, at home, and in your life will follow you to the workplace. Treat school like you will treat your employment. Get to classes on time. Turn your assignments in on time. Always do your best and don't try to slide by and "pass." Build the right habits for success wherever you are, right now. This will help you make the most of your investment in education and position you for a successful career.

emotional intelligence. You will learn about maintaining a positive self-image and a good attitude. In addition, you will gather six other basic tools: motivation, commitment, good habits, patience, integrity, and empathy.

Why You're Here

There are times when all of us have wondered whether the information we learn in a class or a book is really going to help us find a job. Students have probably asked themselves, "What can I do with what I've learned? How will I make use of it in the real world?" Underemployed or unemployed workers have probably wondered, "How will this help me find another job? How will I find the time to take this class and look for a job?" That's where the tool kit comes in.

This text won't teach you how to create an Internet web page or how to build a "green" home, or any other specific career opportunity or trade. We leave that to courses and books tailored to specific purposes. Instead, this text deals with "universal work skills"—general skills that apply to every vocation or job you will ever study or have. These skills ensure that you can work efficiently and effectively in any position. These are the "tools" we talk about throughout this text. Just as an artist needs tools like brushes, paints, and charcoal to create a potential masterpiece, a worker needs universal work skills to create a career. Without the tools, no amount of raw talent alone can guarantee success.

These are also the skills that employers often assume employees already have. In reality, however, many employees and would-be employees lack these skills and have very little time to learn them. Luckily, as you learn the universal skills and put them in your tool kit, you will have what it takes to succeed on the job.

Taking this class and considering your future is the first step in achieving your career goal.

Taking This Class Is the Right Choice

Many of you have spent time thinking about the type of career you want to pursue. Others have already spent years in careers that were not a fit. Or, you may have had a career you liked, but found yourself downsized. Still others have committed time and energy preparing for work in specific vocations or trades.

Perhaps you have chosen a course of study that teaches you the technical skills you need to begin your desired career. Or maybe you are brushing up on skills you hope will let you change careers or get a promotion. Either way, you have already taken an important step—you are focusing your efforts and channeling your energy toward a goal.

Education can multiply your earning power and expand your opportunities. Technological change and global competition are widening the difference in lifetime earnings between those who are educated and skilled, and those who are not.

At School or on the Job?

Going to school to learn your job is a smart move. You are giving yourself an opportunity to make the most of your natural abilities. The purpose of your school or program, and the goal of your teachers and advisors, is to prepare you to intelligently handle situations that will come your way on the job.

What about those of you who already have a job, or had one in the past? You probably learned a lot on the job and we believe you should continue to learn for the rest of your working life. However, school still has something to offer in focused attention and training. For example, suppose you work as a hospital administrative assistant. Your manager has a job to do and cannot spend all day teaching you how to update records in the computer or how to evaluate vendor invoices. Besides, if your manager did spend a lot of time training you, he or she might risk neglecting his or her own duties. You will never get the kind of attention and training on the job that you can get in a school.

When you consider learning at school and learning on the job, you might think of it this way: If you want to learn to play an instrument, you would first have to learn to read music and play simple scales before you could put that knowledge to use and play some easy songs. It would take lots of practice before you could play complicated pieces or compose music. In this analogy, school gives you the knowledge to read music, practice scales, and play simple pieces. The job is

actually learning to play more difficult music, improving your skills, and possibly beginning to compose music.

Your Raw Resources

Your skills and natural talents are like raw resources—they are the nails, wood, and cement that you need to build a house. But something more is necessary. A building plan shows you the best way to use those resources to build a well-made home. This text and the course you are taking make up part of your career-building plan. With this plan, you learn how to develop and organize your mental, physical, social, emotional, and creative skills so you can translate them into a successful career.

Many people don't give themselves the chance to improve basic skills before going out into the world. They dive in without preparing themselves for what lies ahead. But you have chosen a different route by committing to read this text and building your own foundation of basic, universal skills.

Staying Committed Is the Right Choice

It can be tough to fit school into your schedule. We know that many of you are balancing schoolwork with other obligations such as jobs, families, or both. However, the return on your investment is well worth it. The skills you develop today will help you go much farther in your career and progress more quickly in a direction that you choose.

For example, suppose you and a friend recently started working at a customer service center for a national e-commerce company. After watching the system support technicians at work, you believe you might want to do what they do. You ask one of them where to go for a good training program. The system technician tells you about a certificate program at a local technology school and you enroll, still working part time at the customer service center while you take classes.

Your friend sees how tired and overworked you become going to work and school, and feels certain she doesn't want to go through something like that. She figures she will move up in the ranks because she is a dedicated full-time employee.

After a year of feeling tired and poor, scrimping and saving to pay your tuition, you graduate from the program. You are now a certified computer system technician with the papers to prove it. You get a new, higher-paying job at the customer service center working on computers. Your friend feels a bit jealous. After all, hasn't she been working full time for the company while you were working part time?

Here's the difference: There's only so much your friend could have learned by watching the technicians during coffee breaks. Your friend may have the talent to be a technician, but she didn't go out and learn the specifics. She has the raw materials, but lacks the building plans—and she has the lower salary to prove it. It will be more difficult for her to achieve the level of employment that she wants without formal education.

A trained and educated employee has greater freedom of choice. Let's say you worked in sales for a couple of years and then attended a community college or business school. Upon graduation, you have multiplied your options. You know you are still a good salesperson and can do that job any time you need or want. But now you have the option of being a marketing analyst as well. You can make choices that were unavailable when you only had certain sales skills. As a result, you have more power to control your destiny.

Universal Work Skills

When we refer to *universal work skills,* we are not talking about specific skills you learn when you take classes related to a particular career. Universal skills are basic skills that you need for any career, no matter what you do or where you do it.

SCANS, the Secretary's Commission on Achieving Necessary Skills, produced a list of universal work skills that reflects the needs and experiences of real working people. The skills are grouped into eight categories that define the areas of proficiency to assure on-the-job success.

- **Emotional intelligence.** Working with other people on the job (interpersonal skills).
- **Information.** Gathering and making use of information.
- **Systems.** Understanding interrelationships between parts and components.
- **Technology.** Working with various technologies.
- **Basic skills.** Using the everyday skills that keep things moving.
- **Critical-thinking skills.** Using your brainpower to figure out your world.
- **Personal qualities.** Displaying traits that show you are valuable and trustworthy.
- **Resources.** Identifying, organizing, planning, and efficiently using available resources.

Table 1.1 lists the eight categories and the specific skills that apply to each. The table also describes what happens when you don't have skills in these categories. As you look over the "Without Key Skills" column, you can see that without solid skills across the board, prospects look pretty bleak. However, when you develop skills in all categories and know how to use them well, you fill your career tool kit with handy tools for success.

technology *at work*

When it comes to technology, a lot can happen in ten years. Skype, iPhones, and social networking are just a few things that have impacted how companies do business. Computer technology skills are now necessary no matter what career field you are in.

Even more important is the necessity of universal skills. With texting, tweeting, and email becoming more prevalent, people appear to be losing the ability to communicate effectively in person. Reading facial and body language becomes more difficult when you only have experience communicating online. Explaining difficult concepts and solving complicated problems is not easy when you lack the language skills to explain things because you are used to sending short text messages with no punctuation and improper spelling. Finally, handling disagreements and resolving conflicts becomes nearly impossible if you lack empathy and have little or no experience working directly with others. Although technology is important, there are other universal skills that are important if you want to succeed in the business world.

Table 1.1 Universal Skills for School and Work Success

Skill	Without Key Skills
Emotional Intelligence	
Empathy Communication Cooperating as a team member Working with clients/customers Leadership Managing relationships Managing workplace diversity Negotiating and resolving conflict	You have difficulties cooperating with coworkers to complete required tasks. You cannot resolve everyday conflicts that are part of work.
Information	
Evaluating information Organizing/interpreting information Communicating information verbally or in writing Processing information (i.e., on a computer)	You don't know where or how to find critical data for an assignment. Your boss doesn't understand your report and effort.
Systems	
Social systems (human relationships) Companies' organizational systems Systems of technology (i.e., how pieces of equipment work together)	You make mistakes because you don't understand your role on your team. Work and communications occur mysteriously or in code and you feel left out.

(continued)

Table 1.1 (Continued)	
Skill	**Without Key Skills**
Technology	
Choosing equipment and/or procedures to use in a given situation Understanding how equipment and/or procedures work Using equipment and procedures properly	Your boss is upset with your overtime; he doesn't know you are afraid to use the new equipment. You lose your job. You didn't upgrade your skills and they became obsolete.
Basic Skills	
Reading, proofreading, writing, and taking notes Listening Speaking Memory and concentration	You are confused and people don't understand you; everyone is frustrated. You have a difficult time getting and keeping a job.
Critical-Thinking Skills	
Creative thinking Decision making Problem solving Knowing how to learn Visualizing Reasoning	It is hard to grow as the job changes when you don't know how to continue to learn. Your career has stalled and you can't seem to move ahead despite how hard you try.
Personal Qualities	
Self-knowledge Self-esteem Attitude and motivation Integrity and honesty Responsibility and commitment Self-management (habits including self-assessment, goal setting, motivation) Prioritizing	Despite the best technical skills, poor work habits cost you a great assignment. Your boss questions you endlessly about your work; does she trust you?
Resources	
Managing time Managing money Managing material items Managing people	Your personal financial blunders have hurt your attitude and your work. You just can't seem to get to work or meetings on time. Your boss doesn't think you care.

A Quick Look at Emotional Intelligence

You are probably familiar with all the categories in the table, although *emotional intelligence* may be a new term for you. This term was coined by psychologist Daniel Goleman, who wrote a bestseller by the same title. Emotional intelligence is the ability to monitor and control your emotions, thoughts, and feelings, while remaining sensitive to and aware of others' feelings. An emotional quotient (EQ) is a measurement of your emotional intelligence, much like an intelligence quotient (IQ) is a measurement of your intellectual intelligence.

Goleman claims that in business, your EQ is more important than your IQ. In fact, people with a high EQ tend to be more successful in life than those with a lower EQ, even if their IQ is average. In other words, what you know is not necessarily a measure of what you can do. You might have the greatest ideas in the world, but if you don't listen to others, if you become hostile when someone questions your thinking, or if you fail to notice when others cannot follow your thoughts, your potential is wasted and you hinder your chances to succeed.

According to Goleman, people with a high EQ experience the widest range and variety of feelings—from great sadness to great joy and excitement. On the other hand, people with a low EQ, who cannot relate to other people, often have not experienced, acknowledged, or accepted many feelings of their own.

A low EQ can hamper your ability to effectively communicate with others and to succeed in business.

 ## Now You Try It: What's Your EQ?

The following are some items you might consider to gauge your own EQ. In each row, put a checkmark next to the statement that sounds like what you do. If you have more checkmarks in the low column than in the high column, chances are your emotional intelligence needs development.

	High EQ		Low EQ
_____	When I look at another person's face, I can easily tell how they are feeling: angry, happy, scared, worried, etc.	_____	When I look at someone else, I have a hard time figuring out what they are feeling or thinking, unless they tell me.
_____	When people get angry with me, I do not take it personally and give them the benefit of the doubt by trying to figure out what might be going on "behind the scenes."	_____	When people get angry with me, I get upset too and assume they have no right to do that. I either yell at them, hit them, or try to avoid them.
_____	When a conflict arises with another person, I try to figure out a solution that will benefit both of us.	_____	When a conflict arises, I usually think the only way to resolve it is to get my way, no matter what it takes.
_____	When I have the opportunity to work with another person, I make sure the other individual gets equal credit for our success.	_____	When I have an opportunity to work with another person, I'm afraid the other person will try to take credit for what we've done together, so I make sure I get all the credit.
_____	If I have an opportunity to make more money or get more recognition, I make sure that my actions do not undermine the well-being of others.	_____	If I have an opportunity to make more money or get more recognition, I have no problem doing what it takes, even if it means stepping on others.

Working Through the Universal Skills

This text presents all categories of universals skills except those dealing with technology, which you will cover in training courses more specific to your job. The book presents the categories in a different order than they are presented in Table 1.1, however, because the chapters progress chronologically, moving from learning more about yourself and your ability to interact with others, to learning more about conducting a job search, to learning how to be successful at the job you hold. As you progress through the book, you will pick up the various skills that fit under each category, filling your tool kit as you go.

The typical day feature looks at how universal work skills weave into everyday life. Take a look at the words in parentheses. They describe the universal skills Ms. Jackson uses throughout her day—the skills you will study. You will see how useful the skills are in day-to-day life and how they help you achieve your goals, from the tiniest (save money at the grocery store) to the largest (get a well-paying job in your chosen field). They serve you in ways you may have never thought about.

A Typical Day in the Life
of a Master of Universal Work Skills

Alicia Jackson just moved to a new state and needs to find a job. She is an experienced computer operator (technology) and knows that she wants to work at a small business (self-knowledge). She just called two people she knows in the area, a cousin and a friend who graduated from the same school as Alicia (relationships). Both recommended businesses for her to contact. Through newspapers and the Internet, Alicia found two other companies that were hiring (gathering and evaluating information). She called three of the companies (prioritizing) and was able to set up appointments with two.

She spends five minutes over breakfast planning her day so she can accomplish a few tasks before her interview later that day (managing time). One of these tasks is finding a bank. She calls three banks and gets information about the accounts and services they offer (decision making) and chooses one that best fits her needs—with no minimum balance required. She then opens two accounts—a checking and a savings account (managing money).

At noon she goes to the grocery store and buys food for the next few days, stocking up on the items that are on sale and limiting the expensive things (managing money). Back at home, she showers and irons the outfit she plans to wear for her interview (self-esteem and appearance). Next, she puts on small earrings and styles her hair. A little bit of makeup, and she is ready to go.

When she arrives at the company's office, the receptionist greets her and tells her she needs to take two short tests. The first is a written test covering basic competencies (reading and writing). The second is a computer test covering her knowledge of several software applications, including Microsoft Word, PowerPoint, and Excel (technology).

When the tests are done, the supervisor calls Alicia into the office for an interview (speaking and listening skills). First, Alicia gives some background about herself and her life. Then she talks about her education, her specific computer training, the previous jobs she held, and the duties she performed (responsibility and commitment). The supervisor explains the requirements of the posted job position (listening) and asks Alicia where she sees herself in five years. Alicia thinks for a moment (reasoning) and responds by describing what she wants out of her next job and how she expects her duties and skills to grow in the near future (visualization). They chat a bit more, and then it's time to go. The supervisor tells Alicia to expect a call within the week letting her know whether she has the job.

Ms. Jackson gets home later than she expected and pays the babysitter extra for the overtime (integrity and honesty). After changing into more comfortable clothes, she sits down and immediately writes a thank you note to her interviewer (written communication skills). She goes over the interview in her head before falling sleep, thinking about what went well and what she can improve on (self-assessment). She hopes she gets a phone call soon.

Alicia Jackson's story demonstrates how the tools in your tool kit will form the foundation of your success. You will use them every day of your life and never have to ask yourself, "How can I possibly use what I learned from reading that book?"

Tools for Your Kit

Right now your tool kit is empty, but starting with this chapter you will begin filling it with tools associated with both personal and interpersonal qualities. These tools include: positive self-image, attitude, motivation, commitment, habits, patience, integrity, emotional intelligence, and empathy. You, as a whole person with thoughts, dreams, talents, and abilities, will put together the tool kit. These tools are the basics, like hammers and screwdrivers, and you cannot do much without them.

Positive Self-Image

Let's start with how you look at yourself—your **self-image**. How you see yourself colors every aspect of your life—your emotions, your relationships, and your level of success on your career path. Your thoughts are powerful. How you think about yourself and the world affects what you say, and in turn, what you do.

> **Self-image,** *noun*
>
> one's conception or view of oneself (your own identity, abilities, and worth)

Much of how we view ourselves comes from what our parents and other authority figures told us as children. For example, imagine a woman who got in trouble as a child for asking questions about things she did not understand—she may grow up thinking she is stupid and feel uncomfortable asking for help. However, another woman who asked questions as a child may have received lots of answers and praise for being curious. She is far more likely to grow up with a positive self-image, feeling free to ask questions whenever she doesn't understand something.

Seeing yourself in a positive light is your first and most important task. Each of us needs to be our own best cheerleader, our own best friend, and our own greatest resource. If we cannot count on ourselves for support, who else can we turn to? A negative self-image not only paralyzes us, it makes us unreceptive to receiving help from others who believe in us. When we truly know and appreciate our own worth, we have the power to achieve success.

Unfortunately, it isn't always easy to have a positive self-image. We are constantly blasted with messages from the media that we are not smart enough, good looking enough, healthy enough, or wealthy enough. We are encouraged to be dissatisfied with ourselves and feel we are lacking in both personal qualities and material goods. Add to that the negative messages we tell ourselves: "I can't figure that out" or "I'll never be able to do that" or "I'm sure to fail." The result is poor self-image, something anyone can suffer from at any time in his or her life. We become our own worst critics. For example, if you go into an interview convinced that people won't hire you because of your cultural or educational background, you will lack self-confidence. This will come across to your interviewers. Your poor self-image will sabotage you and prevent the actual situation from unfolding as it should.

Sound Bite
For Positive Self-Esteem

We all have gifts. We all have the power to make a contribution. And we all make mistakes. Let's view mistakes as assets, not liabilities. Let's learn from our mistakes, instead of beating up ourselves over them, burying them, or becoming defensive.

There are two parts to a positive self-image. One is *self-esteem*. This refers to having a realistic, but favorable impression of yourself. When you have good self-esteem, you perceive that you are of value. You respect yourself. You are satisfied that you are a capable and worthwhile human being. You know that your qualities and abilities can improve your life, as well as the lives of other people. You believe that you can make a difference in the world.

The other component is *self-confidence*. This refers to having a realistic confidence in your own judgment and abilities. Self-confident people trust and believe in themselves. They believe in their ability to make positive changes in themselves and in the world. Self-confidence allows you to take your positive perceptions about yourself and turn them into action.

Put self-esteem and self-confidence together and you have a solid base from which you can work to achieve anything. One saying conveniently combines both parts quite nicely: "If you perceive and you believe, then you can achieve." If you perceive your own value (self-esteem) and you believe in the worthiness of your abilities and actions (self-confidence), you will achieve your goals and dreams.

We all make mistakes, so how do you keep yourself from feeling like a failure when things don't work out as expected? First, you realize that we all get down on ourselves from time to time.

You are in good company with most of the population. In fact, people who seem super confident all the time are probably hiding their self-doubts extremely well. Second, realize that what most people call "failure" is only disappointment about not meeting expectations. Sometimes those expectations were not realistic to begin with, so failure to achieve them does not mean you are a failure; it simply means you need to adjust the expectations. In reality, as long as you keep on trying, there is no real failure, only ongoing learning. People who never try new things never fail, but they also never learn anything different or move forward.

Sound Bite

If you have to take a test, or things like that, avoid saying to yourself, "I don't think I'm going to be able to pass it." When you have that negative attitude about it, you're always going to do badly. You defeat yourself already from the start. If you have a positive attitude about it, you'll do well.

—J. Wade, computer science student

When you're feeling negative about yourself because of a perceived failure, it's easy to fall into the habit of negative self-talk. Unfortunately, few people realize the devastating effect that negative self-talk has on them. Even thoughts like "That was dumb" or "How could I be so stupid?" or "There I go again. . ." add up and erode your sense of self-worth. Eventually, you won't have the energy to put your talents and your tools to work.

How do you reverse the devastating effects of negative self-talk? First, you need to understand how negative self-talk affects you. In the human body, everything begins with a thought. The thought generates an emotion, which in turn produces various hormones. These hormones make us feel a certain way, which in turn affects how we act. So, change the thought and you'll change the action.

Let's look at a simple example. You volunteer to do a presentation on the use of social networking in non-profits. It's a real interest of yours and you work hard to make the presentation interesting and informative. You're nervous because you've never given a presentation to a large group before, but you forge ahead. After the presentation, your boss tells you that you "messed up" because you forgot to mention some important details. You immediately think, "I'm such a loser when it comes to giving presentations." The next thing you know, you feel a terrible sense of embarrassment and shame. What happens next? Your face turns red and your eyes get watery. When you try to speak, your voice sounds shaky and you dread ever giving another presentation. The thought created an emotion, which created a physical reaction.

Now, what if your boss said "Great job! I can't wait for you do another presentation"? You would probably think, "Hey, I did it. That wasn't so bad." Next, you would feel a sense of pride and happiness. A big smile would appear on your face as you thanked your boss in a confident voice and told her "I can't wait either!" You would actually look forward to opportunities to make presentations, and you would probably be quite good at them.

Get a Grip on Self-Talk

Your private thoughts become an independent voice that can bring you down or build you up. Let's look at techniques for dealing with negative self-talk and turning things around.

Technique 1: If you hear yourself thinking "Boy, am I stupid," stop yourself immediately and change the thought to something like "I can do better than that and next time I will." Replace negative thoughts with positive ones. This means you need to come up with some positive thoughts ahead of time. If you've been thinking negative thoughts for a long time, that might be difficult, but not impossible. Jot the positive thoughts on a piece of paper if you have to and read through them to get them in your mind. That way, when a negative thought pops into your mind, you can

Getting a grip on your own thoughts can take a lot of effort.

Figure 1.1 **Think empowerment**

Use		Avoid	
• I want to	• I promise to	• I have to	• I intend to
• I choose to	• I know I will	• I should	• I think I can
• I will	• I commit to	• I'll try	• I hope to

quickly replace it with one of your positive ones. Don't be too hard on yourself if the negative self-talk keeps popping into your mind again and again. That's natural! Just keep replacing the old negative thought with a new positive thought, congratulate yourself, and move ahead. Remember, it takes a lot of practice over a considerable period of time to make progress.

Technique 2: Try to take a moment to make positive statements to yourself, perhaps when you see yourself in the mirror each morning. Tell yourself, "I am a unique, valuable person, and there's a company out there that needs me." Or get more specific: "I will impress so-and-so with my great skill set at my interview today." Some people complain that the statements don't sound real to them or they don't feel any differently when they say the statements. That doesn't matter. Say the statements enough times and eventually the thoughts will sink in, you will begin to believe them, and then you will begin to feel them. In fact, one way people make the statements seem more real is by adding a little something at the beginning (appears in italics): "*Regardless of appearances, the truth is,* I am a terrific, valuable person, and there is a company out there that needs me." The new words at the beginning of the statement allow you to acknowledge your doubts that maybe things don't seem that way right now, but the statement is true.

Technique 3: One more idea is to replace "have-to" words, which take power from you, with "want-to" words, which give you power and control. The want-to words give us power because they imply a personal decision to act. For example, when you say "I have to work on this project" or "I should finish this assignment," it seems like someone else has the power to tell you what to do. "I want to work on this project" and "I choose to finish this assignment" put you in the power seat—you make the choice, you initiate the move and the decision. The words in Figure 1.1 give you plenty of ideas.

As you learn and grow, you will gain confidence. Each new skill, each job success, each good grade or piece of positive feedback you receive becomes proof that you are valuable. Tell yourself about your accomplishments. Remind yourself of your successes and your steps in the right direction. Focus on your own potential. Those actions will help keep your self-image strong and steady.

Maintaining a positive self-image is a lifelong challenge! You must learn to ignore the negative voices inside and outside your head that make you feel inferior. Positive self-image gives you the power to use your tools with strength and confidence. Don't ever forget how important you and your ideas are, no matter the situation. Carry your own positive vision of yourself and don't let go. It will smooth your way in the world more than any other tool.

Attitude

Attitude can mean your actual mental state, or the behavior you exhibit to express that state. There are infinite kinds of attitudes. Attitudes go with all kinds of feelings. Have you ever heard someone say "She has a nasty attitude" or "He has a good attitude." Those comments refer to the person's mental state. Or maybe you have heard "Don't give me that kind of attitude!" The speaker means a way of acting that shows a mental state.

Your attitude affects everything that you do. It helps you or trips you up and slows you down. It opens up opportunities for you or pushes them away. It even hides them so you don't know they exist. Make your attitude a tool that works for you. Tame it and put it into your tool kit.

Attitude, *noun*

one's disposition, opinion, mental state, etc.

a manner of acting, thinking, or feeling that shows one's disposition

Attitude ties in with self-image. If you have a positive self-image, you will have an easier time projecting a good attitude. A negative self-image often results in a negative attitude that gets in your way. What you feel on the inside comes through to the outside.

The truth is, people would rather be around a positive person than someone who complains or criticizes others. Have you ever heard the term *energy vampire*? They are people who seem to suck all the energy out of the room because of their negativity. People around them feel tired because it takes a lot of energy to combat that negativity. That's why it's so important to think positively and make sure both your conversations and your actions demonstrate that positive attitude.

Tame That Attitude

You may not have control over what happens to you, but you do have control over your attitude about what happens and the way you react. Sometimes it seems like the attitude you wake up with in the morning will dictate your entire day because you have no choice in the matter. That's a myth! Don't be a slave to your attitude. What if you have an important meeting, date, or game on a "bad" day? Are you going to let your attitude be your excuse for not trying your best? Even if you do fail, you will be able to learn from it and move ahead more quickly with a positive attitude. With a negative attitude, you may make the same mistakes over and over again.

Here's an example of thoughts affecting attitude, and attitude affecting action. Raul has just started a radiology program when his school placement director tells him about a part-time job opportunity with a medical clinic that could help him develop some useful skills and make some much needed cash. He applies for and earns a job interview with the clinic. Then the negative attitude sets in. He worries that he has no healthcare or computer experience. This is his first interview for a job other than retail sales. When he wakes up on the day of the interview, he worries some more as he starts thinking "I am not what they are looking for. I have nothing to offer, no experience at all. Everyone else who interviews will be more qualified than I am. I am unworthy of this job. I might as well forget it."

Raul's negative thoughts have generated a negative attitude. He has already convinced himself that he will not get the job, and he hasn't even been interviewed! A negative attitude robs you of the win before you even start the game. What kind of interview do you think Raul would have with this attitude? He would probably have nothing good to say for himself. He would appear unconfident and maybe even unfriendly. When asked why he would be a good choice for the job, he might even say "I don't know." Attitude reflects self-image, and if you don't have a good image of yourself, neither will anybody else (such as your interviewer).

Raul's thoughts with a positive attitude could be quite different: "I may not have any experience, but I am very friendly and intelligent. I love learning and can soon adapt to the office systems at this particular clinic. I enjoy working with people and will treat the patients well, with good service and a smile. My personality is perfect for this job." Raul's good attitude allows him to focus on his good points and makes him feel he deserves this job. In the interview, he will cheerfully volunteer his assets. If the interviewer remarks that he has no computer experience, he might say that he learns quickly and his ability to get along with people will be of great value while he learns the more specific skills of the job.

People prefer spending time with a positive person rather than a negative one.

Having a good attitude can turn things around for you. If you do wake up with a negative attitude, make the choice to turn it around. Use positive thinking. You won't do yourself any good by ruining your opportunities before they even present themselves.

Now You Try It: You and Your Attitude

Think about two important events that occurred in your life in which your attitude had a direct impact on the outcome: one where your attitude was good, and one where your attitude was bad.

1. What was the first event (when you had a good attitude)?

   - What was your attitude?

   - What kind of things did you say to yourself?

   - What were the results?

2. What was the second event (when you had a bad attitude)?

   - What was your attitude?

   - What kind of things did you say to yourself?

   - What were the results?

   - What could you have said or thought differently to change your attitude?

Motivation

Working hard at keeping a positive attitude and focusing on your good points is only the beginning. Next in your tool kit is motivation. **Motivation** gives you the energy and drive to dive in and work toward achieving your goals. This tool keeps you moving when the going gets rough. Motivation comes from many different sources. Did you ever wake up in the morning and not want to get out of bed? What motivated you to finally get up? Did you remember that you had an important test in school? Did you think about the fact that being late to work might cost you some pay that you needed? Were you hungry for breakfast? These are all different kinds of motivation, and they all work!

Motivating yourself can be challenging. If you have ever spent time exercising, you know that some days you feel psyched for it and other days you have to drag yourself to the gym. Even when you feel unmotivated to work out, you usually have a surprise at the end—you feel better, you're glad you did it, and you have a sense of accomplishment. Those surprise

Motivation, *noun*

that which incites or impels; that which provides with a motive

A good attitude gets you nowhere if you don't have the motivation to get up and do something!

feelings of pride and accomplishment come from completing a task that might seem bothersome when you start. It's the light at the end of the tunnel.

The reasons you are motivated to educate yourself and get a good job probably run a little deeper. Perhaps you have dreams of pursing a career that you will really love. Maybe you aspire to live at a certain income level. Or perhaps you have children to support and need a better job. Dreams, financial aspirations, and the need to support family are all strong and valid motivations. Some people are also motivated by the need to prove something to themselves or to others, while other people are motivated by the desire to express themselves or make a difference. No matter where it comes from, motivation is necessary to set your dream in motion.

What if you have a good attitude, but no motivation? Well, you might find yourself lying in bed all day, feeling good about yourself, with a smile on your face. You can hang on to your good attitude forever, but if you never have the motivation to go out and show someone how good it is, you won't be able to find a job. So, how can you get motivated?

Let's work through the motivation process by considering this scenario: What would it take to motivate you to mail resumes to 20 potential employers? Figure 1.2 illustrates the motivation process.

1. **First, set your goals.** You want to send out resumes to 20 local businesses. You want to get names of those businesses from an online job board, your newspaper, bulletin boards, and the placement office at school. You want a cover letter to accompany each resume, and you want everything to be printed attractively on a laser printer.

2. **Next, define what your rewards might be.** Some will come automatically, such as the satisfaction of having done a good job, the relief of being able to cross the task off your to-do list, or the joy of owning a nice stack of professional, well-formatted resumes. Some rewards are beyond your control and may or may not come, such as potential calls requesting an interview or job offers following interviews. And some you can choose to give to yourself, such as an evening out, a new CD, or a shopping trip for new interview clothing.

3. **Before you begin, examine the situation to see what might be blocking your motivation.** What kept you from getting this done before? Perhaps you were a little nervous about actually starting the job hunt, and it always seemed more relaxing to put it off for a while. There's no way to remove that block other than to just start the hunt! Maybe another obstacle is the print quality of your home printer and the trouble you had getting access to a better

Figure 1.2 Motivation keeps you going

1. Set Clear Goals	2. Define Rewards	3. Remove Obstacles	4. Take the First Step
Write down the "whys" for motivation.	Identify benefits.	Define roadblocks and create solutions.	Starting is the hardest part.

printer. Tackle that obstacle by talking to your teacher and scheduling a time after the regular school day when you can use the school's printer. One more stumbling block is that you aren't pleased with the people you currently have as references. To get past this, call three people who have a more current perspective on you and your life and ask if they will consent to being listed as references.

4. **Once you overcome those obstacles, get started.** It's easy to waste time sitting around considering all your goals and wondering where to begin. Choose a logical first step and start there. Here's one: You can't send out new resumes until you have updated your current resume. That means you need to revise your resume on the school computer and then print it out. Next, round up the list of people who will receive your resume and confirm their proper addresses. Third, write a basic cover letter and adapt it for each employer. Next, print the resumes and cover letters, stuff and stamp the envelopes, and mail everything. Finally, call the people you want as references and let them know you're sending out resumes—they may get calls from potential employers. You might even tell them the type of job you're going after and ask them to focus on certain skills or qualities you have. Don't forget to make a list of the references with their names, titles, and contact information. Your potential employer just might need that list. You did it! You have systematically and efficiently motivated yourself to complete a task.

Think through what's motivating you to read this text, and let that motivation drive you toward your goals. Grab the motivation tool and put it in a good spot next to your positive attitude in your tool kit.

Commitment

You are now a motivated person with a terrific attitude and self-image—you know your value in the working world and you have the drive to go out and prove it. But that's still not enough. We now present another tool—commitment.

Any time you make a promise to do something, whether it is to love someone for the rest of your life or to take out the garbage after dinner, you have made a **commitment**. Definition 1 refers to the promise itself: "He made a commitment to meet me every Saturday to go to the recycling center." Definition 2 describes a willingness to dedicate your energy to something over a longer period of time: "Working with that club takes a lot of commitment. You will be busy."

Every job you take requires a commitment. In fact, this class you are taking right now is a very important commitment. You would be wasting your time if you were attending the class without being committed. Commitment means you do what you say you will do. You find out what it takes to achieve a goal and you do what it takes. Saying "I've made a commitment to improve myself" isn't a real commitment until you decide on a clear and specific course of action, such as exercising regularly or reading a book every week.

What if you have a good attitude and strong motivation without commitment? You will be all charged up with no place to go. You will spin all your good intentions (attitude) and energy (motivation) into space because you are not committed to achieving a specific goal. Have you ever known anyone like that? People who rarely commit often seem sweet and well-intentioned, but usually end up spending their lives in a job or in a relationship they don't really like. If we don't commit to anything specific, we tend to take the first thing that comes along. If that first thing is not the right thing, we may never commit to making a change. It can be a real dead end.

Commitment gives you the clearest possible vision of what you want and how you plan to achieve it. It means focusing on that big road sign before you make the decision to move down the exit ramp onto the highway. How can you commit to something and stay that way? Figure 1.3 identifies three key steps in creating and sustaining commitment.

1. **First, define your commitment.** Make a decision about something you want to do: "I want to read this entire book with the rest of the class." The decision always comes first, even if you have no idea how you are going to achieve your goal.

Commitment, *noun*

a pledge or promise to do something

dedication to a long-term course of action

2. **Second, take the first step on the path toward your goal.** In this case, begin reading the first chapter. You have now made a commitment to yourself, to your teacher (who wants you to benefit from the book), and to those close to you who know that everything you do in school will help you to have a more successful career.

3. **Third, stick to your commitment by renewing it regularly.** Why does staying committed usually seem tougher than making the initial commitment? Usually, when you first make the commitment, you have more positive energy to devote to your task than you do a few days or months later. After losing your steam, it's easy to want to quit or to slack off. You might have experienced this feeling if you have ever made a commitment to stop smoking, read the news every day, exercise, keep your home clean, or eat healthy.

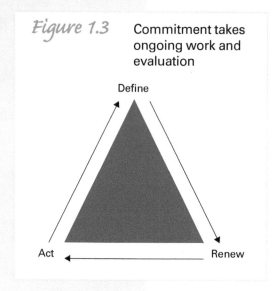

Figure 1.3 Commitment takes ongoing work and evaluation

Renewing your commitment regularly is a way to keep that positive energy high so you can stay committed. When you renew a commitment, think about it almost as if you were starting over. Remind yourself why you made the commitment in the first place. Think about the goal you are trying to reach. Ask yourself how you will feel when you reach that goal. Review your original thoughts about why that goal is important to you. Commitment is vision (a view of your future), and staying committed means renewing that vision and keeping it as clear as possible.

When you develop the ability to make and maintain commitments, you gain a valuable personal quality necessary for career success—responsibility. Committing yourself to something means taking responsibility for completing the steps that lead to the goal. If you are irresponsible, lose sight of your goal, or fail to take one of the steps toward it, you falter in your commitment. Commitment and responsibility are inseparable. When you act responsibly, you earn the respect and trust of others who see that you stick to your commitments and get the job done.

A commitment helps you define your goals and draw the path from where you are today to where you dream of being tomorrow. It probably won't be a straight path, because our lives are unpredictable; things arise now and then that cause us to take a few detours. But if you commit to following the line with good attitude and motivation, you'll arrive at your destination.

Habits

Everybody has habits—good ones and not-so-good ones. When you encourage your good habits and learn to control or change your bad ones, you'll have an advantage in the working world.

Habits belong in your tool kit because they affect so many of your activities. Habits control a lot of what you do, and are stubborn about sticking around, whether you want them to or not! People hang on to habits because they have rewards. You get something in return for sticking to a habit. Sometimes the worst habits bring the most immediate rewards; good habits tend to bring rewards over time. Therefore, you may find it tough both to break the bad habits and to stick with the new ones.

For example, let's look at eating habits. Imagine that Raphael has a bad habit of eating a lot of chocolates. That bad habit has an immediate reward because the chocolates taste good the moment Raphael eats them. In the long term, however, the fat and sugar won't do him much good; in fact, he already has a weight problem. If he begins eating more fruits and vegetables instead of chocolates, Raphael will have to give up that immediate sugar high. He'll probably experience headaches and cravings at first, but feel better later. The reward doesn't come right away, but after time and steady devotion to the new good habit, a more energetic, healthier body would begin to emerge for Raphael, which would be a much longer-lasting and valuable reward.

Habit, *noun*

a tendency to perform a certain action or behave in a certain way; a usual way of doing something

What do we mean by a "bad" habit? A bad habit is one that hinders you as you pursue your dreams, one that pulls you down into a rut and holds you there, even as you try to escape. Procrastination is one of the most common bad habits, and one that constantly keeps people from moving ahead. People can have bad personal habits, bad workplace habits, and bad habits with friends, family, or substances. Bad habits come in all shapes and sizes—from not following through on projects at work, to not eating well, to not communicating with family members. Do you have any habits that keep you from reaching your goals?

As life progresses and as you change, habits that helped you cope in the past may hinder you in the future. Consider Renee, a full-time parent reentering the workforce. In her role as a mother, she developed the habit of putting other people's needs before her own. That made sense when her children were very young and completely dependent on her. But now that her children are older and more independent, Renee's habit is not necessarily a good thing. Renee could jeopardize her job by continually looking out for others before getting her own work done. The habit of putting the needs of others first is no longer appropriate and should be broken.

It takes some strong, constant effort to beat your bad habits. Give yourself time. First you must decide which habits get in your way and what you want to replace them with. Then you must keep in mind the "rule of 21": It generally takes 21 days to even start to change a habit. During those 21 days you'll spend time thinking about the change, trying out the new habit, going back to the old habit, and trying again. In those 21 days you have a chance to think things through and to realize the effort involved in making a change.

How can you break your not-so-helpful habits during those 21 days? Here are seven helpful steps to success.

1. **Recognize the habits that block your success.** Visualize where you want to be and define which habits seem to stand in the way. List the habits you want to break or change, with the most important ones at the top. Identify replacement habits. Then set a path for yourself.

2. **Work on only one change at a time.** You might become overwhelmed by trying to change too many habits at once. Changing even one habit takes a lot of energy; the effort required to change more than one habit might make you want to quit. Focus on changing one habit and give it your all.

3. **Believe that you want to change.** Think it through. Be certain that you will benefit from the change you have decided to make. Write it down; this makes you feel more committed.

4. **Start today.** If you start now, you won't waste any valuable time. The sooner you begin, the sooner you will be on your way to better habits.

5. **Take a little piece at a time.** Don't expect to dump the entire habit in one day. Your mind or body will rebel against that sort of unrealistic expectation. Ease into the change and be kind to yourself. For example, if you decide that your goal is to spend less money, start by making your lunch instead of buying it, or cutting down on those daily fancy coffee drinks. Later, you can make other changes, such as limiting how many times you go out to dinner or the movies, or creating a clothing budget.

6. **Reward yourself when you take a step in the right direction.** Give yourself credit. Do something nice for yourself when you make progress toward making or breaking a habit—a quiet hour, a little purchase, or a bike ride. Be proud of yourself, and feel confident that you have taken the right road. Acknowledging your success is important; if you skip this step, you may begin to wonder why you're even trying to make any changes.

7. **Don't get discouraged if you fall back into old habits from time to time.** It happens to all of us. No one can live up to the expectation of instant success. When you've spent months or years developing a habit, you can't toss it out in a day or a week. Take your time and forgive yourself for slipping up once in a while—it's part of the learning process. You'll make a stronger return to the path of success when you tolerate the occasional detour. If you feel as if you have moved way off the track, reevaluate the original goal you set for changing the habit. Maybe it was too ambitious or too risky. You may need to soften that goal to temporarily take the pressure off yourself.

Now You Try It: What's Your Habit?

Think about three good habits you have and three bad habits. Write them below, along with how long you think you've had the habits. You will be working with these at the end of the chapter.

Good habits

1. _____ 2. _____ 3. _____

Bad habits

1. _____ 2. _____ 3. _____

Patience, *noun*

the state of being able to endure pain, trouble, etc., without losing self-control

the will or ability to wait without complaint

Patience

The importance of taking your time leads us to the next tool in our discussion, patience. **Patience** may seem like an odd choice for a crucial tool, but without it your other tools may fail you. Building your career without patience is like building a house without a level to make sure that every board is flush and even with the next board. Your hammer, saw, and screwdriver may let you build the house quickly, but you won't like what you see when you finish.

Similarly, if you have a great attitude and you are motivated, committed, and working to improve your habits, you still don't have it all. What if you have to go through interviews with 5, 10, or even 15 companies before you are hired in your ideal career field? It may happen. Without patience, you might give up after the third interview and take a job that is readily available that you don't even like. With patience, you will realize that if you don't get hired right away, there is no need to give up or get down on yourself. Patience will help you make improvements in your interviewing skills or to accept factors that lie beyond your control (for example, a job may become unavailable because the manager decides to promote someone from within the company). Patience ensures that you continue on your quest for the right job.

Sometimes it takes a long time—even years—before you finally get the job you wanted all along. You may have to move from job to job, learning more about yourself and what you like, and gaining new skills before you land the job of your dreams.

Staying patient will serve you well. Only a few people catapult to the top of their professions in no time. Ironically, those are the few we read about or see on television! Most of us make the slow, steady climb to the top, and that doesn't get much media attention. A well-known actor once said, "It took me 15 years to become an overnight success." When he finally made a hit movie, everyone treated him like a talented phenomenon who had just arrived on the scene. In reality, though, he had been working at obscure and low-paying jobs for years, perfecting his craft and patiently seeking better opportunities.

The right job will happen, but often not right away. Remember, while you are being patient, continue to use your other tools. Sitting and waiting for the job to fall in your lap won't do you any good. Your positive self-image will help you stay confident in your abilities, your attitude will keep you hoping, your motivation will keep you looking, your commitment will keep you focused on your ideal career field, and working on your habits will improve your rate of success.

Integrity, *noun*

the quality or state of being of sound moral principles and ethics

honesty, uprightness, and sincerity

Integrity

Underneath all your trade skills and work skills is **integrity**, an important personal quality that any employer prizes and rewards. The words in the definition—moral principles, ethics, honesty, sincerity—are probably familiar to you. How do they translate into real life? How do you live when you are a person of integrity? Here are four principles of integrity, each with some examples of how they apply in daily living.

1. A person of integrity makes family and work decisions based on admirable moral principles.

   - You schedule work time so you have dinner each night with your children.
   - When an angry customer confronts you, you choose to discuss the situation calmly and offer the customer a few options on how to resolve the conflict.
   - If a neighbor is having some difficulties with his marriage, you refrain from gossip.
   - You admit to your supervisor when you have made a mistake that cost the company time.

2. A person of integrity deals with others honestly and tells the truth to herself and to others.

   - You tell your spouse when something he or she did has upset you.
   - When your work quality suffers because of a disagreement with a coworker, you take time to discuss the situation with that person and voice your feelings honestly.
   - You praise yourself for jobs well done and you admit mistakes to yourself, while brainstorming ways you could do better next time.
   - You tell your supervisor when you disagree with a work decision he or she made.

3. A person of integrity speaks and acts sincerely, voicing thoughts accurately and doing what feels right.

   - You tell your coworker that you will finish up a project when she has to leave early, and you follow through by completing the work.
   - You tell your mother that she looks wonderful—and she does—when she returns from a relaxing vacation.
   - You voice concerns about rushing a particular project at work.
   - When you feel you must break up with a long-time partner, you do so without waiting too long and express yourself as clearly as you can.

4. A person of integrity considers the needs of others with his own needs when making the decisions that define the path through life.

   - When your best friend at work has a family emergency, you adjust your work schedule so you can help his clients.
   - You decide to vacation as a family at a local beach to satisfy your financial constraints, as well as provide fun for both the adults and the children.
   - You parcel out the duties of a particular project according to the talents of each member of your work team.
   - You give up a few nights out to care for the kids so your spouse can take a night class.

Integrity is one of the most sought-after qualities in an employee, friend, or spouse because it allows people to trust you at the most basic level. When employers know you will do what is asked, speak your mind honestly, and make work decisions based on good principles, they feel confident about assigning responsibilities to you. They also feel comfortable giving you more opportunities to grow and learn because they don't have to spend time reinforcing or redirecting your moral foundation. In any work or personal relationship, trust brings freedom. If people trust how you think, work, and behave, they will let you make decisions freely and act according to your own will.

For example, suppose you work for a manager who does not trust you based on your past behavior and doubts your integrity. As a result, she watches you very carefully and gives you little room for independent decision making, always making sure you check with her first. She only gives you work that she can control and monitor. This lack of trust on the job will inhibit your growth and will paralyze your manager because she will spend too much time keeping an eye on you.

Now imagine your behavior is different. You have exhibited a great deal of integrity on the job. You tactfully say what you think. You do what is assigned to you and what you say you will do. You are honest with your supervisor and other coworkers, and you are always aware of the needs of those around you. In this case, your manager trusts you and your work. She lets you do your regular tasks on your own, only checking now and then to verify the quality. When you have ideas and make suggestions, she listens carefully and gives you the go-ahead on the ones that she feels make sense. Your supervisor is able to complete more of her own work because she is freed of the responsibility to constantly monitor what you do. The trust that integrity brings makes everyone's jobs easier and more productive.

Integrity cannot really be taught. We all learned about the "right" way to behave from parents, teachers, and life experiences. But each of us makes individual decisions about whether we will actually behave the right way. Many people know what honest behavior is, but don't choose to behave that way. Integrity is more than knowing the right way to behave; it is making the independent decision to behave that way. The more people see you make decisions that demonstrate integrity, the more freedom they will give you to pursue your dreams.

If you have integrity, when you do make the occasional mistake, people won't lose their trust in you. For example, did you ever do something wrong and then feel afraid to tell someone close to you about it? Chances are, if you are a trustworthy person, once you told the truth the other person's disappointment wasn't great enough to damage the existing trust he or she had in you. If you constantly strive to speak, think, and act with integrity, you will earn trust from those around you.

Empathy

Every tool you have gathered so far is worthless if you are unable to empathize with those around you. **Empathy** is the ability to put yourself in another's place and imagine what he or she is feeling. This ability helps you make win–win decisions that benefit everyone, rather than win–lose decisions that benefit only you. The problem with win–lose decisions is that the person who loses continues to feel angry and victimized, and looks for a chance to get back at you.

A lack of empathy in the corporate world is certainly responsible for the dog-eat-dog behavior we so often see around us. Think about companies that lose their employees' pension funds due to speculative investments, or pay exorbitant salaries to CEOs while laying off the rest of the workforce, or damage the environment to make a bit more profit. They all do a great amount of damage because of lack of empathy.

Empathy gives you an edge because you understand what other people are feeling and can therefore communicate and negotiate more effectively and achieve lasting results. For example, imagine that you work for a manager who is worried about losing his job. The company has been making layoffs, and the manager feels he will be the next to go. He is concerned because his wife is ill and the hospital bills are piling up. Now, suppose your manager asks you why you are taking so much time finishing up a project. You start to explain, but very quickly the manager starts yelling at you, threatening that if you and your team don't finish the project on time, the whole department will suffer and you will get fired!

If you have no empathy, you will probably react in kind and start yelling at your manager. You may even walk out on him or threaten to quit. Who knows, he might fire you on the spot! And there you would be, out of a job, because of one conversation that ended badly.

If you are an empathetic person, however, you will understand that your manager is under a lot of pressure and is afraid that if his team doesn't perform, he will be fired. As a result, you would be able to take his anger less personally. Instead of reacting to his yelling, you might calmly assure him that the design phase of the project took longer than expected, but as a result, the development phase will take much less time. You will be able to convince him that the project is under control and will finish on time. Best of all, your manager will probably calm down once he knows that the project is proceeding as planned and will make the department look good.

The ability to understand what another person is feeling and to act accordingly goes a long way in making you successful in the workplace, in school, at home, and in the world. That is the power of empathy, the most important tool in your tool kit.

Managing Change and Stress

Before you learn about the rest of the tools in your tool kit, it's good to remember that those tools are only as good as your ability to select the right ones at the right time, and use them correctly. The ability to do so rests on your ability to deal with change and manage stress. We will discuss this further in later chapters, but for now, here are a few things to remember.

- The world is changing at a faster rate than ever before. You need to remain flexible to deal with change, instead of rigidly resisting it, violently reacting to it, or allowing it to control you.
- You may not be able to control changing events, but you can control your reaction to them (your attitude). People who take things in stride, do not assume that change is always for the worst, and do not assume that events occur to deliberately thwart them tend to be more successful.
- Your response to events affects the amount of stress you experience. Stress occurs when you respond negatively to events. As a result of your negative emotional reaction, certain hormones are released in your body, such as adrenalin and cortisol. These hormones were originally intended to give human beings added energy to

"fight or flee" in the face of imminent danger. Today those same hormones are released when you are worried, upset, angry, or scared, even when there is no real danger. Unfortunately, over the long term, these stress hormones have damaging effects on the body, such as decreased bone density, decreased muscle tissue, increased blood pressure, and a lowered immune system.

When you feel stressed, it's important to get oxygen into your system and to work those stress hormones out of your system. Table 1.2 gives you some tips for doing so.

With the basic universal tools in place and a few stress management tips under your belt, it's time to practice what you've learned in this chapter.

Table 1.2 **Tips for Managing Stress**	
Burnout Management Technique	**Actions to Take**
Get some oxygen	We tend to breathe shallowly when stressed. To counteract this, do some slow, deep breathing. Take a walk and get some air. Calming breaths go a long way in alleviating stress.
Change your state	This is a very simple technique that can quickly change your outlook. If you are sitting, try standing while you go about your business. If you have been standing, sit down and relax. Standing, in general, communicates a greater sense of involvement with and control of a situation, but it is harder on the body and simply can't be maintained constantly.
Take a think break	Take time to get away from the interruption-driven environment of your desk or workspace so as to change your state. Take a short walk, even if it's inside the building. Take a stretch break to increase your blood flow.
Establish a system of balance	Listen to the nonverbal ways your body communicates its need for a break. Is your head throbbing? Are your eyes glazing over? Do you get tense in your neck and shoulders? To avoid or get past these symptoms, it's important to balance periods of hard work with breaks.
Know when you need to refuel	Refueling involves more than just a short break. Make time to eat, rest, exercise, and interact with others or take some time alone.

Learning from Experience
A Perspective from the Working World

Taking the High Road

Ray Golding, *molding manager and student of business management*

I really hated high school because I got bad grades and thought it was boring. So in the eleventh grade, I quit. Because I'd always been good with my hands, I worked in a woodshop and later on a construction site. Then I got a job as a machinist for an automation plant. I helped make parts for fixtures that sorted items on the assembly line and packed bottles into cases.

Because I dropped out of high school, I didn't think I could ever go to college. But my supervisor kept telling me to go back to school. He said that if I wanted to get promoted I would need a college education. I didn't really believe him. After all, I kept moving up in the companies where I worked, in terms of money. However, I was never given more responsibility. I wasn't even sure that I wanted to push myself any harder so I coasted, changing jobs from time to time, but always working as a machinist.

Then I got married and had two children. We were living in a mobile home, and I knew I needed to do something different so our lives could be better. The company I worked for hired me to work in a prototype machine shop, building "proof-of-concept" fixtures for an engineering team. I thought this might be the break I needed. But then they started introducing me to concepts and tasks that I'd never heard of before. For example, they wanted me to modify the mechanical drawings of the parts I was building. They even asked me to put together some estimates for manufacturing the parts. I had no idea how to do this.

They also wanted me to manage a team of four machinists, but I didn't know how to manage people. Instead, I pushed the men around and had a terrible attitude. Of course, I didn't have anybody to show me anything different.

And then I got my break. The manager of the company told me that even though I'd quit school, I could still go to college. He suggested I try some computer aided mechanical design (CAD) classes at the local community college. I thought he was crazy, but I gave it a try. Going back to school was a turning point in my life. I was blown away by how hard it was, but I liked the challenge. I learned you have to be very independent in college. It's not like high school, where you're told what to do; you have to motivate yourself. In my first course I had a very great instructor. He made learning CAD software so interesting that I actually found myself enjoying school.

I'm learning things in class that I can apply directly to the job. As I work on class projects, I learn ways to communicate with my team so everyone wants to cooperate. Teamwork is very important if you want to build a prosperous company. I've learned that as a manager, you can't just dictate to people; you have to tell them *why* you want them to do things—*why* it's important to the company. They need to have a vision of where the company is going, as well as know what you expect of them.

I've also learned that there are people out there who really care and want you to succeed, but you have to open up to them for that to happen; you have to ask for their help. I was lucky enough to have an instructor who helped me. Sometimes I'd come to his class after a long day of work, feeling very frustrated. I'd tell him about a problem at work, and he would listen and give me a different perspective. With problem solving you have to be creative, and I'm learning how to think like that.

When I think back to my life ten years ago, I cannot believe how far I've come. I'm very excited about what the future holds for my family and me. I like it that my children are seeing me get an education because it sets a good example. When I come home and tell them I got an A, they are happy for me. Right now I'm shooting for an A.A. degree, but I plan to keep learning all my life.

Your Tool Kit at Work

We all learn by seeing, reading, and doing. Perform these end-of-chapter exercises to give yourself a chance to practice what you learned in this chapter.

1.1 Universal Work Skills

Universal work skills are divided into basic skills and workplace competencies. The basic skills on the list add up to the knowledge you need in the workplace, and the workplace competencies refer to how to put that knowledge to work. Both skills and competencies are necessary if you want to qualify for a good job, succeed on the job, and move forward in your career.

All of the chapters in *The Career Tool Kit* are interrelated, which means the basic skills and workplace competencies appear many times throughout this book, building on and complementing one another. To give you a quick resource, each skill is listed in Table 1.3, with numbers in parentheses ( ) indicating the chapter or chapters focusing on that skill. AC stands for all chapters, which means the skill is a basic theme that runs throughout the book. Read the list carefully. Then check your current interest and skill level. Leave the last column unmarked for now.

Refer to your list as you go through the chapters. Fill in your progress in the last column each time you finish a chapter.

Universal work skills will boost your career. Think about your valuable work experience, including paid and unpaid jobs. For example, you may have worked in a factory and volunteered at the fire department. You may have worked in an office and visited nursing home residents in your spare time. Or you may have groomed horses or mowed lawns while attending school.

Think about your performance on those jobs, specifically your strengths. List three of your job strengths and the universal work skills they required.

1. _____

2. _____

3. _____

On the other hand, we all have areas that could use some work. Look again at the universal work skills listed in Table 1.3. Think of the strengths you needed in the past, but didn't possess. Perhaps you yelled at your boss because you lacked patience, or gave a customer $50 in change instead of $5 because you lacked concentration, which cost you a job.

List three universal work skills that you need to improve. Be specific and honest. The first step on your new career path depends on an honest assessment of yourself.

1. _____

2. _____

3. _____

1.2 Positive Attitude List—Your PAL

Your attitude affects everything you do, so a positive attitude is probably your most essential tool. Your attitude accounts for 80% of your success in your career and in your personal life.

Throughout the end-of-chapter activities in this text, you will build your positive attitude list. We will refer to the list as your PAL. A pal is a close friend who helps you and supports you, and that's the kind of effect your positive attitude list can have on your future.

A new list with related attitudes will appear at the end of each chapter. You may find an attitude that appears more than once if it applies to more than one chapter. We've included some attitudes frequently to highlight their importance in different situations.

Table 1.3   Universal Work Skills Reference Table

Universal Work Skill	My Skills Are: Excellent Good Average Poor	I Want to Improve	I'm Progressing
Basic Skills			
Thinking clearly and creatively (AC)			
Making decisions (AC)			
Solving problems (AC)			
Being responsible (AC)			
Positive self-image (AC)			
Making choices based on values (AC)			
Developing good habits (1)			
Working and living with integrity (AC)			
Empathy and emotional intelligence (1, 10)			
Identifying goals (2, 6)			
Setting priorities (2, 6)			
Knowing how to learn (4)			
Reading (4)			
Writing (4)			
Listening (4, 10)			
Speaking (10)			
Demonstrating sociability (6, 8, 10)			
Workplace Competencies			
Communicating (AC)			
Working in a diverse community (9)			
Managing time (2)			
Managing money (2)			
Participating in a team (6)			
Handling clients and customers (10)			
Negotiating (8, 10)			
Resolving conflicts (10, 11)			
Using resources (6, 7)			
Acquiring information (5, 6, 11)			

Look over the following attitudes and circle the words that best describe you. Then select the one you want to improve first and write it in the space provided.

- **Ambitious.** Actively seeks success.
- **Truthful.** Is honest, sincere, and straightforward.

- **Tenacious.** Holds firmly to ideals and strong values; never gives up.
- **Imaginative.** Brings creativity to the job.
- **Thorough.** Is complete and comprehensive in work.
- **Unique.** Has special qualities and values them.
- **Dependable.** Is reliable and trustworthy.
- **Enthusiastic.** Shows a lively interest in the job and the people.
- **Self-confident.** Has confidence in abilities.

I will develop my ability to be: _____

Here's a way to affirm your positive attitude. Write "I am" at the top of an index card or a sticky note. Below that, write the positive attitude that you want to develop. Place the note where you will see it first thing in the morning. Your bathroom mirror or the refrigerator is a good spot. You can write your attitude on several notes and put them in places where you will see them. Recite your affirmation aloud (if possible) many times each day. Always say it as if you already possess it: "I am dependable," rather than "I will be dependable" or "I hope to be dependable." Remember, we choose our attitudes. Whatever the human mind can perceive and believe, it can achieve. When you repeat your positive attitude affirmation and practice the attitude, you acquire a new PAL.

1.3 The Habit Pledge

It's your turn to give your opinion. Is it more difficult to accept a new habit or to break an old one? Most people say getting rid of an old habit is harder than acquiring a new one.

Analyze your habits. Think back about the ones you identified earlier in the chapter. Which old one would you like to drop? What new habit would you like to adopt in its place?

A new habit I'd like to develop is: _____

An old habit that gets in the way is: _____

Make the commitment—sign your name to the pledge and practice the rule of 21.

I AM PRACTICING THE NEW HABIT FOR THE NEXT 21 DAYS.

Name: _____

Date: _____

The 21-Day Habit Breaker

In the 21-day habit chart (see Table 1.4), list the old habit you identified earlier that interferes with your current life and goals. Then list the new habit you want to develop in its place. Put a check by each day that you practice the new habit. Avoid skipping days. If you do skip a day, start the 21-day cycle over. Reward yourself when you succeed. As you can see from the example, you don't have to reward yourself every day—just enough that you show some appreciation for your hard work.

1.4 Habits for Work That Work

You probably already have habits that will help you achieve career success if you apply them to your working life. Perhaps you get to school or work ten minutes early, maybe you lay out clothes for the next day just before bed, or perhaps you help a coworker when you have a break.

Table 1.4 **21-day Habit Chart**			
Old Habit	**New Habit**	**Day**	**My Reward**
Example: Watching television 9–10 p.m. on weekdays	Study 9–10 p.m. on weekdays	1	Watch television 9–10 p.m. on weekends
		1	
		2	
		3	
		4	
		5	
		6	
		7	
		8	
		9	
		10	
		11	
		12	
		13	
		14	
		15	
		16	
		17	
		18	
		19	
		20	
		21	

On line 1 of Table 1.5, write a useful habit that you already have and a situation in which you want to apply it. Perhaps you get to class early, but you always rush into work just after 9:00 a.m. In this case, you need to apply your school habit to your work behavior. Extending the useful habit into the rest of your life requires a conscious decision and repetition. However, in 21 days you'll make strides. After all, you already have a habit that works. Fill the additional spaces with more habits as you think of them. Use tally marks to keep track of how many days you are able to extend your habit.

1.5 Technology Is Now Universal

Answer yes or no to the following technology checkup questions.

1. Do you know how to open different types of attachments you receive through email?
2. Do you know how to collaborate on a document through programs such as Google Docs?

	Good Habit	Where/When Used	Where/When to Extend	Days	Reward
1.					
2.					
3.					
4.					

Table 1.5 **Useful Habits**

3. Do you have your own Internet provider and email account (either through your home, school, or work)?
4. Are you comfortable electronically formatting and editing professionally written material?
5. Have you submitted an electronic resume, cover letter, or application online for a job?
6. Have you used a spreadsheet program such as Excel or Lotus 123?
7. Have you used software programs to develop professional visual or audio presentations?
8. Do you know how to do online searches for images that you can use in reports, articles, or presentations?
9. Have you ever developed a website or created content for one?
10. Are you a member of any online forums or social networking sites?

If you answered yes to:

- 7–10 questions, you use technology as a tool and understand its importance. Keep it up.
- 4–6 questions, you are technologically aware. Consider deepening your use of different technologies.
- 0–3 questions, you might consider setting a goal of increasing your knowledge of technology.

1.6 Take New Tools on the Road

Choose the three most important tools you gained from reading this chapter and write them here.

1. _____
2. _____
3. _____

For each tool you just listed, write how you will apply that tool to achieve success in your career. You can write about changes you might make, as well as existing behaviors that you want to reinforce and continue.

1. _____
2. _____
3. _____

Here's an example to get you thinking:

Tool: Positive self-talk

- **How to apply:** I will put notes all around and talk to myself about my positive attributes because I tend to have low self-esteem. I will work hard to keep supporting myself and reminding myself that I am valuable and smart. When a negative thought about me pops into my mind, I will replace it with a positive one.

Unlock Your Personal Power

Keys to the Tool Kit

Be yourself. There is something that you can do better than any other. Listen to the inward voice and bravely obey it.

Unknown

 learning objectives

- Why is self-understanding important for your personal and professional future?
- What are the four categories of the Myers-Briggs Test Indicator and how do they create a personality profile?

- What roles do talents, abilities, likes, and dislikes play in a career choice?
- What are "SMART" goals and how do you set them?
- How can you best manage your time?

Melanie and Justin are two very different people who both work at Westward Solar, a company that develops software controllers for solar panels. Melanie is a software tester who is very organized and likes things planned and scheduled. She doesn't like loose ends and she is a very detail-oriented person. She is good at meeting deadlines, as long as she can focus on the task at hand without being interrupted. She likes doing what she's assigned and working by herself in a quiet office. She loves being able to explore the software, find hidden problems, and make sure they get fixed. Melanie is dedicated to making sure that every software application the software team releases is easy to use and bug free.

Justin is a graphics designer who is a very "go with the flow" kind of guy. He's quite creative and likes to work on a variety of things at the same time. He doesn't like deadlines or schedules, and often comes up with things to do that are not associated with his job assignments, just because he thinks they need to be done. All the departments at Westward Solar use him from time to time—and sometimes at the same time. He is used to switching back and forth between projects, working on brochure covers and logos for the marketing team, toolbar icons for the software team, and illustrations for the technical writers. As long as he has a chance to express himself and interact with lots of people, Justin is happy.

Luckily, both Melanie and Justin work at jobs that make the most of their talents and suit their personalities. Can you imagine if they had to do each other's jobs? Poor Melanie would go crazy, being constantly interrupted, never being allowed to focus on one task until it was completed, and reporting to so many people. Justin would be bored to tears, sitting in his office by himself, forced to work on only one assignment at a time.

This chapter is all about understanding who you are. Although you may not think so, you have something unique to offer the world, and it is up to you to figure out what that is. The more you understand yourself—your ideas, thoughts, likes, dislikes, interests, dreams, skills, and talents—the closer you get to unlocking your personal power and becoming the person you were meant to be. It is never too late to delve within and learn who you are or can be. This chapter walks you through the process of better understanding yourself so you can set meaningful goals and priorities, and then manage your time to accomplish those goals.

myth

"I have a hard enough time thinking about how to get all my stuff done today. Thinking about career and life goals and my mission is a waste of time."

reality

Having goals and a mission is vital for success. Without them we are easily sidetracked, caving in to the smallest disappointment and giving up. Without them we cannot prioritize our many daily tasks and manage our time. Goals and a mission give us direction, motivation, and a way to know if we are making meaningful progress.

Understanding Yourself

If you've ever used a power tool, you know it can't serve you well unless you know how it operates. For example, suppose you need to use a power drill, but have never seen one before. You would probably read the manual first (hopefully). Next, you might try out the drill to see what grip works best and how to balance its weight. You would study which materials were safe to drill and which ones were unsafe. You would become aware of the drill's limitations and its capabilities. In short, you would get to know your tool inside and out, and develop a healthy respect for its power.

Your brain is a far more powerful tool than a drill. That's why it's so important to get to know yourself and respect yourself. Self-knowledge and self-respect should be your main focus right now. Until you know who you really are, you will have difficulty expressing your full potential and sharing your gifts with the world. That's why this chapter gives you permission to turn your focus inward.

It's time to build a solid core of self-knowledge and self-respect, for a number of reasons:

- You cannot believe in yourself without knowing what you are believing in.
- You cannot set smart and realistic goals for yourself without knowing where your strengths and weaknesses lie.
- You need to learn how to care about yourself before you can care for others.
- Other people take their cues from what you project. If you act like you care about and respect yourself, they will follow your lead.
- A solid, grounded base of self-knowledge and self-respect will stay with you through the tough times and keep you strong.
- The more you know about yourself, the better you can determine your ideal job and lifestyle.

How can knowing about yourself help your career? Once you have a good idea of your personality, you will have an easier time setting goals and making smart decisions for yourself. With a better understanding of your likes and dislikes, you will gain insight into what kinds of jobs would be a good fit for you. Recognizing and using your own talents and abilities will make you feel more fulfilled and will help you in your career. Ultimately, the best job for you is one that: (1) fits your personality, (2) makes the most of your abilities, and (3) fits your likes. By making a conscious effort to discover the real you, you can learn to focus your natural strengths and interests into a career you will love for as long as you choose to work.

How do you start to know yourself? The self is a pretty vague idea, but you can break it down into three primary categories—(1) personality, (2) talents and abilities, and (3) likes and dislikes.

Personality

Personality, noun

habitual patterns and qualities of behavior as expressed by physical and mental activities and attitudes; distinctive individual qualities

Other people in your life might have an easier time describing your personality because they observe you from the outside. They see how you relate to people and how you react to situations. Chances are, you are so busy relating and reacting that you don't often step back to take a good look at yourself.

Personality is a way of describing who you are by looking at your external actions and views. Why is personality important when it comes to your career? What if you decided you wanted to be a police officer, but were extremely shy and preferred to work indoors? You might go through all the training only to learn that you really disliked your job. If you were aware of your tendencies ahead of time, however, you could have found a more suitable niche in the police or legal fields. What about a legal assistant, an analyst in a crime lab, or a court stenographer?

Many people go into a particular line of work because of pressure from family and friends, media hype, or the promise of high pay. Later on these same people may learn they dislike the work and are not suited for it. Do you really want to spend the rest of your life doing something you don't like or aren't good at? It's never too late to find out who you are so you can do the kind of work you are naturally meant to do. A good way to figure this out is through a personality test.

Myers-Briggs Personality Test

In 1773, a Swedish botanist named Carolus Linnaeus thought of a system for classifying all plants and animals: kingdom, phylum, class, order, family, genus, and species. In 1943, Katherine Cook Briggs and her daughter, Isabel Briggs Myers, began working on a system to classify personality types. In 1962 they published the Myers-Briggs Type Indicator, a widely-used and valued personality test that measures psychological preferences in how people perceive the world and make decisions.

The Myers-Briggs personality test asks simple questions about how you would handle situations and what you like or dislike. The result of the test is a personality "type." Your teacher may choose to have you take the Myers-Briggs test and have the results interpreted by a trained professional, but in this book, we will simply talk about the categories (or "dimensions") that make up your personality type so you can begin to find your niche. Even though we call it a test, you cannot fail it. The scores aren't numbers that measure ability; they are letters that stand for words that describe your personality. Figure 2.1 lists the various letters used to describe personality type. As we look at the dimensions, think about which you seem to naturally prefer.

Figure 2.1 Four dimensions of personality types

Introvert	vs.	Extrovert
Sensing	vs.	Intuitive
Thinking	vs.	Feeling
Judging	vs.	Perceptive

Extrovert or Introvert. These terms refer to whether a person gets energy from the outer world or the inner one.

- An extrovert is a person who receives energy from interaction with the outer world, who enjoys working with people and things, and who is happy and comfortable interacting with people in the outside world. People might call an extrovert "outgoing" or "charismatic."

- An introvert is someone who receives energy from his or her inner world, who enjoys spending time alone, and who often enjoys ideas and concepts. People might call an introvert "quiet" or "a listener."

Consider several famous people and try to determine which category fits them—extrovert or introvert. Look at what they do and where they seem to find their energy. How about Shaquille O'Neal, the basketball player? He's an easy talker, probably an extrovert. Oprah Winfrey, the talk show host and interviewer? Her whole job is talking to people, probably an extrovert as well. Jodie Foster, the actress? She is a thinker who usually avoids the press, perhaps an introvert. Think about your family members and friends too, and see if you can decide how to categorize each one.

Sensing or Intuitive. These terms refer to how you perceive things, or how you look at and discover the world.

Did You Know? Katherine Cook Briggs and Isabel Briggs Myers began creating the Myers-Briggs indicator during World War II. They did so because they believed that a knowledge of personality preferences would help women entering the industrial workforce for the first time—so they could identify the sort of wartime jobs in which they would be "most comfortable and effective."[1]

[1]Myers, Isabel Briggs, with Peter B. Myers. *Gifts Differing: Understanding Personality Type.* Mountain View, CA: Davies-Black Publishing, 1995.

- A sensing person views the world primarily with the five senses. This person takes in information based on hearing, seeing, tasting, touching, and smelling, and looks at the world in terms of facts that can be measured and proven through those senses.

- An intuitive person goes with a gut feeling. This person views the world through the emotions, relationships, and deeper meanings he or she feels—things that senses alone could not necessarily explain.

Here's how these two types might react to the same situation. First, we'll imagine you're the intuitive type. You wake up in the morning after a good night's sleep and have a good feeling inside. You just know it's going to be a great day. Never mind that it's raining outside, your job review is coming up, and you have bills to pay. Your inner feeling is unrelated to outside circumstances.

Now imagine you're a sensing type. You wake up, see the rain, remember your job review, and worry about your finances. You now feel stressed and unhappy. Outside circumstances have determined how you feel.

Thinking or Feeling. The Myers-Briggs system uses the words *thinking* and *feeling* to describe how you behave and decide to act on what you see happening in the world. In the Myers-Briggs system, *thinking* does not refer to intellect and *feeling* does not refer to emotions.

- Thinking people make decisions based on objective principles—facts and figures. They place more value on consistency and fairness than on how others will be affected, and they want to be able to concretely explain any decision they make. They tend to make decisions more analytically and impersonally. You might call these people logical, measured, or calculated.

- Feeling people make decisions based on how they feel about the situation. They tend to make decisions more subjectively, according to their personal values and their relationships. You might call this kind of person sensitive or compassionate.

How would a thinker and a feeler react to the same job offer? Let's look at Melanie and Justin. Melanie is a thinking type (T) and Justin is a feeling type (F). Both live in the same apartment complex in the suburbs just outside the city line. They have similar experience using computer-aided design systems and comparable skill levels. Suppose they both interviewed for the same job at Adaptive Interface. The job involves designing websites and online marketing brochures. Adaptive Interface offers a moderate salary, limited benefits, a downtown office, and an outgoing and congenial staff of 15 employees.

Although Melanie likes people at Adaptive Interface, she quickly decides the moderate salary and benefits package just aren't enough to make the job worth it. She makes a logical decision based on the facts.

Justin immediately feels at home with the staff and can easily imagine working with them day in and day out. The fact that the salary and benefits are moderate can't compete with how he feels about the staff. Even the commute into the city doesn't affect his feelings, which dominate his decision.

Judging or Perceptive. The last category looks at how you relate to your outer world. In the Myers-Briggs system, judging does not mean judgmental or opinionated, and perceptive does not mean insightful.

- If you are a judging person, you typically like to make decisions as quickly as possible and you feel more comfortable when issues are resolved and plans are made. This type of person prefers a more structured life and is uncomfortable leaving things open-ended. Words to describe this person might include decisive, controlled, and structured.

- If you are a perceptive person, you prefer living day-to-day and leaving things open and flexible, rather than making decisions or creating plans. This type of person is probably not comfortable making a decision because it means all other choices are closed. Words to describe this kind of person might be spontaneous or flexible.

It's easy to imagine a perceptive person carrying around a short scribbled list of ideas, while the judging one has a detailed list of tasks to accomplish during the day.

Do What You Are and Find a Fit

Within each Myers-Briggs category, you will typically be more comfortable or prefer behaving or viewing the world in one way rather than the other. These preferences become your personality type. For example, a personality type of EIFJ means you are an extrovert who is intuitive, feeling, and judging.

Figure 2.2 shows the 16 possible Myers-Briggs personality types based on the categories. The information in the table is grouped first by introvert and extrovert types, and then by judging and perceptive types.

Even without taking the Myers-Briggs test, you can put together a basic personality type for yourself by thinking about the descriptions you read. Let's say you are a very outgoing person—an extrovert. You are also emotional and act on your feelings, rather than taking the time to find out the facts. So you are probably an intuitive and feeling person. But you like your life organized, so that means you would choose judging for the last category. Your personality profile is ENFJ.

The final letter of your personality type, P or J, probably has the greatest impact on your job choice because it affects how you handle the outside world. This determines your work style and preferred work environment. Knowing whether you are a P or J can help you choose a job that supports rather than frustrates you.

- Judging types like structure and organization, well-defined assignments and schedules, the opportunity to focus on one task at a time, and a chance to analyze and solve problems.
- Perceptive types prefer fewer rules and regulations, flexibility and change, switching gears frequently to prevent boredom, and plenty of opportunities to interact with others and think creatively.

Once you know your personality profile, it becomes easier to consider the types of careers for which you might be suited. The rest of this section looks at each personality profile, describes it, and lists a few example professions that would appeal to that type of person.

The information comes from a popular book, *Do What You Are,* by Paul D. Tieger and Barbara Barron-Tieger.[2] Both are experts in personality type and career development and have trained groups and individuals, including career counselors, over the last 25 years. Whether you are already in a profession you love, are feeling unsatisfied with your job, or are just starting out on your career, the information should prove valuable. It is presented in the order of the rows you see in Figure 2.2.

ISTJ: Introvert-Sensing-Thinking-Judging

This personality type is serious, responsible, and sensible. People fitting this profile are trustworthy and honor commitments. They are also practical, realistic, matter-of-fact, accurate, and methodical, with good powers of concentration. This personality type makes up about 7 to 10% of the U.S. population. These individuals are happiest with jobs that let them:

1. Work on technical projects with explicit objectives and use their abilities to remember facts and details.
2. Work on projects in a logical and efficient way, following standard operating procedures.

Figure 2.2 Myers-Briggs personality types

16 personalities view and interact with the world in different ways				
Introverts	ISTJ	ISFJ	INFJ	INTJ	Judging
	ISTP	ISFP	INFP	INTP	Perceptive
Extroverts	ESTP	ESFP	ENFP	ENTP	Perceptive
	ESTJ	ESFJ	ENFJ	ENTJ	Judging

[2] Tieger, Paul D., and Barbara Barron-Tieger. *Do What You Are.* Boston, MA: Little, Brown, and Company, 2001.

3. Work independently with plenty of time alone, in an environment that rewards practical judgment and experience.

4. Produce tangible, measurable results.

Here are some sample professions that tend to suit the ISTJ personality type:

- **Business:** Auditor, office manager, accountant, word processing specialist, efficiency expert, regulatory compliance officer, bill collector, statistician
- **Sales/service:** Police officer, detective, IRS agent, military officer, real estate agent, corrections officer, ship captain, pilot, farmer, musical instrument maker
- **Finance:** Investment securities officer, tax preparer, estate planner, budget analyst, treasurer/controller
- **Legal/technology:** Law researcher, electrician, engineer, software tester, technical writer, geologist, meteorologist, judge, court clerk
- **Healthcare:** Veterinarian, surgeon, dentist, nursing administrator, pharmacist, orthodontist, optometrist, coroner, public health officer, physician

ISFJ: Introvert-Sensing-Feeling-Judging

This personality type is loyal, devoted, compassionate, and perceptive of how others feel. People fitting this profile are conscientious and responsible and enjoy being needed. They tend to absorb information, enjoy using a large number of facts, and have good memories for details. They are also patient with follow-through. This personality type makes up about 7 to 10% of the U.S. population. These individuals are happiest with jobs that let them:

1. Use their careful observation skills, accuracy, and ability to remember facts and details.
2. Work on tangible projects in a traditional, orderly environment.
3. Work behind the scenes, yet be appreciated for their contributions.
4. Focus their energy on one project or person at a time, while adhering to standard procedures.

Here are some sample professions that tend to suit the ISFJ personality type:

- **Healthcare:** Dental hygienist, nurse, optician, medical records administrator, pharmacy technician, hospice worker, occupational therapist, dental technician
- **Service/education:** Preschool teacher, librarian, social worker, substance abuse counselor, child welfare counselor, religious educator, guidance counselor, instrument repair, farmer, fish and game warden
- **Business/service:** Secretary, bookkeeper, computer operator, paralegal, lawn service manager, franchise owner, museum research worker
- **Creative/technical:** Interior designer, electrician, artist, merchandise planner, jeweler

INFJ: Introvert-Intuitive-Feeling-Judging

This personality type inhabits the world of ideas. People fitting this profile are independent and original thinkers. They also have strong feelings, firm principles, and personal integrity. This personality type makes up about 2 to 3% of the U.S. population. These individuals are happiest with jobs that let them:

1. Produce products and services they are proud of.
2. Think of new ways to solve problems.
3. Take ownership of their contributions.
4. Work independently, but with the opportunity to share with others in an environment free of interpersonal conflict.

An INFJ personality type might enjoy being a religious worker.

Here are some sample professions that tend to suit the INFJ personality type:

- **Counseling/education:** Career counselor, special education teacher, employee assistance counselor
- **Religion:** Director of religious education, religious worker
- **Creative:** Graphic designer, design architect, genealogist, educational software developer
- **Healthcare/social services:** Nutritionist, speech therapist, massage therapist, occupational therapist
- **Business:** Customer sales representative, outplacement consultant, translator
- **Technology:** High-tech customer relations manager, technology consultant, project manager

INTJ: Introverted-Intuitive-Thinking-Judging

This personality type is logical, critical, and perfectionist. People fitting this profile have a strong need for autonomy and personal competence. They are not particularly bothered by criticism and have an unshakable faith in their own original ideas. This personality type makes up about 2 to 3% of the U.S. population. These individuals are happiest with jobs that let them:

1. Solve problems that improve existing systems.
2. Work with other competent, conscientious people whom they respect.
3. Produce products according to their high standards and get credit for, and control of, their own ideas.
4. Get exposed to new ideas on a regular basis.

Here are some sample professions that tend to suit the INTJ personality type:

- **Business/finance:** Telecommunications security, budget analyst, real estate appraiser
- **Technology:** Scientist, electronic technician, software developer, biomedical researcher, pharmaceutical researcher, webmaster, database administrator, systems analyst
- **Education:** University professor (computer science or math), administrator, mathematician
- **Healthcare/medicine:** Psychiatrist, neurologist, cardiologist, coroner, pathologist, surgeon
- **Professional:** Attorney, judge, aerospace engineer, civil engineer, pilot, intelligence specialist

INTP: Introvert-Intuitive-Thinking-Perceiving

This personality type is straightforward, honest, and pragmatic. People fitting this profile prefer action to conversations. They have a good understanding of how things work. They tend to be analytical and more interested in the underlying principles of things. They also have an innate understanding of how mechanical things work. This personality type makes up about 4 to 7% of the U.S. population. These individuals are happiest with jobs that let them:

1. Develop, analyze, and critique new ideas.
2. Focus their attention on a process rather than an end product, working with a small group of highly regarded associates.
3. Remain challenged with complex problems and use unconventional approaches to solve them.
4. Set their own high standards and perform their work in a flexible environment without excessive rules and regulations.

Here are some sample professions that tend to suit the INTP personality type:

- **Computers/technology:** Software designer, systems analyst, database manager, network integrations specialist, webmaster
- **Healthcare/technical:** Neurologist, physicist, plastic surgeon, pharmacist, chemist, veterinarian, microbiologist
- **Professional/business:** Lawyer, economist, psychologist, architect, psychiatrist, biophysicist

- **Academic:** Mathematician, anthropologist, archaeologist, historian, college faculty administrator
- **Creative:** Photographer, creative writer, artist, entertainer, dancer, agent, inventor, music arranger, producer, director, film editor

ISFP: Introvert-Sensing-Feeling-Perceiving

This personality type is gentle, caring, and sensitive. People fitting this profile tend to keep personal ideas and values to themselves. They express their passions through actions, rather than words. They are modest and reserved, yet warm and enthusiastic with people they really know. They are also patient, flexible, and easy to get along with. This personality type makes up about 5 to 7% of the U.S. population. These individuals are happiest with jobs that let them:

1. Work in harmony with their own personal values and beliefs, helping others grow and develop.
2. Develop their own in-depth knowledge of a subject.
3. Work by themselves with plenty of uninterrupted time, and still have the chance to bounce ideas off others.
4. Work in an environment with few rules or regulations.

Here are some sample professions that tend to suit the ISFP personality type:

- **Creative/arts:** Graphic designer, magazine editor, website editor
- **Education/counseling:** Special education teacher, bilingual teacher, substance abuse counselor, social worker
- **Religion:** Religious leader or educator, church worker, religious counselor
- **Healthcare:** Nutritionist, physical therapist, occupational therapist, geneticist
- **Organizational development:** Human resources consultant, outplacement consultant, labor relations specialist
- **Technology:** High-tech customer relations manager, technology consultant, project manager, human resources recruiter, educational software developer

INFP: Introvert-Intuitive-Feeling-Perceiving

This personality type values inner harmony above all else. People fitting this profile are sensitive, idealistic, and loyal. They have a strong sense of honor concerning personal values. They are also are motivated by a deep belief or devotion to a cause. This personality type makes up about 3 to 4% of the U.S. population. These individuals are happiest with jobs that let them:

1. Work at something that is consistent with their inner values and beliefs.
2. Work with others in a supportive, affirming environment in which they are part of a loyal team.
3. Pay attention to detail and help make others comfortable.
4. Work independently without restrictive rules, yet have others nearby that they can assist as necessary.

Here are some sample professions that tend to suit the INFP personality type:

- **Creative/arts:** Fashion designer, carpenter, jeweler, gardener, potter, painter, dancer, tailor, instrument maker
- **Healthcare:** Visiting nurse, physical therapist, massage therapist, radiology technician, home health aide, exercise physiologist, art therapist, pharmacist, registered nurse, hospice worker or director

An INFP personality type might enjoy being a visiting nurse.

- **Science/technical:** Surveyor, forester, botanist, geologist, marine biologist, zoologist, soil conservationist, archaeologist
- **Sales/service:** Elementary teacher, police officer, corrections officer, crisis hotline operator, cleaning service operator, travel sales, customer sales representative, child welfare counselor, animal groomer or trainer, teacher's aide, horticulturalist, train engineer, recreation worker, florist
- **Business:** Paralegal, legal secretary, insurance appraiser

INTP: Introvert-Intuitive-Thinking-Perceiving

This personality type consists of conceptual problem solvers. People fitting this profile are intensely intellectual, with flashes of creative brilliance. They are outwardly reserved and detached, but inwardly absorbed with solving problems. This personality type makes up about 3 to 4% of the U.S. population. These individuals are happiest with jobs that let them:

1. Identify and use available resources as efficiently as possible.
2. Practice and master acquired skills, and then apply them in the real world to solve problems.
3. Follow clear directions and work independently, with plenty of quiet time to concentrate, and without much supervision.
4. Do their work without following excessive rules or bureaucracy, with time to pursue their hobbies.

Here are some sample professions that tend to suit the INTP personality type:

- **Technology:** Computer programmer, new product developer, research specialist, Internet architect, computer security specialist
- **Healthcare:** Neurologist, physicist, microbiologist, geneticist, chemist
- **Business/finance:** Intellectual property attorney, psychiatrist or psychologist, entrepreneur, investigator, anthropologist
- **Academic:** Mathematician, archaeologist, philosopher, astronomer, historian
- **Creative:** Photographer, creative writer, inventor, producer, music arranger, director

ESTP: Extrovert-Sensing-Thinking-Perceiving

This personality type rarely worries. People who fit this profile are active, easygoing, and spontaneous. They enjoy living in the present moment. They are realistic, curious, trust their senses, and are observant. They also tend to be open-minded and tolerant of others. This personality type makes up about 6 to 8% of the U.S. population. These individuals are happiest with jobs that let them:

1. Use their keen powers of observation and ability to remember facts.
2. Meet and interact with many people throughout the day, and respond to unplanned situations in a fast-moving, fun environment.
3. Search for solutions to problems using their experience.
4. Organize themselves as they go along and respond to high-pressure situations as they arise.

Here are some sample professions that tend to suit the ESTP personality type:

- **Sales/service:** Police officer, firefighter, paramedic, detective, corrections officer, flight attendant, insurance fraud investigator, personal fitness instructor, flight instructor, military officer, criminalist and ballistics specialist
- **Finance:** Personal financial planner, auditor, stockbroker, investor, insurance broker
- **Entertainment/sports:** Sportscaster, news reporter, promoter, tour guide, agent, dancer, bartender, professional athlete, musician, actor
- **Trades:** Carpenter, craftsperson, farmer, general contractor, construction worker, chef/cook, technical trainer, repair engineer, aircraft mechanic, computer support, soil conservationist, wilderness guide, travel agent, ecotourism specialist
- **Business:** Real estate broker, entrepreneur, wholesaler, car sales, management consultant, Internet marketer

ESFP: Extrovert-Sensing-Feeling-Perceiving

This personality type enjoys people and has a real zest for living. People who fit this profile are playful, energetic, and make things fun for others. They are adaptable, easygoing, warm, friendly, and generous. They also tend to be extremely sociable, like being the center of attention, and can juggle several activities at once. This personality type makes up about 8 to 10% of the U.S. population. These individuals are happiest with jobs that let them:

1. Learn from hands-on experience and work directly with clients or customers out in the field, rather than away from the action.

2. Work with lots of people in an active, social environment, with lots of fun and spontaneity.

3. Juggle multiple projects and activities, easing tensions between groups, and getting recognized and rewarded for their work.

4. Work in a friendly, relaxed environment without hidden political agendas.

Here are some sample professions that tend to suit the ESFP personality type:

- **Education/social service:** Elementary school teacher, child care provider, home health social worker, educational software developer, special education teacher
- **Healthcare:** Emergency room nurse, medical assistant, dental hygienist, dental assistant, licensed practical nurse (LPN), massage therapist, emergency medical technician (EMT), veterinarian or veterinary technician, hospice worker, art therapist
- **Entertainment/arts:** Travel agent, photographer, film producer, musician, performer, promoter, costume specialist, painter/illustrator, sculptor, animator, sketch artist
- **Business/sales:** Retail merchandiser, public relations specialist, fundraiser, human resources manager, home healthcare sales
- **Service:** Police officer, flight attendant, waiter or waitress, receptionist, secretary, interior designer, chef/cook, aerobics instructor, ecotourism specialist
- **Science:** Environmental scientist, zoologist, marine biologist, geologist

ENFP: Extrovert-Intuitive-Feeling-Perceiving

This personality type is full of enthusiasm for new ideas. People who fit this profile are optimistic, spontaneous, creative, and confident. They have original minds and a strong sense of the possible. This personality type makes up about 6 to 7% of the U.S. population.) These individuals are happiest with jobs that let them:

1. Work with a diverse group of people on a variety of projects.

2. Create new ideas and products.

3. Work in a friendly, relaxed environment that rewards imagination and enthusiasm.

4. Work at their own pace without focusing on a lot of details.

Here are some sample professions that tend to suit the ENFP personality type:

- **Creative:** Reporter, editor, educational software developer
- **Marketing:** Public relations specialist, marketing consultant, advertising director, copy writer
- **Education:** Special education teacher, bilingual teacher, social worker, guidance counselor
- **Healthcare:** Nutritionist, holistic health practitioner, massage therapist, physical therapist
- **Business:** Team trainer, outplacement consultant, environmental attorney
- **Technology:** High-tech customer relations manager, project manager, human resources recruiter

ENTP: Extrovert-Intuitive-Thinking-Perceiving

This personality type loves excitement and challenge. People who fit this profile are enthusiastic, talkative, clever, and good at many things. They constantly strive to increase competence and personal power. This personality type makes up about 4 to 6% of the U.S. population. These individuals are happiest with jobs that let them:

1. Practice creative problem solving and implement their own innovative solutions.
2. Receive encouragement for creativity, competency, and improvisation.
3. Have constant interaction with many different types of people and increase their professional power.
4. Work in an environment that is casual and unstructured.

Here are some sample professions that tend to suit the ENTP personality type:

- **Business:** Entrepreneur, inventor, venture capitalist, outplacement consultant, property manager, employee relations specialist, hotel manager
- **Marketing/creative:** Creative director, sports marketing, radio/TV talk show host, producer, copy writer, columnist, reporter
- **Planning/development:** Real estate agent, investment broker, financial planner, urban planner
- **Politics:** Politician, political manager, political analyst
- **Professional:** Detective, criminalist and ballistics expert

ESTJ: Extrovert-Sensing-Thinking-Judging

This personality type is great at getting things done. People who fit this profile like to run the show and make things happen. They are responsible, conscientious, and faithful to commitments. They also like structure and can remember and organize many details. This personality type makes up about 12 to 15% percent of the U.S. population. These individuals are happiest with jobs that let them:

1. Work systematically while organizing information and people.
2. Use skills they have already mastered, doing a job that has clear expectations and a well-defined reporting hierarchy.
3. Work in a friendly environment with other hardworking people who do not share personal issues at work.
4. Work on projects that are realistic, with practical applications and concrete results.

Here are some sample professions that tend to suit the ESTJ personality type:

- **Sales/service:** Insurance agent, computer sales, funeral director, cook, military officer, paralegal, government employee, technical instructor, budget analyst, underwriter, sound technician
- **Technology/physical:** Mechanical engineer, general contractor, farmer, construction worker, pharmacist, auditor, database administrator
- **Management:** Office manager, administrator, factory supervisor, database administrator, chief information officer (CIO), bank manager or loan officer, credit analyst, bill collector, nursing director
- **Professional:** Dentist, physician, stockbroker, judge, electrical engineer, paralegal, school principal

ESFJ: Extrovert-Sensing-Feeling-Judging

This personality type is motivated to help others in real and practical ways through action and cooperation. People who fit this profile are responsible, friendly, and sympathetic. They value relationships with others and are popular, gracious, eager to please,

technology at work

"I know how to use Google, but I can never find what I'm looking for!" This is a common complaint people voice when looking for information on the Internet, especially information about possible careers. When they get their list of results and start clicking on links, the websites they land on just don't give them the information they need. This is usually because the keywords they entered in the search were not specific enough.

When searching for information, try entering a string of specific words. For example, if you want to find out more about a career as a graphic designer, don't just type *graphic designer*; try a more specific keyword search, such as "graphic design career" or "how to become a graphic designer." When you put quotes around words, the search engine will look for those words as a group, rather than individually.

Even if you are very specific with your keywords, you may end up with a list of search results that are not as useful as you hoped. In fact, when you click some of the links near the top of the results list, you may arrive at websites that are not relevant at all. This is because search results are not always listed in order of relevance; results often show up at the top of the list because their sponsors paid more money to have them appear there. You may want to try items lower down the list of results.

and talkative. This personality type makes up about 11 to 14% of the U.S. population. These individuals are happiest with jobs that let them:

1. Establish and maintain warm interpersonal friendships with people at work.
2. Do work with practical benefits for people and have a chance to learn new things.
3. Work on projects with clear expectations in a cooperative environment without conflict.
4. Make decisions and interact with many people.

Here are some sample professions that tend to suit the ESFJ personality type:

- **Healthcare:** Medical/dental assistant, speech pathologist, physician, nurse, dentist, veterinarian, home health aide, radiation therapist, dental hygienist
- **Education:** Elementary school teacher, child care provider, athletic coach, nursing instructor
- **Social service/counseling:** Social worker (for children and the elderly), welfare worker, religious educator, minister/priest/rabbi, child welfare counselor, substance abuse counselor
- **Business:** Public relations, sales representative, office manager, retail owner, credit counselor, merchandise planner, health club manager, hotel manager, food service manager, nursery and greenhouse manager
- **Sales/service:** Flight attendant, funeral home director, hairdresser, cosmetologist, fundraiser, caterer
- **Clerical:** Secretary, receptionist, bookkeeper, typist

ENFJ: Extrovert-Intuitive-Feeling-Judging

This personality type consists of real people lovers. People who fit this profile place the highest importance on people and relationships, and are naturally concerned about others. They are also very loyal, like to promote harmony around them, and can be self-critical. This personality type makes up about 3 to 5% of the U.S. population. These individuals are happiest with jobs that let them:

1. Develop creative solutions to projects they believe in, in which they can see the positive effects of their efforts on others.
2. Work in an environment where expectations are clear, contributions are appreciated, and activities are interesting and varied.
3. Be part of a team of creative people they can trust.
4. Have time to explore new ideas, develop creative solutions, and share them with others.
5. Work in a well-planned manner and use their organizational skills.

Here are some sample professions that tend to suit the ENFJ personality type:

- **Communication:** Advertising executive, public relations specialist, writer/journalist, TV producer, graphic designer, magazine editor
- **Counseling:** Psychologist, facilitator, career counselor, clergy, substance abuse counselor, guidance counselor
- **Education/human service:** Teacher, librarian, nonprofit organization director, special education teacher, social worker (elderly), music director, adult day care coordinator, sociologist
- **Healthcare:** Holistic health practitioner, nutritionist, chiropractor, occupational therapist
- **Business/consulting:** Management consultant, team trainer, outplacement consultant, ecotourism specialist, sales manager, set designer, hotel and restaurant manager, talent director

We all have unique talents and abilities that we can share with others in our work.

ENTJ: Extrovert-Intuitive-Thinking-Judging

This personality type consists of great leaders and decision makers. People who fit this profile can easily see possibilities in all things and are happy to direct others toward their vision. They are also ingenious thinkers and long-range planners. This personality type makes up about 3 to 5% of the U.S. population. These individuals are happiest with jobs that let them:

1. Lead, be in control, and organize people.
2. Perform long-range strategic planning.
3. Work in a well-organized environment with clearly set guidelines.
4. Work with others they respect who are goal oriented.

Here are some sample professions that tend to suit the ENTJ personality type:

- **Business:** Executive, senior management, network integration specialist, technical trainer
- **Finance:** Investment banker, personal financial planner, corporate finance attorney, venture capitalist
- **Consulting/training:** Business consultant, management consultant, labor relations manager, corporate team trainer
- **Professional:** Judge, intellectual property attorney, environmental engineer, psychiatrist
- **Technology:** Network administrator, systems administrator, database administrator, systems analyst

Remember, the Myers-Briggs personality profiles and their recommended professions are not exact and nothing is set in stone. The point of the personality profile is not to box you in, but to broaden your self-knowledge. When you know your preferences and strengths, you can build on them and use them in your career.

 ## Now You Try It: Who Are You?

Now's your chance to guess your personality profile based on the descriptions you read earlier.

1. Do you think you are an E or an I? Why?
2. Do you think you are an S or an N? Why?
3. Do you think you are an F or a T? Why?
4. Do you think you are a J or a P? Why?
5. Based on the answers to your questions, what is your four-letter Myers-Briggs personality profile?
6. What jobs have you held in the past that fit well with your personality profile? Have you had jobs that were not a good fit? What were they?
7. Moving forward, what types of jobs might suit your profile? (Refer to the information presented earlier in the section.)

Talents and Abilities

As you think about your personality, your talents and abilities will come to mind. Although many tend to use the terms interchangeably, there is a subtle difference between "talents" and "abilities." **Talents** are skills you come by naturally. Even if you do not practice them, they remain with you. **Abilities** are skills that you learn and must continually practice so you do not lose them.

Be True to Yourself

Give yourself time to consider your talents and abilities. What have you always been good at? What have you learned to do well? What earns you praise from others? Use your knowledge of your personality type to help you.

Talent, *noun*

an apparently natural power or gift in the learning or doing of something

Ability, *noun*

the power to do something, either physical or mental; skill

It's important to be true to your talents and abilities when searching for a job. Otherwise, you may find yourself in a job that you want to be good at, but you know deep down that you aren't. This can happen for a number of reasons:

- Your family or friends push you to go into a certain field.
- You think you will make a lot of money.
- You are trying to prove something to someone.
- Everybody's doing it.
- It is somehow convenient or easy.

It's unrealistic to imagine that these reasons never enter into your career decisions—they do from time to time. Just make sure they don't form the entire basis of your decision. If they do, you will neglect your true talents and wear yourself out trying to fill in the gaps in your abilities. Challenging yourself to do things you are not naturally good at is terrific, but not all the time.

Getting to Know Your Strengths and Weaknesses

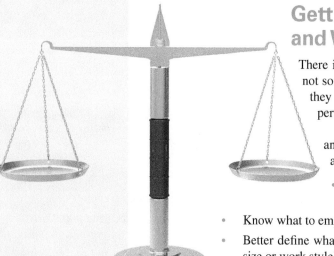

There is another side to what you're good at, namely, what you're not so good at! All of us have strengths and weaknesses. Together they form our complete and complex personalities. Nobody is perfect and nobody is going to be good at everything.

Knowing yourself means knowing where you do not excel and where you do. When you know these details, you will be able to:

- See the areas where you need to improve so you can begin to work on them.
- Know what to emphasize in a job application or interview.
- Better define what kind of environment will suit you (for example, company size or work style).
- Determine what kind of job you should take within your field (for example, if you are studying fashion, you could go into design, sales, textile marketing, or photo styling).

Getting a handle on your strengths and weaknesses helps you make better choices about your career. It's best to focus on a career that takes advantage of your strengths because you will be more useful, more successful, and happier doing something you do well.

Likes and Dislikes

There is more to a career than simply doing something you are good at; there is also doing something you like. Many people have been pushed into a career because they were "naturally good at it," only to find out they were not really that interested in the job. Ultimately, you will be best at doing the things you like to do. Interest often plays a more important role in career choice than skills. Someone who is interested and passionate about a job will do what it takes to gain the necessary skills to excel, even if that individual initially lacks the natural talents to do so.

> *Did You Know?* Sometimes people think that because they have certain skills, they should perform a certain job, whether they like it or not. This is not true. For example, someone may have excellent mechanical skills, but have no desire to be a mechanic. This is okay. That individual can hold a different job, but use his or her mechanical skills on personal projects. It's not necessary to make a living from those skills.

Now it's time to take a concrete look at what you like and dislike to help clarify your thoughts about potential employment. There is clear evidence that you perform best in your areas of interest. Think about high school or college. Where did you succeed most in your classes and extracurricular activities? You probably got your best grades in the classes that you liked the most, and you probably excelled in your favorite activities. When something really matters to you, you're more likely to give it your all. That holds true as you get older, and it especially holds true in the workplace.

Someone who goes into a job for the money, when he or she has little or no interest in it, often ends up hating the job and leaving it, or staying in it and becoming bitter and ineffective. In reality, people who like their jobs perform better at them, are happier, and are typically more successful than people who do not like their jobs. Of course, you may know people who work because they have to, without paying much attention to whether they like what they do. You may know others who have worked all their lives at jobs that they do not particularly like. Perhaps they put up with those jobs because of salary or stability. Maybe their skills are limited or they have no time to look elsewhere.

Whatever their reasons for staying at jobs they do not like, the longer they stay, the tougher it is to leave. This is because they become comfortable with their discomfort. Even though they dislike their jobs, they know every single aspect of those jobs. The idea of finding a new job—a better job—is actually uncomfortable to them because it is an unknown.

Now You Try It: What Do You Like?

Here's a chance to find out more about yourself and what you look for in a job.

1. Start by answering these questions about yourself.

   - What are you good at?
   - What do you like to do (whether you're good at it or not)?
   - What are you interested in (whether you've done it before or not)?

   Review your answers and notice whether you are interested in something you never do, or like doing something you're not very good at, or are good at something you don't really care about.

2. Circle the statements below that apply to you.

   - I prefer to do only those things I know how to do, using well-developed skills, so I do not have to learn or try something new.
   - I prefer to do things I have never done before, so I can learn something new.
   - I prefer doing only those things that I enjoy.
   - I do not mind doing things that are not completely enjoyable to me, as long as I do them well or can do them with people I like.
   - I prefer doing things I am interested in, even if those things are difficult to do or are things I do not do well—I can't stand being bored.
   - I do not mind doing things I am not that interested in, as long as I do them well and they are well-structured.

3. Based on your answers, prioritize the characteristics you look for in your ideal job (1 = lowest priority, 3 = highest priority):

   - _____ I need to be good at what I do.
   - _____ I need to like what I do.
   - _____ I need to be interested in what I do.

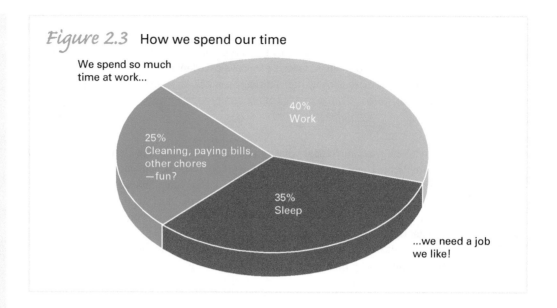

Figure 2.3 How we spend our time

We spend so much time at work...

40% Work

25% Cleaning, paying bills, other chores —fun?

35% Sleep

...we need a job we like!

Sound Bite

You never know where your work is going to take you. I did data entry work part time when I was at school and it was so boring. But I did learn to coordinate paperwork. When I graduated, I was in a bottom-level position in a company some distance away and I hated the commute, so I decided to accept a job at a company close to where I lived. I stayed there for five years, working my way up from secretary, to marketing, and finally to vice president of operations.

Later, I left the company and took a position in sales for a pet cemetery. I did a lot of work on my own. I even did sales for the cemetery. After awhile, I realized I've always wanted to do independent contracting work, and now we're starting this floral shop. It's going to be my company. I'm going to be a business owner!

—K. Mitchell, independent consultant

Do Yourself a Favor

It's sad to imagine the wasted time and energy of doing work you don't like for years and years. Consider this: You will spend 8 or more hours a day, 5 or more days a week, 50 or more weeks a year, as a working citizen. This will continue for perhaps 30 or 40 years. If you spend 40% of your time at a job you dislike, and around 35% of your time sleeping, that leaves 25% of your time left for your own activities ("you" time), as illustrated in Figure 2.3.

However, almost 25% of your "you" time goes toward less than desirable, but necessary, activities such as cleaning, paying bills, and doing other household chores. That means you have less than 19% of your lifetime to do things you like. Besides being unhappy, people in this kind of situation tend to take out their frustrations on those who care about them. And that's a bad situation no matter what the cause.

Wouldn't you rather spend 40% of your waking hours doing work you enjoy? Do yourself and everyone around you a favor, and let yourself have the kind of job that will keep you satisfied. This satisfaction can come from any combination of factors: atmosphere, tasks, and coworkers. Be on the lookout for it, because you deserve a job you enjoy. This doesn't mean you will find work that makes you deliriously happy all the time. It simply means you can spend your working time in a manner that is usually pleasant to you. When looking for a job, take your own happiness into account.

Horizontal Moves

Once you find something you like, you can still switch jobs and careers, as many people do, but those switches will probably be "horizontal moves." This refers to switching jobs, but staying within a particular line of work that feels most comfortable to you.

For example, suppose you have an interest in computers. What might be your horizontal range? You could program computers, repair them, or build them. You could also write manuals for using computers or teach computer classes. Or, you could use computers to design logos or fashions. The range of jobs within a particular career or interest category can be quite wide. Other factors, such as your self-knowledge and your personal needs, will help you to narrow your choices.

Identifying Meaningful Goals

At this point you should have a better idea of your abilities, likes, and dislikes. The next logical question to ask yourself is, "What do I do with all this knowledge?"

Before you unlock the secrets of your working life, you need another key: the ability to identify goals for yourself. This is one of the most important job (and life) skills you will ever learn. Think of a **goal** as a dream with a deadline—a result you want to achieve.

You are already a goal setter and may not even know it. Think about the small goals you set for yourself each day: buy groceries, drop off the recycling, go to the doctor, turn in a project, or pay a bill.

These goals generally begin with a decision to do something, followed by the commitment to follow through and by daily reminders. These daily reminders may be as simple as writing a shopping list for groceries, making a to-do list for errands, or marking dates on your calendar or smartphone for appointments, project due dates, or bill payment.

Your job is to apply the daily goal-setting skills you already have to your larger purposes in life, and eventually learn to prioritize those goals. By doing so, you will set a clear a path to your future. Figure 2.4 illustrates the relationship between your abilities, likes, and dislikes with the establishment of goals and priorities.

Goal, *noun*

an object, aim, or end that one strives to attain

Roadblocks to Goal Setting

It's tough to make your way through life if you get lost in the possibilities. Setting goals keeps you on track so you don't get lost. But, if setting goals is so important, why do so many people avoid them? Here are a number of possible reasons. See if any of them apply to you.

- **Lack of role models.** Perhaps your parents or other adults around you did not know how to set goals, so you never learned.
- **Lack of encouragement and support.** Perhaps others in your life made fun of your goals, or told you that you would never achieve them, or tried to sabotage your efforts.
- **Lack of confidence.** Perhaps you have not been very successful at setting and achieving goals in the past, so you feel insecure about doing so.
- **Overwhelming fear.** Perhaps you are afraid of failing, so you don't even try.

Figure 2.4   **Unlocking your personal power**

Understand Yourself	Identify Goals	Set Priorities	Manage Time
• Personality • Talents and abilities • Likes and dislikes	• Long-term • Short-term	• Essential • Regular • Optional	• Time log • Weekly schedule • Daily to-do list

Setting SMART Goals

Even if any of these reasons have stopped you from setting goals in the past, you can move beyond them by using the SMART method to define goals:

• **Specific.** Make sure your goal includes as many details as possible to make it real to you. The more specific the goal, the easier it is for you to focus on its achievement. Suppose you want to improve your health because you feel stiff and tired. Consider these goals:

Vague: "I want to be healthy."

Specific: "I want to increase my flexibility and stamina."

• **Measurable.** Define your goal in such a way that you can measure your results. After all, if you cannot measure your goals, how will you know you have achieved them? Suppose you live in a different state from your sister and you want to stay in touch with her:

Vague: "I want to communicate more with my sister."

Measurable: "I want to phone or email my sister twice a week. "

• **Achievable.** Make sure you have what it takes to achieve the goal; otherwise, you are likely to give up. This may mean developing the attitudes, abilities, skills, and the financial capacity to reach the goal. If the goal is too far out of your reach, you probably won't commit to doing it. For example, suppose you enjoy reading mystery books and decide to write a book of your own; however, you have never done much writing in any of your jobs:

> **Not achievable:** "I want to get my first mystery novel published in 9 months." (You don't even know if you can write!)

> **Achievable:** "I want to attend at least two hands-on writing workshops this year and attend the regional writer's conference."

• **Realistic and Relevant.** Realistic means doable, given your ability, time, and energy. When goals are too difficult, we become frustrated and unmotivated, and we stop trying. Relevant means meaningful to you; it has nothing to do with what other people think. If the goal doesn't really matter to you, you probably won't stick with it for long. For example, suppose you have a full-time job, but also enjoy playing tennis on the weekends. Consider the following goals:

> **Unrealistic:** "I want to become a tennis pro and quit my job." (Sure you love weekend tennis, but do you love it that much, and do you have the time to become a pro?)

> **Realistic:** "I want to start taking private tennis lessons at the club and participate in the masters' tennis tournament."

• **Timely.** Set a time frame for your goal so you have something to work toward. You can set one big deadline for when you want to achieve the entire goal, or set mini deadlines along the way. Plus, you can adjust the deadline as you learn more about what it takes to achieve the goal.

> **No time frame:** "I want to get money for my research trip." (You forgot to mention how much money, how you are going to get it, or when your research trip will occur.)

> **Time frame:** "I want to develop a grant proposal for submittal in one month, requesting $10,000 for a three-month research trip."

Take the time to set SMART goals in both your personal and professional life.

Making the Goal Stick

Once you create your SMART goals, there are a number of things you can do to make sure those goals stick. By *stick*, we mean maintaining the energy and interest to achieve your goals.

1. **Write down your goal.** By writing your goal, it is no longer just an idea or words; it becomes tangible. Put it somewhere where you will see it every day as a constant reminder.

2. **Make sure the goal has a beginning, an end, and a defined first step.** We all procrastinate. Getting started is the biggest challenge. By establishing a starting date and a completion date, we create a reason to begin—a sense of urgency. It also helps if you define a first step—an initial activity that you can accomplish in a short amount of time. For example, consider this goal: "I want to develop a grant proposal for submittal in one month, requesting $10,000 for a 3-month research trip." You might decide that the first step is to begin researching funding organizations online today and then download proposal forms from three potential organizations by the end of the week. This is a fairly painless way to start your grant proposal process immediately.

3. **Break a big goal into little goals.** Some goals may be very large in scope, so it's always a good idea to break a large goal into smaller practical goals that are more easily achievable. As you achieve the smaller goals, you will gain confidence in achieving the larger one. For example, think back to the "unachievable" goal of writing a mystery novel in nine months while working full time. Smaller, more practical goals might involve any of the following: attending writing workshops, conducting background research online, visiting possible story locations in person, interviewing real-life detectives, transcribing notes, developing an outline, drafting the first chapter, and so on. Of course, each smaller, practical goal would have to be written as a SMART goal.

4. **Create an action plan.** To the best of your abilities, identify the steps that need to happen to achieve your goal and write them down. Some people like to work backward by imagining the end result, writing down what needs to happen just before that occurs, and then writing down what has to happen before that, and so on. Without an action plan, you will have difficulty knowing what to do and whether you are moving in the right direction.

5. **Periodically review your goal.** Revisit your commitment. As time passes, we tend to forget the meaning of the goal, lose our enthusiasm, and stop expending any effort. Set time aside to reflect on your goal and think about why you established it in the first place. Remind yourself of the excitement you felt when you first created the goal. Imagine the satisfaction you anticipate in achieving it. This will help sustain your commitment.

Follow these five steps, and you will be able to achieve your goals with a sense of pride and accomplishment.

Types of Goals

Now that you know what a SMART goal is and how to maintain one, let's look at the type of goals you might be interested in setting. There are a variety of areas in your life in which goals are important. Following are some examples. These questions are relevant whether you're just starting out on a career or have been in one for awhile.

- **Personal.** What changes do you want to make in your ideas, thoughts, tendencies, habits, and abilities? Do you want to change or improve your relationships? Do you want to improve your physical health and/or appearance? Do you want to rekindle or alter your spiritual life and practices? Do you want to develop certain talents or skills or explore new interests?

- **Family.** Do you want to marry? Do you want to have a family? How many children do you want? How much time do you want to be able to spend with your spouse and children? Do you want to live near your parents, siblings, or other extended family? Do you want to strike out on your own?

- **Career.** What specifically do you want to be doing on the job? Are you happy doing what you are doing now? Do you want to manage others? Do you want to own a business? Do you want to work as an independent contractor? Do you want to be your own boss? What kind of hours would suit you best? What salary level? What benefits?

- **Money.** How much do you want to earn? Do you want to invest some of your earnings? Do you want to pay off loans? Do you want to make major purchases such as a car, home, education, insurance, vacation, or appliances?
- **Living.** Where do you want to live—city, country, or suburb? What style of housing do you want? Do you want to rent or own? What kind of community do you seek?

Time Frame

Regardless of the area of your life for which you set goals, you are bound to set goals with different time frames. Long-term goals are goals that you intend to work on for quite a while and achieve over time. They typically take months or even years to achieve. For example, you might set a goal of owning your own business in 10 years, learning a new language, or purchasing an apartment. Long-term goals keep you looking toward the future.

Short-term goals are smaller and more concrete, and can be reached in the more immediate future. They can be independent from your long-term goals, or steps to achieving them. For example, suppose your long-term goal is to own your own home. Your short-term goals might be setting aside some savings each month, looking for a better-paying job, and exploring the real estate section of the paper for possibilities and prices. Short-term goals also help long-term goals feel less overwhelming. Each time you accomplish a short-term goal, you get to check it off and feel successful.

Getting Help with Goals

No matter how well-defined your goals, there is always a chance you will encounter an obstacle as you attempt to achieve them. Internal obstacles could include reduced motivation, negative self-talk, or poor organizational skills. External obstacles could include changes in the economy, lack of money, or geographical distance.

Here are some tips regarding what you can do when you encounter an obstacle.

- **Remind yourself of the benefits of the goal.** Focus on the positive outcome of the goal and imagine how you will feel when it's accomplished.
- **Consult role models and mentors.** They may be able to offer concrete suggestions based on their own experiences.
- **Get support.** Talk to friends and family who can offer positive suggestions and who believe in you when you don't even believe in yourself. Don't waste your time on people who drag you down with negative feedback.
- **Replace negative self-talk with positive self-talk.** It's common to fall back on bad habits, like negative self-talk, when you feel afraid or doubtful. Every time you think, "I don't how I'm going to do this," replace that thought with, "I may not realize it right know, but I actually do know how to move forward," or something similar.

No matter what the obstacle, the key to success is believing in yourself and moving forward, a little bit at a time.

If you don't set any goals, you may end up like many people who say, "I should have. I could have. But I didn't." These are sad words that mean you had opportunities and abilities, but you did not use them. Don't let your fears freeze you into a life of regrets. Challenge yourself. Challenge your dreams. Set goals for yourself.

Now You Try It: Backward Goal Setting

To give you practice setting a long-term goal, we're going to let you work backward and set some short-term goals.

1. Identify a long-term goal from one of these categories: personal, family, career, money, or living. Write it down in general terms.
2. Estimate a date when you would like to achieve the goal.
3. Work backwards from the goal and identify smaller, short-term goals you must accomplish before you can achieve the long-term goal. Add an estimated time of completion for each.

Short-Term Goal   **Estimated Date of Completion**

These short-term goals become milestones that you can aspire to and use to gauge your progress. In fact, as you move toward your long-term goal and learn more about what is required to achieve it, you will probably want to adjust those milestones so they are more realistic.

Setting Priorities

You know all about exploring who you are and what you can do. You know how to set goals that are meaningful and important to you. Before you begin achieving those goals, you need to set your **priorities.**

If you don't set priorities and you work on your goals in no particular order, you may reach some smaller goals but you won't meet the big ones. Setting priorities defines what is most important to you. It helps you decide to work first (and maybe hardest) on the most crucial goals, leaving others for later. Following are some ways that people prioritize:

> **Priority,** *noun*
>
> something that takes precedence in time or importance

- Goals may be a higher priority because other goals cannot be accomplished without them.
- Goals may be important because they remove obstacles to future goals.
- Goals may be more important because they yield a great return for your investment of time.

Like goals, priorities are unique to each individual. The differences come from circumstances and preferences. For example, if you like athletics, you may make working out a priority. If you prefer less physical activities, you may focus on reading. Or, if you are a parent, you will probably make your children a priority.

Some of your priorities will change on a daily basis, whereas others may change on a weekly, monthly, or yearly basis. Still others may remain throughout your life. Figure 2.5 illustrates a prioritized list of life priorities for Brianna, a working mother of two.

Priorities and Your Job Search

Whether you are going to school, are employed or unemployed, you can make good use of your ability to set priorities right now. Defining daily priorities helps keep you organized and focused as you work toward your goals. Following is a list of sample priorities for a student. Think about which of these might be your priorities, and how you might rank them in order of importance.

- Class
- Study time

Figure 2.5 **What are your priorities?**

Priority
Work at a job I like
Take good care of my family
Travel the world
Act in an environmentally responsible manner
Help others
Stay healthy
Buy a home
Write a book

Learning from Experience
A Perspective from the Working World

The Tenacity of Success

Andrea Selena,
*FedEx service rep and
real estate agent*

When it comes to your life, it's never too late to start over. After high school, I enrolled in a community college because I thought I wanted to be a dental assistant. Since I had a number of dental issues that year, I spent a lot of time at the dentist and got to be pretty good friends with the dental assistant. Based on my own experiences and what she shared with me, I realized dental assisting was not for me. I kept taking classes at community college to fulfill general education requirements, but I didn't know what I really wanted to do. I just hoped something would click.

Along with school, I worked part-time at a grocery store. It didn't pay much, and the bills were mounting. My mom told me that a friend of hers had a son who worked for FedEx. I talked to him and found out the pay was decent and so were the benefits. He suggested I apply for the part-time package handler position. I got the job.

At that point I dropped everything, including school, because nothing had clicked. I worked nights and the job was pretty tiring. When a full-time customer service associate position became available I applied for it and got the job. Working with people during the day in the FedEx store, in both the shipping and computer copying departments, was much more fun than handling packages at night.

But after a few years I started to lose interest. I began thinking about going back to school and doing something else. One of my frequent customers at the FedEx store was a real estate broker. I asked her how she liked it. She was very enthusiastic about her work and told me there was nothing like running your own business.

Not long after our discussion, I signed up for courses at a community college to become a real estate agent. It was fun to be learning again, even though it was sometimes difficult to work around my job schedule. The next hurdle was taking a state exam. I studied hard, but failed the exam. I was so discouraged that I didn't go back to school.

Luckily, my customer, the real estate broker, did not let me give up on my dream of being a real estate agent. She urged me to retake the exam and even helped me study. And this time I passed!

I asked the broker if she needed another real estate agent in her office, and she said, "Absolutely—how would you like the job?" That's when I quit FedEx and started selling homes full-time. During my first year, I sold over one million dollars in homes.

Through this job, I've discovered who I am. I like talking with people and I know how to make them feel comfortable. My clients like me because I'm truthful and I really try to find what they want. My clients ask me what I think and it feels good to share information that I know will help them. Buying a home is a major commitment in anybody's life and I get to be involved in that process.

I also like the freedom of setting my own hours. I'm never bored because I get to meet different people, see different kinds of houses, and handle various forms of contracts. I also enjoy taking classes every year to stay current in my profession.

The best part of my career is knowing that *I* did this. Nobody did it for me. *I* went to school. *I* took the tests. *I* met the people. *I* had an idea and *I* followed it through. Finishing what *I* started gave me a great sense of accomplishment and purpose.

Learning gave me the courage to believe I could change my life. I wish I'd had that kind of motivation when I was in high school because I would have pushed myself harder to succeed. Thankfully, it wasn't too late and I now have a satisfying career and life.

- Part-time or full-time job
- Parenting
- Being a partner or spouse
- Chores
- Sleep
- Exercise

If you can prioritize life priorities, you can prioritize job search priorities. It's best to prioritize your career goals, such as location, wages, and work environment, to help you find a job that best fits who you are and what you need. Setting priorities for yourself *before* you search for a job will help you determine what you want from the outset. This will help you rule out jobs, businesses, and areas that don't fit your personality, needs, and lifestyle. In the end, you will save time and energy because you prioritized.

Priorities and Your Job

Prioritizing is vital once you find the job that suits your needs. A company will value you more as an employee if you know how to identify daily, weekly, and long-term tasks, set priorities, and plan your work schedule accordingly. Companies prefer self-regulating employees who know how to get things done without constant reminders.

Prioritizing at work involves not only what you believe is important, but what your supervisor and coworkers tell you is important; therefore, you must take more points of view into account. Sometimes you have to shift priorities. For example, you may work on one project and then receive word from someone else that another task is more pressing for the day. Which task should you work on? It probably depends on who requested those tasks. It may be a higher priority to do work assigned by your supervisor than to take care of a task given to you by a coworker.

Understanding your company's organizational structure will help you make smart choices. If you receive too many requests from too many people and priorities conflict, you can always ask your supervisor for some help in prioritizing.

Managing Your Time

To efficiently achieve the goals you have prioritized, you must manage your time. Without time management skills, whole days may go by without you accomplishing a thing.

Time remains constant and cannot be controlled; you must adapt and plan accordingly to work within the limits of time and use it as motivation. There are only 24 hours in a day. Once you take away your sleeping time, you have about 16 hours left. How can you manage that time so you accomplish goals without making yourself crazy, overestimating, or scheduling so tightly that you can't deal with surprises? It depends on your personality.

Personality Profiles and Time Management

Take some time to consider what you already know about yourself. Remember your personality profile? It will tell you much about how you handle time and can help you decide what to do to manage it more efficiently. Following are two examples of how different personality types manage (or don't manage) time.

ISTJ and Time Management. If you are an ISTJ type, you may be a natural-born list maker. The **T** for thinking and the **J** for judging combine to create a thoughtful, deliberate person who likes to write a schedule on paper. If you make reasonable lists and stick to carrying out the duties on the lists, your tendencies will serve you well.

The **I** in your personality profile means you are an introvert, and introverts like to think. If you find yourself spending more time thinking through everything you could do rather than doing it, try to cut down on your plotting and get on with moving through the schedule.

ENFP and Time Management. If you are an ENFP type, you probably are on the go a lot and you may not spend much time organizing your schedule. Your disorganization may slow you down. You could take a lesson from the list makers, just as they can take a lesson from your drive and enthusiasm. Keep a small calendar with you all the time, and write a few essentials down daily.

The **E** in your profile means you are an extrovert, and extroverts tend to like to socialize. If you love to talk and it interferes with getting things done, take a few steps to improve your chances of success: unplug your phone (or set it on vibrate) while you study or work, or let your calls go to voicemail. At work or school, go straight to your desk or work area—don't stop for a drink or to talk. If you try hard to stick to a schedule but your friends take up your time anyway, cheerfully and gently say no to any invitations to visit or take a break. You can suggest another time to talk that will fit into your leisure time.

How to Successfully Manage Your Time

When it comes to managing time to accomplish tasks, different methods work for different personality types. Regardless of personality type, you must learn to tell the difference between an important task and an urgent one. An important task is one of value or significant worth. An urgent task is one that needs immediate attention. Spending too much time on urgent tasks actually takes away time you could spend on important ones. You end up constantly putting out fires, instead of preventing them.

Urgent tasks that interrupt your work can distract you from things that are truly important.

Have you heard the saying "There's never enough time to do it right the first time, but there's always enough to do it over and over?" That saying deals with people who are always in a time crunch, reacting to some last minute request to perform an urgent task. As a result, they never do the task well, and end up having to do it over, which takes time away from other important tasks they need to perform.

How do you manage your time so you can focus on the important tasks and not just react to the urgent ones? Following are some useful tips. Not all of them may apply to you, but some of them are bound to work very well.

1. **Keep a time log.** Find out how you are actually spending your time.

2. **Look at your week as a whole.** Get the big picture.

3. **Find a time management system that works for you.** Use a print or online system to keep your schedule.

4. **Create a daily to-do list.** Establish a routine, know what's coming up each day, and set realistic expectations of what you can do.

5. **Plan for free time.** Don't forget to relax and make sure to use your free time effectively.

6. **Expect the unexpected.** Learn to adjust and go with the flow, as well as say no.

7. **Take time to think about time.** Plan and be efficient.

8. **Avoid procrastination.** It's always best to just do something.

1. Keep a Time Log

> **Note:** You will typically do this activity only once to help you understand how you spend your time.

Before you can manage your time, you need to figure out how you are spending it in the first place. If you were creating a financial budget, you would first look at how you were spending money and then decide where to spend less or more. The same is true for a time budget or schedule.

Most people keep a daily time log for a week to learn about their habits. For one week, write down everything you do each day in 15-minute increments (if this seems too time consuming, try 30-minute or 1-hour increments). Some people enter the information online; others prefer to

> **Did You Know?**   Successful people typically spend 65 to 85% of their time on important activities, whereas the rest of the population spends the majority of their time on urgent ones.[3]

---

[3] Miller, Lucy. *Career Development Strategies*. Fort Collins, CO: McKinely College, 2008.

Figure 2.6 **How do you spend your time?**

Day	Date	Activity	Time Start	Time End	Total Time
Monday	8-23	Get up and exercise	7:00	7:30	0.50
		Shower and get ready for work	7:30	7:45	0.25
		Eat and brush teeth	7:45	8:15	0.50
		Commute	8:15	8:30	0.25
		Arrive at work and return phone calls and emails	8:30	9:30	1.00
		Start editing one chapter of new textbook	9:30	11:30	2.00
		Lunch	11:30	12:30	1.00
		Do research/surf the Internet	12:30	1:00	0.50
		Attend sales meeting	1:00	2:15	1.25
		Respond to emails/surf the Internet	2:15	3:00	0.75

write it on paper. However you do it, be specific and honest. This is a way for you to see how you actually use your time, how long it takes for you to perform certain activities, where you are efficient, and where you are wasting time.

For example, you might note that you started doing Internet research for an assigned paper at 8:30 pm, switched over to watching YouTube videos at 9:30 pm, and did not stop until 11:30 pm. After a week, you could examine your time log and see that you spent 5 hours working on your assignment, but 10 hours watching YouTube videos. Sometimes you have to see it on paper to believe it!

Figure 2.6 shows parts of a weekly time log for Krista, a former technical writer who is now working part-time as an assistant at a publishing company while she attends college to get her master's degree in creative writing. This incomplete log only covers part of the day, but you get the general idea. From this log we see that Krista spends a lot of her time at work on the phone, reading email, and surfing the Internet.

2. Look at Your Week as a Whole

Once you have tracked your time with a daily time log, you probably have a good idea of where your time goes each day and where you might want to make changes. Now is your chance to create a general (not detailed) schedule of the activities for a typical week. For example: work, commuting, errands, exercise, meal preparation, chores, reading, and entertainment. Write this schedule on paper or online.

Remember, each of us has exactly 168 hours a week (24 hours, 7 days per week). Once you calculate how much time you spend per week on everything, you can look at how much time you have left over and plan your extra time more wisely. Just make sure you schedule enough time for sleep!

Depending on your age, health, and life situation, you probably have 60 to 80 quality hours per week available for work, study, and other important commitments. After using your quality hours you lose your efficiency, which means you take longer to accomplish tasks and may make careless mistakes. Unfortunately with our busy lives, many people find themselves with commitments that exceed the 60 to 80 hours per week.

Seeing your entire week laid out will give you a picture of how you spend your time at home and at work. How many hours of commitments do you have? Do you find it difficult to maintain your concentration? Do you find yourself having to reread the same paragraph several times? That understanding will help you decide where you might want to devote more time and where to spend less.

Figure 2.7 shows an example of a weekly schedule for Terence, a divorced father of one. Terence goes to school at night and works part time during the day. He shares custody of his child with his ex-wife and lives one hour away from school.

3. Find a Time Management System That Works for You

Do you work best with a paper-based calendar or an electronic organizer? There are plenty of options out there, so experiment until you find something that works well for you so you can jot down your schedule. Remember, if you forget to charge your smartphone or the battery to your computer is drained, your schedule is lost. That's why a hardcopy version of your schedule is always a good idea.

You will find two major types of printed or online date books: one that lets you see a day at a time and one that shows a week at a time. The books that display one day at a time give you more room to write in the day's activities, but don't give you a good look at what is to come. You may forget important events scheduled for a day you cannot see. With a week-at-a-glance book, you have less room to write about your day, but you have perspective on the whole week. Decide which type of calendar will work better for you, then write your schedule for the week. Most people jot down only the essential tasks. However, if you have more space or are more detail oriented, you might want to note regular and optional tasks as well. Figure 2.8 explains the three types of tasks: essential, regular, and optional.

You probably noticed that categorizing tasks is a form of prioritizing. This is crucial on the job. Within your workday, you will have any number of tasks to complete, all at different priority levels. You must manage your daily work time by deciding how long the essential tasks will take, scheduling them into your day where they best fit, and then planning your regular and optional tasks around them.

Figure 2.7 How much time do you have for a life?

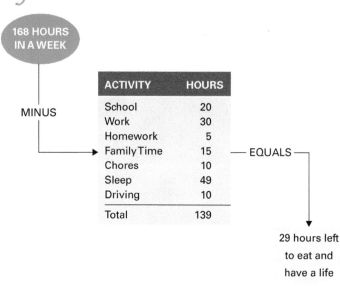

168 HOURS IN A WEEK

MINUS

ACTIVITY	HOURS
School	20
Work	30
Homework	5
Family Time	15
Chores	10
Sleep	49
Driving	10
Total	139

— EQUALS —

29 hours left to eat and have a life

Figure 2.8 What types of tasks go in your schedule?

Task Description	Examples
Essential tasks are things that have to get done, no matter what. They differ from person to person, and from day to day. For example, on a certain week, laundry might not be essential on Monday, but by the following Sunday it is essential because you have nothing clean left to wear.	Typical essentials include: dropping off or picking up a child from school, business appointments or events, attending class, taking the car for a major repair, mailing bills on time, or going to a medical appointment. Write your essentials first to make sure you have time to accomplish them.
Regular tasks are things you do each day or each week at approximately the same time. You might be able to adjust or miss these activities if you have to, although you'd rather not because they make things run smoothly.	Typical regular tasks include: a weekly trip to the grocery store, laundry, household chores, a favorite TV show, or a Sunday night dinner at a relative's home. Add these to your schedule and think about how to balance them with the essentials of that day.
Optional tasks are those you want to do "if there is time." It would be nice to do these tasks, but you can sacrifice them or bump them to the next day or week if you can't fit them into your schedule.	Examples of optional tasks include: a shopping trip, a hair appointment, a movie, and calling or visiting a friend. Some of these could become essentials, depending on the situation. Take a look at your schedule and see what you can fit in after you write your essential and regular activities.

4. Create a Daily To-Do List

Once you set your weekly schedule, it's still important to plan each day. In a daily to-do list you list all the things you have to do (or would like to do) on a given day.

Some people create a to-do list with items in the order they must be done; others create the list more randomly. Either way, it's a good idea to prioritize the items on your list to make sure they get done:

A = high priority (you must get them done, or else!)

B = medium priority (you should get them done to make other tasks easier)

C = low priority (if you don't get them done, you can move them to the next day)

If you are having trouble keeping track of your time or making schedules, you might try using your computer to help budget your time. Software programs such as Daytimer Organizer or Microsoft Schedule+ are designed to help you manage your time. Or you can use a spreadsheet program such as Excel to develop a daily schedule, a weekly plan, and a place to write your goals, priorities, and to-do lists.

Imagine you are Tanya, a software manager at Noraya, Inc. Your to-do list might look like this *(italicized material in parentheses explains why an item is categorized a certain way)*:

A

- Complete project plan for department meeting at 2:00 pm *(you must do this today)*
- Fill out W-4 form for new employee *(if you don't fill it out, your employee won't get paid)*
- Deposit checks in bank *(if you don't deposit, a personal check might bounce)*

B

- Write annual evaluation for one team member *(you still have two days, but you're worried about finishing on time)*
- Get birthday card for your son *(his birthday is tomorrow)*

C

- Send in mail-in ballot *(you still have two weeks)*
- Exchange your new shoes for a different size *(you can do this anytime this week)*

Some people like to make their to-do list in the evening, as they review their day; others like to do it in the morning, before they begin their new day. Either way, a to-do list helps you achieve your goals by reminding you of tasks that can easily slip your mind.

You can also keep a long-term to-do list of activities you want to accomplish when your schedule lightens up. You don't assign these activities to a certain day. Instead, you write them and keep the list handy to remind you of what you want to do. That way you can take advantage of unexpected free time. A long-term to-do list might include:

- Buy a new garden hose
- Fix screen door lock
- Sort through clothes, give unused clothing to the needy
- Put photos in album
- Wash car
- Update phone numbers
- Sort through old records

It doesn't matter how many items are on your long-term to-do list; the longer it gets, the more variety you have when you have time to choose something to do.

5. Plan for Free Time

Whether you keep general or detailed schedules and to-do lists, it's a good idea to allow free time for yourself every day. We call it *downtime* or *me time,* and you can fill it with whatever relaxes you: having a cup of coffee or tea, reading, writing, daydreaming, playing a sport, watching television, or just doing nothing.

People who schedule every moment of their day may find they get irritated, frustrated, and exhausted. Everyone needs some unscheduled time to themselves. The littlest bit of downtime will refresh you and give you a chance to reenergize. Your brain will benefit from turning off for a few moments, even if it's only for 15 minutes. And you'll feel another benefit, even if you don't realize it—taking time for yourself helps you to get to know yourself a little bit better.

6. Expect the Unexpected

No matter how well you plan your day, you do not have control of what happens, only how you respond to it. Events are sure to occur that foul up your plans. Maybe a storm comes up and you can't get out of your house to get things done. Perhaps your car's transmission conks out. Your supervisor might surprise you with an urgent project, which means you have to drop everything else you had planned for the day. Whatever the unexpected event, it can instantly throw you off balance.

You can expect the unexpected by keeping your mind open and your plans flexible. If you schedule your day so tightly that not one crack of unused time shows through, you make yourself less able to adjust to a sudden change of plans. Try to leave some open spaces in your day. Then you have a chance to shift things around, if the need arises.

Accept the fact that your to-do list and daily schedule do not control the events of the day. Be open to change and willing to go with the flow. If something unexpected happens and you have to abandon some other scheduled activities, be calm. Give yourself a break and don't sweat over what you might not get to do. If your child falls ill and you have to miss a meeting at work to take him to the hospital, you have done what is truly most important. Work can wait. Or, conversely, if you suddenly have to work overtime for a sick coworker and miss a trip to the park with your child, again, you have set your priorities. There will be more times to go to the park, but only this one chance to substitute for the coworker who had an emergency and had to leave. Go with the flow.

7. Take Time to Think about Time

We all have days when we feel there just isn't any extra time to sit down and plan everything. Interestingly enough, taking time to plan will actually save time in the long run. Try getting up a few minutes earlier in the morning and quickly sketching out your day. It might save you hours! For example, suppose you work at the north end of town. During your workday, one task is to go to the office supply store, located 10 miles away on the south end of town. At some point you also need to pick up a personal prescription at the pharmacy, only 2 miles away from the office supply store. Without plans, you might end up driving to the same part of town twice to complete your errands.

However, if you take time to plan, you will figure out the best route to take so you can visit both stores and save yourself some time. No matter how pressed for time you feel, make a plan.

Sound Bite

> Look into all of the schools that you are interested in so you don't limit yourself. When you do find a school, don't keep putting it off. If you put it off too long, you won't go back. I know that from experience, because I was almost there. Just go ahead and do it. It's hard to keep up with it but you'll be really glad once you did it. You'll be glad when it's over too because you can move on with your life.
>
> —C. Hartlove, computer science student

8. Avoid Procrastination

Following all the tips we've provided only works if you actually do something! Putting things off, known as *procrastination,* is time management's number one enemy.

Sometimes we get creative, inventing odd and unimportant tasks that get in the way of starting the activity we are avoiding. Often that creativity takes up more energy than just finishing the job. Have you hidden a difficult project under other papers on your desk, and decided that you couldn't start working on it because you didn't have a big enough block of time available that week? Or, maybe you avoided making a difficult phone call by telling yourself that you were expecting someone else's call and needed to keep the phone free. Both are creative, normal, and crafty ways to trick yourself into thinking that procrastination is a good move.

People have many reasons for procrastinating. We procrastinate because we lack goals or set unrealistic goals that we cannot reach. We also procrastinate because we lack confidence in our ability to complete a task or we see that the work ahead seems hard and are afraid to fail. Luckily, there are a number of ways to banish procrastination.

- **Ask for help with projects.** Teachers, tutors, coworkers, and supervisors are great sources of information and assistance.
- **Keep in mind that no one does anything perfectly.** Better to try your hardest and do your best, even if it isn't perfect, than do nothing.
- **Set reasonable goals and write them down.** Put goals on a sticky note or an index card. Put the cards where you can see and refer to them.
- **Talk to yourself positively.** Put a positive self-talk card with the goal cards.
- **Break up a big task into very small tasks.** Completing one small task helps you feel successful so you are willing to try the next tasks.
- **Tell yourself you will start working on the task and then quickly evaluate your progress.** Check your progress in about 15 minutes. Getting started is the hardest part. Once you start, you will find it easier to keep going. And if you keep going, you will win the battle with procrastination.
- **Think about how you will feel when you complete this task.** Will you feel relieved? Proud? Excited? Imagining that feeling can provide the emotional energy to get you started on the task.

Hang On to Your Key Ring

You now have a solid grip on a collection of keys that will make your personal and professional life more efficient: self-knowledge and self-management. Understanding yourself, identifying your goals, setting your priorities, and managing your time are the keys to a successful life, in and out of the workplace.

Your Tool Kit at Work

2.1 Your Goals: Past, Present, and Future

Here is a chance to look at some goals you accomplished in the past and to set some new goals to work on now. Reaching goals can be a long process. Writing what you plan to do will help you structure your time and stay on track.

1. In the space provided, write goals you've accomplished in the past month. You can include personal accomplishments, such as eating a well-balanced diet or exercising regularly, as well as business or school accomplishments. Write what you think each accomplishment means to your career success.

My Accomplishments	How They Will Help My Career
I lost five pounds.	I have a more professional look.
I stopped smoking.	I will be able to work in a smoke-free environment.

2. Fill in the following worksheets to help define your future goals and lay out plans for achieving them. Use one for a career goal, one for a school-related goal, and one for a personal goal. As you work, you will discover how to achieve success in all three aspects of your life.

Life Area: Career

Goal—Be specific and positive (for example, instead of writing "I will stop being late," write "I will be prompt at all times.")

_____

_____

Obstacles—Why haven't I reached my goal by now?

_____

_____

Possible solutions to obstacles

_____

_____

Action steps—Things I will do and dates to be completed

_____

_____

Benefits I will receive—What will it mean to me when I accomplish this goal?

_____

_____

What I have accomplished and by what dates these accomplishments confirm for me that I am serious

_____

_____

Life Area: School

Goal—Be specific and positive

_____

_____

Obstacles

_____

_____

Possible solutions to obstacles

_____

_____

Action steps—Things I will do and dates to be completed

_____

_____

Benefits I will receive

_____

_____

What I have accomplished and by what dates

_____

_____

Life Area: Personal

Goal—Be specific and positive

_____

_____

Obstacles

_____

_____

Possible solutions to obstacles

_____

_____

Action steps—Things I will do and dates to be completed

_____

_____

Benefits I will receive

_____

_____

What I have accomplished and by what dates

_____

_____

2.2 Plug Your Knowledge into Real Life

Demands on your time in the workplace continually crop up. You need to devise different ways to handle these demands. As an example, put yourself in Manuel's place:

> Manuel is a hairstylist. One morning, the salon manager tells Manuel he has two appointments scheduled that evening, although he planned to leave at 6:00 p.m. In addition, another hairdresser, Amber, is sick today, and Manuel has to take a couple of her appointments. Manuel has worked at the salon for only two months. Keeping on the manager's good side and making a little extra money are important to him.

1. What would you do if you were Manuel?

_____

_____

2. If you chose to reschedule your day, how would you do so?

_____

_____

3. Consider a slightly different scenario: Manuel has worked at the salon for more than three years (as opposed to two months), and he is the manager's right-hand person. What, if anything, would you do differently if you were Manuel in this situation?

_____

_____

4. While in class, break into pairs and discuss your solutions together. See what you can learn from each other. If you like, construct a new solution by combining the best elements of your two solutions.

2.3 Your Time—Spend It Like Money

This activity combines daily time logs, weekly time logs, and a weekly schedule. You may never be this organized in real life, but the activity should give you some real insight into how you're spending your time.

1. You already had a chance to track your time for a day in the earlier "Now You Try It" mini-activity. Now try tracking it for a week by creating and using a daily log form that looks like this. You can create it on the computer, with as many lines as you like, and print multiple copies. Then keep track of your time and activities on it each day. The first few lines shown are just examples. Use any of the activity categories listed in step 2 or make up your own.

Daily Time Log

Day	Date	Activity	Start	End	Total Hours	Category
Monday	Sept. 13	Get up and do exercises	7:00	7:30	0.50	Exercise
		Shower, dress, get ready for work	7:30	8:00	0.50	Personal Hygiene
		Eat breakfast	8:00	8:30	0.50	Meals
		Commute to work on bike	8:30	9:00	0.50	Exercise

2. At the end of the week, transfer your information from your daily logs to this simplified weekly log form to see where the time went. You may decide to add other activity categories.

Current Weekly Time Log

Activity	Mon	Tue	Wed	Thu	Fri	Sat	Sun
Work							
Family time and childcare							
Class time							
Study							

Activity	Mon	Tue	Wed	Thu	Fri	Sat	Sun
Sleep							
Meals							
Commuting							
Personal business							
Household duties							
Communication							
Leisure activities							
Religious activities							
Dealing with the unexpected							
TOTALS:							
GRAND TOTAL (Add totals):							

a. During the week, did you feel like you had too little time, too much time, or just enough time to accomplish things?

b. Examine your daily logs and your weekly log. Do you notice any places where you waste your time? What are they?

3. Now's your chance to spend your time like money—carefully and realistically. Fill in a revised weekly time planner based on what you learned in the previous portion of this activity.

a. Now that you know how you spend your time, how can you change your schedule to accommodate your responsibilities? Look over your current time allocations and make cuts and increases where needed. Television, telephone, email, and Internet are often the major time wasters. Cut back on those culprits, but don't shortchange leisure time or time that can help you handle unexpected events.

b. If you are currently unemployed and plan to get a job, have you left enough hours open? If not, go back and make more cuts. If there are no more cuts to make, realize that you may have to live this way temporarily until your life situation changes or some of your goals are accomplished.

Revised Weekly Schedule

Activity	Mon	Tue	Wed	Thu	Fri	Sat	Sun
Work							
Family time and childcare							
Class time							
Study							
Sleep							

(continued)

Activity	Mon	Tue	Wed	Thu	Fri	Sat	Sun
Meals							
Commuting							
Personal business							
Household duties							
Communication							
Email, phone, and Internet							
Television							
Leisure activities							
Religious activities							
Dealing with the unexpected							
TOTALS:							
GRAND TOTAL (Add totals):							

4. OPTIONAL: If you are a detail-oriented personality type, you might want to transfer the hours from the previous step onto a weekly master time chart. Fill in your activities under the best times for you to accomplish them. Of course, you need to put the actual times you work, go to school, and complete your other time-specific tasks and activities.

Master Chart

Time	Mon	Tues	Wed	Thur	Fri	Sat	Sun
7:00 a.m.							
8:00 a.m.							
9:00 a.m.							
10:00 a.m.							
11:00 a.m.							
12:00 p.m.							
1:00 p.m.							
2:00 p.m.							
3:00 p.m.							
4:00 p.m.							
5:00 p.m.							
6:00 p.m.							
7:00 p.m.							
8:00 p.m.							
9:00 p.m.							
10:00 p.m.							
11:00 p.m.							

2.4 To Do or Not to Do

We all know about to-do lists, but not everyone consistently uses this tool. Writing major tasks is a must if we plan to get things done. To start a habit of making to-do lists, jot down everything you need to do tomorrow. Do this each day for a week and see how it goes.

1. _____
2. _____
3. _____
4. _____
5. _____
6. _____
7. _____

Look at your list. Which three items are the most important things to do? Put an A, B, and C by those items according to their order of importance.

2.5 Your Positive Attitude List

Your PAL for Chapter 2 takes another look at your personality. The traits on the list are considered necessary personal qualities for today's successful employee.

1. As in the last chapter, circle the skills where you feel confident, and identify the skills you need to develop.

Skill	Description
Adaptable	Adjusts well to new situations
Truthful	Is honest and sincere and straightforward
Thoughtful	Takes time to think things through before acting or passing judgment
Industrious	Works hard and steadily and completes tasks efficiently
Tenacious	Holds firmly to ideals and strong values; never gives up
Understanding	Has perspective on the needs and situations that affect self and others
Dependable	Is reliable and trustworthy
Empathetic	Can put self in another's shoes and see a situation from that perspective
Self-controlled	Knows how and when to act, and can defuse anger when necessary

2. These skills are essential for your success, so don't stop improving the ones you already do well. Make a note of the traits that need extra work, and set goals for you to work on them.

   a. I will develop my ability to be:

   _____

   _____

   b. Write the ability you want to develop on a sticky note or index card. Put it with your other cards from the earlier chapter.

2.6 Technology Exercise

Deciding what career is right for you is challenging. One of the difficulties can be a lack of firsthand knowledge of the different types of jobs. Students just out of school often suffer from this, but so do long-time employees who have never explored job alternatives. This is an assignment to help expand your workplace horizons.

1. Identify a possible entry-level job for a career that might interest you. For example: Web designer, Web content writer, auto mechanic, or dental technician. Perform an Internet search for information about your career of interest.

2. Select several items from the search results list and go to their websites to see what you can learn about the career. Write down what you learn.

_____

_____

_____

3. Next, interview three people who are doing work in the career you have selected. Include in your interview questions about: job qualifications, a typical workday, good versus challenging aspects of the job, what distinguishes successful versus unsuccessful people doing this type of work, and how the people got into their lines of work. Summarize your findings in writing.

_____

_____

_____

4. Did you notice any difference between how the job is described on the Web and how people who perform this job describe it? Why do you think that is?

_____

_____

_____

3

Manage Your Time and Money

Make the Most of Key Resources

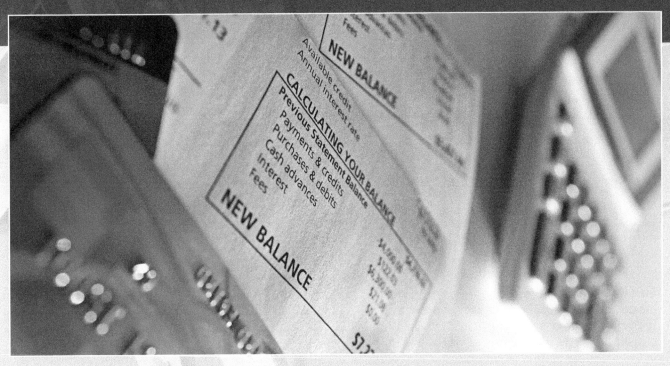

There is nothing so degrading as the constant anxiety about one's means of livelihood. Money is like a sixth sense without which you cannot make a complete use of the other five.

William Somerset Maugham

 learning objectives

- How do you budget your income and expenditures?
- Why is it a good idea to live beneath your means?
- What are ways to pay yourself first for everyday saving?
- How do you establish a good credit history?

- How did credit cards come about and how do credit card companies make money with their cards?
- How can you solve credit card problems?
- What is identity theft and how can you avoid it?

Janelle didn't set out to be in debt. But somehow, after she graduated from college, started moving up the career ladder in her profession, and later married and had a child, debt just seemed to happen, one purchase at a time.

Janelle got a promotion and she and her husband decided to celebrate with a number of big-ticket items for their home: a flat-screen television, new laptops, and a new car. Next, Janelle started upgrading her wardrobe. After all, she was now a senior sales representative who flew back and forth across the country, wining and dining customers. And then there were the home renovations: new furniture for her son to replace her parents' hand-me-downs, and paint, molding, and curtains for the rest of the house. In addition, her husband decided to get new skis, boots, poles, a mountain bike, and a motorcycle.

The expenses mounted until one day it all fell apart. Janelle's husband got laid off and could not find work for six months. During that time, the family lived on Janelle's salary, but the credit card debt from all those purchases and the accumulating interest were just too much. Janelle and her husband could barely sleep at night because they were worrying about the bills. In desperation, they visited the county consumer credit and debt counseling office. They were immediately told to stop all further credit card purchases, keep a spending log, cut back on expenses, and go on a budget. The organization also helped them contact creditors and consolidate their debt. The process was eye-opening and painful, but over the next two years Janelle and her family learned a lot about living frugally, making conscious decisions about purchases, and ignoring media and friends who urged them to buy, buy, buy.

Today, Janelle's husband is working again and their debt is almost gone. They continue to live beneath their means, however, because they will never forget the financial and emotional weight of that debt. They have vowed never to go into debt again, no matter what!

myth

"I've never used a budget and don't like keeping track of expenses; it's too restrictive. But look at me—I'm doing just fine."

reality

Success brings more responsibilities and often a greater income. At some point, we need to learn to manage our money. We can't afford to simply buy, buy, buy—we have to save as well. We need to use tools to help us track our expenses and our savings. Prepare yourself for success and start using a budget.

How you manage your money will directly affect the opportunities available to you, as well as your ability to pursue and achieve your personal and career goals. If you are not worrying about how to pay your bills or avoiding creditors, you can better focus on your work. This means you can consider job opportunities that require learning new skills or moving to a new location or employer—opportunities you might not consider because of the additional risk they appear to have when you are under financial pressure.

You already learned the importance of identifying meaningful goals, setting priorities, and managing your time. In this chapter, you will develop skills to manage your money—skills that are crucial for achieving your goals.

Good money management means more than simply watching the money come in and go out again (even though that's how it often feels). Money management tools are strategies for maximizing and saving your money. In this chapter you will learn how to budget and how to spend and save wisely. You will read about the pros and cons of credit cards, and how to avoid identity theft. After taking in all this information, you will be able to evaluate it and make choices that best fit your needs.

Going into Debt: An American Pastime

Today it seems that buying (especially with credit cards) and going into debt is an American pastime. According to the Federal Reserve's monthly G.19 report, total U.S. revolving debt (98% of which is made up of credit card debt) was $852.6 billion in March 2010. That's $54,000 in total debt (credit card, mortgage, home equity, and loans) for every U.S. family.[1]

Debt is an equal-opportunity destroyer. It occurs among college students, white-collar and blue-collar workers, and corporations. Spend some time watching television or going through your junk mail and you'll see how easy it is to go into debt. In fact, you are encouraged to do so—consider the number of "priceless" credit card ads on television, the number of credit card offers in the mail, and the volume of "no interest until . . ." offers from stores (especially around the holidays).

The message consumers receive is that it's their right to buy anything they want with credit, and nothing bad will ever come of their spending behavior. We call this magical thinking because it has no basis in reality. Companies that promote this message are interested in only one thing: profit. If they can get people hooked on using credit cards to purchase things they cannot afford and make them go into debt, those companies can make millions, perhaps billions, from the interest payments.

So, five years after you finally pay off that Caribbean vacation (that you can barely remember), the big screen TV (that no longer works), and a new wardrobe (which is now out of style), and you've racked up even more debt, what happens when a new financial crisis hits? What will you do when a balloon payment comes due on your house, or your children get sick and have to go to the hospital, or you have to come up with your child's college tuition, or you have to take care of an elderly parent? You can only handle these kinds of situations by spending and saving wisely.

Why Do Companies Care about Money Management?

Using money wisely is an important life and business skill. Financial literacy is just as important as general literacy (the ability to read and write). When you learn how to manage your money, you are less likely to overspend and go into debt. You will also be more of an asset to the company for

---

[1] Woolsey, Ben, and Matt Schulz. "Credit card statistics, industry facts, debt statistics." Accessed on October 7, 2010, from www.creditcards.com/credit-card-news/credit-card-industry-facts-personal-debt-statistics-1276.php

which you work. Getting things done on time and within a budget is a valuable skill. The ability to prioritize, evaluate costs, and make decisions about what to buy or not buy is what keeps a company in business. The more you learn about managing your personal finances, the better able you will be to deal with project budgets in your professional career.

Managing Your Money

Money plays a crucial role in our lives. We know that money isn't everything—it will never equal love, family, education, and a satisfying career. But it still pays for the wedding; feeds, clothes, and houses the family; and finances the education that leads to a great career. Money is a basic resource, and knowing how to manage your finances lets you function successfully in our society. Figure 3.1 illustrates key factors in money management. You don't necessarily need a huge flow of money—just a well-managed one. A small amount of money handled well will go much farther than a lot of money spent carelessly.

Figure 3.1 Building your financial foundation

Expand Opportunities!
- Manage Spending
- Control Credit Cards
- Save
- Create a Budget
- Set Priorities

Putting all your energy toward making money, at the expense of the more important things in your life, won't get you very far. It's important to strike a balance between expecting money to appear on its own and becoming obsessed with earning as much as you can. It's important to control your money without it controlling you. Because you probably already have a paying job, why not start learning how to manage that ebb and flow of cash? A budget is a great way to do this.

Budgeting

Budgeting is something we all do, even when we don't think about it. It is the simple act of realizing, "If I spend this money on X, then I won't have money for Y." However, it takes some thought and energy to do it well. As easy (and fun) as it is to spend your money without a thought for tomorrow, you will thank yourself later if you put some of it away. A smart **budget** is an investment in your own future.

You are budgeting when you go to the grocery store and think to yourself, "I have 20 dollars. That means I can pick up food for dinner and get some soap, but I will have to wait until next time to get laundry detergent." You are budgeting when go to the movies and have to decide what you can buy with the money left over after you purchase a ticket: a large popcorn and a small drink, or a small popcorn and a large drink. You are budgeting when you decide how much you can spend on each member of your family during the holidays.

You can see that you've already had some practice with budgeting. But it is important to look at the bigger picture—to budget over a period of a week, a month, or a year. Budgeting means setting goals with your money. The earlier you set your goals, the more in control you will be.

Money Trouble Often Equals Lack of Control

Losing control of spending rarely means you are incapable of controlling your spending; it usually means you haven't tried. More important, it usually means you lack long-term vision. When you look ahead, you will be able to control your funds.

Here's an example. Mark has a job with a company that does not give employees paid vacation time. It is March, and Mark plans to take a week off in April. He decides he wants to go someplace warm, and he makes plans to fly to Cancun the first week of April because an airline is running a special cheap fare. By the end of April, he has a stack of bills that he is unable to pay. He wonders, "What just happened?"

Mark didn't plan ahead. He didn't consider the fact that he would lose a week's pay during his vacation. He also forgot that April 15 was tax day and he needed extra money to pay taxes he

Budget, verb

to plan activities and expenditures according to the amount of income available

noun

a list of expenses and the money spent on each

owed. Unfortunately, he didn't spend his money according to how much money he actually had available.

What could Mark have done differently? Even though he planned the vacation around an inexpensive flight, he forgot to factor in the costs of living, eating, and recreation for the week. How about changing the vacation week altogether? If he traveled in March or May, he could have avoided the clash with tax day. If he had to be someplace warm, what about going to Florida or the Florida Keys instead of Mexico? What about taking the train instead of flying? Making a money decision requires taking a hard look at all the expenses and weighing what options make the most sense. Taking the train to Florida in May would have provided a warm-weather vacation and allowed Mark to save money.

How to Budget

It isn't hard to budget. It simply takes time to think about your expenses and income, and catalog your information. How often should you do it? Budgeting once a month makes sense, because bills and bank statements arrive monthly. After learning the monthly budget process, you can project your annual expenses. Following the budgeting process can be done in a few easy steps:

1. Determine approximately how much money you will make in the coming month.

2. Determine your most basic expenditures (food, gas, heat, water, electricity, phone, Internet, rent or mortgage, loans, credit cards, prescriptions, car payment, and tuition) based on figures from previous months.

3. Subtract these expenditures from your income, and look at how much you have left over. If you have money left over, this becomes a "buffer" for emergencies. If you do not have money left over, you are probably living beyond your means.

4. Make decisions about how to allocate your money for next month.

   a. Shift more money to areas that need it.

   b. Decide how much you can spend on not-so-necessary items such as entertainment.

   c. Plan to spend less in areas that are unaffordable right now.

   d. If you perform actions a through c, but still come up short, you may need a different job that will increase your income.

   Now let's look at each step in more detail.

Step Will 1: Determine How Much You Will Make

You can do this by adding your pay stubs from last month, if you currently have a job, or your paid invoices from the last couple of months if you are self-employed. If you receive any financial aid, loan funding, or scholarship money that

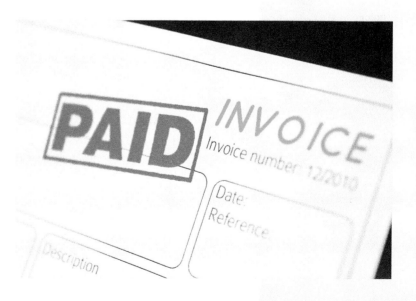

does not go directly to your school, determine how much of that you can allow for each month's spending and add it to your income.

Step 2: Figure Out How Much You Actually Spend

You may think, "I haven't the slightest idea what I spend in an average month!" That's okay. If you never pay attention to what you spend, you need to take some time to track your spending habits before you can successfully budget. Take two weeks or even a month to look closely at your spending. Buy a small notebook or tack a piece of paper to a bulletin board, and write what you bought and how much you paid each time you spend money. This is called a spending log. It is similar to a food log that a person might keep when he or she is trying to figure out how to adjust eating habits. It is also similar to the time log you learned about in the previous chapter. However, the spending log tracks the money, rather than the time, you spend. It is an effective way to find out where your money actually goes so you can adjust your spending habits.

When you finish tracking daily expenses for a week or two, it's time to get down to work. Start by looking at your list of expenditures and grouping them into categories, such as:

- Rent or mortgage
- Tuition or school loans (If you don't pay monthly, figure out what it would be per month. For example, if you pay for a half year at a time, divide that amount by six.)
- Regular bills (heat, gas, electric, phone, car payment)
- Credit card or any other loan payments that you make
- Food
- Toiletries
- Household supplies
- Childcare expenditures
- Entertainment and other related items (eating out, books and magazines, coffee)
- Insurance
- Transportation

Next, calculate your average weekly expenditures. For each category, estimate what you spend each day, multiply the amount by how many days per week you have that particular expenditure, and use that as the amount for the week. Think carefully about small items you might have forgotten, which tend to add up. If you have a mid-afternoon snack regularly, or buy a newspaper every day, the resulting monthly expense might surprise you. For example, if the cost of your daily café macchiato ranges from $3.50 to $4.50, you could easily spend $20 a week for coffee (averaged to $4 per day for a five-day week).

The whole point of a spending log is to get a general idea of what you spend. Don't worry if you haven't added each penny from your receipts. Just be sure to estimate the amount of money you spend, and then bring that amount to the table when you begin to plan your budget.

Step 3: Look at How Much Money Is Left Over

If there is any leftover money, you should figure out a way to save it (the section on saving is coming up later in this chapter). Some months you may not have any left over. Because you are budgeting for the following month, you aren't in trouble yet; take it as a sign to be especially careful not to overspend during that next month. If you end up with a negative number, you are spending more than you make. Move on to Step 4 and adjust your budget so you won't overspend. When you have a negative number and you realize that you're looking at a typical month, you might start thinking about adjusting your budget over the long term.

Step 4: Make Changes in Your Spending According to Your Needs

Certain areas of your budget may need more money some months, such as when you go for your twice-yearly dental visit. You may need to adjust other areas if you run short of funds. Adjusting doesn't mean cutting out your rent or heating bill. It means looking carefully for unnecessary expenditures. Do you go out to lunch too often? Perhaps you should cut back and make your own lunch. Do you pay for a premium channel in your cable service? Perhaps you can eliminate this channel (or the cable service) and watch DVDs you already own or rent them free from the library.

What it comes down to is this: Be smart. If you cannot comfortably afford extras, cut them out. You will be glad you did in the long run. Of course, the other solution to this problem is to get a higher-paying job. You're working toward that right now by studying.

A student's budget probably looks quite different from that of a full-time employee. And a working, single professional's budget probably looks different from a professional with a family, or an unemployed professional. Your money picture shifts depending on the circumstances of your life, and you have to shift your budget accordingly.

Figures 3.2 and 3.3 show two sample monthly budgets for Roy and his two-year-old son, Taylor. Figure 3.2 shows the budget while Roy is in school, living with his parents, and paying them a small rent. Figure 3.3 shows the budget when Roy graduates and is a full-time employee with his own apartment.

Roy made some tough choices so he could afford going to school. He asked his parents if he and Taylor could move back in while he was a student; they agreed to him moving in if he could pay a small stipend each month. Roy was able to save on childcare costs (his parents looked after Taylor), as well as heat and electric bills. He still paid his share of the phone bill and provided a lot of his own food (but his parents made some family meals, so that helped).

Money was tight for Roy during that time. As you can see in Figure 3.2, he often went over his budget and had to spend more than he made. In this situation, his parents often helped when that happened. In general, he had to cut back on his entertainment a lot, he had to shop carefully in the supermarket, and he made an effort to do a clothing swap with other parents when Taylor grew out of his clothes. He avoided buying lunch by making his lunch every day. He could not afford a car and took the bus instead.

Let's take a look at Roy's budget after he finished school and found a good full-time job in his desired field (see Figure 3.3). What a difference a job makes! Figure 3.3 reflects these changes:

- Roy's job brings in a much more substantial salary.

- He no longer has to pay tuition. Instead, he has a monthly payment toward his student loan.

- Because he moved into his own apartment, he now has to pay rent, heat, electric, and water bills.

- He bought a used car and now has monthly car payments and gasoline expenses.

- His food and phone bills are slightly higher because he must take care of them on his own.

- Taylor now goes to preschool, but Roy's parents still babysit Taylor whenever necessary.

- He can put a little bit more money into fun things to do with his son.

Sometimes all it takes is eating a bag lunch several times a week to change your spending habits and save up the money you need.

Figure 3.2 Sample monthly budget while Roy is in school

Expenditures	Amount
Tuition ($8,500 per year)	$ 708
Public transportation	$ 60
Phone	$ 30
Food	$ 200
Rent paid to parents	$ 200
Taxes (about one-fourth of salary) Note: This entry is necessary only if your employer withholds no taxes or not enough taxes from your paycheck. If taxes are automatically withheld, list your income after taxes and eliminate this entry.	$ 300
Entertainment	$ 60
Total expenditures	**$1,558**

Income	Amount
Part-time salary ($5.00 per hour, 20 hours per week)	$1,200
Student loan ($3,600 per year ÷ 12 months per year)	$ 300
Total monthly income	**$1,500**

$1,500 (income) − $1,558 (spending) = $58 (over budget)

technology *at work*

Try using your computer skills to create a budget. List your income and expenses on a spreadsheet program such as Excel, and let the program do the calculations. You'll find it easy to make some changes to your income or expense assumptions and see how this will affect how much you have left. In addition, making a 12-month budget is a snap with this program.

You might also want to check out some money management programs such as Intuit's Quicken or Microsoft Money. If money is tight (which it often is), consider some of the free budgeting services online, such as Mint.com and BudgetTracker.com.

Because Roy's job brings in more money, he finally has some money left over at the end of the month. Some of the left-over money will probably go toward the unplanned purchases that come up each month—a new car part, new shoes, a birthday gift for a family member, medicine, and so on. But before any of that happens, Roy should save some of that money for the future.

Think about it: If Roy can save $150 a month, that will become at least $1800 by the end of the year—and interest will add even more. Saving money is difficult and requires a lot of discipline. But the payoff is big. You are investing in your future! If you can budget your own finances well, you have a skill that will serve you well in many types of jobs.

Like Roy, your financial circumstances will change over time. You'll have a positive financial change when you start a full-time job in your career field, get a promotion, or land a higher-paying job. Other changes may crop up, such as a move to a cheaper or more expensive dwelling, a loss of financial responsibility due to divorce, or a gain of financial responsibility due to the birth of a child or having to care for an ill parent. You might experience a change in part-time employment or a good-sized tax return in April—anything can happen. Plan to revise your budget any time your financial situation changes.

Figure 3.3   Sample budget after Roy graduates

Expenditures	Amount
Rent	$ 800
Heat and electricity	$ 60
Water	$ 45
Car payment	$ 200
Food	$ 400
Phone and Internet	$ 60
Entertainment	$ 100
Loan payment	$ 200
Taxes	$ 875
Gasoline	$ 100
Preschool	$ 400
Total monthly expenditures	**$3,240**

Income	Amount
Full-time salary ($42,000 per year ÷ 12 months per year)	$3,500
Total Monthly Income	**$3,500**

$3,500 (income) − $3,240 (spending) = $260 (left over)

 # Now You Try It: Create a Daily Spending Log

Here's your chance to try tracking your expenses for a day. Later you'll have a chance to do so for a week, but this should give you a taste of the process.

1. Today, as you go about your daily business, make a conscious effort to write down everything you spend money on. This includes small purchases, big purchases, and bills. Make sure to keep all your receipts as well. Jot down the items and amounts in a small notebook. This notebook will become your spending log.

2. At the end of the day, go through your receipts to ensure you did not forget anything.

3. Review your spending and answer these questions:

   a. Was today a typical day in terms of your spending? If not, why was it different?

   b. What did you notice about your spending?

   c. Do you tend to pay by cash, check, or card?

   d. Did you buy anything you didn't really need?

One More Way to Plan Your Budget

If the idea of tracking your expenses with a spending log and developing a comprehensive, detailed budget feels overwhelming, you are not alone. People with different personalities handle budgeting differently.

Figure 3.4   Terra's annual budget

Expenditures	Amount
Tuition	$ 6,000
Rent (12 × $700)	$ 8,400
Car payments (12 × $200)	$ 2,400
Car insurance (4 × $450)	$ 1,800
Renter's insurance	$ 300
Phone (12 × approximately $50)	$ 600
Electricity, including heat and air conditioning (12 × approximately $70)	$ 840
Total annual expenditures:	**$20,340**

Income	Amount
Student loan	$ 6,000
Wages (after taxes are subtracted)	$15,000
Total annual income:	**$21,000**

$21,000 (income) − $20,340 (spending) = + $660

Think back to what you know about your personality and your strengths. How well do you work with details and schedules? Those with an S, T, J, or any combination of the three traits in their personality profiles probably compute monthly budgets with relative ease and appreciate the control it gives them. Others whose profiles weigh heavily on the P or F sides may not get such a kick out of budgeting, and may find it to be more trouble than they think it is worth. If you have trouble maintaining a monthly budget, a simpler and broader method is to look at your finances for the whole year:

- Some amounts, such as salary, wages, or tuition, are easy to determine for a year.
- Some expenses, such as rent or car payments, involve multiplying by 12 (or by however many payments you make during the year).
- Some bills require you to estimate before you multiply, such as your phone and energy bills.

Although you won't get as much information from a general yearly budget, it might satisfy your need to know where your money is going and help you make some financial decisions. In fact, even if you work well with monthly budgeting, you should look at the big picture of your annual budget. Sometimes items get lost in monthly planning (insurance, taxes, and other quarterly or once-yearly payments), but they show up more clearly in a yearly budget.

Let's take a look at Terra's annual budget as an example (see Figure 3.4). She is single, rents a studio apartment, and works nights and weekends while taking classes four days a week. Terra knows that she is not overspending. That's good, but she must remember that she hasn't included food, entertainment, or needs such as clothing and gasoline; these costs are hard to estimate using this particular kind of budget. Terra really doesn't have the funds to pay for food and all her other incidental needs for the year. She knows she must search for additional income to live comfortably this year, and she needs to consider how she might do this. Maybe she can move into a shared living space and reduce her rent, or try to do some more part-time work at her school during the day to earn extra money. If you were in her place, what changes could you make in your life to increase your money resources?

Spending and Saving Wisely

Once you review your spending log and establish a budget, you'll know where your money goes. This puts you in control of your money, not the other way around. The next step is to control how you distribute that money. That's where wise spending and saving come into play.

The Golden Rule of Smart Spending and Saving: Live BeneathYour Means

To live *beyond your means* is to spend more money than you make and to create debt. To live *beneath your means* is to spend less than what you make. For example, if you make $2,000 a month, you would spend only $1,800 and save the $200 difference. That savings, however small, provides you with a buffer that will come in handy when emergencies or bigger expenditures arise. This doesn't mean you have to give up everything but your basic needs; it simply means you need to look at possible expenditures intelligently and decide whether you can afford them at the time or need to defer them. It means weighing the pros and cons of an immediate purchase and thinking, "If I buy this now, I won't be able to. . . ." It means making

Learning from Experience
A Perspective from the Working World

Setting Priorities

Eton Jackson
*GIS software project
manager and officer in
army reserves*

Life is a journey with many challenges. To overcome future challenges, I decided to get a college education, which turned out to be a challenge in itself! I earned a degree in Computer Science, with a focus on GIS (geographic information systems), but I learned far more from college than just the courses I studied, especially when it came to managing time and money.

There is an old saying, "The more you put into it, the more you will get out." The things that a person puts in are time, money, and personal effort. As a student, I did not initially put much into it. The freedom of student life allowed me to give in to the temptation to spend and waste both time and money. However, over time, I learned how to manage my time and live within my means. This wasn't easy because I had to learn how to set limits on what I spent. This meant creating a budget, something that was pretty alien to me.

To help me keep track of what I spent, I started saving receipts. I kept whatever cash I had in a system of envelopes, each with a designated use. One envelope was for school supplies, one was for personal use, one was for food and entertainment, and another was for emergencies. It probably wasn't the most high-tech system imaginable. I suppose I could have used any of the online budgeting systems to help me, but being a hands-on kind of guy, I liked those physical envelopes.

While budgeting, I discovered that wanting something isn't the same thing as needing it, and living simply does not mean living in poverty. I also learned that something urgent is not always important, and available money is better saved and invested. I bought things I thought I couldn't live without, but after a while many of those things lost their appeal.

Although I did not have a credit card for a long time, I saw many students around me get into dire financial difficulties with plastic money. With a credit card, it's too easy to buy things with money you don't really have, which sets a dangerous trap. I saw friends barely making their credit card minimum payments each month and ending up with thousands of dollars of debt when they graduated.

I also struggled with time management in college. My biggest problem was participating in too many activities. At the beginning of college, I enrolled in the Army ROTC (Reserve Officer's Training Corps) scholarship program. School, ROTC, and sports had me on the go all the time, making it difficult to fully commit to things that really mattered.

Fortunately, ROTC taught me about time management and decision making. I had to prioritize, plan, and execute the work to get the mission accomplished. I learned how to identify needs, issues, and possible problems. I had to start thinking ahead and acting wisely. I gradually learned to establish goals, set priorities, and maintain a schedule. Learning how to budget my time became easier once I knew how to set priorities.

After graduation, I worked for a GIS company as a software developer, and later as a project manager. In college, I thought things couldn't get any worse in terms of lack of time and money. How wrong I was. In the world of software development, documentation, and support, it was a daily struggle to realistically estimate project release dates and necessary resources. It was even harder to get things done within budget and on time because of the number of people involved. Fortunately, the lessons I learned in college helped tremendously.

Although I still struggle with time and money, all of those learning experiences are helping me become more proactive. I'm learning how to look ahead and think long-term as well as short-term. The lessons have not stopped because learning is a lifelong endeavor— "The more you put into it, the more you will get out."

informed decisions about purchases, rather than acting impulsively. Most importantly, it means not overspending and overconsuming. Even if you spend $1 less than you make, you're moving in the right direction.

When you live beyond your means, you run the risk of being unprepared for the unexpected. Jonathan is an example of a person who tried to live beyond his means and got into trouble for it. Specifically, he got a new job that paid $30,000 a year, $5,000 more than the job he had previously. That's an extra $833 per month. To celebrate, Jonathan bought the expensive new car of his dreams.

The company that hired him was bought by another firm only two months after Jonathan joined the staff. Jonathan lost his job when the buyout happened because he was a new hire and the purchasing firm was more loyal to employees who had been there longer. Jonathan found himself unemployed and back on the job market, with a steep monthly car payment he couldn't afford.

What if Jonathan had restricted his celebration to one nice dinner out and maybe a new suit, instead of a new car? Then, when he lost the job, he would have had no extra debts. Plus, he still would have earned an extra $833 for each of the two months he worked. If he had saved this money, it would have helped him stay afloat while he looked for another job.

 ## Now You Try It: Underspending on Entertainment

Do you wonder whether you can start underspending instead of overspending? Try making some adjustments in the entertainment category of your budget. Think of some free or almost free entertainment possibilities that you enjoy. Videos and DVDs from the library beat the cost of going to a movie theatre. Parks are free, and some museums are free on designated days or in certain cities. If you live near a lake or reservoir, swimming is often free. Bartering entertainment is another option. You might go fishing on your friend's boat one weekend, and invite her for a cookout in your backyard the next. Using Figure 3.5, write down the following:

1. Brainstorm and write down free or inexpensive entertainment ideas. Be creative!
2. Estimate how much money each activity will save you in a month's time.
3. Go back and make a check mark by the ideas you plan to use this month.

Figure 3.5 Underspending on entertainment

Ideas for (Almost) Free Fun	Money Saved	Use This Month
	$	$
	$	$
	$	$
	$	$
	$	$
	$	$
	$	$
	$	$
	$	$
	$	$
Total money saved on entertainment:	$	

The Silver Rule: Pay Yourself First

Paying yourself means putting money away in your savings, where it can grow until you need to use it. When you have an extra dollar (or more, we hope) left over after all your expenditures, put it in your savings account. You owe it to yourself to save that money—it could become your security as you grow older, help send your children to college, help you survive a crisis or job loss, or contribute to a large purchase, such as a house or car.

We all like to spend "extra" money on things that we don't really need—things we *want* to buy, such as entertainment or dinners out. What good will a new television do if you have a financial crisis? Even if you sell it, you won't receive what you paid for it. Your investment will shrink. Better to save the money, keep an eye on it as it gains interest and grows, and buy the television when you have more of a surplus.

Another important tip is not to think of your post-bill leftover money as "extra." Instead, think of it as a reinvestment, just like companies do. Well-run companies do not spend their profits indiscriminately; they often reinvest a large portion of that money in machinery, research, and training for the future. Honor your commitment to yourself by including your leftover money in your budget as a payment to yourself that carries equal weight with your mortgage or rent payment.

When we talk about ways to budget and save money, we don't mean you should sacrifice all the little extras that make life enjoyable. Life is too short to restrict all your fun activities so you can save money. At that rate, by the time you retire, you will have worked so hard that you'll be too tired to enjoy the money you have saved! Instead, we hope that even if you don't have to worry about money right now, you will stay conscious of where it goes. You never know what the future holds.

We encourage you to deal with money matters intelligently, reason through your financial needs, apply budgeting strategies, make wise decisions, and work toward financial goals. Do you want to go to a nice restaurant, a show, or basketball game? Do you want to buy a new outfit or a television? Don't deny yourself; just do yourself a favor by thinking before you buy. For example, eat inexpensive dinners at home all week to save up for the restaurant. Find opportunities to walk instead of drive, or take public transportation, and put the savings toward your concert tickets. Give up buying sugary foods for a month and spend the saved money on that new outfit (see how great you look in it after giving up sugar). Or justify the new television by watching Monday night football in your own living room (much cheaper than going to a bar).

Get in the habit of "if . . . then" thinking when it comes to spending money: "If I want to buy X, then I need to do Y." This means asking yourself questions, such as where is your surplus money going? Where do you think you could cut back? There are many ways to have your fun in life without strapping yourself financially. You just need to think about it.

Credit Cards

Heads up! A credit card can be an incredible lifesaver or a black hole of debt. It depends on how you decide to use **credit**.

Some businesses or stores offer credit in the form of accounts—your purchases go on the account and you pay for them in installments. But most credit comes in the form of a little plastic card.

A credit card allows you to make a purchase with money you don't have at the moment, and then pay off the debt later. If you pay it off at the end of the month, you are charged no interest; otherwise, you pay anywhere from 11% to 24% interest. That interest can really add up over time, especially if you keep making purchases. In fact, some people end up with so much credit card debt that their monthly payments barely cover their interest payments. Before we get into the pros and cons of credit cards, however, let's look at the history behind them.

Sound Bite

I think knowing that you need to put some money away is the most important idea. Opportunities will come up later and you will need money to take advantage of them. You don't always need to buy that extra this or that; you need to put some money away in savings or investments and watch it draw interest. I know that a lot of people coming out of school are younger, and they're not thinking about investing their money. But if you're making enough money and you can save some money, then by all means, do it. When I was younger I was so busy, and at that time life was very simple and I didn't have a lot of bills. Things get more complicated— you're not buying new shoes, you're buying new furniture, and there's a big difference in price.

—K. Mitchell, independent consultant

Benefits of Credit Cards

Credit, *noun*

a sum of money made available by a bank or credit card company, on which a specified person or firm may draw

If credit cards cause so much trouble, why have them? If used wisely, they can be beneficial. Let's take a look at the benefits.

Establishing a Good Credit History

Having a credit card that you use moderately and pay off regularly (on time) can give you a good credit rating. Equifax, Experian, and Transunion are companies that track credit histories and ratings of everyone who has any sort of credit. The history is the record of your credit use, and the rating is the score that the company gives you based on how good or bad your history is. Your credit rating becomes important for both job hunting and major purchases (for example, cars and homes). Many prospective employers look into the credit histories of applicants to see if they reliably pay their bills and keep their debt under control. If your credit rating is good, it can help you qualify for a job. Also, when you want to make a major purchase, you may need a loan from a bank. Banks are more likely to loan money to someone who has a good credit rating because it shows responsibility and reliability.

How do you know what your credit card rating is? You can contact Equifax, Experian, or Transunion (visit their websites) and request a credit report. Most states allow you to request one report a year for free; there may be a charge for more frequent requests. When you receive your report, study it to make sure it's accurate. Common inaccuracies include listing cards you no longer have or use, or indicating that a credit card company terminated your account when you requested the account be closed. Contact the individual credit card companies to resolve the issues. You will probably need to get another credit report at a later date to verify the inaccuracies have been corrected.

Sound Bite

These are challenging times financially because of the instability of the work world. You have to prioritize—pay the most important things first, because it's not always realistic to be able to pay off all your bills all of the time. As for the other bills, pay a little bit this month, a little bit that month. It's like building a house. Build your finances brick by brick, and you will eventually come to a point where everything is being paid consistently and you are on some kind of schedule.

When I had my first job in New York I was starving! I got a second job selling real estate part time at night, and then I just knocked off one bill at a time. I would focus on my Visa, pay as much as I could, and only pay minimum on the others until Visa was paid off. I'm not a financial expert, but that's how I did it.

—L. Durden, career counselor

Handling Emergencies

Credit cards can come in handy if you are caught somewhere without cash and need to pay for something. These kinds of situations can happen anytime you run out of gas, you get stuck somewhere and need to stay in a motel, or you need to find transportation in a hurry. Perhaps you get injured and need to stay in a hospital. If you don't have health insurance, your credit card can get you out of a jam.

Keeping a Record of Purchases

Some people like to use credit cards because they get a record each month of the purchases they made, where they made them, and exactly how much they paid. This can be useful if you make purchases for work on your credit card and need to keep records for tax purposes.

Getting Bonuses from Credit Card Companies

Many companies offer bonuses to attract more people to their particular credit card. For example, most major airlines offer credit cards that give you frequent flier miles in exchange for dollars spent. Other universal cards may offer cash rewards when you spend a certain amount within a particular time frame. (Beware, the purchase amount is usually high and the cash reward is low.) Still others offer a rebate when you use the card to purchase gas. If you know that the bonus will be useful to you, and you use the credit card consistently and pay it off each month, obtaining the card may be worthwhile.

Pitfalls and Problems

In spite of their many benefits, credit cards can get you into trouble if you aren't careful. Pay particular attention to this section if you find yourself using credit cards more often than you should.

You Are Spending Someone Else's Money

Until you pay it back, the money you spend is not yours. It belongs to the credit card company and the credit card company pays it to the retailer. Retailers also have to pay a percentage to the credit card company for use of the credit service (this is why some retailers do not accept credit cards). Credit card companies count on you to pay them for your purchases, but they really don't *want* you to pay the money back on time. Instead, they want you to keep a running balance so they can make money on the interest. If you don't like paying interest, pay off your balance each month.

It can be very tempting to overspend using credit cards. Because you don't have to pay with your own money right away, you may feel free to spend more than you should. This can lead to trouble later if you are unable to pay off your cards or even make your minimum payments.

You Are Taking Out a High-Interest Loan

When you make purchases using a credit card, it is the same as taking out a loan. You are using money with the promise to pay it back. In exchange for the privilege of using that money, you pay interest and fees if you don't pay your balance in full each month. Credit card companies are businesses that are interested in making a profit, and they do this with high interest rates and fees.

Let's say you have $2,000 in your savings account and owe $2,000 on a credit card that charges 18% interest. You decide not to touch your savings and make only the minimum payment of $40 each month. At this rate, it will take you 30 years to pay off the debt (assuming you make no other purchases) and you will end up paying $4,927 interest, more than twice the original debt.

Instead of giving all that money to the credit card company and staying in debt for much of your life, you could pull $1,000 from your savings to cut the debt in half, and make double payments of $80 each month. As a result, you would be debt free in about 14 months versus 30 years. Additionally, you would pay only $116 in interest versus $4,927. And if you continued to put some money into your savings account during those 14 months, it would gradually rebuild to its former size over time, and then continue to grow.

Generally, try to keep your credit card debt lower than the amount of money you have saved. If you need funds for a large purchase, try a bank loan. The interest rates will be lower than those on a credit card.

Credit Is Addictive

Spending money can be like a drug. It's fun and seems painless, because you don't see the damage (the bills) for a while. But if you get hooked on it and your material desires get the best of you, you can wind up thousands of dollars in debt to credit card companies. You will see your debt grow by leaps and bounds because of the high interest.

Harold Pruett, UCLA's director of student psychological services, said he and his fellow counselors have been deluged with students concerned about their finances. "I often talk to students who run up $4,000 or $5,000 on a credit card in a year," said Pruett. "Then they stress and worry and some of them have to drop out of school for a quarter to pay it off. It starts a crazy cycle."[2]

---

[2] Weiss, Kenneth R. "Survey finds record stress in class of 2000." *Los Angeles Times*, January 13, 1997, p. A18.

Carrying a large amount of debt will hurt you in many ways: Your credit rating will fall, you will be unable to take out loans or mortgages, you will lose the ability to use your credit cards, and money that you could spend on things you need will have to go toward repaying your debt.

A Bad Credit Rating Can Haunt You

With many credit cards, the first time you make a late payment, your interest rate goes up and you suffer a late payment penalty. Over time, increased interest rates and penalties can increase your credit card debt substantially. Then, when you miss a payment, default on a payment, or misuse your card, a black mark shows up on your credit history, which lowers your credit rating. If a prospective employer checks your credit, that employer may be less likely to trust you. And if you apply for a bank loan, the bank may refuse the loan if you have a history of late or missing payments, or other credit card problems.

Do yourself a favor—don't create unnecessary stress by getting into credit card trouble. It can be tough enough to get by in this world without getting financially strapped! Save your money so you can pay back a house or car loan, help a family member through a tough period, pay back education loans, or pay medical bills. Don't lose your savings by getting into a hole with credit cards.

You Can Draw Your Financial Picture

Getting control of your finances helps you get control of your life!

You are in control of your finances, even though it may not always seem that way. With your current salary, you may be making just enough to get by. Despite not liking your job, you might not feel that you can make a change. You feel locked in by the monthly payments you have to make.

Rather than feeling paralyzed, you now have the tools to open up your options. You know how to set goals and priorities. You know how to keep a spending log and establish a budget. You know where to cut spending and start saving, and you know how to control your credit card use.

Getting your financial facts together will give you a solid base from which to make decisions. When you are job hunting, you will know what knowledge to use and what actions to take, no matter the situation. Perfecting the use of your personal finance tools will prepare you for your first job or when you get a new one.

Your Tool Kit at Work

3.1 Where Your Money Goes

As with your time, you need to know how you're spending your money to make changes and improvements in your budgeting. A good plan requires a solid starting point: a weekly spending log that you keep for four weeks to get an idea of your monthly spending.

You already had a chance to track your spending for a day in the "Now You Try It" mini-activity. You know how to track your daily expenses in a spending log and collect your receipts.

1. At the end of each day, go through your receipts to be sure you did not forget anything.

2. At the end of the week, transfer the amounts from your spending log to the appropriate categories on the weekly spending form (Figure 3.6). Note that you may choose to use slightly different categories.

   a. What do you notice about your spending from week to week? (Do some expenditures vary from week to week? Are some expense categories greater than others?)

   b. What are your greatest expenses?

   c. What are your lowest expenses?

   d. Which areas are problem areas in which you are overspending?

Figure 3.6 **Your weekly expenses**

Expense Category	Week 1	Week 2	Week 3	Week 4
Rent or mortgage	$	$	$	$
Utilities (electricity, gas, water)	$	$	$	$
Food (groceries)	$	$	$	$
Dining out	$	$	$	$
Telephone and Internet	$	$	$	$
Loan payments (student, bank loans, car)	$	$	$	$
Insurance (car, health, home/renter's, life)	$	$	$	$
Car expenses (repairs, parts)	$	$	$	$
Gasoline	$	$	$	$
Public transportation	$	$	$	$
Home expenses (furniture, household items, repair)	$	$	$	$
Clothing/personal items	$	$	$	$
Salon and personal services	$	$	$	$
Entertainment	$	$	$	$
Childcare (caregivers, clothing and supplies, other fees)	$	$	$	$
Medical care (prescriptions, doctor visits, hospitalization)	$	$	$	$
Miscellaneous/unexpected	$	$	$	$
GRAND TOTAL:	**$**	**$**	**$**	**$**

3.2   What's Your Cash Flow?

Now that you know what you are spending each week, it's time to estimate your monthly expenses, income, and cash flow (see Figure 3.7).

1. Take the average of the four weekly amounts for each category to determine your monthly average.
2. Calculate the money you earn each month (see Figure 3.8).
3. To find out your cash flow each month, subtract the grand total of your expenses from the grand total of your income (use the bottom portion of Figure 3.8).

3.3   Make Some Adjustments

Now that you have determined your cash flow, you are in a position to take steps to improve your situation. If you have a negative cash flow (more money goes out per month than comes in), you have two choices: make more money or spend less money. You need to look at both alternatives. Your budget will probably reflect ideas for both earning more and spending less.

1. Start with spending cuts, because it can be tough to take on more work while you're in school or working full time. Look at all your current expenditures for places to "trim

Figure 3.7   **Your monthly expenses**

Expense Category	Monthly Average
Rent or mortgage	$
Utilities (electricity, gas, water)	$
Food (groceries)	$
Dining out	$
Telephone and Internet	$
Loan payments (student, bank loans, car)	$
Insurance (car, health, home/renter's, life)	$
Car expenses (repairs, parts)	$
Gasoline	$
Public transportation	$
Home expenses (furniture, household items, repair)	$
Clothing/personal items	$
Salon and personal services	$
Entertainment	$
Childcare (caregivers, clothing and supplies, other fees)	$
Medical care (prescriptions, doctor visits, hospitalization)	$
Miscellaneous/unexpected	$
GRAND TOTAL:	**$**

Figure 3.8 **Your monthly income**

Income	Monthly Amount
Regular work salary (full- or part-time work or self-employment)	$
Grants or work-study payments	$
Monthly assistance you may receive from family members or other sources	$
Private sale of items (for example: in person or on eBay or Craigslist)	$
Other	$
GRAND TOTAL:	$

My income is:	$	per month	
My expenses are:	$	per month	
		Income	$
		– Expenses	– $
		Cash Flow	$

Choose one:

☐ I have $ ___ positive cash flow.

☐ I have $ ___ negative cash flow.

☐ I break even.

the fat." Your rent or mortgage is a fixed amount, but it can be lowered by moving or sharing your home. Loans can be refinanced (restructured so that your payments change), or cars can be sold. Everything is fair game. If you live frugally now and give yourself every opportunity to succeed, you'll receive the dividends of excellent financial skills and self-confidence.

2. List the spending you will reduce or eliminate, and the amount you estimate you will save per month by doing so.

3. Revamp your budget accordingly (see Figure 3.9).

4. Recalculate your cash flow based on your income and revamped expenses (use the bottom portion of the figure). If you had a negative cash flow before, have you moved into the positive?

3.4 Your Financial Resources

We've looked at your monthly income; now it's time to broaden the view and examine all your financial resources. Here's the difference between income and resources: *Income* means the money you earn; *resources* refer to all the money available for you to use. Resources include income, but they also include money you can borrow or use for a period of time (credit or loans), or money that is given to you (a gift from a parent or an educational grant).

1. At the top of Figure 3.10, fill in the amount of money you need to increase your income per month if you are still in the red, or if you are just breaking even and would like a buffer zone.

Figure 3.9 Your revamped budget

Expense Category	Monthly Average
Rent or mortgage	$
Utilities (electricity, gas, water)	$
Food (groceries)	$
Dining out	$
Telephone and Internet	$
Loan payments (student, bank loans, car)	$
Insurance (car, health, home/renter's, life)	$
Car expenses (repairs, parts)	$
Gasoline	$
Public transportation	$
Home expenses (furniture, household items, repair)	$
Clothing/personal items	$
Salon and personal services	$
Entertainment	$
Childcare (caregivers, clothing and supplies, other fees)	$
Medical care (prescriptions, doctor visits, hospitalization)	$
Miscellaneous/unexpected	$
GRAND TOTAL:	$

My income is: $ per month

My expenses are: $ per month

Income $

– Expenses   – $

Cash Flow $

Choose one: ☐ I have $ positive cash flow.

☐ I have $ negative cash flow.

☐ I break even.

2. Fill in the first column (**Current Amount**) with the amount you currently have for each resource. If you were given a certain amount for the year, divide by 12 to get an amount for the month.
3. Next, put a checkmark in the **Explore** column for any resource from which you may be able to seek increased funds.
4. Finally, enter an amount in the **Request** column for the resource you want to explore. This is the amount of money you would like to request from that resource.
5. You are now ready to sign the money pledge provided in the figure, but only if you resolve to carry out your requests in the next week.

Figure 3.10 **Your monthly financial resources**

I need $ _____ more each month.

Resources	Current Amount	Explore	$ Request
1. Grants or work-study payments	$		$
2. Educational loans	$		$
3. Scholarships	$		$
4. Full-time employment	$		$
5. Part-time employment	$		$
6. Self-employment	$		$
7. Financial assistance from personal contacts (family, friends)	$		$
8. Services or products I can trade or sell	$		$
9. Credit/loans (from banks and/or credit unions)	$		$
10. Other	$		$
TOTALS	$ _____		$ _____

**ADD TOTALS FOR PROJECTED MONTHLY INCOME
IF YOU ARE ABLE TO INCREASE RESOURCES AS INDICATED:**

Grand Total $ _____ $ _____

Within seven days I will contact the person(s) and institution(s) that can help me live within my budget and without financial stress.

Name: _____

Date: _____

3.5 Balance Your Budget

In the previous exercises, you learned where you are financially (whether you have a positive, negative, or balanced cash flow), where you want to go (toward having a balanced or positive cash flow), and how to work toward that goal. You followed the same steps that businesspeople do before they write financial plans and budgets. You are now ready to write your complete monthly personal financial plan.

Feel free to document this budget using software that you might already have, such as Microsoft Word (create a table), Microsoft Excel (create a spreadsheet), or Intuit (create a budget).

1. Here's a chance to fill in your expense chart again (see Figure 3.11). Revise the numbers based on your reduced spending.

2. Revise your income amount, based on how you increased your financial resources (see Figure 3.12).

3. To find out your cash flow each month, subtract the grand total of your revised expenses from the grand total of your revised income (see bottom portion of Figure 3.12).

4. Compare that number with your first cash flow amount from Figure 3.8. Even the tiniest bit of progress is a step in the right direction.

It's your money. Budget it like your time—carefully and realistically.

Figure 3.11 Your revised monthly expenses

Expense Category	Monthly Average
Rent or mortgage	$
Utilities (electricity, gas, water)	$
Food (groceries)	$
Dining out	$
Telephone and Internet	$
Loan payments (student, bank loans, car)	$
Insurance (car, health, home/renter's, life)	$
Car expenses (repairs, parts)	$
Gasoline	$
Public transportation	$
Home expenses (furniture, household items, repair)	$
Clothing/personal items	$
Salon and personal services	$
Entertainment	$
Childcare (caregivers, clothing and supplies, other fees)	$
Medical care (prescriptions, doctor visits, hospitalization)	$
Miscellaneous/unexpected	$
GRAND TOTAL:	**$**

3.6 Plug Your Knowledge into Real Life

Companies, like individuals, must budget and reforecast (re-budget) as circumstances change. Many businesses fail because they don't take steps that would prevent financial collapse, such as cutting back or generating more revenue. Companies in financial trouble must decide whether to increase revenue, decrease expenses, or to employ a combination of the two.

Let's apply what you've learned about personal finances to a corporate situation. Wonderful Widgets is in trouble. It lost $250,000 last year. That means its budget is in the red (in debt) by $20,833 per month.

Troy is the bookkeeper at Wonderful Widgets. He wants to curb expenses by making cuts in inventory, personnel, and advertising. Gina is the business developer. She sees a way out of the predicament by increasing sales through additional advertising and hiring a few more salespeople.

1. What would be the more efficient way for Wonderful Widgets to get out of debt?

2. Which approach do you endorse, or would you use a combination of the two?

3. What factors influence your decision? Even though you don't know the specific numbers for the budget of Wonderful Widgets, with your knowledge of today's salaries

Figure 3.12 **Your revised monthly income**

Income	Monthly Amount
Regular work salary (full- or part-time work or self-employment)	$
Grants or work-study payments	$
Monthly assistance you may receive from family members or other sources	$
Private sale of items (for example: in person or on eBay or Craigslist)	$
Other	$
GRAND TOTAL:	$

My income is:	$	per month
My expenses are:	$	per month
	Income	$
	– Expenses	– $
	Cash Flow	**$**

and a guess at inventory and advertising costs, you can still estimate the steps it would take to save the amount per month by which the company needs to correct the budget ($20,833).

4. Explain your solution.

3.7 Managing Your Credit Cards

Earlier in the chapter, you had a chance to begin looking at your credit cards and their use. Now you will assess your credit card situation in more detail.

1. Collect all your credit cards, along with the most recent statements (one to three months). Then fill out Figure 3.13 to the best of your ability.
2. Which cards have the highest balances? Consider paying off these cards first.

Figure 3.13 **Your credit card details**

Card	Interest Rate	Penalties for Late Payment	Average Charges	Average Monthly Balance	Average Interest Payment	Credit Limit

3. Which cards have the highest interest? When you have a high-interest card, consider negotiating with the credit card company for a lower rate. If you cannot get a lower rate, consider getting rid of the card (if it is paid off), or focus on paying off the balance and then getting rid of the card.

4. Which cards have the highest credit limit? Consider keeping these for emergencies, but only if they do not have the highest balances and they do not have the highest interest.

5. Based on your answers, fill out Figure 3.14 with the list of cards you plan to get rid of and why.

6. Based on your earlier answers, fill out Figure 3.15 with the list of cards you plan to use, in the order you plan to pay them off. Also indicate the average payment you plan to make for each.

7. Based on the work you just completed, when do you estimate you will have your cards paid off (in weeks, months, or years)?

3.8 Keeping Your Identity Safe

As you learned earlier, identity theft is a real problem in today's online society. This exercise will help you explore identity theft and its ramifications.

Have you had your identity stolen? If you answer no, please do some Internet research to find someone who has had his or her identity stolen so you can answer the following questions about the theft. Write up your answers in a short essay.

1. How did it happen?

2. How was it discovered?

3. How was it resolved?

4. What could you (or the other person) do in the future to prevent identity theft?

Figure 3.14 Credit cards to get rid of

	Card	Reason
1		
2		
3		
4		
5		

Figure 3.15 Estimated card payments

	Card	Planned Payment
1		
2		
3		
4		
5		

3.9 Your Critical Resource Quotient

Answer yes or no to the following questions:

1. I never receive a "surprise" bill I forgot about.
2. I invest money each month in a savings account, IRA, investment account, or some other savings vehicle.
3. I pay all my credit card balances in full each month.
4. I balance my checkbook every month.
5. When I have an unexpected expense (for example, my car breaks down or I have a doctor's visit), I do not have to borrow money or use a credit card.
6. I save a certain amount or percent of money from each paycheck.
7. I never or rarely have insufficient funds (or bounce a check) in my checking account.
8. I typically have money left over at the end of the month.
9. I use a monthly financial budget.
10. I shred all documents that contain personal and financial information before I recycle them or throw them out.

All answers should be "yes." How did you do?

If you answered yes to

- **7–10 questions:** Congratulations! Your critical resources will provide a foundation for your school and career success.
- **4–6 questions:** You are aware of your critical resources. Strengthen your management of them.
- **0–3 questions:** You need to grasp and use your tools for management of your critical resources.

3.10 Technology Exercise

Go online and search for free, web-based personal budgeting tools. Examples of budgeting tools include BudgetSimple.com, Mint.com, and others.

1. Compare the features of these tools and write them down (see Figure 3.16). For example, some download and categorize your online transactions every day, others chart and graph your spending, and others generate reports on spending and income.
2. Which one would you like to try?

Figure 3.16 Website budgeting tools

Website Tool	Features

4 Your Basic Skills

Sharpen Your Tools

Let us . . . cherish, therefore, the means of knowledge.
Let us dare to read, think, speak, and write . . .
Let every sluice of knowledge be opened and set a-flowing.

John Adams, 1765

learning objectives

- What are ways to practice active listening?
- How can you improve your concentration?
- How do mnemonic devices help your memory?
- What are "think-links" and how can you use them when you take notes?
- How can you improve your reading comprehension skills?

- What are the three Cs for writing?
- Why is proofreading important?
- What are some effective hints for test taking?
- How can you work more effectively with teams?
- What are some techniques for managing stress?
- Why is lifelong learning essential to your career?

Jenna considers herself a very tech-savvy person. She tweets, texts, updates her profile on a social networking site, and keeps in touch with friends and family by cell phone. In fact, that phone is never far from her hand.

Lately she has noticed that her one-on-one interactions with coworkers are suffering. During meetings, she can't seem to stop checking her cell phone for messages. When her manager meets with her to go over a new assignment, she finds it difficult to concentrate while she thinks about her to-do list. Later, she can't even remember what her manager said. Worse, her already short attention span is getting shorter, and she finds it difficult to read or write the brief reports that are part of her daily work. In fact, she often feels so overwhelmed with all the different things she has to do at work and at home that she loses her temper with people and can't sleep well at night.

Jenna is rapidly realizing that unlike the shows she watches on television, daily problems at work cannot be solved in 10 minutes. Unlike the texts she sends to friends, issues at work cannot be documented in 40 words or less. And unlike the ads she likes to scan in magazines, reports at work must actually be thoroughly read, analyzed, and understood.

Jenna's abilities to read, write, remember, work with others, and manage stress are all suffering. What can she do?

Up to now, we've looked at self-focused actions and behaviors. Now we'll begin to look at effective ways to interact with others. To avoid finding yourself in Jenna's situation, you can use certain building blocks to help you succeed. In addition to all your abilities, ideas, and talents, you need the basic skills of reading, writing, listening, team building, and stress management to successfully function in the working world. Regardless of one's profession, everyone needs these skills.

myth

"I just can't write. Writing is just too hard."

reality

Writing is a skill—a very important and necessary skill. Writing is the means by which we communicate in a more permanent fashion with those around us. The way you write says a lot about you. Most of us will not become famous journalists or novelists, but with practice, writing gets easier, becomes less of a chore, and can even be fun.

Words are everywhere. Being able to hear them accurately, read them easily, and communicate them clearly on paper will serve you in any profession. More important, you need to know how to share what you know with a team and manage the stress that is sure to arise from time to time when working with others, especially under tight deadlines or budgetary constraints.

There's no escaping reading and writing—or any other basic communication skill. Just think about how often reading and writing come into play on the job:

- Reading and writing emails and memos to or from superiors, colleagues, subordinates, suppliers, and clients
- Reading workplace rules, your contract, and your job description
- Reading sales orders
- Reading directions for use of equipment
- Writing purchase orders

- Writing telephone messages
- Filling out forms

Before we launch into basic skills, there is one skill you need to consider that involves many aspects of the basics. That skill is called *knowing how to learn,* and you may remember it from Chapter 1. The techniques involved in knowing how to learn can free your mind to take in the knowledge you encounter. They enable you to evaluate, retain, and use what you have studied.

At the end of this chapter, you will look at a list of how-to-learn skills in detail, and you will evaluate your aptitude level for each. Some of them involve the basic skills of reading, writing, listening, team building, stress management, concentration, memory, and test taking. Others address the kind of study environment you set up for yourself as well as your attitude toward your studies and your habits. Used together, they help you open your mind to knowledge at school and on the job.

Now it's time to start looking at the basic skills that are so important to your success.

Listening

Everyone can listen to some degree or another. Even most people who cannot hear can essentially "listen" by reading lips or hand and facial expressions. We are not really taught how to listen in school, although our teachers often say "listen up." We know we should listen, but we often don't listen as well as we should because we don't know how.

In today's fast-paced world, people seem to be losing the ability to listen because they insist on doing more than one thing at a time. Consider this example. You worked hard to complete an important project and scheduled a half-hour appointment with your boss to review it. You are now meeting with him, but he doesn't seem to be paying attention. As you talk, he reads other material on his desk and sends a few texts. Worse, he not only picks up the phone when it rings but is now making a phone call. How do you feel? Your boss seems to have no idea how rude he is being and how poor his listening habits are.

As an employee or supervisor, don't make the same mistake as this boss—learn to listen. Not only will it help your performance, but listening well lets others know you care about their work and respect what they are doing.

Did you know that the ability to listen well is one of the most sought-after qualities in employees of all professions (and friends, too)? It comes down to two basic facts. First, we all love to be understood. When we talk, we want to know that someone hears us and understands our message. Don't you feel good when you pour your heart out to a friend who focuses on you attentively? Don't you feel annoyed when you try to communicate to people who constantly interrupt and use your words as springboards for telling stories about themselves? It's frustrating to feel like no one really hears what you say.

Second, the success of a company depends on the level of communication among its employees, from the top level down and from the bottom level up. When people listen well as someone communicates ideas and instructions to them, things roll along as they should. If people do not listen well, communication breaks down and the company's operations may be in jeopardy. For example, consider two coworkers, Mario and Nell. Nell has been at the job for two years and Mario was just hired, which means Mario looks to Nell for instructions and guidance. Following is an exchange that happened between the two of them.

Nell: Tomorrow you can take care of the last section of that draft. But today I need you to finish up these purchase orders so we can get them out by 5 P.M.; otherwise, we won't get the equipment in on time and it will stall out the whole project.

Mario: Sounds good.

Unfortunately, Mario was concentrating on his computer and didn't give his full attention to Nell. This is what he heard:

Nell: Tomorrow you can do the last section of the draft and finish up those purchase orders so the equipment will come in on time for the project.

Oops! Mario's focus on his computer work prevented him from hearing the key word *today*. He knows what he has to do, but he didn't pick up on the necessary scheduling; he thinks he can wait until tomorrow to finish the purchase orders. What will happen? Unless Nell realizes that Mario did not hear her correctly, the project will be delayed.

Miscommunication happens often in the workplace. Many avoidable mistakes occur because people don't always listen well or because people do not check to see if their audience is actually listening. A small amount of effort can make a big difference when it comes to listening. For example, Nell could have asked Mario for his full attention before she started speaking to him. That would have pulled him away from the computer screen. Even if she did not ask, Mario could have turned to look at Nell and forgotten about the computer for a few minutes. By doing so, he could have focused on what she was saying.

If you are a good listener, you will find that people will listen to you in return. It's simply another application of the golden rule: Do unto others as you would have them do unto you. It will pay off. Figure 4.1 identifies key steps for listening success.

Figure 4.1 Enhance listening skills

Stop talking

+

Quiet your brain and only listen

+

Focus on the source of words

+

Repeat the message

=

Listening SUCCESS!

Guideline 1: Close Your Mouth

It seems simple, but one of the most effective ways to listen attentively is to stop talking. It's very hard to hear what others are saying when you are talking. Close your mouth and concentrate. Don't interrupt. When you let someone else speak, you will better hear what they have to say because you won't be throwing your own words into the mix.

If you get restless, don't worry. The more you let someone else have a turn, the more likely it is that you will have a turn to speak and people will listen to you as well.

Guideline 2: Focus on the Source of the Words

It is crucial to focus on the source of the message, whether that source is a person, a television program, or a voice over the phone. Even if you stop other activities, you may still find your mind wandering or your eyes turning away from the speaker. Unfortunately, both actions will divert your attention.

It's amazing what visual focus can do for the quality of your listening. When you look directly at the person speaking, you guide your energy toward that individual, allowing you to take in the information freely. Plus, focusing on the speaker helps you ignore distractions. Take listening one step further by using open facial expressions and body positioning to show your interest, and you will encourage the other person to open up even more.

For example, crossing your arms and frowning while listening is a defensive posture that makes the person speaking think that you don't believe what he or she is saying. This often creates tension in the conversation as the individual tries to convince you by becoming more and more animated or forceful. Sitting with your hands in your lap and an interested expression on your face is an open posture that makes the person speaking feel like sharing more with you. This reduces tension and improves communication.

What if you are talking on the phone? When you can't see the person who is speaking to you, how can you focus on that individual? Some people find it helpful to focus on an image of the person in their mind. It works well, but only if you know what the person looks like and are good at visualizing. A more useful idea is to make sure your eyes are not focusing too hard on anything else, such as your computer monitor, a book or memo, or another individual. Eliminating other distractions will help you concentrate, even though you cannot see the other person.

Guideline 3: Remember the Value of Repeating

This technique adds a few more steps to the listening process, but it is quite worthwhile. After you listen to someone, take a minute to repeat the message in your own words to see if you heard it right. Repeating gives you a chance to check your understanding of the message and gives the other person a chance to correct any confusion.

We are not suggesting you repeat the message word for word. For example, suppose your supervisor says:

> Cancel the 2 o'clock appointment for Ms. Altamont. She is going to have to stay longer with a customer. But see if you can reschedule the appointment for tomorrow. Confirm the 3 o'clock; she'll be free by then.

You might respond:

> Let me make sure I got that right. Cancel the 2 o'clock appointment and reschedule it for tomorrow, and confirm today's 3 o'clock.

Wait to hear a verbal response that indicates you are right. If you don't receive one, politely ask, "Is that correct?" If you are wrong, the person will tell you, and it's up to you to make the correction right away. Repeating serves three purposes:

- You assure the speaker that you are listening.
- You reinforce what you heard by saying it aloud.
- You get a chance to correct a misunderstood direction before acting on it.

The benefits of repeating mean you keep your clients and customers happy, which makes your supervisor very happy!

 ## Now You Try It: Active Listening

1. Monitor your conversations today and ask yourself these questions afterward:

   - Do I tend to do most of the talking or does the other person?
   - Do I interrupt? Why do I do that?
   - When I listen, am I thinking of other things at the same time? Like what?
   - Do I easily understand and remember what the other person said?

2. What have you learned about your listening skills? Are they adequate or do they need work?

Concentration, *noun*

the act of collecting one's thoughts and focusing them toward one center; the act of increasing something in density or intensity

Concentration

Being able to actively listen depends on your ability to concentrate. The dictionary lists two definitions of **concentration,** and what you need to know involves both.

When we talk about concentration, we're referring to the first definition—the act of focusing your thoughts on one thing or concept. But the very act of focusing brings in the second definition, because it increases the intensity of your thought power.

Think about this: You have a certain amount of available brainpower at any given time. Suppose you're in class, and the teacher is talking, but you have three or four other things on your mind: Your father is sick, you deposited a check that bounced, and you have a tough project at your part-time job coming due at the end of the week. All those things compete in your head with the need to listen to the teacher, and the listening ends up with only one-quarter of your brainpower. You won't get nearly as much out of the class as you would if you focused 100% of your thoughts on the teacher.

When it comes to concentration, consider yourself a participant in a bicycle race. A successful racer has only one thing in mind: to keep going and move ahead. If the racer worries about how fast the other racers are going, who is ahead, or how many miles are left to go, his concentration would scatter. Ultimately, he will be unable to find holes in the pack to plough through with increased speed, and he will be unable to improve his position. The racer will lose a bit of his brainpower, which will hinder his success. Next, let's look at some guidelines for improving your concentration.

Guideline 1: Keep a Single Focus

You will always get more out of whatever you do if you let your brain focus on one thing at a time. We've all experienced worrying about 10 things at once. Have you noticed that during those times you rarely solve any of your problems? That's because you cannot concentrate. Your thoughts flit around. You seem unable to take any action and all you manage to do is conclude that you have a lot of worries, which you already knew.

Instead of letting your thoughts flit around for an hour, divide and conquer. Concentrate your energy on one issue at a time. So you have six concerns? Focus on *one* concern for 10 minutes and don't let your mind wander during that time. As we mentioned before, the human brain is only capable of focusing on one task at a time. What we think of as multitasking is actually "switchtasking," which means our brains are switching back and forth between one task and another, with less time spent on each task. Eventually, with enough interruptions and swapping back and forth, none of the tasks get completed. Respect your brain by letting it work on only one issue at a time. It will reward you with good progress.

Guideline 2: Be Here Now

Concentration thrives best in the here and now. Thinking about something that happened in the past or something that concerns you in the future takes you away from what you should concentrate on in the present. Don't shortchange the present. It's all that you have at any given moment; it is the solid opportunity you hold in your hand.

For example, consider two people, one caught up in the future and one caught up in the past. Tanya was so looking forward to her weekend trip that she daydreamed about it all day and forgot to complete two important tasks that needed to be done before the weekend. Ben was so caught up in feeling angry with himself over a mistake he made yesterday that he couldn't bring himself to make the phone calls today that might have partially corrected the error.

Did you know that most people spend up to 90% of their time thinking about the past or the future? This means we often spend only 10% of our brainpower on the present. Think of what we could accomplish if we focused 100% of our brainpower on the present!

Staying in the present also saves you time. If you concentrate on what is happening in the moment, you won't need to spend as much time remembering it later. The more energy you devote to the information in front of you at the moment you take it in, the less time you will spend trying to recapture it later. This is especially good advice for those of you who feel the need to text or check your email while performing another task—anything from taking a walk, hanging out with a friend, or attending a business meeting. Since your mind is never fully engaged on the current event, you are likely to forget many aspects of it.

Guideline 3: Use Proven Concentration Techniques

Have you ever noticed that sometimes your brain can relax and focus, but other times it's just too busy to focus? This is when it becomes hard to concentrate. However, there are a few techniques you can practice to improve concentration. Try them all, and see what works for you. You may like some better than others or find that some work better in certain situations.

Breathe. It's amazing what a few minutes of deep breathing can do. Breathe slowly and deeply, exhaling your busy thoughts as you blow out your air. Close your eyes so that what you see doesn't get in the way of clearing your head. Don't do this for too long—you may end up hyperventilating or taking a nap! Just a few minutes of deep breathing should calm you down and clear your head so you can choose your focus.

Focus. Focus your eyes on an object. Sometimes gazing at something intensely and narrowing your vision can help bring your thoughts into a similar focus. Looking at something may naturally lead you to think about what you are seeing, and other thoughts may fall away. When you feel focused, you have more power to turn your thoughts in your chosen direction.

Find a relaxing environment. Certain places make it hard to concentrate—perhaps for you it's a busy lunchroom, a family room where children are playing, or somewhere with a loud television or stereo. You know yourself, and you know what kinds of distractions bother you. If your environment makes it hard to concentrate, move somewhere else or change your environment. Build yourself a "bubble of peace." Find a quieter room or a café, or ask someone to turn down the music or television. Find someone else to watch the kids for an hour. Give yourself the best chance to concentrate by minimizing your distractions.

> It is important to incorporate relaxation time into your busy work or school schedule so you remain effective.

Guideline 4: Give Yourself a Break

All work and no play can make anyone antsy. It's tough to concentrate when you're tired and would rather be doing something else. This can easily happen if you study, work, or concentrate for long periods of time. Listen to your mind's hints. If you cannot concentrate because you keep dreaming about getting outside, going shopping, or taking a long lunch, go ahead and take the break that you need. Enjoy yourself, and when you return to your work later, you will be able to concentrate once again.

It's important to include leisure time in your schedule. Plan ahead so you know when to work and when to play. That way you won't waste valuable time and energy wishing you could escape to some more pleasant activity. You free your mind to concentrate when you know you have fun time scheduled later. It may be hard to schedule breaks when you're coming up on a project deadline and you are worried that you won't have time to finish the project. The truth is, a short 15-minute break will not stop you from meeting your deadline. Taking that time to stretch or take

---

Did You Know?

When you're studying or working at home and become too tired to concentrate, give your brain a rest and try one of the following:

- Read or watch television.
- Do a mindless task such as cleaning up, raking, or organizing your desk.
- Take a nap or turn in for the night.
- Do some deep breathing, stretches, or yoga poses.

When you return to your task, you will feel refreshed and ready to go.

a quick walk may be just what you need to keep your brain working at top efficiency. Without that break, you may become tired and your mind fuzzy, making it even harder to finish that project.

Think back to your work history, and try to remember a day that was so hectic you hardly had time to breathe. Did you feel efficient, or did you feel like you were rushed and had trouble concentrating on everything? Keep in mind your mental state on that day. Now think of a day when you worked a full day but took regular, full-sized, relaxing breaks. How did you feel when you returned to your work? How well did you function during the day? Your mind was probably more refreshed and ready to attack your duties with renewed energy and focus. Compare your mental state on the no-break day with your state of mind on the regular-break day. Which would you prefer to experience more often?

Memory

Memory is a tool that people use many times a day. Many people have trouble remembering names, phone numbers, or directions. There is so much information to take in each day that it's tough to retain it all.

Good memory skills save time, and time is one of the most valuable commodities in the workplace. The more you accomplish in the time you have, the more efficient you become. If you retain information and are able to recall it quickly without always having to refer back to something or someone, you end up saving your company a great deal of time and money.

Your memory saves you time by eliminating extra steps. Memorizing phone numbers means you don't have to look them up. Memorizing dollar amounts saves your time hunting for them through stacks of purchase orders. Memorizing names saves the embarrassment of asking a client to refresh your memory because you have forgotten his or her name. Here's another example. Suppose you are a legal assistant, and over a period of time you memorize which drawers contain which files and which books discuss which cases. You will no longer have to look things up or ask questions when you need to find a file or case. Multiply that time saved by the number of times you have to hunt for something and it adds up quickly.

Guideline 1: Use Your Other Tools

A couple of other basic skills give memory power a jolt. The first is concentration. It's tough to remember things that you hear or read unless you focus on them at the time. The more you concentrate on something, the more you will ingrain it into your memory. The second is listening. If you don't listen well, you won't know what you need to remember.

Have you ever read an entire page of a book and then realized you couldn't remember a word of it? Because you didn't concentrate the first time, you have to go back and read it again to glean the information. During conversation you may hear phrases such as "Come again?" or "Could you repeat that?" or "What?" These words often indicate that someone hasn't been listening. When you don't listen to the information the first time, it has to be repeated for you to remember it.

Guideline 2: Repeat

When you repeat something verbally, to yourself or others, you increase your chances of remembering information. For example, reading your own notes aloud helps you remember them. Verbal repetition also works especially well with remembering names of people you meet. Try using the name right away when you meet someone: "It's a pleasure to meet you, Kayla." Just saying the name, letting your mouth and tongue form the words, helps inscribe it in your memory.

Guideline 3: Associate

If you can associate new information with something you already know, you will remember it more easily. For example, radio broadcasting students better understand and remember program scheduling concepts when they associate them with what they already know from listening to different programs, announcements, and advertisements on the radio.

Association can also be helpful in recalling certain names. Suppose you meet Stacey Long, and she is tall. You have a natural association that helps you remember her—her height and her last name. Or perhaps she reminds you of your best friend, Tracey. In that case, the association of rhyming names helps: Stacey and Tracey. You can even make up an association to help you, such as "Stacey lives a *long* way from me." Any of these associations works.

Guideline 4: Write

For many people, writing helps them remember what they've heard. This goes for rewriting as well. For example, if you take notes during a staff meeting and want to remember certain key points, take a clean sheet of paper and rewrite a simple list of those points. If you take notes in class, type them afterward. Write down important numbers or names. The more you write, the more you will remember.

Guideline 5: Mnemonic Devices

Mnemonic devices are word tricks that help you memorize information. Mnemonic devices work well for those with strong memory skills, as well as those who could use some assistance.

Mnemonic devices help you remember specific sets of information. One type of mnemonic device uses the first letters of words to make a unique sentence. Those of you who have studied music probably remember the mnemonic device "Every Good Boy Does Fine," which helps you remember the names of the notes on the lines of the treble clef: E-G-B-D-F. Another device, called an *acronym,* uses the first letters of words to create an unusual and memorable word. For example, suppose you need to remember the names of the five major suppliers to your company. Their names are Eagle, Lester, Smith, Lowe, and Switchell. You could shift the first letter of each name around to make a catchy acronym, SELLS. Or you could make a sentence from the first letters of the names: Easy Living Should Love Selling. Whatever makes sense to you will work. Mnemonics are easy to remember because they are designed to be catchy, and they are especially effective when you make them up yourself.

How about using a mnemonic to help you remember the skills involved in having a good memory? We have to CRAWL before we can RUN.

Crawl	Run
Concentrate	Remember
Repeat	Unlimited
Associate	Names
Write	
Listen	

 ## Now You Try It: Concentration and Memory

Think about the way your mind works and answer these questions.

1. Do you tend to think about more than one thing at a time?
2. When you are doing one activity are you often thinking of another?
3. Do you ever have difficulty falling asleep because so many thoughts are going through your mind?
4. Do you easily forget names of people you have met?
5. Do you often forget appointments?

If you answered yes to more than two of these questions, chances are you have difficulty focusing. Based on what you learned in this chapter, what could you do to improve your focus?

Although you may think you can leave note taking behind when you finish school, this skill goes beyond the classroom. Just think about activities in the workplace for which note taking is important.

- An orientation meeting when you start a new job
- Learning rules of your workplace
- Learning how to operate equipment or software
- Staff meetings
- Interviewing others
- Taking phone messages
- Learning essential information, such as lock or alarm combinations, emergency phone numbers, or intercom numbers

Specific jobs have other opportunities to take notes. Use this list as a springboard for your own ideas about when you will need to write things down. Figure 4.2 identifies actions you can take to improve your note taking. Start from the bottom of the visual and work your way up.

Right now, taking good notes is important as you pursue your studies. You are investing valuable time and money to train yourself for your future career. Taking good notes allows you to take physical copies of the lessons with you so you can think about them later. This gives you a second chance to internalize what the teacher covered in class.

Note taking helps you gather information and remember it.

Guideline 1: Listen Carefully

Refer back to the "Listening" section. You cannot take good notes if you don't listen. You have to hear the message before your brain translates it to your writing hand. A fuzzy brain means poor notes. Have you ever been so tired in class that you could hardly take notes? Later, you probably realized how much your notes suffered when you compared them with those of a classmate who was alert during class. Your fatigue reduced your listening power and closed you off from much of the information.

Guideline 2: Use Good Penmanship

Suppose you listened well and wrote all the important things you heard, but could not read what you wrote. What good would it do? Not much! If you use good penmanship you will benefit from what you write. To do so, follow the guidelines that appear later in this chapter in the "Writing" section.

Guideline 3: Follow the Leader

Whether your teacher, manager, trainer, or a coworker is the leader of a meeting or class, follow that person's example when taking notes. If this person writes something on a board, copy it. If this person repeats something or says it will be on a test, write it down. If this person emphasizes

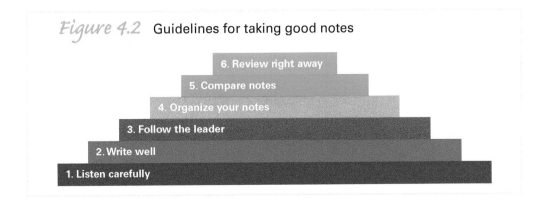

Figure 4.2 **Guidelines for taking good notes**

6. Review right away
5. Compare notes
4. Organize your notes
3. Follow the leader
2. Write well
1. Listen carefully

something, write it down and maybe even put a star next to it. The emphasis might occur when the speaker talks louder, slows down, or shows excitement. Follow the leader. It is the speaker's job to lead you in the right direction.

Guideline 4: Organize Your Notes

Even if your notes are legible, you won't get the most out of them unless they are organized. Perhaps you use an outline format when you take notes, complete with Roman numerals. Or maybe you use a method of your own that is more effective. It doesn't really matter because your notes are mostly for your own purposes. Choose an organizational method that you understand, and use it consistently.

As you take notes, make good use of space on your paper. If you cram everything together, you may have trouble reading it later. You can isolate important bits of information by surrounding them with white space or circling them. You can also connect related information by drawing lines or arrows.

Figure 4.3 shows a couple of ways to organize your notes. The one on the left is the standard outline form. The other is called a *think-link* or *bubble diagram,* developed in 1965 by Dr. Frank Lyman, a learning theorist. It is a creative, visual way to connect related ideas and examples by using geometric shapes and lines. Experiment with these methods and see what works best for you.

You can even use a think-link to make notes about your daily plans. Figure 4.4 shows an example of how to organize a day in think-link style. Do you see how white space and indenting help you better see various parts of the notes? They draw your eye to important points.

Guideline 5: Compare Notes

This step is particularly useful when you are in school or taking a training class. After class or during a break, compare your notes with your peers. Did you miss anything? Did you emphasize something that others missed? An episode of daydreaming, a brief loss of focus, or even a trip to the restroom can cause you to miss an important point. Together, you and your coworkers or classmates can help fill in the gaps. Many heads are better than one.

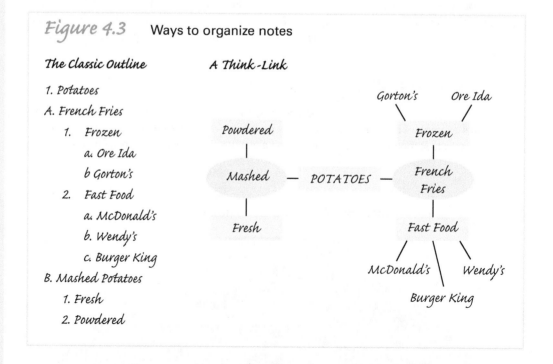

Figure 4.3   Ways to organize notes

The Classic Outline

1. Potatoes
A. French Fries
   1. Frozen
     a. Ore Ida
     b Gorton's
   2. Fast Food
     a. McDonald's
     b. Wendy's
     c. Burger King
B. Mashed Potatoes
   1. Fresh
   2. Powdered

Figure 4.4 A sample think-link

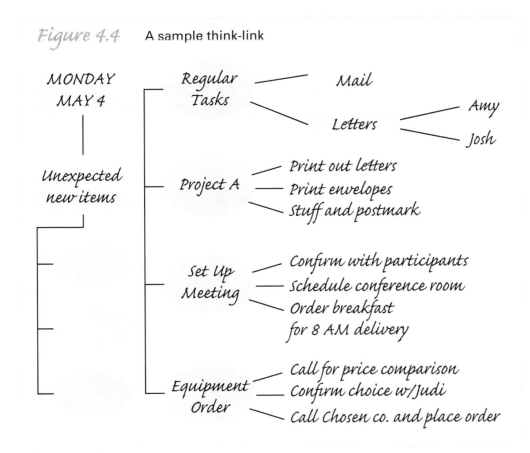

Guideline 6: Review Right Away

Always review your notes as soon as possible after you take them. If you look at them within 24 hours, filling in any blanks that you have, you will stand a much better chance of retaining the information. We lose 50% of what we hear in the first day and 80% within two weeks.[1] Keep everything fresh in your mind by reviewing soon and often.

If your job or class assignment involves interviewing someone, it is particularly important to review your notes as soon as possible. Otherwise, you may later forget something you heard, misinterpret the meaning of what you wrote, or document your interviewee's words incorrectly.

Reading

You probably learned to read a long time ago. You may still be working on your reading skills, or you may have stopped trying to improve your reading skills because you think you're already a good reader or don't believe you need reading in your career. No matter what, keep on reading. Like any physical skill, your ability to read declines when you don't use it. The more you read, the more words you know, and the more you know about putting words together.

Take a look at the world around you, both inside and outside your workplace. Words are everywhere. They help you find out which way to go, how to use things, what facts to know, and what to do. Information comes to you constantly in the form of the written word, and you can receive it only if you know how to read.

What if you work as an electronic technician, a hairdresser, or a cook? Do you really need to be a good reader? Of course! You need to read directions to install computers, use a hair-coloring

---

[1]"Note Taking." *Counseling Center of North Carolina State Univeristy.* Accessed on August 23, 2012 from http://www .ncsu.edu/stud_affairs/counseling_center/resources/academic/study%20skills/note_taking/note_taking.htm

kit, or operate the meat slicer. Without proper reading skills, you might assemble the computer incorrectly so no one could use it. You might mix the wrong amounts of colorant and destroy your customer's hair. Or, you might insert the slicer blade incorrectly and injure someone. In all three cases, you could lose your job.

Good reading skills are not just for librarians, journalists, or authors. Everyone should continue to improve their reading skills, even if they do not have trouble reading. People who spend most of their evenings poring over a book are improving their reading skills just by using them. They are also improving their spelling skills. The more you read, the more you are exposed to words and their proper spellings. The ability to read will serve you well throughout your life as long as you keep it in good condition through regular use.

If you didn't grow up reading and speaking English, remember that English is the business language of the United States, as well as for much of the world. (Of course, your native language will help you communicate with customers or clients who speak that language.) To succeed on the job, you need to know how to read and speak English well. The more you read, the more you will learn.

Some of you may not like to read. You may find it boring, slow, or too quiet. You may not believe you need to improve your English skills for your particular career. You may think you are no good at reading and your reading skills will never improve. Don't sell yourself short. You are all capable of improving your reading skills. Let's take a look at guidelines that help good and poor readers alike.

Guideline 1: Read a Lot

The most important boost you can give to your reading skills is to read as much as you can. The more words that sift through your brain, the more you find out about them, and the faster you will be able to read. With any skill, one primary way you learn it is by doing. If you associate reading with boring books that you are forced to read in school or at work, start reading books you enjoy. Read for entertainment. Some of you may find that fiction intrigues you because it lets you escape the world around you. Others may find that nonfiction books about people, activities and hobbies, or machines are much more fun and useful. Go to the library and explore!

Guideline 2: Make a Decision to Read

How can you include more reading in your day? It takes a conscious effort. You have to make a decision, just like deciding to go grocery shopping and fixing dinner. If reading is not currently an important part of your life, you need to be very deliberate about saving time, energy, and attention for it.

Reading what your teachers assign you for school is a good place to start. When you need to complete a reading assignment, try using the next guideline to find a time when your mind is alert.

Guideline 3: Look for Time to Read

Once you make the decision to read, search for the time you need. Life moves quickly. Most of your time is taken up by work, family, and everyday tasks. Hunt through your schedule for time when you can read while doing something else. Here are some ideas:

- Read during breakfast or lunch.
- Read during your commute by bus or by train.
- Read as dinner cooks.
- Read when you use a stationary bike at the exercise club.

You may also discover hidden pockets of unused time when you can squeeze in some reading. Here are a few examples:

- Read before you go to bed (or in bed, before you fall asleep).
- Read during a break between classes.
- Read for an hour instead of watching television. Reading may not seem as appealing at first, but it will boost your mind power and creativity. Television watching is passive—it involves no effort on your part. When you sit in front of the television, you take in someone else's images without thinking. Television viewing actually reduces higher brain activity and suppresses your ability to analyze information. Reading, on the other hand, is highly interactive. When you read, your imagination creates its own pictures and expands to take in the information that you are reading. You analyze and assess the information to form your own conclusions.[2]

To make more time for reading, think about what times might be convenient for you, and then make a commitment. Keep in mind what you read earlier about procrastination, habits, and time management—the key is to simply get started. Once you do, it won't be so hard to continue. Try devoting an additional 15 minutes each day to reading material of your choice, and progress from there. Those additional 15 minutes a day will add up to hours of reading practice over time.

Some people may feel too distracted when they try to read during short periods of spare time. In that case, don't worry about fitting your reading into the tight spaces. Instead, try scheduling a longer block of time for your reading. Many people also prefer, and even require, a quiet place to read to minimize distractions. What conditions do you prefer when you read?

Guideline 4: Read What You Like to Read

If you don't like reading, chances are you only associate it with school and work assignments. But outside of school and work, you can choose anything to read. Read what you enjoy reading. If you don't enjoy it, you won't continue reading, and you won't reap the benefits.

You benefit from almost anything that you read: newspapers, magazines, fiction or nonfiction books, cereal boxes, pamphlets, or instruction books. Do you like astrology? Find a book on it. Do you like to fix things around the house? Pick up a book on home repair. Do you like the outdoors? Find a book on places to hike or a magazine on gardening. Mysteries, fitness magazines, self-help books, and sports books can all help you learn things and enjoy yourself.

Guideline 5: Use Specific Techniques

This guideline contains techniques for reading for work and school, rather than for leisure. The more you use specific techniques as you read, the more quickly you will improve your reading speed, efficiency, and information retention. Remember what you just read about mnemonic devices? We have one for you as the first technique.

Be a CHARTER member of the reading comprehension club:

- Concentrate by following the guidelines presented earlier.
- Highlight important passages, use a pen to write in the margins (if you own the book), and take notes.
- Associate (relate what you read to ideas and events in your own life).
- Reread one page before beginning new material. For example, reread the last page of the preceding chapter before proceeding to the next chapter.
- Take as much time as you need.
- Enjoy something in everything that you read.
- Review right after reading if you need to recall the information for a test or to perform a job function. (Statistics show that reviewing within 24 hours of reading greatly increases your information retention.)

---

[2]"The Effects of TV on the Brain." *EruptingMind Self-Improvement Tips.* Accessed on September 20, 2010, from www .eruptingmind.com/effects-of-tv-on-brain

Here are a few more techniques you can try:

- Don't read out loud. It will slow you down.
- Don't go back over words. Read at whatever speed you need to get all the information the first time.
- Read groups of words. Let your eye take in a group of words together (it will speed up your reading without sacrificing your understanding).

The more you structure your reading with these techniques, the more your reading will improve.

Now You Try It: Reading

It's a good idea to get familiar with your own reading preferences. Answering these questions will help you.

1. Do you typically read because you have to, or because you want to?
2. Do you prefer reading in print or online? Why?
3. What do you wish you could read if you had time?
4. How long do you typically read before you feel fatigued or bored? Does the time depend on what type of material you are reading? Explain.
5. Are you happy with your reading skills? If not, what do you wish you could do better?

Your answers will help you better plan your reading activities.

Writing

Knowing how to write flows from knowing how to read. When you are a good reader, you gain a sense of how to combine words in a way that make sense to others. Certain professions require strong writing skills, such as marketing, technical writing, journalism, and legal work. But you need good writing skills at any job.

There are many situations in which you need to communicate to others in writing. For example, you might need to write a business email, report, or memo. As we will discuss further in Chapter 10, successful work situations and relationships are built on good communication, of which writing is one form.

Regardless of what kinds of items you have to write, you will find that writing clearly and directly makes your job easier. With good writing skills, you save yourself the extra step of having to explain yourself again in person, on the phone, or with another written communication. You become an efficient and understandable worker. Think about a typical day at your job. What do you have to write, and when? What important tasks do your written communications perform?

If you don't have good writing skills, it won't matter how brilliant, educated, or clever you are—people will not understand your messages. You won't be able to get your point across by email, on paper, or on a Web page. In fact, poor writing skills are likely to cause your readers to draw the wrong conclusions about you. If your writing is awkward and clumsy, readers may think you are disorganized and don't know your topic very well. Poor grammar and spelling may make people think you're uneducated or careless. Worse, readers might think you don't care about what you're writing, so why should they? Good writing is powerful. The better you are at it, the better you will be at your job.

The following guidelines are essential to successful writing. These apply to those who like to write, as well as to those who do not.

Guideline 1: Write Legibly

Although computers allow us to type everything, there are still plenty of times that we have to write things by hand, such as filling out forms, receipts, or orders. When writing by hand, people frequently write things that others cannot read. If no one can read your writing, your message

Adjusting to Change

Amy Lee,
Part-time Apple sales associate and graphics art student

During my first year of college, I got a part-time job at the local Apple store, the Mac Shack. As an accounting major with a lot of computer experience, I thought I was pretty knowledgeable about iPads, iPhones, apps, and Macs … that is, until customers started asking me questions about resolution, processors, pixels, processors, memory controllers, and graphics. It was a good thing the store had a training program.

Over time, I noticed that a lot of graphic artists used Macs. I talked to them about how they used their computers, what they did for a living, and how they learned to do what they did. They often shared their latest projects with me. I was amazed by their photos, illustrations, and animation. I was in awe of their creativity. I wished I could do something like that.

At the time, I was enrolled in the accounting program because I thought that was what my parents expected of me. However, there was something about those computers and those graphic artists that I could not get out of my head. I felt stifled by my major and wanted to be more creative. That's why I decided to change my major to graphic arts with an emphasis on online design. I could use a computer to exercise my creative talents.

Coming from a world of numbers and facts in accounting, I felt overwhelmed when I attended my first graphics course and encountered visual design terms and concepts I'd never heard before. There was so much information to learn that I felt like my brain was exploding. Listening to lectures took a lot out of me because I tried to focus on all the details before I could figure out how the pieces fit together. And there were plenty of details to take in. I knew that if I were going to adjust to my new learning experience, I would have to relax and just concentrate on doing my best. Easier said than done!

Over time, I figured out things that helped me learn and continue to help me learn today. I am a hands-on learner: I have to *do* things to learn them. Hearing or seeing them is not enough. In class, I often draw and doodle to help internalize the design ideas I'm hearing. When I work on a project, I always clear my study area of distractions so I can focus. I also I like to study alone where it's quiet. Consistency helps me learn, too. I try to study and work on my graphics projects a little bit every day, at about the same time, instead of waiting until the last minute to do everything. I find that making notations while I'm reading, such as highlighting sentences and circling key words, helps me remember things.

I also find that previewing the chapter before class really helps me. When I do this, I get an idea of what the instructor will discuss and at least get familiar with a few new ideas. Since the instructor posts notes and examples online, I always look at those materials as well. I constantly comb the Internet for examples of creative websites and videos, and review the latest apps available for my cell phone. That keeps me current with what other graphics artists and app developers are doing. Plus, I always test myself at the end of each week to see if I understand what has been covered in the reading and in class.

When I first started the graphics art program, I felt like a left-brained, analytical foreigner visiting the land of right-brained creatives. I felt lost. I had excellent computer skills, but no artistic talents, or so I thought. However, in the last three years, armed with a passion for graphics, excellent discipline, and well-exercised study skills I have designed websites, apps, mini-videos, and even some anime—something I never thought possible!

Switching from accounting to graphics art was a challenge, but I'm glad I stuck with it. With each class, understanding the material gets easier and easier, and my projects are looking better and better. I'm a wiz on any Apple computer and I'm still working at the Mac Shack. If I had given up too soon, I would have never gotten this far. I feel more confident about my artistic abilities, which makes it all worthwhile.

will not be communicated, no matter how perfect the spelling and grammar. Have you ever tried to interpret someone's messy handwriting? It can be frustrating and time consuming. In fact, you probably know people who cannot read their own handwriting minutes after they've written something.

To improve your handwriting, try writing in whatever style makes you the most comfortable (unless your job requires you to write a certain way). Is your cursive sloppy? Then print instead. Do you like writing straight up and down, instead of slanted? Then do it. If you use a writing style that is more comfortable for you, chances are your writing will improve. And don't forget to slow down when making handwritten notes for others. The faster you write, the more likely your handwriting will be messy and difficult to read.

Guideline 2: Find Opportunities to Write

Writing is a lost art these days. The world moves fast and furiously. The speed of cell phones, email, and texting has established them as the leading modes of communication. No wonder good writers (and readers) are hard to find.

You can change the situation. Look for opportunities to write something. Here are some ideas for chances to write.

- Lists (for example, things to do and groceries to buy)
- Letters to relatives or friends (many people like to save personal letters)
- Thank you notes (friends and businesses value handwritten notes more than emails)
- Summaries of meetings
- Letters to companies praising good products or telling them about problem ones
- Cover letters to accompany job applications
- Thank you letters after job interviews
- Recommendations for friends or relatives trying to get a job or get into a school

You may even find other reasons to write by hand as you go through your daily routine. Take advantage of them.

Guideline 3: Keep a Personal Journal

Perhaps you're great at talking to people, but for some reason you have difficulty communicating what you think and feel in written words. If this is the case, a journal is a great way to improve your writing. Write in your journal as often as you can. Every day would be ideal, but is not always realistic. When you run out of space in the supplied journal, get yourself a blank notebook and keep going. It doesn't matter what you write. You can write about people, events, things that happen to you, your thoughts about the world, poems, angry feelings, song lyrics, meaningful phrases, jokes you want to remember, anything. Just write.

You don't have to pressure yourself to write every day. At times you may be too busy or just not feel like it. But you may discover that writing helps organize your thoughts, let off steam when you're upset, and spur creative ideas. If you don't force the art of writing, you may end up enjoying it. Writing is a means of relaxation and an emotional release for many people.

Guideline 4: Consider Your Audience

Unless you are writing in a personal journal, you are writing for someone other than yourself—someone who is not exactly like you and doesn't have the advantage of knowing what's in your head. This means you need to write in a way that makes sense to your audience. The first question to ask yourself is: "Who is my audience and why am I writing this?"

If you don't know the purpose of your message or who it's going to, stop right now and ask yourself these questions:

- What do I want my readers to do after they read my message?
- Is my audience familiar with the technology I am using to deliver the message?
- What knowledge does my audience already have? Do I need to include more background information?
- What experience does my audience have that could impact their understanding?
- How much does the audience already know about an issue?

Armed with answers to these questions, you can create a written message that engages your audience and gets your point across. More important, you can limit your message to only what your audience needs to read, rather than including everything you want to discuss.

Guideline 5: Remember the Three Cs

Here is a mnemonic to remind you of three practical hints for efficient writing: **C-C-C**.

- **C** is for *clear.* Write what you need to say and nothing else.
- **C** is for *concise.* State your case in as few words as possible.
- **C** is for *concrete.* Keep your message simple and understandable.

For example, here is a poorly written memo that does not consider the three Cs:

Bad Example

There will be a meeting this evening, October 5, at 6 P.M. for all those who might have an interest in participating in the volunteer group this fall. If you want to participate but you can't make the meeting tonight, please let Mel McFadden know and he will talk to you at another time. Leave your evening conflicts on his voicemail so that he can see if you will be available for the scheduled activities. We will be in the conference room and we need to finish by 7 so that the office can close. Thanks—see you soon.

And here's a better written version that uses the three Cs:

Good Example

MEETING TONIGHT—All Welcome

5 October, 6:00–7:00 P.M. in the Conference Room

Topic: Fall Community Activities for Volunteers

Interested persons not able to attend: Contact Mel McFadden at x213

The reader gets the picture much more easily and quickly when you remember the three Cs. If you are not used to doing a lot of writing, you might be asking yourself, "How do I go from the bad example to the good example?" The rest of this section discusses steps that will improve your three Cs.

1. **Write in active voice, not passive.** Do you want your readers to stay awake when they read your writing? Do you want them to understand what you're saying? Then use active voice whenever possible. Active voice means the subject of your sentence is performing the action. Passive voice means the subject is not doing the acting—it's receiving the action. Passive voice sentences are typically longer than active voice sentences. Figure 4.5 shows examples of each.

2. **Use fewer words for greater impact, and keep them simple.** No one likes to wade through lengthy sentences and then reread them to understand the point. Shorter sentences generally convey messages better because there is no confusion about their meaning. Simplify the words

Figure 4.5   Passive voice versus active voice

Passive Voice	Active Voice
Receiver ⟵—— Action	Actor → Action
The following items must be returned.	You must return the following items.
Receiver ⟵ Action	Actor ⟶ Action
The open house was hosted by the *Sustainable Living* magazine.	The *Sustainable Living* magazine hosted the open house.

Table 4.1 Simplified Wording for Ease of Understanding

Wordy and Complicated	Concise and Simple
Teachers facilitate the education of students.	Teachers help students learn.
Complicated, verbose sentences tend to discourage full comprehension in readers.	Wordy sentences are difficult for readers to understand.
It is vital that email be used for the communication of all requests.	Please use email to communicate all requests.

Table 4.2 Friendly, Clear Writing Using Second Person

Third Person	Second Person
This form helps the buyer document the purchase price, accurately record terms, and professionally submit her offer to purchase a home.	This form helps you document your purchase price, accurately record terms, and professionally submit your offer to purchase a home.
The employee might consider speaking with a human resources representative to advise him or her about how to pursue a discussion with a manager regarding a poor performance review.	Consider talking to a human resources representative about how to talk to your manager about a poor performance review.

that make up the sentences. Although some people believe that longer words make them look smarter, long words actually interfere with understanding. Table 4.1 provides some examples.

3. **Write directly to your audience.** Whenever possible, refer to your reader as *you*. This is called *second person*, as opposed to *third person*, in which you refer to your reader as *he* or *she*. By writing directly to your audience, people who read your writing feel like you are having a conversation with them on paper. This style of writing is more friendly, easier to read, and takes up less room. Table 4.2 provides some examples.

4. **Keep sentences and paragraphs short.** Readers often have short attention spans or may be busy with other work. They tend to scan, rather than read closely. Help them out by breaking up long blocks of text with white space to make things easier to read. Table 4.3 provides some examples.

Guideline 6: Writing Goes with Reading

Good writing comes from knowing about words and how they fit together, which comes from reading! The more you read, the better writer you will become. When you observe how others write, especially good writers, you will begin to notice what works well. You can learn to write from an author's good example.

Did You Know?

We have a number of ways to communicate: in person, by phone or voicemail, by email or text, as well as through written notes and letters. Whenever possible, put good news in writing and communicate bad news in person.

When it comes to good news, write a personal note when you want to congratulate or thank someone. It will mean a lot more to that person, and he or she can keep the note and reread it later. When it comes to communicating a negative message such as delivering bad news or discussing a conflict, sit down and talk with that person. A personal conversation softens the blow. Even a phone call helps if you can't talk in person.

Most importantly, avoid using electronic media like text messages, IMs, email, or phone messages to communicate bad news. These media are too impersonal and leave a bad impression.

Table 4.3 Shorter Paragraphs and Sentences for Better Readability	
One Long Sentence	**Two Short Sentences**
We process thousands of requests for information each month, estimating that it takes approximately one hour to respond to each request.	We process thousands of requests for information each month. We estimate it takes approximately one hour for each response.
One Long Paragraph	**Two Shorter Paragraphs**
When you write a report for others to read, always keep in mind that your readers are not you. They may have different backgrounds, different experiences, and different reading skills. The more you know about your readers, the better. That way you can tailor your message to their needs, using words that are meaningful to them. By doing so, you avoid writing about things they don't need to know (but you love to discuss) or using terms your readers don't understand (but you are familiar with). In the end, writing simply and clearly, with your readers in mind, makes you a successful writer.	When you write a report for others to read, always keep in mind that your readers are not you. They may have different backgrounds, different experiences, and different reading skills. The more you know about your readers, the better. That way you can tailor your message to their needs, using words that are meaningful to them. By doing so, you avoid writing about things they don't need to know (but you love to discuss) or using terms your readers don't understand (but you are familiar with). In the end, writing simply and clearly, with your readers in mind, makes you a successful writer.

Proofreading

After writing something on the job you must proofread it, even if it's only a phone message. Read it again and check for any mistakes. If it's longer a phone message, it's also a good idea to give it to someone else to read to make sure it's clear and free of mistakes. It always helps to get another perspective—another pair of eyes sees things the writer cannot.

In our discussion of proofreading, we won't go into the specifics of proper syntax, grammar, or detailed punctuation. Instead, we will address the basics of proofreading that will help you in any kind of job that you take, whether you proofread your own work or someone else's.

Guideline 1: Always Proofread

No matter what you write, always take a moment to review it before you pass it on. Text messages, IMs, emails, phone messages, or purchase orders must all be proofread. It's too easy to make a mistake.

Can you remember a situation in your working life when a problem occurred because someone didn't proofread? It happens. The wrong item got shipped, someone showed up at the wrong time or wrong address, or a letter was mailed to the wrong person. That's not only embarrassing; it's a serious problem.

Guideline 2: Put It Away for a Moment

If your message is brief and you have to send it now, make sure to read it through at least once before you send it. However, if you write a longer message, report, or article, give yourself some time before you look at it again—a day, an hour, even a few minutes. By doing so, you will be able to look at it with fresh eyes, from the perspective of someone else who has never seen it. Pretend you are that person. Do you understand everything you are reading? Does it make sense? Would you know what to do if you were the person receiving the written information? Be honest and objective, then make any necessary changes.

Guideline 3: Pay Attention to Detail

Proofreading is all about details. You are looking for small ways to correct and improve what you have written so it's easy to read and understand. *Correcting* refers to checking over information and fixing it if it is wrong. Commonly used information that should be corrected includes phone numbers; addresses; name and word spellings; time, dollar, and product amounts; and street directions. *Improving* refers to bettering your writing by using complete sentences and proper punctuation, addressing people formally with proper titles, and writing clearly and directly so people understand what you're saying without having to read your words over and over.

Correcting

Check yourself against your sources—your notes, the telephone book, the person who read it to you over the phone, or the colleague at work who told you. Check your spelling as well.

Using a computer spell-check function is rarely adequate for finding *all* spelling mistakes. It cannot tell you that you are using the wrong word when it's spelled correctly. That's why you need to read and check the spelling yourself. For example, the following humorous paragraph would actually pass the spell-check test (we marked the mistakes in red):

I have a spell-checker,

It came with my PC;

It marks **four** my **revue**,

Mistakes I cannot **sea.**

I've run this poem **threw** it,

And I'm sure you're pleased to **no**,

It is letter perfect in **it's weigh**,

My checker **tolled** me **sew**.[3]

It's best to use spell check for a rough spelling check only, but then proofread your material to find any other spelling errors. Also, be sure to look at the words the spell-check program suggests when it finds a spelling mistake; it often tries to substitute the wrong word.

Improving

Put yourself in your audience's shoes to see if everything makes sense. Or, ask a colleague to read over what you have written. He or she can tell you if your message is clear or identify where the writing becomes unclear.

When you proofread your own work, try using these reading methods:

- From top to bottom
- From bottom to top
- In chunks
- In several passes (looking at high-priority items, spelling, punctuation, formatting)

Figure 4.6 shows an example of a quick email with a lot of mistakes. These mistakes have been corrected and the writing improved with some proofreading.

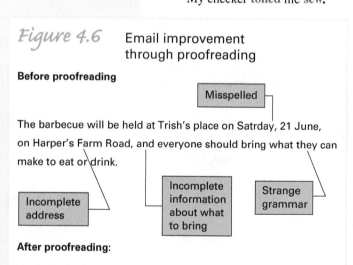

Figure 4.6   Email improvement through proofreading

Before proofreading

Misspelled

The barbecue will be held at Trish's place on Satrday, 21 June, on Harper's Farm Road, and everyone should bring what they can make to eat or drink.

Incomplete address

Incomplete information about what to bring

Strange grammar

After proofreading:

You're Invited to a Barbeque
- **Date:** Saturday, June 21
- **Time:** 4:00 p.m. to 6:00 p.m.
- **Place:** Trish's home (3942 Harper's Farm Road, #6)

Please bring either one bottle of something to drink (soda, water, juice) or one food item to share (chips, salad, casserole).

Note: You might also want to read your work aloud to catch any errors.

---

[3]Harper, Pennye. "Spell Checker." *The Write Advice.* Pensacola: University of West Florida Writing Lab. Accessed on April 13, 2009, from http://uwf.edu/writelab/advice/documents/wa-goodgram1.htm

Notice how bolding, bullets, and white space make a difference? Correct spelling and grammar, along with more complete information, communicate the message more clearly.

 ## Now You Try It: Writing and Proofreading

1. Have you ever sent an email or a text without reviewing it?

   a. If so, were there mistakes in it?

   b. Did the mistakes cause a problem or embarrass you?

2. Think about examples of written messages you have recently read in emails, texts, books or magazines, memos, or letters. Some of them were probably easier to read than others, and some were probably poorly written.

   a. What things made some materials hard to understand?

   b. What things made materials easy to understand?

3. Examine your own writing. Do you ever find any of the things you identified in 2b? What are your most common mistakes?

Test Taking in the Workplace (Worker Assessments)

We've covered the basics: listening, concentration and memory, reading, and writing. But what about taking tests? You probably received a lot of advice about dealing with tests in school. It's time to extend your knowledge to testing in the workplace. You might encounter tests as a job applicant because employers in certain fields use tests to determine the most qualified applicants.

One example is the field of word processing. Many administrative assistants and data entry personnel must take typing tests, spelling and grammar tests, or tests using certain software applications to be considered for a job. Employers in some technical fields, including software programming, also test basic skills and knowledge before hiring.

Check with teachers, your school's placement director, personnel directors, and other people in the field to find out if you will have to take tests when you apply for a particular job. If you will, ask questions about the tests. Here are some questions to consider:

- What kinds of skills will be tested?
- How long will the test(s) take?
- What kinds of questions will be on the test: direct answer, true–false, multiple choice, complete answer, technical? Will you be tested on typing or other skills?
- Can you bring any reference materials with you?
- How important is the test in relation to other factors (experience, education, personality)?

Find out as much as you can. Sometimes your school or workforce center will have sample tests so you can practice. At the very least, find out enough so you know what material to study.

As for test anxiety, it happens to all of us to different degrees. The best way to fight it is to study, question, and prepare as best you can, which includes getting enough sleep. If you use your time wisely and prepare as well as you can for the test, don't ask any more of yourself. And don't ask others how much they prepared or studied. Comparing your studying with that of others may make you feel like you didn't prepare correctly or enough. Everyone is different. Someone else may need to study more or less than you because he or she has different knowledge and experiences. Stay focused on your own studying needs. You are the best judge of how you should prepare.

Think about your past test-taking experiences. Do you tend to get nervous or are you fairly relaxed? Do you generally prepare well or cram at the last minute? Can you concentrate? Afterward, do you feel depressed about your performance or are you confident you did what was required? Knowing your test-taking personality will help you improve your preparation and attitude in the future. Following are a few effective guidelines for taking tests.

Guideline 1: Stay Healthy and Alert

Get enough sleep and eat healthy and regular meals on the day of the test. Don't risk being drowsy, hungry, or low on energy. Give yourself a chance to do your best.

Guideline 2: Don't Study Too Much

You probably know the material better than you think—you've been learning it over a long period of time. Trust yourself. Study enough so that you feel confident, but don't cram to the point of feeling overloaded. The night before the test, just before bed, relax and visualize yourself confidently taking the test. Imagine yourself finishing the test and leaving with a big smile of success on your face.

Guideline 3: Plan Ahead

Make sure you know the date, time, and location of the test. Plan to arrive early so you can feel prepared and calm.

Guideline 4: Relax When You Take the Test

Relaxing during a test is sometimes easier said than done, but it is possible. Sit down and take a few deep, calming breaths. Focus your mind. Take your time. Remember that you know the material and feel confident that you will complete the test in the time allowed. You are in control.

Guideline 5: Keep in Mind Your Basic Test-Taking Skills

Some of you may have taken tests quite recently; others may not have done so for years. Here is a summary of some excellent test-taking basics.

- **Look over the whole test before you start.** Notice the number of questions and their point values. This gives you a general idea of the scope of the test and helps determine how much time to allow for each question.
- **Read directions carefully.** Listen carefully, too, if the test administrator reads the directions aloud. There are important clues in the directions about how to complete the test.
- **Answer the easiest questions first.** Unless your test is on a computer, you usually don't have to do the questions in order. This warm-up will give you confidence and extra time to tackle the tougher questions.
- **When in doubt, go with your first guess.** It is often fairly accurate.
- **Don't waste time pondering.** If you get stuck, go on to another question and come back when you are ready (if you have time).
- **Check over your answers before you hand in your test.** It's easy to make careless errors.
- **Don't change answers unless you are positive you made a mistake.** As you read earlier, first answers are usually correct.

Guideline 6: Be Kind to Yourself

Give yourself a pat on the back when you finish a test. You got through it. Don't be hard on yourself if you feel you did badly. You did the best you could at that time. Besides, you don't yet know the results for sure. If you do receive disappointing results, take it easy. You are not a failure simply because you fail one test. You are still you, with as much value and worth as you had before the test. You simply didn't do well on that particular test. Look at what went wrong—maybe you got nervous or didn't know the material well enough. Then think about what you can do to improve for the next time.

These guidelines apply to both tests you take in school and those you take at work. Use them to your best advantage!

Working on a Team

Many of the skills you've learned so far, such as reading, writing, and test taking, are things you typically do by yourself. Even listening is solitary in the sense that you do the listening by yourself, although you are listening to another person. You will not be successful, however, until you learn how to be part of a team. Why? Because very few jobs involve you sitting all by yourself, never interacting with another soul—they involve **teamwork**.

Today, companies use teams for a number of reasons. Some companies are desperate to develop products and get them to market as quickly as possible, and no one employee can accomplish that. Other companies have offices in different locations around the world, and employees must learn to operate as virtual teams to get things done, communicating by video conference, instant messages, emails, and phone conferences. Still other companies are small start-ups with few employees, and these companies require employees to do multiple jobs and work together to ensure the company succeeds. That's why the best companies look for employees who are good team players.

Of course, working on a team is not always easy. There are both advantages and disadvantages to teamwork, as you can see in Table 4.4. Working on a team can be a challenge, but in reality, how you communicate with that team can make or break your career. As Lee Iacocca, the businessman credited with reviving the Chrysler Corporation in the 1980s, once said, "A major reason capable people fail to advance is that they don't work well with colleagues."

So, what can you do to work well with colleagues and become a better team player? Following are some guidelines that will help you.

> **Teamwork,** *noun*
>
> cooperative or coordinated effort on the part of a group of persons acting together as a team or in the interest of a common cause

Working effectively with teams is an essential part of any career and requires patience, communication skills, and plenty of emotional intelligence.

Guideline 1: Know What You Have to Offer

To be an effective team member you need to know your gifts—those skills and talents you bring to the table that can help the rest of the team. Think back to Chapter 2, in which you identified your traits and skills. Armed with this knowledge, you will know when to say yes to a

Table 4.4 Advantages and Disadvantages of Teams	
Advantages	**Disadvantages**
Teams generate multiple ideas for solving problems, making it easier to tackle large tasks.	The problem-solving process can slow down as teams grow larger, and deadlines may be missed.
Teams allow members to share their talents and work together.	Working together can frustrate employees who prefer working alone.
Teams strengthen bonds between employees and improve their job satisfaction.	Some team members may not participate as much as others.

request and when to say no. If someone asks for assistance and you know you have the ability to help, say yes. If you know you don't have the skills, won't be able to make much of a difference, or don't have time, say no. People who say yes to every request often end up burned out and resentful, unable to help anyone.

Guideline 2: Use Emotional Intelligence and Personality

Remember what you learned in Chapter 1 about emotional intelligence and in Chapter 2 about personality profiles? A team is the best place to put this information to work.

By developing emotional intelligence, you gain the ability to monitor and control your own emotions, thoughts, and feelings, while remaining sensitive to and aware of others' feelings. This is particularly important in a team environment because it's easy to get frustrated or step on others' toes. You will be a lot more effective when you can see things through your teammates' eyes.

As for personality, understanding your own personality profile can help you avoid uncomfortable situations. For example, if you are an ESTJ, you probably know you have a tendency to talk a lot, value facts and thoughts over feelings, and be judgmental. Knowing this, you can make an extra effort to let others speak while you listen (instead of interrupting), consider others' feelings, and curb your natural tendency to criticize. By doing so, you allow others to contribute and the team works together more smoothly.

Conflict is bound to arise in a team from time to time, so it's important to know how to react when someone gets angry with you or has an emotional outburst. Regardless of your personality profile, you must remember to listen for the words underneath the emotion. Think of the emotion as static and try to tune it out while you listen for the real problem. The person probably has a valid concern, but it's hard to figure out when the individual is emotionally distraught. Once you recognize the actual concern, you will be able to respond to the problem with empathy. By staying calm and taking the other person seriously, you are a lot more likely to diffuse the situation.

Guideline 3: Understand the Stages

Most teams go through several stages of development. Some stages may last for minutes or hours; others may last for days or weeks. The better you understand the following stages, the better you can work effectively with your team during each stage.

1. **Forming.** This is the chaotic stage in which members of the team are getting to know one another, figure out their strengths, and determine a direction for the team.

2. **Storming.** This is the uncomfortable stage in which conflicts arise because people begin to show their real selves to one another and disagree. It's vital that people keep communicating during this stage.

3. **Norming.** This is the comfortable stage in which the group recommits, accepts its roles and responsibilities, and begins to build consensus.

4. **Performing.** This is the dynamic stage in which the team actually accomplishes things. Members have a good understanding of the strengths and weaknesses and are able to get work done on a project.

5. **Adjourning.** This is the final stage when the team finishes its project, members discuss how things went, and then the team dissolves. Or, in some cases, the team gets ready for another project!

Guideline 4: Use an Agenda

As a team member, you may have to set up meetings from time to time. To keep the meetings effective, consider sending out an agenda that answers these questions:

- **Purpose.** Why are you holding the meeting?
- **Outcomes.** When the meeting is over, what do you hope the outcome will be?

- **Expectations.** What do you expect your teammates to bring to the meeting? What do you want them to contribute?
- **Logistics.** When are you holding the meeting and how long will it be?

Remember to follow the agenda during the meeting, and your teammates will love you for it.

Guideline 5: Practice Meeting Etiquette

Being part of a team means attending meetings. There are certain behaviors you can practice that will make you a more effective attendee or leader and help get your point across. They are also useful when dealing with people one-on-one.

- **Show up on time.** It's rude to arrive at a meeting after it has started. If you know you'll be late, call and let people know. If you are unexpectedly detained, apologize for showing up late, but do not give a long, drawn-out explanation.
- **Be prepared.** Make sure you have all necessary materials (both printed and online) for the group. Always do a "tech check" ahead of time to make sure your equipment is working, such as your computer, software, and video projector.
- **Don't interrupt.** This is the hardest thing for most people. However, if you follow the guidelines in the earlier "Listening" section, the rest of the team will appreciate you even more. A teammate who listens is one who is respected.
- **Use polite language.** No matter how angry or frustrated you might feel, do not let your words convey extreme emotion. The minute you shout or swear, you lose your credibility. Always speak the way you would like to be spoken to.
- **Respect confidentiality.** If someone says something in the meeting that needs to stay confidential, do not spread the word when you leave the meeting. People will no longer trust you if you do.
- **Discuss issues in person, not in front of the team.** If you have an issue with someone on the team, do not complain about the individual in front of the rest of the team. Instead, talk to him or her alone after the meeting. Once you berate a colleague in front of the rest of the team, your team members will automatically assume that you will do the same to them. As a result, they will be far less likely to interact, offer ideas, or participate.
- **Acknowledge teammates.** Give credit where credit is due. If you feel you were mostly responsible for something, be the bigger person and mention others as well, even if they were only peripherally involved.
- **Avoid sending text messages, emails, or instant messages or taking phone calls during a meeting.** Besides showing up late, this is the rudest thing you can do in a meeting. It is vital that you focus on the meeting without distractions. Otherwise, it's highly likely that you will not pay attention, will forget things, and will irritate others. Some companies are even making it mandatory for attendees to drop their cell phones and PDAs in a box before they sit down to a meeting!

Follow these five guidelines to make you a more valuable team player and help your team become more effective.

Now You Try It: Working on a Team

Think back to a time you participated in a team activity (do not include sports). Your answers to these questions will help identify your team behaviors.

1. What kind of project was it?
2. What part did you play?
3. What did you like about being part of the team? What did you not like?
4. What kinds of problems did the team have?
5. Did the team accomplish the project? Why or why not?
6. Do you prefer to work alone or as part of a team? Why?

Managing Stress

Stress, *noun*

physical, mental, or emotional strain or tension (for example, "Worry over his job and his wife's health put him under a great stress"); a physical factor, such as injury, or a mental state, such as anxiety, that disturbs the body's normal state of functioning

Part of being a successful professional is learning to deal with the **stress** that comes from working with others (especially on teams), dealing with deadlines, and handling unexpected events.

Stressful situations are bound to arise in your life—at work, in school, at home, and in your community. Although you cannot always control the events or people around you, you can control your reaction to them. This is called *stress management.* Table 4.5 lists some useful tips for dealing with stress.

Table 4.5 Stress Management Techniques	
Stress Management Technique	**Actions to Take**
Change your state.	Change your outlook by changing your physical state. If you are sitting, try standing or walking. If you have been standing, sit down and relax.
Take a think break.	Take time to get away from your work, school, or home environment. Take a short walk, even if it's inside the building. Take a stretch break to reactivate your blood flow. Do some deep breathing to calm yourself.
Establish a system of balance.	Pay attention to your body and know when it's time for a break. Is your neck sore? Are your shoulders tight? Is your breathing shallow? Do you feel irritated or angry? It's time for a break! Learn to balance periods of hard work with breaks.
Know when you need to refuel.	Refueling involves more than just a short break. Make time to eat, rest, breathe deeply, exercise, interact with others, or take some time alone. All work and no play can make you a very stressed out person!

Did You Know? What makes stress so toxic is the variety of ways the body processes it. Stress may contribute to the development of some illnesses, including heart disease and cancer. Research at the University of Florida showed how mental stress can decrease blood flow to the heart. The *Journal of the American Heart Association* equated stress with bad cholesterol and smoking as risk factors for coronary heart disease. In addition, stress hormones, such as adrenaline and cortisol, inhibit the immune system and cause high blood pressure.[4]

---

[4]Lam, Kevin. "Sickness Can Be Price of Unbridled Stress." *MindBodyHealth,* October 18, 2010. Accessed on October 30, 2010, from www.mindbodyhealth.com/stressillness

Now You Try It: Stress Management

1. Who do you know that handles stress well?

   - What does that person do in stressful situations?
   - Have you ever done those things to handle stress?

2. Think of a situation in which you felt very stressed.

   - How did you handle the stress?
   - What could you have done differently?

Thinking about your own reactions to stress can help you identify stressful situations and better respond to them.

These tips can help momentarily reduce stress. However, for long-term stress management, it's important to have a proper diet, take part in physical activities, manage overloaded schedules, and learn to tune out distractions and focus on the task at hand.

By practicing these techniques, you will be better able to deal with the unexpected events that so often arise in our busy lives.

Lifelong Learning

No matter how good you feel you are with the basic skills we've covered in this chapter, you can always learn more. In the real world, people who succeed are those who are willing to keep learning and remain open to new ways of doing things.

It is not unusual for a company to fire 25 to 50% of its workforce during "downsizing." Layoffs and pink slips are everyday news. Having a career and keeping a job are bigger challenges in today's competitive world.

What determines who keeps a job and who gets fired? How long will it take for those laid-off employees to find new jobs? What might help an employee find a job of equivalent pay sooner rather than later?

These questions confront an ever-increasing number of employees as companies seek to keep their advantage or simply survive increased global and technological competition. Ask First Interstate Bank employees after Wells Fargo acquired their bank. Talk to GTE employees who experienced a number of reorganizations over recent years, or the General Motors employees who were laid off when the assembly plant closed and still can't find jobs with comparable pay.

There was a time when excelling at your job meant an annual pay raise and long-term employment. There was an unwritten employment agreement: I do my work and you will pay me. If I keep on doing this, I will have a job (and probably make more money). However, times have changed. Doing your work well is no longer enough. Today, lifelong learning is an essential ingredient to sustaining a career or finding comparable employment.

Lifelong learning means keeping abreast of how technology and competition are changing job requirements and then participating in, rather than fighting, the resulting changes. Lifelong learning means developing new, relevant skills on the job or at workshops or in school. Lifelong learning means embracing the learning process as fun and not work. Lifelong learning also means recognizing learning myths.

Myth 1: After I Graduate or Get My Certificate, My Education Is Done

Shanna just finished her program. All the studying is behind her. She can just concentrate on what is important—work. Wrong!

We often equate our early life (formal schooling) with education and learning. This compartmentalized view of learning gives us a false sense that our learning is complete when we finish school. Today, people can expect to have at least five to seven jobs, if not different careers, during

their working lives. Is it realistic to believe these job or career changes can be made successfully without learning new skills? No way.

Myth 2: Learning Is Not Necessary

After years of school and five years of hard work, Tyler finally got the promotion toward which he had been working. He earned it. Now he can relax.

Does this career game plan sound familiar? Unfortunately, this is not reality in today's working world. Rapidly shifting demands, fierce global competition, and rapid technological innovations make lifelong learning a necessity. Jobs and skills are becoming obsolete at an increasing rate. Lifelong learning is essential to sustain a career of good jobs, rather than facing prospects of downgraded jobs in terms of pay and your ability to add value.

Myth 3: Learning Can Wait

Have you wondered why some people take months to find employment after getting laid off, when others have recruiters pounding on their doors to present incredible job opportunities? The big difference is often the development of relevant skills and experience, based on continuous learning.

We are creatures of habit. Once you start procrastinating and telling yourself that learning can wait, it becomes all too easy to continue to defer learning opportunities. Once you stop trying to learn, it is hard to start again. On the other hand, once you understand the value of learning and actively engage in learning activities, learning becomes a habit and an important part of your life.

Just as you can find a number of excuses to not visit your dentist, you can find any number of excuses to not engage in learning experiences. Learning takes time, effort, and commitment. Don't let time run out on you—learning is worth it. Learning not only creates employment opportunities and options, but it also provides the keys to a better life. Through learning you can unravel the mysteries of new ideas and business processes, fill the skill void created by technological innovation, and remove the fear of change. Make learning a lifelong habit.

Hang On to Your Basics

You now have a large set of valuable basic tools. All of them, separately and together, will serve to make the other items in your tool kit more useful to you. Take time to discover how each tool works and to test it out. The exercises at the end of the chapter will help you do that. You will find that you will use your tool kit every day, both in and out of your work environment. Your tools will always be there to make what you do easier and more successful.

Your Tool Kit at Work

4.1 Knowing How to Learn

Honest appraisal of your learning skills is critical for your success. Knowing how to learn is vital for success in school and in your career. Unless you know how to learn, you will have trouble building the workplace know-how that helps you adapt to different situations. The knowledge you find in courses and books is useful only if you can efficiently learn and retain it.

Review your how-to-learn skills in the following exercise by checking the answer box that applies to your present skill level. In this chapter we focused on how-to-learn skills as they apply to your school experience; later, in Chapter 11, you will complete a similar exercise that shows how these skills function in the workplace.

Skill	Rarely	Sometimes	Often	Almost Always
I have a regular place to study.				
I have a regularly scheduled study time that corresponds to when I'm most alert.				
I plan my study time and set priorities.				
I read the table of contents before beginning a textbook.				
I scan reading assignments first and then reread them carefully.				
When I read, I underline, highlight, or make notes in the margins.				
I ask myself questions on what I just read.				
I look up words that I don't know in the dictionary.				
I attend class.				
I come to class early.				
I listen intently in class.				
I keep a notebook for class notes.				
I take notes in class.				
I know how to determine the key points my teachers make.				
I include these points in my notes.				
I write assignments in the teacher's exact words.				
I review my notes within 24 hours of class.				
I study my most difficult subjects first.				
For a writing assignment, I write a first draft.				
I proofread.				
My concentration is good; I am able to focus on what I read and study.				
I know and use memory aids.				
I review my notes and assignments weekly rather than cram for a test.				
I ask a teacher, the dean, or a tutor for help when the need arises.				
I reward myself when I finish studying.				
I arrive early for tests.				
On a test, I answer the questions I know first.				
I check all my answers before I hand in my test.				
I spend more time studying than I do worrying about school.				
I know that ultimately only I am responsible for how much I learn.				

Give yourself the following number of points for each answer: 4 points for Almost Always, 3 points for Often, 2 points for Sometimes, and 1 point for Rarely.

Total Score: _____

- **110–120:** Congratulations! You have excellent learning skills. Keep working on making your skills even better.
- **100–110:** You have good learning skills. Try new learning ideas to achieve excellence.
- **90–100:** You have average learning skills. If you change some habits, you'll do better in school and feel more confident in your career.
- **Below 90:** Your skills have weaknesses that most likely cause you difficulty. Increase your potential by putting learning skills to work.

4.2 Are You an Active Listener?

Assess your listening skills by checking the appropriate boxes. You will notice other skills mixed in with the listening skills; these are primarily communication skills that you will study in Chapter 10. This shows how closely good listening skills and successful communication are linked.

Listening Skill	Rarely/ Sometimes	Often	Almost Always
I avoid interrupting others.			
I start listening with the first word.			
I put away what I'm doing when someone is talking.			
I encourage others to talk and say what they think.			
I ask questions.			
I listen even if I don't particularly like the speaker.			
If I don't understand, I ask the person to clarify.			
I respect other people's right to their opinions.			
I think of a disagreement as an opportunity to share opposing views.			
I think of a disagreement as an opportunity to understand a person better.			
I enjoy listening.			
I use eye contact.			
I listen to the tone of a person's voice and watch gestures to understand the real meaning of the words.			
I look for points on which we agree and not for points on which we disagree.			
I realize the speaker's meaning is not necessarily what I would mean with the same words.			
I listen equally well to a person of a different age, gender, race, or culture as I do to a person similar to me.			
When appropriate, I take notes.			
When I respond, I avoid lecturing, prying, or topping the story with my own experiences.			
If I don't hear the speaker, I ask politely for the information to be repeated.			
I know listening is an important success skill, and I continually work to improve it.			

Give yourself 2 points for every Almost Always and 1 point for every Often.

Total Score: _____

- **30–40:** You're all ears. You clearly hear what others need to communicate to you in any environment.
- **20–30:** You're a fair listener, but you may be missing some important points.
- **0–20:** If you activate your listening skills, you'll do much better at school and at work.

Whether you scored high, low, or in between, list the five listening skills that are most difficult for you:

1. _____

2. _____

3. _____

4. _____

5. _____

In the next two weeks, concentrate on improving these skills. Reread the "Listening" section of this chapter for help. At the end of the two weeks, briefly discuss two situations in which your improved listening skills paid off.

1. _____

_____

_____

2. _____

_____

_____

4.3 How Much Do You Read?

People often fail to realize the importance of words and reading, and the volume of information they take in each day through the printed word. This is a chance for you to find out how much you actually read.

1. Today, use the following chart to monitor the number of times you read to get through the day. Keep a log of all the materials you read online or in print at work, school, home, and elsewhere.

   - **Time** = time of day (morning, afternoon, or evening)
   - **Material** = title of the actual item read
   - **Type** = sign, menu, book, magazine, advertisement, comic book, online article, e-zine, blog, etc.
   - **Reason** = school, work, personal entertainment, personal research, personal education, etc.

Time	Material	Type	Reason

Time	Material	Type	Reason

2. Examine your log in the evening.

    a. Do you typically read online or in print?

    b. What types of materials do you typically read?

    c. Do you read more materials for personal reasons or because of school or work?

    d. What would you like to read more of?

    e. Do you do most of your reading at a particular time of day, or do you typically read throughout the day?

    f. When are you most alert for reading?

    g. When could you squeeze in more reading during the day or evening?

4.4 Do You Know What You Are Reading?

To determine your skill in concentrating and understanding while you read, quickly scan the following paragraph and then carefully read it through *once*. After you finish, cover the paragraph and answer the questions.

Ergonomics

With most Americans spending 70% of their waking hours at work, the office environment should be as safe, healthy, comfortable, and productive as possible. Then why don't we feel more at home in the workplace? Because, traditionally, workplaces have expected *us* to conform to *them*. However, workers have not conformed as expected.

One reason is because of computers. As computer technology advanced and more office workers began using computers, problems of user comfort arose. Since the introduction of personal computers in the 1980s, an entire market of products has evolved to support the use of computers. As more and more people used computers, more experienced various physical discomforts, and the field of ergonomics evolved. *Ergonomics* is the science of fitting the workplace to the worker to meet the physical and psychological needs of the worker. Everything that affects the worker must be considered—layout, decor, furniture, lighting, amount of workspace, quality of air, heating and cooling, acoustics, and placement of equipment.[5]

[5]Paraphrased from Jennings, Lucy Mae, Sharon Burton, and Nelda Shelton. *Procedures for the Automated Office.* Upper Saddle River, NJ. Prentice Hall, 1994, p. 8.

1. What percent of their waking hours do most Americans spend at work? _____

2. Your office environment should be: (enter three qualities)

   _____

   _____

   _____

3. What have workplaces expected us to do in the past?

   _____

4. When we began to use computers, problems related to worker comfort rose.
   True _____ False _____

5. The field of ergonomics is: (select one)

   a. The science of advanced computer technology.

   b. The process by which the worker becomes accustomed to the workplace.

   c. The science of fitting the workplace to the worker.

6. The workplace needs to meet only the physical needs of the worker.
   True _____ False _____

7. Name four office factors that affect workers.

   _____

   _____

   _____

   _____

Go back to the paragraph and check your answers. How did you do? Don't feel down if you didn't answer all the questions correctly. To remember what you read, scan the material first, read it carefully a second time, and then ask yourself questions about what you just read. Also, review often. Use this process every time you pick up a textbook.

4.5 Are You a Team Player?

Get into groups of four. Each group should imagine its members work for a popsicle company and all the companies are competing. Summer is just around the corner, and each company is gearing up for increased sales due to hot weather. With all the other fast foods on the market and concerns about childhood obesity and nutrition, each company is concerned about how to get parents to buy more popsicles for their children.

1. Within your group, think of all of the things it would take to launch a successful new popsicle campaign. Consider areas like product development (shape, color, flavor), marketing, finance, and distribution. Allow 10 minutes for the discussion.

2. After 10 minutes, go through the first three stages of team development discussed earlier. Ask each team try to pinpoint when each stage occurred and what occurred during that stage.

   Forming: _____

   Storming: _____

   Norming: _____

3. For the fourth stage, performing, have each group present its popsicle idea to the class. After all the groups present their ideas, the class members will vote on which popsicle they would most likely buy.

4. After the best popsicle is chosen, get back in your groups and perform the last step, adjourning.

   * What was the result of your concept?
   * Looking back, was there something your group could have done to make the performing step more successful?

5. Now consider how you worked within your group.

   * What did you notice about yourself and how you related to others?
   * How hard was it to come up with an innovative concept with other people?
   * Could you have come up with the idea on your own?
   * What did you like about working with a group? What did you dislike?

Throughout your career and your life, you will find that teamwork is essential to getting things done. You will almost always have to work with other people. In the end, cooperation in a group always gets things done better!

4.6   How Do You Manage Stress in Your Life?

People often fail to realize how stress impacts them. This exercise should help you learn to identify key stressors and figure out how best to respond to them.

1. Think about situations you've been in that you considered stressful. List the primary causes of stress in your life right now, as well as things that historically stress you out.

   _____

   _____

   _____

   _____

2. How does your body feel when you are stressed out? Are certain parts of your body affected more than others?

   _____

   _____

   _____

3. How do you typically try to deal with stress? Does it work?

   _____

   _____

4. Review the stress-reducing actions from Table 4.5.

   * Which ones have you tried?
   * Which ones worked?
   * Which would you like to try?

In the future, remember that stress is your reaction to a situation, and you have a choice about that reaction. Learn to recognize your body's reaction and attempt to practice the stress management techniques to keep your reaction more positive.

4.7   Calibrate Your Basic Skills

Answer yes or no to the following questions:

1. Remembering names is easy for me, even when meeting a lot of new people.
2. I rarely, if ever, daydream at a meeting at work or in a class at school.

3. I read a newspaper, online or in print, on a regular basis.
4. I write notes, underline, or highlight as I read this book.
5. I have taken tests when applying for jobs.
6. I am comfortable learning new computer software and technology on the job.
7. I tend to take notes at meetings at work and during classes.
8. I use the spell-check feature as I write, but then set aside what I have written and reread it later to make any additional changes.
9. I take a short break when I find myself losing my concentration and practice stress reduction techniques whenever I recognize the symptoms of stress in my own body.
10. I work well with others and enjoy working with teams.

All answers should be "yes." How did you do?

If you answered yes to

- **7–10 questions:** You have a grasp of basic skills. Keep it up!
- **4–6 questions:** You have a foundation for your basic skills. Use your tools to build on it.
- **0–3 questions:** You will significantly benefit from working on your basic skills.

4.8 Technology at Work

Use a word processing program of your choice to format, edit, and improve the following cover letter, written by a programmer who was recently laid off and is hoping to find another job.

Remember to use the three Cs and the proofreading guidelines. In particular, focus on adequate white space, short sentences and paragraphs, and active voice sentences.

October 30, 2012

Dear EarthWired,

I was talking to a coworker the other day who told me about a job position you had called a Web Usability Specialist and I am very interested in applying for that job.

My name is jennifer sharone and your company is the kind of company I want to work for because you really value your customers and think its important to make websites as easy to use as possible. The last 6 years were spent with me working for Athena Web Solutions in Savannah, Georgia, working with software developers, graphic artists, and marketing departments to develop websites that were attractive, intuitive, friendly websites. When looking at my combined experience, youll see I have 15 years of doing website design, marketing writing, and training. A creative company like yours is where I want to put my experience to use. I can help you do any of the tasks you identified in your job description:

Audience analysis

website evaluation and design

developing website content

presentations and reports

I am a versatile person with multiple skills, who feels strongly about making a difference. I am comfortable with working with people in different departments and with people in different geographic locations, and with communicating in in person and in writing. I am also an empathetic person and I know how to put myself in the users' shoes and understand there wants and needs. Thats why I consider myself a valuable addition to any team.

I look forward to hearing from you,

Jennifer Sharone

Jen.sharone@comcast.net

770-555-1212

102 Holly Street

Savannah, GA 31420

Here is a possible solution with spelling corrections, more white space, active voice, and shorter sentences. In additional, we broke up the very long second paragraph into two paragraphs.

October 30, 2010

Dear EarthWired,

A co-worker forwarded me your job description for a Web Usability Specialist, and I am very interested in applying for the position.

My name is Jennifer Sharone, and I would like to work for a company that values its customers and strives to make websites as easy to use as possible. I spent the last 6 years at Athena Web Solutions in Savannah, Georgia, working with software developers, graphic artists, and marketing departments to develop attractive, intuitive, friendly websites.

I have 15 years combined experience in website design, marketing writing, and training. I would like to put my experience to use in a creative company like yours. In particular, I can assist with any of the tasks you identified in your job description:

Analyzing audiences

Evaluating and designing websites

Developing website content

Making presentations and writing reports

I am a versatile person with multiple skills, and I am passionate about making a difference. I am comfortable working with people in different departments and different geographic locations. I am an excellent communicator in person and in writing. I am also an empathetic person who can put myself in the users' shoes and understand their wants and needs. I consider myself a valuable addition to any team.

I look forward to hearing from you.

Sincerely,

Jennifer Sharone

Jen.sharone@comcast.net

770-555-1212

102 Holly Street

Savannah, GA 31420

4.9 Plug Your Knowledge into Real Life

You've seen the need for effective concentration, listening, and note-taking skills at work and at school. Now apply these skills to solve Raymond's problem.

Raymond repairs computers. He has difficulty remembering all the intricate parts of one of the computer models he services. It's a new model that he needs to study, but he hasn't made the time to do so. As a result, Raymond made two mistakes this week, which shut down the computers at a major client's office.

His supervisor, Ms. Tanaka, was angry. She threatened to fire Raymond if he made one more mistake. Once she calmed down, Ms. Tanaka told Raymond to meet with her tomorrow morning before starting his service calls.

Raymond is so upset he doesn't think he'll be able to improve. All he can think about is the possibility that he will be fired.

Write a paragraph showing how Raymond can have a productive meeting with Ms. Tanaka tomorrow and save his job. Use what you know about basic learning skills, such as active listening, concentration and memory, note taking, reading, teamwork, and stress management.

_____
_____
_____
_____
_____
_____
_____
_____
_____
_____

4.10 Your Positive Attitude List—Your PAL

1. This basic skills PAL is different from the positive attitude lists that you have seen so far. Circle the items that reflect your current behavior and write in the trait that you need to develop now.

   - Produce good notes
   - Attend all classes
   - Listen in class
   - Study class notes and materials

   I will develop my ability to: _____

2. Write the ability you want to develop on a sticky note or index card. Put it where you keep your other cards, in a place where you can see it every day.

3. Now reinforce those skills with another pledge. Make a study pledge to help you prepare for your career efficiently (using waste-cutting, productive ideas) and effectively (using methods and skills that bring excellent results).

Sign the study pledge only if you have every intention of living up to the guidelines.

I will attend all my classes. In class, I will listen attentively and take notes. I will review the notes within 24 hours of the class.

Name : _____

Date: _____

4. How can you stick to your pledge? By avoiding distractions. Unless you concentrate in class, on the job, and when you study, you may waste time. No one can afford to lose time. When your mind is distracted, you can't concentrate on what you're studying. What's on your mind right now that might interfere with your concentration? You may be letting the date you had last night, the phone call you hope to receive tonight, the project at work that you hope to complete, or the errands you have to run after school interfere with the present.

For one minute, jot down everything you're thinking about right now. These are your "interfering thoughts."

I am distracted by:

- _____
- _____
- _____
- _____
- _____

5. Now, leave all those distractions on the page. Turn to the next page of your study material. Close your eyes. Bring yourself into the present with a clear mind and be ready to concentrate. After you finish studying, the interfering thoughts will still be waiting for you on the paper where you wrote them. That's when you can feel free to think about them all you want.

This is an excellent exercise whenever thoughts about the past or the future seem to block out the present. Quickly jot them down and then forget about them while you study. You can always go back to them later when you finish.

Explore the Job Market

Find a Fit

Find a job you like and you add five days to every week.

H. Jackson Brown, Jr.

 learning objectives

- How can you get a sense of the local job market?
- What do we mean by job "trends"?
- What are four excellent ways to conduct job research?
- What are the four phases of job creation?
- What is the "hidden job market"?
- How can you find time for your job research?
- Why is it important to stay flexible and set boundaries during your job research?

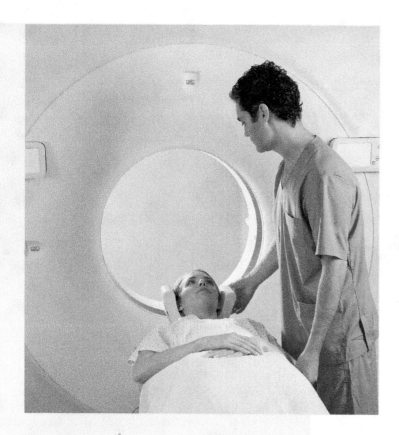

myth

"There are no jobs out there."

reality

Every region of the United States has its own economic challenges, as do certain industries. The truth is, there are jobs out there you have never even heard of—jobs that might be perfect for you, jobs that need someone with your skills and experience, and jobs that would really suit you. Your job is to figure out what they are!

myth

"The best way to find a job is to check the classified ads in the newspaper or the job postings online."

reality

By the time a job makes it to the classifieds or a national job posting site, the competition is fierce. If you really want to find a job without all that competition, you need to explore the hidden job market. In fact, 80% of all jobs are not even advertised.

Todd worked as an X-ray technician for years at several hospitals. But during his latest stint with a hospital in the Pacific Northwest, he's realized something. He doesn't want to be an X-ray technician any more. He wants more time to interact with patients and have the opportunity to help them heal, rather than simply read X-rays.

He thinks he wants to be a registered nurse, but he's not sure—after all, that would require more schooling. But maybe there are other positions that would suit him; he just doesn't know what they are or whether they even exist in the city where he lives. Todd decides it would not be wise to quit his job until he figures out what he really wants to do.

Lucky for him, there is a workforce center nearby where he can do some exploring. He decides to drop by during his lunch hour and finds out about a great website where he can research different professions and find out what type of work they involve, what kinds of skills and experience are necessary, what education is required, whether the profession is growing, and what personality types are best suited to the different jobs. He's not sure what personality type he is, so he signs up for a Myers-Briggs personality profile workshop. The next thing you know, he's signed up for a "hidden job market" workshop because he just learned most jobs aren't advertised. Todd is well on his way to discovering the best job for him and how to go about getting it!

Todd is a good example of someone who understands how important it is to find out what kinds of jobs are out there and which ones might fit well with his talents, abilities, values, and needs. In this chapter you are going to grab a whole new set of tools to help you hunt for the right job. This involves researching jobs by looking at local job market trends and economic factors. It means getting exposed to publications and websites that can help identify jobs and careers you may have never considered. And, most important, it means discovering the importance of the "hidden" job market and job hunt flexibility, which will give you a big advantage among job seekers.

Note: This chapter is a short chapter that focuses on research to whet your appetite for the job hunt. However, it does not get into the nitty-gritty of the job hunt, such as networking, resumes, and interviews. Those topics are covered in Chapters 6, 7, and 8. Let's start by looking at factors that affect the availability of jobs.

Looking at the Local Job Market

A quick way to get a sense of your local job market is to read the classified or business sections of your local paper. Are there a lot of ads for certain types of jobs, but few for others? Is there mention of companies moving to town and opening new facilities? Are companies laying off workers? This information can help you pinpoint jobs and companies of interest.

You might also try using a national job search engine like Indeed (www.indeed.com). Enter the name of your city and the search engine will comb through all job postings and job websites, such as Monster and Dice, to show you what's available. Your chamber of commerce and local workforce center can also provide you with information about your local job market, such as names of organizations that might be able to help you network, products and services your area is known for, and names of companies moving into or out of the area.

Remember, just because you do not see certain jobs listed does not mean they don't exist. They simply may not be advertised. You'll learn more about unadvertised jobs in the later section of this chapter, "Tapping the Hidden Job Market."

Just because your local job market may be going through a slump does not mean you won't find a job. For example, suppose a large electronics company in your city just laid off 25% of its workforce, and you lost your job. You might naturally assume that you are doomed because there are no other large electronics companies in the area. However, perhaps a small, little-known, start-up company is looking for an electrical engineer to help develop a new product. You just need to be open to possibilities. When one door closes another opens!

Did You Know?

Some geographic areas are known for their unique job markets. Here are just a few:

- Los Angeles and New York City are great for actors and actresses.
- Silicon Valley, California, is best known for computer technology jobs (think Google).
- Seattle, Washington, is known for jobs in the high-tech industry (think Microsoft).
- Wyoming needs oil field workers.
- Orlando, Florida, is a wonderful city for hotel and hospitality workers.

Do you know for what jobs your city may be known?

Checking Out Job Trends

Knowing your local job market is important, but so is knowing national career **trends**. You're probably familiar with trends in fashion, cars, and television shows, but trends in careers exist as well.

Career trends deal with general directions in the economy that may result in fewer or greater numbers of jobs in different areas. For example, the Bureau of Labor Statistics (BLS) conducts research on labor economics and statistics. As a result of its research, the BLS believes that the

Trend, *noun*

general tendency or direction; fashion, mode

following 10 jobs will be in high demand by 2014, due to the high percentage of baby boomers in those jobs who will be retiring from the workforce:[1]

The Bureau of Labor Statistics keeps track of career trends each year.

- Bookkeeping, accounting, and auditing
- College and university teachers
- Educational and other administrators
- Elementary school teachers
- Farmers
- Heavy truck drivers
- Janitors and cleaners
- Registered nurses
- Secondary school teachers
- Secretaries

It's important to remember that trends are merely general tendencies; they may or may not pan out. However, try to avoid pursuing careers that are so trendy that they will be short-lived (for example, Twitter proofreader), or jobs that will be a dead end in the future (for example, oil roustabout). Your best bet is to pursue a career that allows you to gain a variety of skills that you can apply to different situations and transfer to other jobs over time.

Conducting Job Research

Once you have a sense of your local job market and trends, it's time to get to work. This section looks at a variety of resources you might explore to learn about possible jobs.

Professional Organization Websites and Publications

Almost every industry has a professional association that produces an industry publication. Most of the publications are in print, as well as online. Conduct an online search of your industry or career of interest to locate professional organizations. A quick way to do this is to go to any of the following websites first.

WEDDLE's Association Directory. WEDDLE's lists several thousand associations from around the world by their primary professional and occupational focus or by industry. This site is maintained by WEDDLE's, a research, publishing, consulting, and training firm.

Website: www.weddles.com/associations/index.cfm

Gateway to Associations Online. This website provides a comprehensive directory of business and professional association websites. If you don't know the full name of the organization you are looking for, you can enter the part you do know and a list of potential organizations will appear. This site is maintained by the American Society of Association Executives.

Website: www.asaecenter.org/Community/Directories/associationsearch.cfm

Associations on the Net. This website lists organizations that have a web presence so you can explore groups you might want to join. All you have to do is select an area of interest and you'll find a lot of links. This site is maintained by the Internet Public Library.

Website: www.ipl.org/div/subject/

---

[1]Dohm, Arlene. "Gauging the labor force effects of retiring baby-boomers." *Monthly Labor Review.* July 2000: page 18. Online (PDF)

Table 5.1 **Sample Professional Associations**	
Association	**Website**
American Society for Information Science and Technology	www.asis.org
International Council of Shopping Centers	www.icsc.org
Academy of Laser Dentistry	www.laserdentistry.org
National Restaurant Association	www.restaurant.org
American Nursing Association	www.nursingworld.org
National Association of Science Writers	www.nasw.org
Center for Software Development	www.center.org

Table 5.1 lists just a few professional associations located through the WEDDLE's site, but you can find many more on your own. Most have professional publications you can read. Once you locate a professional association of interest and visit its website, find out whether the association has a magazine or journal you can subscribe to. This often involves paying a membership fee, but it can be worth it in terms of finding out about jobs and trends. Also find out whether there is a local chapter of the organization in your geographic area. Perhaps you can attend a meeting as a guest.

Being a member of a professional organization is a great way to make contacts for your job hunt. Even if you decide not to attend meetings, you might still find the meeting minutes, e-newsletters, and magazines very helpful in your job research.

Job Posting Websites

In addition to industry publications and websites, there are job posting websites that list jobs all over the United States and abroad. By the time jobs hit these websites, the competition can be pretty great. By visiting these sites, however, you will learn about what different companies are looking for. Even if a particular job is not listed, you may decide to proactively contact the company and ask about other jobs you are interested in. We will discuss this further in Chapter 6, in which we discuss networking.

Because national websites post so many jobs and get so many replies, you might have to wait weeks or months for a response. Plus, the website may not provide the name of any real person for you to contact. That's why it is sometimes more effective to use smaller job posting websites that are specific to your geographic region or type of work. Table 5.2 lists some example websites. Even though smaller websites may not post as many jobs, they are more likely to provide better information about whom to contact and they will respond to you more quickly than larger

Table 5.2 **Example Job Posting Websites**	
Website	**Description**
www.monster.com	General
www.dice.com	General
http://careerbuilder.com	General
www.coloradojobs.com	Colorado jobs
http://jobs.37signals.com	Software programming, design, and usability jobs
www.geosearch.com	Geographic information systems (GIS) jobs
http://freelanceswitch.com	Freelance writing jobs

sites. In addition, once you have a contact at the site, you may be able to explain the type of work you're looking for so your contact can keep an eye open for you. Yes, it's true—there are actually real people maintaining these smaller websites and they will respond to your emails and answer your questions! For example, one U.S. college student contacted a New Zealand university website about a typo and a broken link on the site, and ended up having a long email conversation with a lab assistant. This eventually led to the student hearing about a teaching assistant position at the university which he applied for and got!

Agencies

If you are new to a geographic area or a career field, you might prefer to talk to someone in person about job opportunities. Following are some good sources of information.

Workforce Center. These centers are typically located in each county in your state. A workforce center is an excellent resource for any job hunter. It provides a wide variety of job search aids, such as workshops that focus on career development and transition, networking, job interviewing techniques, and more. It also lists job postings as they become available in the area. Counselors are available to assist you with resumes, cover letters, and interviewing techniques. Many workforce centers also provide information about grants and job training. Best of all, services at your workforce center are typically free!

Website: Varies by location. Enter something like this in your browser search field to find the nearest workforce center: "[your_county_name] Workforce Center"

Small Business Development Center (SBDC). These centers are typically found in each city in your state and are funded by the U.S. Small Business Administration. The SBDC provides assistance to current and prospective small business owners. The center generally has a wide variety of information and affordable workshops on business-related topics. The SBDC is a great place to learn about small businesses in your area.

Website: www.sba.gov

To locate your nearest SBDC, go to the website and follow these links:

- Local resources
- Small Business Development Centers
- SBDC locator

Chamber of Commerce. Every city or county has a chamber of commerce. This is typically an organization of local business owners who join together to help their business interests. The chamber of commerce provides statistical information about employment in your geographic area. It also hosts networking events business training. Although it costs money to become a member, guests can usually attend networking events for free.

Website: Varies by city

Online Research Tools

If you like doing research on the Internet, there are plenty of great sites where you can explore the **labor market** in greater detail. For example, you might want to find out what kinds of jobs exist for someone with your personality profile and interests, what education and skills are required for those jobs, and whether those jobs have a future.

All of the following online tools are updated annually and contain the latest and greatest information about occupations in the United States.

O*Net Online. This comprehensive website lets you browse for occupations by category to learn what jobs exist in those areas. You can also find out the demand for a particular job; the type of tasks you would be performing; the skills, knowledge, and education required; the tools and technology used; and even the work styles of people who do well in the job!

Website: www.online.onetcenter.org

Labor market, *noun*

available supply of labor considered with reference to the demand for it

America's Career InfoNet. This website lets you examine reports to learn which industries and occupations are growing or declining in your state. The site also provides career assistance, such as finding financial aid for education required for a career transition, writing resumes, and exploring career options.

Website: www.acinet.org

Occupational Outlook Handbook. This Bureau of Labor Statistics handbook provides valuable information about hundreds of jobs. You can learn about training and education, earnings, expected job prospects, working conditions, what people do on the job, and more.

Website: www.bls.gov/ooh

Riley Guide. This website provides free career and employment information, including how to plan your job search, how to target employers, how to write resumes and cover letters, and more. It also includes a career research center where you can find out about salaries, growth, and education associated with various jobs.

Website: www.rileyguide.com

Researching information online, reading news articles, and visiting the workforce centers are good ways to learn about different jobs and companies. However, you might want to get the inside scoop and find out what other job seekers are saying about various companies. If you know someone who works for a company you're interested in, you can always call or meet with him or her. This is a great way to find out about the work environment and corporate culture, as well as salaries and business growth. If you don't know anyone, there are also "insider" websites that provide information from both current and past employees of large, national companies. (These sites typically do not provide information about small, local companies.) These sites change all the time, but two popular ones are www.vault.com and www.wetfeet.com.

 Now You Try It: Surfing O*Net

Now's your chance to try a bit of Internet research through O*Net. You'll have a chance to do much more at the end of the chapter, but this will help you gain some familiarity with the site. Currently, green energy is an industry that is greatly expanding. In this exercise you will find out more about it.

1. Go to the O*Net website, www.online.onetcenter.org.
2. Go to the **Green Occupations** section on the right side of the screen.
3. Click **Learn More** and the Green Economy page appears.
4. From this page, select the **Green Sectors** tab for a list of sectors associated with green energy.

   - Click each sector for a description.
   - Decide which sector you are most interested in.

5. Return to the Green Economy page and click the **Online Search** tab.

   - From this tab, select your area of interest to see a list of associated jobs.
   - Click any job for a detailed description.
   - Find one or two jobs you're interested in.

6. Now return to the Green Economy page and click the **Green Occupations** tab.

   - This lets you find out which occupations have increased demand, which require new skills, and which occupations are new and emerging.
   - Do the jobs you selected fit any of those categories?

7. Just for fun, visit the Bureau of Labor Statistics Occupational Outlook Handbook website and research opportunities in wind energy.

   - Go to www.bls.gov/green/wind_energy.
   - Explore the information about wind energy and where the greatest opportunities exist.

Hopefully this short exercise will help familiarize you with O*Net and the Occupational Outlook Handbook. These are great sites for learning more about the myriad of occupations available to you.

Learning from Experience
A Perspective from the Working World

From Layoff to Freelance

Marilyn Roberts,
freelance writer and
usability specialist

Getting laid off is never pleasant, but sometimes it opens up opportunities you never thought you had. At least that was my experience.

For years I'd worked for various high-tech firms as a technical writer and trainer, writing computer manuals and developing training courses. I'd also developed quite a reputation as a software usability specialist, helping companies design more friendly and intuitive software. After all, when you spend most of your time trying to teach people how to use complicated software, you come up with some good ideas about how to make the software easier to use.

Each time I worked for a new software company, I gained more skills and got better at what I did. At some point, though, I would come to the conclusion that there was nothing left to learn and it was time to move on. I gave each job my best and each company was sorry to see me go. I always got rave letters of recommendation and felt good about the experience.

I believe I was doing excellent work and making a difference in the world of software. But then my entire department was laid off. Let me tell you, being told to leave was a lot different than *me* telling a company I planned to go. After the layoff, I felt battered, angry, and in shock. I couldn't think. I didn't want to talk to anyone. I didn't even have the energy to update my resume. How could I possibly explore new job opportunities when I felt like that?

Thank heavens for a slip of paper in the folder my former employer gave me when I was laid off. The paper listed the address, phone number, and website of our local workforce center. It turns out the center was only four blocks from my home and I never knew it existed!

I visited the workforce center website and discovered a number of helpful workshops on resume writing, cover letters, interviewing, networking, and nontraditional job searches. As a writer and presenter, I felt very comfortable with resumes and interviews. But the other stuff—networking and job searches? I felt very uncomfortable with them. After all, my jobs had always fallen in my lap. I never had to look for them. And after being laid off for the first time in 25 years (and six jobs), my self-confidence had really plummeted. I needed to find out how to talk to people and find out about jobs.

I signed up for the nontraditional job search workshop. During that workshop I was introduced to O*Net, and that website really opened my eyes to the fact that there were lots of other types of writing I could do besides technical writing—Web content writing, marketing writing, textbook writing, magazine writing. I also learned that my natural tendency to open up to people and talk about myself (and ask questions about them) made me a natural networker. And I learned that my personality would allow me to easily move into self-employment, something I'd never considered.

As odd as it may seem, it took a layoff to make me see all the other great opportunities out there that I'd never even considered! I suddenly realized I could be a freelance writer. All I needed to do was find a client. It took about four more months, but I eventually found my first freelance writing client, a correspondence school, and I began writing and editing their textbooks. Next, I found a college that needed help with a website. Then I found a clinic that needed marketing materials and a software company that needed help with its manuals. I was on my way!

It's been eight years since my layoff, and I've expanded my writing skills and my client base considerably. I like what I do, I like my clients, and I feel I'm making a difference. And to some extent, I owe it all to a layoff, the workforce center, and O*Net!

Understanding Job Creation

Up to this point, you've looked at the different places where you might learn about possible jobs. But have you thought about how jobs are created in the first place? A good understanding of the job creation process helps you realize where and when to look for a job, instead of waiting until it hits the local newspaper.

There are four phases to creating a job within any company, as shown in Figure 5.1:

- **Stage 1.** There are no job openings because all personnel needs are met. This is still a good time to talk to people within the company to find out more about the company culture, its products and services, and its hiring practices. The very act of talking to managers at the company may get them thinking about some unmet needs they didn't even realize they had. When the company decides to meet that need, they will remember you because you stopped by to talk to them and dropped off your resume.

- **Stage 2.** No formal openings exist, but managers know of a job that will become available. For example, maybe someone is moving to another state or taking maternity leave. Maybe a new project is starting up and the team will need another member with specific skills. Or, maybe the company has been having problems in a certain area and knows it will eventually need to hire someone to help resolve the issue. This is a great time to talk to people. You might learn that someone is leaving, a new project is starting up, or a department is expanding. You'll be able to submit your resume long before anyone else does.

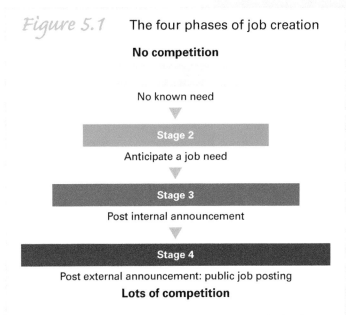

Figure 5.1   The four phases of job creation

- **Stage 3.** The human resources department announces a job opening internally. People within the company are aware of the opening, but it hasn't been posted externally for the rest of the world to see. The company is hoping that its own employees may know someone who's right for the job. If you hear about a job at this stage, submit your resume immediately and beat the rush!

- **Stage 4.** The opening is now official. The job description has been posted online and in print. You are now competing with everyone else who can read the job advertisement. It's now a bit tougher to stand out from the crowd and get noticed because you have a lot more competition.

What can you do to minimize your competition during the job hunt process? Get involved during stages 1 through 3 to tap the "hidden" job market. Read on to find out how.

Tapping the Hidden Job Market

When it comes to jobs, one of the most important things to realize is that by the time a job is advertised online or in print, hundreds, if not thousands, of other people are reading the ad and getting ready to apply. That's a lot of competition, and it exists because you are dealing with the open job market—jobs that are formally posted.

However, there's a whole other job market you can explore to reduce the competition: the hidden job market. The hidden job market consists of jobs that have not yet hit the classified ads in the newspapers or the online postings. In fact, companies may not even realize they need people to do these jobs.

Think of an iceberg. Approximately 20% of the iceberg is visible, while 80% lies beneath the surface. The open job market is the tip of the iceberg that's visible and the hidden job market is what lies beneath the surface. This means that only a small portion of potential jobs are advertised.

Did you know that companies dislike hunting for new employees as much as people dislike hunting for new jobs? Finding the right person takes time, and many employers never advertise their openings because they prefer to hire someone who is referred to them by their employees, business associates, friends, and families. These are the people they trust. In other words, the hidden job market

A large hidden job market lies beneath the surface of a relatively small advertised job market.

depends on word-of-mouth advertising—people who know about these opportunities tell other people, who tell others, and so on.

For example, suppose Lauren is considering leaving her current job because it offers little opportunity for advancement or creativity. She shares an idea with her friend, Elisha, that she'd like to try her hand at graphic design. Lauren's been doing design work in her current job on an informal basis, and thinks she has a knack for it. However, she has no formal training. When Elisha gets home, she shares Lauren's story with her husband, Darnell. The next day at work, Darnell learns that the marketing communication department at his company is looking for an entry-level graphic designer to assist with online and print materials. The manager has not yet posted a job opening and is trying to figure out the best way to find a qualified candidate.

You can imagine what happens. Darnell comes home that evening and tells Elisha about the position. Elisha gets on the phone and tells Lauren. And the rest is up to Lauren!

Of course, you may not find a potential job in the hidden job market as quickly as Lauren did, but you can talk to people from companies you're interested in and look for opportunities such as the following:

- Positions that are still in the planning stages
- Positions that may become available because of employees moving, resigning, or retiring
- Positions that will be created because of new or expanded projects
- Positions that will result from new corporate plans or reorganizations

If you're not sure how to talk to people about these opportunities, you're not alone. Talking to strangers is not something with which everyone is comfortable. However, to successfully conduct your job hunt, you will have to become comfortable networking with people you don't know. That's why we have devoted the entire next chapter to the fine art of networking!

---

[2]Fraser, Jane E. "How long should you stay in your job?" *The Big Chair: Career Couch.* Aug. 29, 2010. Accessed 8 Nov. 2010 from http://thebigchair.com.au/news/career-couch/when-to-move-on

Now You Try It: Taking Advantage of the Hidden Job Market

Think back to a job you got that was not advertised. This can be a part-time or full-time job that you had as an adolescent or as an adult.

1. What was it?

2. How did you find it?

3. How did you get it?

That was an example of you tapping the hidden job market—and you probably didn't even know it at the time.

Finding Time

Trying to contact employers during the early stages of the job creation process can be time consuming. Some experts estimate that a job search can take 1 month for every $10,000 you want to make.[3] Some people find jobs in much shorter periods of time, and for others it takes longer.

To maximize your chances of finding the right a job, you need to commit yourself to the task at hand. If you can only dedicate a couple of hours to your job search, expect the process to take longer than someone who can dedicate eight hours a day. Researching your ideal job is not a race—it takes as long as it takes. Be realistic about the amount of time you can dedicate to your job search and carve out a few hours a week to work on your job search. Be persistent and consistent in your job research. Sure, the desire to spend an hour watching television, calling friends, or listening to music might be strong, but it will only distract you and take time away from your job research. In the next chapter you'll learn how to make your job research time really count by using effective networking.

Staying Flexible

Finding jobs in the open or hidden market can be stressful. To reduce the stress, you'll need to practice all the stress management techniques you learned earlier in Chapter 4. In addition, you'll need to learn to stay flexible, yet set boundaries.

Flexibility can help when you don't get exactly what you want. For example, perhaps your online job research turns up a job that sounds absolutely perfect for you. When you talk to someone within the company, you learn the position requires more experience than you have or a different level of education. However, an entry-level position is available for which you're highly qualified. The problem? The entry-level position has a much lower salary.

What do you do? Give up on the original job and look elsewhere? Apply for the original job and lie about your experience? Apply for the entry-level job? Hopefully, the first two options do not appeal to you. Instead, you might consider applying for the entry-level position and, if the company really likes you, negotiate a higher salary. Or, you might be able to negotiate for a raise within a certain amount

Finding the right job can be stressful, so it's important to stay flexible.

[3]Barrett-Pointdexter, Jacqui. "Failing in Your Job Search? Here Are 5 Things You Must Do." *U.S. News,* August 20, 2012. Accessed on August 29, 2012, from http://money.usnews.com/money/blogs/outside-voices-careers/2012/08/20/flailing-in-your-job-search-here-are-5-things-you-must-do

of time. Or, perhaps your employer might be willing to financially assist you in getting a certification that would allow you to apply for the higher-paying job later. You never know.

If you have flexible expectations about wages, location, hours, and job titles, you will probably find employment more quickly. You will learn about salary negotiations later in this book.

Of course, there is such a thing as being too flexible and settling for a job you do not really want or that is wrong for you. That's why it's important to know your boundaries. You do this by identifying your minimum requirements. These might include:

- The minimum salary you can live on
- The area(s) of the country where you are willing to work
- The type of work environment (people and physical surroundings) that you can tolerate
- The work style that works best for you (for example, highly structured vs. informal)
- The length of commute you can handle without excessive stress
- The maximum number of hours you can work without harming your health or family relationships

By clearly identifying your limits, you will be better able to negotiate for what you want when a potential job opportunity does arise.

 ## Now You Try It: Your Job Search

1. Have you ever quit a job, been laid off, fired, or desperate to find a job?
2. How long did it take to find the next job?
3. Was the job you eventually got one you really liked or one that you took because you needed it at that time?
4. Did you negotiate at all for the job tasks, salary, or hours?
5. How long did you end up spending in the job you took?

Your answers to these questions may show that during a job hunt, we can forget what our minimum requirements or limits are if we're feeling desperate.

Exploring Your Options

Careers are all about possibilities, and we hope this chapter has provided you with a few tools to explore your options. When you are considering careers, it helps to know where to go to find the information you need. By doing upfront job research, you increase the possibility that you will find the right job for your geographic location, skill set, personality profile, and future plans. Once you decide on the right career and job, it will be time to start the hard work of networking, putting together resumes and cover letters, and interviewing. As we mentioned, all of these things will be addressed in the upcoming chapters.

Your Tool Kit at Work

Now it's time for some hands-on practice—a chance to do some career exploration on your own.

5.1 Find the Site, Find the Publication

When you are interested in a particular career, it's always a good idea to learn more about it through professional organizations and publications. Of course, if you don't know what the organizations or publications are, it's tough to know where to start. This activity should help you find those organizations and publications by using WEDDLE's.

1. Go to www.weddles.com/associations/index.cfm.

2. Look through the Association Directory for a category that interests you and click that job category.

3. Scroll through the list of resulting associations and select one.

4. When you arrive at its website, explore the site. Then answer these questions:
   - How do you become a member?
   - Can you subscribe to its publication?
   - Where is its nearest chapter?
   - Are there any events you can attend?

5.2   Conduct Your Online Research

Whether you've never had a job, love the one you're in, or want to find another job, it never hurts to learn more about what's out there. In this activity you have a chance to explore occupations you may have never considered by visiting the three online career websites mentioned earlier in this chapter. This should give you a chance to find out more about various careers, as well as discover which website works best for you.

O*Net

1. Go to www.online.onetcenter.org.

2. Under Advanced Search, select **Skills Search** and click the arrow.
   - From the Skills Search page, put a checkmark next to each skill that you currently have and click **Go**. A list of all occupations using those skills appears.
   - Click any specific occupation to learn more about it (view both its **Summary** and **Details** tabs).
   - Write down what you learn.

3. Return to the home page.

4. Under **Find Occupations,** select a particular career cluster and click the arrow.
   - From within that cluster, browse for a particular career area (for example, **Education and Training**).
   - Select a particular career and check out its **Summary** and **Details** tabs to learn more about tasks, wages, and career trends.
   - Find out the average salary for your state.

5. Write down what you learn.

America's Career Infonet

1. Go to www.acinet.org.

2. Click Industry Information.
   - Find out the fastest-growing industries and industries with the highest employment rates.
   - Select one of the industries that interests you and study its **Industry Profile**. In the **Industry Description** section, note the various occupations within that industry.

3. Return to the home page and select **Occupation**.
   - Look for one of the occupations you identified and study its description.

4. Write down any key information.

Occupational Outlook Handbook

1. Go to www.bls.gov/ooh.
2. Hover over one of the occupational categories in the list on the left side of the page. If a pop-up menu appears, click the category of interest.
   - From the resulting list of occupations, select one of interest.
   - Read about the nature of the work, necessary training, and job outlook.
3. Write down anything of interest.

Based on your experiences with the three websites, which one was easiest to use and provided the most valuable information for your needs? We hope you return to it later to assist you with your personal job research.

5.3 Setting Limits and Finding Time

Sometimes the most difficult aspect of career exploration or a job hunt is figuring out the minimum requirements for the job of your dreams and finding the time to explore that dream.

1. Let's start by setting some limits. Based on your current or anticipated needs, what are your minimum requirements for a job? Sometimes it's also useful to write down what you *won't* accept in addition to what you *will*.
   - Hourly wage or yearly salary
   - Location
   - Commute
   - Travel
   - Physical environment
   - Type of work
   - Type of people
   - Hours per day
2. Based on the career exploration you did in Activity 5.2, what careers might be a good fit? Feel free to revisit the occupations on any of the research websites with your minimum requirements in mind.
3. What days of the week and times of the day are best for you to conduct your career exploration and job hunt? Even if it's only 15 minutes a day, write it down.

Day	Time(s)

Now that you have a particular career in mind and a set of minimum requirements, you should be able to make better use of your time for further exploration.

5.4 Plug Your Knowledge into Real Life

Let's take what you've learned about career exploration and apply it to the situation that Maya finds herself in.

Maya currently works as a receptionist at a GIS (geographic information systems) company. Most of the people she sees each day are computer programmers developing software that is supposed to help the average person view and print maps. Occasionally, the programmers ask Maya to be their informal software usability tester. They ask her to test the new software and tell them how easy or hard the software is to use. The programmers tell Maya she is a great software tester because she always finds problems with the software they never knew existed. Maya really enjoys testing the software. She likes being able to sit quietly and concentrate on the computer, instead of being interrupted by phones, people, email, and faxes, which is what her normal day as a receptionist is all about.

However, Maya knows she doesn't have a degree and isn't sure if she has the skills to be a software tester. Plus, she doesn't know what possibilities exist in the GIS field or how she would ever be able to get into the field.

Pretend you are Maya's friend and she shared her dream of being a GIS software tester with you. Based on the information you learned in this chapter, what would you suggest that Maya do? Write a paragraph describing what you would tell Maya.

5.5 Moving Beyond the Computer

Most of the activities you've performed have involved using websites to explore careers, and this one starts out this way. The difference is, you will actually have to get away from your computer and do some real interacting with people!

1. Use the Internet to search for a workforce center near you. Once you are on the workforce center's website, find out what types of workshops and services they have. Do any sound interesting? If so, sign up for one.

2. Next, explore the site to discover any job tools and tips.
   - Does the site require you to register to look for jobs?
   - Are there job counselors you can talk to?

3. Call the workforce center to make an appointment to visit it so you can personally meet some people there and find out what's available. After your visit, write down the different ways you plan to use the workforce center.

Get the Hang of Networking

Tools That Create Opportunity

Many hands make light work.

John Heywood

learning objectives

- What is networking and how is it valuable?
- Where do you find people to build your network?
- What is a mentor and how can a mentor help you in your job hunt?
- What is an elevator pitch?
- What is an informational interview and why is it important?
- How does shadowing work?
- What are street smarts and how do they help you?
- How do you evaluate the job opportunities you find?

For the first time in their lives, Tina and her daughter Ashley find themselves in very similar situations. Tina recently was laid off from a large electronics manufacturer where she worked as a technical writer, and Ashley just graduated with a degree in ecotourism. Both are looking for jobs in a "down" economy. Tina knows she's going to have to look for work in a different field, because there is only one electronics manufacturer in town and she has no intention of moving. Ashley doesn't care where she lives; she just wants to get a foot in the door somewhere doing the type of work she believes she will love—taking people on guided tours and sharing her love of the natural world with them.

Both mother and daughter attend a workshop at the local workforce center and decide that to find jobs they will have to tap the hidden job market because the open market has so few jobs. The only way to do that is through networking. They each work on a list of possible contacts, starting with friends and family. They slowly work through their lists, using the approach the workforce center suggested—developing an elevator pitch and playing detective by following every lead. Within a few weeks they are actually starting to enjoy their job detective work. They have each managed to find friends of friends of friends who have provided them with some excellent leads.

Tina talked to a number of writers in town, one who worked for a marketing company, one who worked for a magazine, and one who worked for a technical college. Tina realized she would probably enjoy writing course workbooks even more than she'd enjoyed writing electronics manuals. Ashley talked to several professors in the environmental sciences and sustainable business departments, one of whom had stayed in touch with a graduate student now working in Puerto Rico. Ashley contacted the grad student by email and learned about several ecotourism outfits there. She realized that working in Puerto Rico would be a dream come true.

Now mom and daughter are ready to put together their resumes and cover letters to approach the companies they discovered.

Tina and Ashley are good examples of people who effectively used networking to tap the hidden job market and learn more about job opportunities. Even in a difficult economy, they were able to find some excellent leads, and so can you.

By now, we know you've gained valuable insight into your own personality and improved the basic skills that will let you think and communicate clearly. We also hope you've gained the self-confidence that comes from understanding your own skills and talents. Better yet, by now you've spent some time researching possible careers that would suit you. Now is your

myth

"The best way to find a job is by posting your resume on Monster.com."

reality

This is a common but incorrect belief. The most effective way to find a job is through your people connections: your family, friends, teachers, and so forth. Life is about helping each other and building and sustaining relationships with others. Build your relationships. Help others. Create a network.

chance to put your abilities to the test in the real world and find the right job in the hidden job market through the magic of networking.

This chapter shows you how to network effectively to learn more about your chosen field and discover jobs in the hidden job market. It shows you how to seek help from a variety of sources, including friends and family, school, organizations, and social networking groups. It explains the ins and outs of informational interviewing and shadowing, and helps you develop the street smarts to evaluate what you learn during your networking activities.

Networking: The People Connection

Network, *verb*

to develop contacts and exchange information with others, as to further a career

Networking is an informal way to meet and stay in touch with people so you can give and get help as needed.

Let's say that you've done your research and know the kind of career that will best suit your skills, talents, and interests. Now what? How do you find a job in that career? As you learned in the last chapter, looking through the want ads or checking the job postings on Monster.com is probably not your best bet. Instead, you should be tapping the hidden job market. But how do you do that? You **network**!

For many people, the idea of networking sounds difficult, time consuming, and uncomfortable. That's because many people mistakenly think that networking means going to business functions, flashing a business card, and making small talk with strangers. In reality, networking is nothing more than reaching out to people you know and people you don't to learn something about them while they learn something about you. It's about making connections and exchanging information. In fact, you probably network every day and just don't realize it. Any time you have lunch with a friend, talk to a relative, or strike up a conversation with someone in the grocery store or dry cleaners, you are actually networking. Sure, the conversation may not be about work, but it is networking nonetheless.

The nice thing about networking is that even when it's about finding a job, it can easily be part of your daily life. For example, perhaps you tell your hairdresser or bank teller about the type of work you are looking for. They come in contact with lots of people on a daily basis; maybe they know someone you can talk to. Or maybe you share some information about your job hunt with another parent at one of your children's sports or school events. You never know what will come of these conversations. That's what networking is all about—putting yourself out there.

Giving and Getting

Networking is more than asking people for a favor or trying to get something, and it is certainly not something you do only when you are looking for a job. Networking is about giving and getting help any time. After all, a network of people helping each other is what makes the entire business world go around—people helping each other learn on the job; people finding jobs through connections, references, advice, and recommendations; and people making contacts and boosting business for one another. Networking is all about people working together, cooperating, and helping each other succeed.

The basic guideline of networking is simple: Treat others the way you would like to be treated. Don't just think about what you can get from others; think about what you can give. Sure, you're looking for a job, but so are lots of people. Maybe there is something you could do to help another person find a job. Perhaps you have some inside information from a former employer or know someone who might be a good contact. Maybe you could look over the person's resume or have coffee with the individual while he or she bounces ideas off you. We call this "giving to get." When you offer your time and energy to someone with no expectations, they are much more likely to help you in the future.

This doesn't mean that every individual you meet in your working life will help you (although many of them will). However, you might be surprised at how casual acquaintanceships develop into mutually rewarding relationships simply by staying in touch, or how sharing ideas and helping one another transforms professional relationships into lifelong friendships.

The Value of Networking

Still not convinced that networking is for you? Think about people in your life who have been important to you. Now consider how many of these people you are still in contact with. If you are like most of us, you may have lost contact with a number of these people. We regret losing these friends and relationships, but somehow they have slipped away. To maintain contact or reconnect we need to network on a regular basis.

Networking can be as easy as periodically picking up the phone to talk, sending an email, or getting together for coffee. As you network with others, you might discover a great restaurant or a nearby weekend getaway. You might hear about an exciting new job opportunity or learn how to fix an annoying problem at work. Networking offers you the opportunity to give or receive advice. Maybe a friend is considering a move to a different company and wants your perspective. Perhaps another friend is looking for a job and needs your help. Or maybe you've been asked to work on a project you know little about and need to ask a coworker for assistance. The more you open up to others and expand your network, the greater the chance that you will be able to help others or they will be able to help you.

Your life is enriched when you network and share ideas day after day, week after week, year after year. By doing so, you will enlarge your world of experiences and multiply the number of opportunities you see in your lifetime—opportunities that will help you fulfill your potential and achieve your dreams.

Building Your Network

Now that you understand the importance of networking, let's look at ways to build your network. It's best to start with people you know or have known—friends, family, teachers, former employers, members of community organizations, or team members from recreational activities.

When you network, it's natural to turn to people you know and in whom you have confidence. These are people you feel comfortable asking for help, and people who feel comfortable helping. The idea behind networking is to put yourself out there and talk to people without the expectation that any particular contact will lead to employment. Networking is kind of an organic process—you talk to one person who puts you in touch with another person, who leads you to another person, and so on and so forth. Just like a detective following leads, you never know which lead dead ends and which will help you solve the case—or in this situation, find you a job.

So, where does your network come from? Let's look at Figure 6.1 for some possible networking sources. The rest of

technology *at work*

As you meet more and more people, keeping track of names, addresses, and phone numbers becomes increasingly difficult. You can organize this information any number of ways: in a card file, in an address book, in your email address book, in your PDA, in a file on your computer, or in your cell phone. Remember, it's always wise to have a hard copy of your contact list in case any of your electronic devices fail!

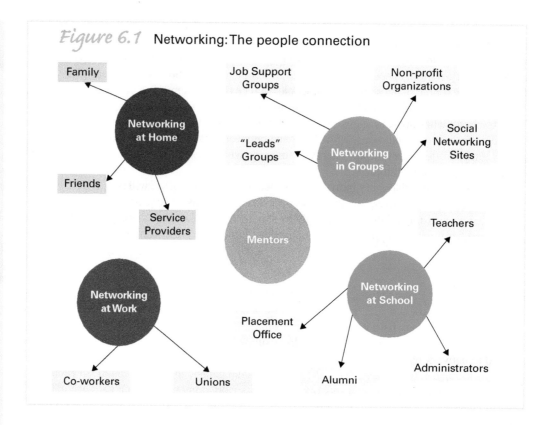

Figure 6.1 Networking: The people connection

this section will help you identify possible networking sources, but it will not delve into what to say as you network. That comes later in the chapter.

Networking at Home

It's always a good idea to start networking with the people you know the best—your friends and family. These are people you already feel comfortable with, so it shouldn't be too difficult to talk to them.

Family

There may be quite a few people in your circle of acquaintances who work in a field that interests you. First, think of your family. Do you have a family member who works at a job that you may like? If you do, make a point to set up a little appointment to talk with them about what they do. That way, you'll be focused enough to take advantage of the knowledge that they can offer you.

Family networking is a good thing. Think about family businesses, or people you know who work with friends or members of their family. People like to hire other people that they know they can trust. As a friend or family member, you have already built a base of trust, respect, and affection. It makes sense that you would have a jump on the competition. Make the most of such a situation if it comes your way.

Friends

What about your friends? Do you have a friend who knows a lot of people? Even though he or she may know nothing about the kind of work you want to get into, that individual may know someone who does. Do you have any friends who work in the field where you plan to seek employment? Perhaps this is the time to "talk shop" with them, discover more about what they do, and find out about opportunities that might exist at their companies.

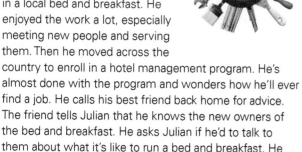

A Networking Tale

Back home, Julian spent summers working as a waiter in a local bed and breakfast. He enjoyed the work a lot, especially meeting new people and serving them. Then he moved across the country to enroll in a hotel management program. He's almost done with the program and wonders how he'll ever find a job. He calls his best friend back home for advice. The friend tells Julian that he knows the new owners of the bed and breakfast. He asks Julian if he'd to talk to them about what it's like to run a bed and breakfast. He says they're very friendly and might have some advice or contacts for him. Julian is very glad he called his friend.

Did You Know?   If your world only consists of your family, work, and school, you will have a more difficult time identifying and evaluating employment in a new field or a different industry. That's why it is important to keep current by reading news magazines or newspapers (in print or online) on a regular basis. This will help you understand important trends and better identify and evaluate employment opportunities. Stay in touch with your world!

Even if your friends don't work in your field, ask them about opportunities anyway. You may find certain companies that specialize in one product or service, but need people with all sorts of backgrounds or training. For example, a tax preparation firm needs both tax preparers to work with tax returns and administrative assistants to keep track of the work and the clients. A computer repair firm needs computer repair persons to do the technical work and customer service personnel to take phone calls. Don't rule out anything until you have explored your options.

Service Providers

When people network, they often think they should only talk to people in jobs that are similar to theirs. But in reality, many professionals work so hard at their own jobs that they have little time to do anything else and are often unaware of other jobs around them. They know their coworkers, and that's about it. However, people in service professions, such as bank tellers, hairdressers, nurses, and doctors, typically come in contact with a large number and a variety of people every day. That's why they make such great initial contacts in your networking efforts. The next time you're talking to your insurance agent or bank teller, you might ask if he or she has any customers who might be good contacts for you.

Networking in Groups

As you reach beyond your friends, family, and service providers, you might consider networking within already established groups. These are usually organizations comprised of people with similar goals, interests, or backgrounds who get together on a regular basis.

Job Search Support Groups

Job search support groups are very helpful when you are transitioning from one career to another, or after you have been fired or laid off. These groups provide a safe environment for people to talk about their experiences, share job leads, and network with others. Many people are more comfortable networking in a group in which everyone is in the same situation—without a job. These groups often bring in speakers from around the community who provide valuable information about the local job market, job search techniques, and resources. Check with your local workforce center for a job search support group near you.

Community and Nonprofit Organizations

Volunteering is a great way to network. Not only do you have a chance to use your skills and talents in new ways that help others, you get the opportunity to learn new skills and experience a different type of work. Plus, you get to meet a lot of people. Sometimes the people you meet know other people who can assist you with your job hunt. Sometimes a volunteer activity opens your eyes to a different career than you intended to pursue. And

A Networking Tale

Marianna did some volunteer gardening and yard cleanup for a local neighbor-to-neighbor organization. She enjoyed the experience and offered to help once a month. Each month that she volunteered, she learned more about the organization and visited many of the apartment buildings it maintained for low-income tenants. She noticed that a particular janitorial service, Mighty Clean, handled all apartment cleaning when tenants moved out. Marianna chatted with some of the cleaning personnel and learned that Mighty Clean hired people on a part-time basis with flexible hours, and even provided healthcare benefits.

Marianna decided to talk to the owner of Mighty Clean to learn more about the company and mentioned that she had a lot of housecleaning experience herself. A few months later, the owner contacted her because neighbor-to-neighbor added another apartment complex to their roster and the owner of Mighty Clean had to expand his staff to accommodate cleaning 12 additional units. Was Marianna interested? Of course she was!

sometimes, a volunteer organization may eventually hire you if they like the work you've done. You never know.

"Lead" Organizations

There are actually organizations out there that specialize in helping people network by generating leads for one another. These organizations often target self-employed people who need to constantly acquire new clients. The organizations usually host networking events to attract new people, and then put people into small groups where they can help one another without competing. (Some networking organizations have a membership fee, while others are free.) For example, one group might consist of a hairdresser, realtor, insurance salesperson, and auto mechanic. The idea is that each member of the group generates leads for the other members of the group. For example, suppose the auto mechanic has a client who comes in for a tire rotation and mentions she's trying to sell her house. The mechanic could refer her to the realtor in his networking group.

Social Gatherings

Though you might not think so, a holiday party, a BBQ, or a birthday party can be the perfect place to do some networking. People are relaxed and more willing to listen to strangers. Of course, in these social situations, it's probably more important that you keep your personal introduction short and set up another time to discuss your job search in more detail. After all, people are coming to the party to enjoy themselves, not listen to a sales pitch.

A Networking Tale

Troy takes his son, Casey, to a neighborhood birthday party. They arrive early and Troy helps the hostess, Lynne, move tables and chairs to the backyard. She is very thankful for his help and Troy tells her it's no trouble—after all, it's what he does for a living. He mentions that he and his brother just started their own moving company after working for one of the largest moving companies in the nation for 10 years. He gives her a business card and asks her to please tell her friends. Troy has no idea that Lynne's parents are moving in a month or so and desperately need some assistance, and Lynne plans to tell them about Troy.

Social Networking Sites

For those of you who might be more introverted, have only a small circle of acquaintances, or feel uncomfortable talking to strangers in person, you might try visiting business-related social networking sites to expand your network.

In general, social networking sites allow you to do three things: (1) set up an account with a username, password, and profile; (2) identify others on the system with whom you have a relationship (friends and contacts); and (3) view your list of connections and those made by others within the system.

LinkedIn is a popular business-oriented social networking site with more than 70 million registered users, spanning more than 200 countries and territories.[1] This social networking site helps professionals connect with past and present colleagues, discover jobs and business opportunities, connect with people within their network, join online groups, and ask and answer business-related questions.

Many businesses "troll" LinkedIn profiles, searching for individuals with the skills and experience they need. That's why it's so important for LinkedIn users to keep their profiles up to date. Companies also post job openings on LinkedIn. In addition, many LinkedIn users join special-interest groups for people in their career fields. This lets them meet other professionals in their field, widen their network, and ask or answer questions related to their professions.

A typical LinkedIn profile consists of the information listed in Table 6.1. It is valuable to collect this information even if you do not plan to join LinkedIn. Figure 6.2 illustrates part of an actual profile on LinkedIn (the individual's name is missing). Once the profile is created, it will be up to you to begin contacting people to join your network, and then to ask people in your network to write you a referral. Many companies look at this information when evaluating potential job candidates.

---

[1]Neal, David. "LinkedIn claims 70 million users worldwide." June 10, 2010. Accessed July 20, 2010, from www.v3.co.uk/v3/news/2264529/uk-businesses-link-linkedin

Table 6.1	LinkedIn Profile Information
Section	**Description**
Executive Summary	This is where you make some key statements about who you are, what you're good at, what you like to do, and where your experience lies. The idea behind the summary is that if someone decides to read your profile and only scans it for a few seconds, the executive summary will tell them enough about you to get them curious and make them want to read more.
Key Skills or Specialties	This is where you list the things you are good at, the skills you have, and how you have used those skills to help people and businesses accomplish their goals.
Experience	This is where you list your three most recent jobs or positions (employee, freelance, or volunteer). Briefly cover the skills you used, what you accomplished, and how your work benefited the individual or company.

Figure 6.2   Sample LinkedIn profile

Name, Technical Writer and Usability Consultant

Summary

My goal is to make the complex simple.

- I work with high-tech, low-tech, and no-tech companies to create easy-to-read documents, easy-to-navigate websites, and easy-to-use software.
- I take esoteric and philosophical material and make it engaging and understandable for the layperson.
- No fluff, no filler, no fanfare—just plain and simple writing and design. That's my style.

Specialties

- Websites and software interfaces: audience definition, site organization and layout, visual mock-ups, website content, usability evaluation
- Educational materials: user guides, manuals, online help, training, textbooks
- Proposals: contract bids, responses to corporate or government RFPs and RFQs
- Technical and marketing materials: data sheets, case studies, success stories, white papers, brochures, press releases, resumes, cover letters
- PowerPoint presentations: sales, technical, educational

Experience
Freelance Writer and Usability Specialist (self-employed)
UI Writer

January 2007–Present (3 years 11 months)

Develop educational and informative materials, websites, and software that are attractive, intuitive, and easy-to-use to ensure a positive customer experience.

Currently providing the following services to clients:

- Technical and marketing writing, editing
- Textbooks and training materials
- Website planning and content
- Software interface design mockups, usability tests
- Articles and press releases
- Proposals and presentations

Usability and Technical Communications Specialist
OPTIMUS Corporation

May 2005–December 2006 (1 year 8 months)

(continued)

Figure 6.2 *(Continued)*

Proposal Writing:

- Co-wrote winning proposals for new commercial and government business software projects (valued at over $1.2 million)

Marketing Writing:

- Wrote customer-focused data sheets, white papers, case studies, and ads for flagship products

Website Design and Usability:

- Led corporate website makeover project (evaluation, information architecture, navigation, wire frame mockups, and content) for company "reinvention"

Interface Design and Usability:

- Developed compelling wire frame mockups for commercial and government applications to ensure usability and accelerate the development cycle (valued at over $800 K)

Learning Materials:

- Developed easy-to-read user guide for military personnel who typically had little time to learn the software

---

Did You Know? Your LinkedIn profile is public. Anyone can view it, even if he or she is not a member of LinkedIn. Be sure your profile contains only information that you want the public to see. Keep it updated so people who view it are not looking at outdated information. If you join a lot of groups, you may receive a large amount of email from members asking questions or responding to them. Reading those emails takes time, so use discretion when deciding which groups to join.

 NowYou Try It: Social Networking 101

Whether you already are a member of a social networking group or not, this is your chance to visit LinkedIn and learn more about it. Even existing members may learn a thing or two.

1. Visit the LinkedIn website, www.linkedin.com.
2. Go to the bottom of the page and click the **About** link.
3. When the **About Us** page appears, look at the contents listed on the left side.

   - Find the **Company Overview** category and click **Company History** to learn more about LinkedIn. Then click **Back** to return to the About Us page.
   - Find the **Resource Center** category and click **FAQs and Stats** for some quick facts about LinkedIn. Then click **Back** to return to the About Us page.
   - Find the **Related Links** category and click **Learning Center**.

4. When the Learning Center page appears, the table of contents changes. This is a great section of the website where you can get more details about how to use LinkedIn. Click any of these links:

Site Features
- Profiles
- Groups

User Guides
- New Users
- Students
- Job Seekers

This should give you a good idea of the power of LinkedIn. You'll have a chance to become a member of LinkedIn at the end of this chapter.

Networking in Industry

If you are already employed, it's never too late to start networking. You probably already know some people at your current job or former job who can become part of your network.

Company Contacts

If you are currently employed and thinking about changing jobs, you may be able to talk to people within your own company who do the type of work you are interested in. This is your chance to learn more about the opportunities and challenges in a particular field of interest. Your coworkers might also know people within the company whom you can contact.

Past work acquaintances are also important contacts. They have worked closely with you and are familiar with what you can do, so they can offer advice tailored to your own particular talents and needs. When it comes to helping you find job opportunities, they are more likely to put you in touch with potential employers if they feel they trust your work enough to recommend it.

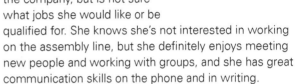

A Networking Tale

Krista works as an administrative assistant at a large electronics manufacturer. She would like to move up in the company, but is not sure what jobs she would like or be qualified for. She knows she's not interested in working on the assembly line, but she definitely enjoys meeting new people and working with groups, and she has great communication skills on the phone and in writing.

Krista has noticed that people in marketing often hold conferences and make presentations onsite. But beyond that, she has no idea what they do. She decides to talk to a friend of hers who is an administrative assistant in the marketing department. Her friend gives her the names of several folks in marketing, but Krista is concerned that they won't want to talk to her. "Don't worry," her friend says. "Marketing people love to talk about themselves. Ask them anything you want!"

Unions

If you are studying for a trade or are already in one (for example, machinist, electrician, construction worker), unions are a great networking source. Unions are formally organized groups of workers within the same trade who negotiate for good work standards, salaries, and benefits for their members. They have a lot of knowledge about the trade and the job market because they are directly involved. They monitor job conditions and take action when trouble arises.

Find out if your trade has a union; not every trade does. If there is a union, find out whether there is a local chapter in your area. Call the union's main office for information. Most unions have their national offices in Washington, D.C. If you know the exact name of the union, you can call Washington, D.C., information (202-555-1212) and get the phone number for the local chapter.

Once you have the location and phone number of your union, take initiative—call and ask to be transferred to the organizing or membership department. Make an appointment to talk with someone. Talk about your interest in this particular trade and what you are currently studying. The new ideas and energy that you'll bring to the trade may spark interest in you. Find out if you can talk to a member of the union about what it's like to be in the trade. This is called an *informational interview,* which you will learn more about later in the chapter.

Networking in School

Your school is not only the classes that you attend. It is also a network of people who can give you all kinds of practical advice about your career path. People at your school can help you broaden your network in many different directions. Who are they?

Teachers

Many of your teachers have worked, or may still be working, in the field they teach. They've had their own experiences and have learned valuable lessons that they can pass on to you. They can often offer valuable advice about what it's like to work in a particular field or how to break into that field. Teachers also have their own network of friends and business associates, and they can refer you to these individuals. By getting to know your teachers well, you may be able to hook into the network that they have already established. Ask teachers when they have some free time to talk, and make yourself available.

Administrators

Most school administrators are where they are because they've worked their way up through the ranks and demonstrated outstanding knowledge in the programs the school offers. Because their decisions about the school's direction strongly influence its success, their knowledge of the business world has to be up-to-the-minute. Take advantage of their business knowledge. They are there to help you.

Like teachers, administrators have an extensive network of contacts in place. If you have a particular kind of job in mind, don't be afraid to ask them if they could recommend any companies that you could contact. You have nothing to lose. Contact the school office and make an appointment to see an administrator.

Alumni

Some schools have alumni associations that continue to provide support, information, and job leads to its graduates and former students. Make a point to involve yourself in the alumni association once you graduate. Some alumni associations are free to join; others may charge a small yearly fee. Alumni associations hold regular meetings and often send newsletters to members. They usually have a website or a social networking site where members can connect with one another, post job opportunities, or respond to job postings. Some associations even hold workshops and other informational gatherings.

If your school does not have an alumni association, it may still have a list of successful working alumni who maintain contact with the school. Some of them may make an effort to hire graduates from the school and most will be happy to talk to you about your job aspirations. Alumni are a bridge between school and the outside world because they have experienced both sides.

Placement Counselors

Unlike your teachers, who are hired to teach and often give advice in their spare time, placement counselors are hired to advise you about the working world. A counselor's full-time job is to keep informed about all kinds of career opportunities and to pass that information on to you. Most schools employ one or more placement counselors full time. Meeting with them may even be part of your classwork.

If you are a working student, you may think that because you already have a job, you don't need career counseling. Your experience is valuable; however, since you are presently enrolled in this program, you probably want to make a change or take a step up your career ladder. Counselors can help you by looking at where you are and advise you on how you can get where you want to be.

When you visit your counselor, your meeting will most likely focus on current job opportunities. Counselors know about all kinds of

opportunities in your area and can often arrange interviews at company offices or even at your placement office. They will often point you toward internships or part-time jobs while you are still in school. Ask about internship and work-study programs with companies in your field of interest. If none is available, consider volunteering your time to an organization in which you can not only gain real-life experience in your area of interest, but also expand your network. Some counselors may take your resume and do a preliminary interview with you to decide which of the job opportunities they have may best suit you.

Placement counselors often keep in touch with graduates of your school who now make hiring decisions. It always helps to walk into an interview with a good recommendation from a respected and well-informed person—a dean, a counselor, an advisor, or a faculty member—at your school. Help them help you by seeking out their services.

Mentors

During your job hunt, there is often no better wisdom and advice than that which comes from a **mentor**. A mentor is someone you feel comfortable with who can offer advice and be your friend. Mentors develop a special interest in you and your success, and go out of their way to help you along your career path. A mentor watches over your progress and offers advice and support, often over a long period of time. Above all, a mentor is there for you when you need him or her, and always has your best interests at heart.

> **Mentor,** *noun*
>
> a wise, loyal advisor; a teacher or coach

You may already have a mentor, or a few, in your life. Your mentor may be a parent, an older brother or sister, a friend, or another family member. Your mentor may be a current or former employer, or a faculty member. No matter who you are, there are people in your life who know more than you do and have had more experiences. You need to respect that knowledge and be open to learning from it.

It's often hard to take advice from others. Having a mentor takes some courage because it requires you to be open to new ideas. It's an exchange; your mentor gives you words of wisdom and educational stories. Remember, you don't have to follow all of the advice that comes from your mentor. A true mentor would not expect you to do so. The most a mentor expects is that you will listen respectfully and consider the ideas offered.

If you don't yet have a mentor, don't force the issue with anyone. Mentoring relationships sprout on their own when you least expect them. Trust your gut instincts to lead you to a mentor you can trust. Your most important role with your mentor, or potential mentor, is to seek advice and be open to what you receive. You may develop a friendship that will be a part of your life for many years to come. Your mentor may learn from you as well, in which case, you both will be able to grow and develop together.

Pooling Your Resources

Dolores Nero
*Boutique owner and
culinary student*

My dream has always been to open my own restaurant. My grandmother loved to cook, my mother loved to cook, and so do I. Plus, people love my cooking. Although I work as a manager of a local boutique, I've done a lot of catering in my free time: special events at my church and local schools, festivals in the community, and a wedding for my best friend where over 100 people attended. All these jobs have given me real-world experience. And my "day job" has given me plenty of experience with marketing, negotiating with buyers, customer service, and order tracking. This kind of knowledge can help me in the future as well.

Since I'd like to eventually open a restaurant that serves foods related to my heritage, I've been collecting unique Caribbean recipes online and from my family and friends here and in the West Indies. Other people are helping me realize my dream, too. One of my salesgirls talked me into enrolling in culinary school. She brought in brochures for different cooking institutes and I did my own research to find a school that fit my budget and my schedule. I checked into financial aid at the school and they helped me get a grant toward my education. I still had to take out a small bank loan, but my longtime reputation as a successful business owner kept the interest rate low. I'm now going to class two nights a week so I can earn a certificate in restaurant management.

In addition to school, I know that networking is key to starting and maintaining a successful business. That's why I've been talking to my customers at the boutique, as well as making contacts with people in the restaurant and catering industry. The culinary school even helped with some of these important connections. For example, one of my school assignments was to interview the head chef of a unique vegetarian restaurant in town. I asked him lots of questions about what his job was like, how he got into his line of work, and what his plans were for the future. After the interview, he invited me to volunteer in his kitchen so I could learn more about meal preparation. I'm pretty sure I can use him as a reference when I finally set out on my own.

As I think about starting a new restaurant, I feel safer knowing that everything I've learned in the boutique business and all the customers I've gained will help me be successful. Of course, I will probably need some mentors along the way. When I look around at possible mentors, I realize that people have different strengths and weaknesses, and I admire them for who they are. For example, I look up to my minister's character and spiritual commitment. I admire the efficiency of a good friend who runs a local bakery. I've catered alongside a member of our Downtown Business Association who has a lot of business sense, and we get along really well. I know I could trust her as a business partner. Any of these people would be great mentors.

Unfortunately, it sometimes feels like school is taking over my life. When I'm not at work, I need to study; and when I'm not studying, I have to attend class. There are days when I wonder if the sacrifice is worth it. But then there are days when I know I'm doing the right thing. For example, one day I unexpectedly got a certificate of completion for my purchasing class in the mail. The certificate reminded me that I'm already on my way toward reaching my dream. With every step I take, I'm moving closer toward my goal. I don't plan on stopping now.

Connecting with Your Contacts

Now that you have your list of networking contacts, get in touch with them. What do you say? This section looks at different ways to communicate with your contacts and "dig" for information.

Initial Brief Personal Contacts

Some networking starts with a brief personal contact. For example, suppose you know that your dentist has many clients who are working professionals in your town. After your teeth cleaning appointment, you tell your hygienist that you just got laid off from a machinist job and are looking for contacts in the high-tech industry. You even think you could do other types of work besides machining. Although your hygienist might not know a lot about machining or the high-tech industry, she may know other patients who work for high-tech companies in the area. She might even be able to give you some names and contact information, or share your contact information with others.

Sometimes it helps to put together a short "elevator pitch" to help you communicate your information as clearly and quickly as possible when you network. The name comes from the fact that you could give your pitch to a stranger in an elevator during the short time you were traveling between floors. The key points to cover are:

* Name
* Type of work you do or your field of study
* Interests and skills you have
* Assistance you need

Figure 6.3 provides sample elevator pitch templates you might use as a working professional or student. Figure 6.4 provides a sample elevator pitch that the machinist could give the hygienist, using a customized version of template A.

You may never use your pitch in an actual elevator, but an "elevator pitch" is a great way to introduce yourself to people you meet.

Figure 6.3 Elevator pitch templates for working professionals (A) and students (B)

A

"Hi, my name is _____.

I have over _____ years of experience in _____.

I am interested in _____."

OR

"I'd like to _____.

Are you aware of any _____?"

B

"Hi, my name is _____.

I will be graduating/I just graduated from _____ with a degree in _____.

I've been studying _____ and am interested in _____.

Are you aware of any _____?"

Figure 6.4 Sample elevator pitch

"Hi, my name is Lamar Douglas. I'm a journeyman machinist at A-Line Assembly and have been machining for more than 10 years. The company recently laid off 25% of their employees and I was one of the people let go. I know I'm an excellent machinist, but I also think I'd be great as a manufacturing engineer. I've worked closely with a lot of design engineers to make sure that their designs can be easily manufactured before they're actually machined.

I'd like to put that knowledge to work in another high-tech firm. Do any of your patients work for a high-tech firm that uses machinists or manufacturing engineers? I'd love to talk to them."

Figure 6.5 **Example networking email**

Hello Michael:

Dr. Highland's hygienist, Lisa, gave me your name as someone I could contact to learn more about Technotronics. My purpose is to do some networking and gain an understanding of local high-tech firms.

My name is Lamar Douglas and I'm a journeyman machinist at A-Line Assembly and have been machining for more than 10 years. The company recently laid off 25% of their employees and I was one of the people let go. I know I'm an excellent machinist, but I also think I'd be great as a manufacturing engineer. I've worked closely with a lot of design engineers to make sure that their designs can be easily manufactured before they're actually machined.

Are there engineers or machinists at Technotronics that you could point me to? I'd like to talk to them about what they do and what it's like to work at Technotronics.

I'll give you a call at the end of the week to follow up.

Thank you for your assistance,

Lamar Douglas

[email]

[phone]

Informational interview, *noun*

meeting in which a job seeker asks for career and industry advice rather than employment

Email and Phone

Once you have a quality contact in mind, it's time to get in touch with him or her. The easiest way to do this is through an introductory email and a follow-up phone call. Don't forget your own contact information at the bottom of the email!

Let's continue with the machinist scenario. Suppose you decide to get in touch with the person that your hygienist recommended (Michael). Your email might look something like Figure 6.5. You'll notice that much of the email leverages the earlier elevator pitch.

It's always a good idea to put a "call to action" at the end of your email that specifies what you plan to do, or what you want the recipient to do. In Figure 6.5, Lamar's call to action is "I will call you at the end of the week to follow up." Following up by phone gives you a chance to speak with the contact, give your elevator pitch again, and find out if he or she might be interested in talking to you. It's also a great opportunity to ask about an informational interview, which you'll learn about next. Figure 6.6 provides an example of a follow-up phone call.

Informational Interview

Often, to get the most accurate information about what it really takes to succeed in a field, you have to network with people currently on the job. They have the most current picture of the job because they do it each day. They can share the tough situations they encounter, the benefits of the job, the way that they are treated, and what they are paid. They are insiders. If you refer to Figure 6.6, for example, the engineer and machinist that Lamar plans to contact by email are insiders in his field of interest.

This is where informational interviews come into play. The **informational interview** is the heart of networking. This is what all your contacts should lead to. This is an interview that you conduct to gather information about a job, a company, or a profession. The informational interview enables you to tap the hidden job market by talking to:

- People who are doing the job you want to do
- People who teach and educate people in a particular field
- People who are responsible for hiring people in your field of interest

The idea behind the informational interview is that *you* get to ask the questions and gather the information. There is no pressure on you to sell yourself and get the job, nor is there pressure on the other person to find you a job. The informational interview is an opportunity to make a contact and find out what it's really like to be in a particular job at a particular company.

The informational interview process involves the following steps:

1. Contact the person and set up the interview.
2. Prepare for the interview.
3. Conduct the interview.
4. Follow up with your contact.

Step 1. Make Contact and Set Up the Interview

You typically set up the interview after corresponding by email and speaking by phone. The email usually explains who you are and what you are trying to accomplish (and how long it will take) (see Figure 6.7). The phone call allows you to verify the purpose of the interview, the location, and the duration.

As you can see, the email requesting the informational interview is very similar to the email shown in Figure 6.5. The main difference is that you are asking for an informational interview and trying to find out a convenient time to hold it. It is very important that you provide your contact information and then follow up by phone so that you can settle on a time, date, and location.

Meeting in person is always best because it gives you a chance to speak face-to-face. You can meet in a neutral location or at the person's place of work. If you meet at a neutral location like a coffeehouse, you should pick up the tab, if possible. You should also ask for a description of the person if you have never met him or her, as well as offer a description of yourself. There's nothing more embarrassing than waiting in a coffeehouse to interview your subject, never realizing that he or she is sitting right there waiting for you—but neither of you know what the other looks like.

If you meet at the individual's place of work, you get to see his or her work environment, which can be helpful when exploring job possibilities. If the individual is unable to meet with you in person, you can always conduct the interview over the phone.

Figure 6.6   **Sample follow-up phone call**

Hello Michael, this is Lamar Douglas. Did you get my email about doing some networking at Technotronics?

[Michael received it.]

Great! Were you able to think of any engineers or machinists for me to talk to?

[Michael thought of one engineer and one machinist.]

Really—that's wonderful. Do you want to contact them first and let them know I'll be getting in touch?

[Michael says that's not necessary; Lamar can contact them directly.]

Okay, I'll contact them directly. Which is better, email or phone?

[Michael says email is better.]

Great! I'll send each of them an email. What are their email addresses?

[Michael spells out the email addresses.]

Michael, thank you so much for your help. Let me know if there's anything I can help you with in the future. I really appreciate the contacts.

Step 2. Prepare for the Interview

Once you set up the interview, you need to prepare a list of questions. The questions you ask should be about things that matter to you and will help you find out if the type of work is a fit for you. The questions should revolve around work responsibilities, personal perspective, company culture, education and background, and future trends. Figure 6.8 lists some common questions you might consider. You will probably never have time to ask all of them, but you can certainly select some of the questions from the list (or add your own).

Step 3. Conduct the Interview

Before you conduct the interview, make sure you have verified the location and time of the interview, as well as what your interviewee looks like. If you are conducting the interview by phone, be sure to call the person on time. If you are conducting the interview in person, always arrive a few minutes early. Greet your interviewee by name and introduce yourself. Make sure to thank the person for his or her time. Always be respectful. After all, you may end up working for or with this person some day.

The next step is to review the purpose of the interview: You are gathering information that will help you with your job search or career planning. Next, talk a bit about yourself so the interviewee understands what you've been doing or studying, what interests you, what your skills are, and what your plans are. You might even share a job-related experience. Keep it short; you want to leave plenty of time for your questions and you don't want to run over time.

The most important part of the interview is asking questions. Let your interviewee know that you've prepared a list of questions, but you understand that you may not be able to ask all of them because of time constraints. You might also let the interviewee know that you'll be taking notes so you don't forget anything important. If you don't want to be distracted by note taking, you can always bring a tape recorder. (Do not take notes with a laptop—the screen and the typing will be both

Figure 6.7   Setting up an informational interview

Hello Devan:

Michael Brandon at Technotronics recommended you as a great contact for me, and I'm following up on the recommendation.

My name is Lamar Douglas and I'm a journeyman machinist at A-Line Assembly and have been machining for more than 10 years. The company recently laid off 25% of their employees and I was one of the people let go. I know I'm an excellent machinist, but I also think I'd be great as a manufacturing engineer. I've worked closely with a lot of design engineers to make sure that their designs can be easily manufactured before they're actually machined.

As part of my career exploration, I would like to conduct an "informational" interview with you to learn more about Technotronics and the work you do there. It would probably take about 30 to 45 minutes, and would involve me asking you a lot of questions. I could do it by phone or in-person, depending on your preference.

Would you be available for such an interview? I am happy to work around your schedule, so please let me know days or times that would work for you.

I'll give you a call to follow up and answer any questions you might have about the informational interview.

Thanks in advance for your assistance,

Lamar Douglas

[email]

[phone]

An informal informational interview is a great way to network and learn more about what other people do on the job.

rude and distracting to your interviewee.) As you proceed, be aware of the time. You may need to cut out questions if you're running short of time.

During the informational interview, gather facts, stories, and opinions regarding the challenges involved in the profession. The more that you know, the more you will be prepared to handle any situation successfully when you get there.

Take any negative information with a grain of salt. This information is one person's subjective view of events and not necessarily what is really happening. Listen to what your interviewee has to say, process the information, and continue to investigate for yourself. The informational interview is not the time to evaluate; it's a time to gather information. You'll do the evaluation later.

When you finish, be sure to thank your interviewee for his or her time and the information they've given you, and offer to help them out in the future. You should also ask your interviewee if he or she can think of anyone else with whom you could speak. Finally, ask for a business card (if you have a card, you should share it as well). And if your interviewee happens to ask for your resume, by all means give it to him or her!

Step 4. Follow Up

Once the interview is over, you need to send a thank you note. It should be handwritten, rather than emailed or typed (unless you have very bad handwriting). This is a common courtesy. You might also call the person who provided the lead and thank him or her as well.

Next, you need to transcribe your notes (people often like to type them) so you can read and study them. Later in this chapter, you will learn how to evaluate what you've learned.

Figure 6.8   Common informational interview questions

General

1. What is your job title?
2. How long have you been in this position?
3. How did you get started in your field?

Work Environment and Culture

4. Do you work from home, an office, or in the field?
5. Do you work by phone, email, or in person?
6. How many hours per day do you work? How many days per week?
7. How would you describe the atmosphere at work?
8. How often does your supervisor check up on your work?
9. Are you formally evaluated? How often?
10. Do you feel over- or undermanaged? If so, what is your personal preference? (If the interviewee's personal preference is similar to yours, you can determine that you might feel the same way about the management style.)
11. What kinds of breaks can you comfortably take during your workday? What forms of relaxation are acceptable?
12. How are deviations from plans or structure received? Are new ideas welcomed and used right away, or shelved until they can be coordinated with the existing structure?

Responsibilities

13. What are your primary work duties?
14. What skills do you have that make you good at what you do?
15. What do you like most about your work?
16. What do you like least?
17. What are the most interesting and challenging aspects of the job?
18. What is a typical day like?

Salary and Benefits

19. What is the starting salary range?
20. What is the salary range at different levels of advancement?
21. What benefits might I expect?
22. Are there provisions for childcare?
23. Do I need to participate in a union?

Future Trends

24. Are jobs readily available in this area, or will I need to commute or relocate?
25. What kind of growth is projected for this field in the next 5 years?
26. What are the possibilities for promotion?

Requirements

27. Are there skill and/or physical requirements?
28. Will I need a car? A uniform? Any other equipment?
29. What background do you recommend for an entry-level position in this field?
30. What is your education? What did you learn after you finished your formal education that helped you succeed at your job?
31. What education or training can help a person get into this line of work? Is a degree necessary? A certificate?
32. What courses should a person take, or what experience should they have for this type of work?

Now You Try It: Warming Up Your Networking Engines

Sometimes it's hard to start networking "cold turkey." Here's a mini-activity to warm up your networking engines.

1. Think about a particular job or career that you are very interested in. What are some things you've always wondered about the job? Write down specific questions that you've always wanted to ask about a particular job or career.

2. Now, think about people you might want to talk to about that particular job or career.

   - Write down their names.
   - If you do not know any of them by name, write down their titles (for example, "machinist at a wind turbine company").
   - If you cannot think of anyone, write down the types of people you might be able to contact who could eventually lead you to the people you want to talk to. For example, talk to friends and family, then talk to your hairdresser or your bank teller, then talk to their friends, and then talk to their business contacts.

   You will have a chance to do more work on networking at the end of the chapter.

Shadowing

Shadow, *verb*

to follow a person in order to keep watch over his or her movements

Talking to people about their jobs and what they do is one thing; watching them do their jobs is another. If you want an even more hands-on approach than informational interviewing, you may want to **shadow** someone on the job.

Shadowing refers to following an individual to see what he or she does on the job. It's a great way to get firsthand experience about what it's like to perform a particular job. Think about it—you can ask someone what they do on the job and how they like it, or you can actually watch them go about their job and come to your own conclusions about whether that type of job is for you.

Small companies are usually more open to the idea of shadowing than large ones. Finding someone to shadow is similar to finding someone to interview. Use your networking contacts to find someone in the line of work you're interested in. Then, contact that person, let him or her know who you are, and explain that you would like to spend some time as a silent observer to learn more about what it's like to work in that field. Reassure the person that you will not interfere with his or her work or ask lots of questions. Instead, you'll be more like a detective tailing a suspect—you'll try to be as unobtrusive as possible. Let them know you would like to ask a few questions at the end of the shadowing activity to clarify what you have seen. We think you'll find that many people are more than happy to show off what they do and to have you tag along.

How long you shadow depends on you, the person you plan to shadow, and the type of work they do. An hour or two is probably the least amount of time to spend shadowing, and a day is probably the most amount of time. The idea is to spend enough time with the individual to observe him or her performing the most common tasks the job requires so you get a sense of the skills used on the job, the level of personal interaction, and the workplace environment.

When you finish shadowing, you can always ask the person if they have time for you to ask a few questions. If so, ask the same questions you would ask during an informational interview. The answers you receive and the observations you made during your shadowing should give you a sense of whether you would like to pursue this line of work.

Evaluating Your Choices

All of us would love to have work that brings us joy, makes the most of our talents, and fulfills our needs. Finding that ideal work situation, however, can take a lot of time and energy. After you make networking contacts, hold your informational interviews, and possibly do some shadowing, the next step is to evaluate your leads and decide which you will pursue, as illustrated in Figure 6.9.

Did You Know? You may look for a job for so long that you take a job that's not really a good fit, just to avoid having to look any longer. In that case, you trade some of your priorities for the relief of having a steady job and income. Sometimes that makes a lot of sense—at least you have a job and you can keep your eyes and ears open for other possibilities in the future.

The evaluation process starts with reviewing the information you collected during your informational interviews or shadowing and analytically examining the facts you uncovered. It continues as you use your intuition to discover how you really feel about what you learned.

Getting Clear: Look at the Facts

Take time now to get clear on what you want or don't want in a job. If you think things through now, you won't waste time pursuing jobs that don't suit your lifestyle. You will have a chance at the end of the chapter to indicate your preferences in these areas. Table 6.2 lists common criteria to consider as you look at different jobs. Read through the items to discover what works for you.

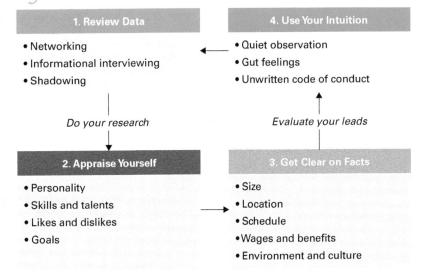

Figure 6.9 Launching your career

Remember, too often we focus on compensation and benefits, functional requirements, and location, without much thought about potential fit or compatibility with an organization's culture. If you're not sure what kind of work culture you feel comfortable in, ask yourself this question: In school or work, do you slack off when no one keeps a strict eye on you, or do you thrive on being able to push yourself and progress on your own? Some people have the discipline to move forward on a project without outside encouragement; they are likely to do well in an unstructured work environment. Others need deadlines and people checking on them to make progress. They are likely to do better in a structured work environment with a manager watching over them. Knowing your own work style will help you evaluate the right work culture for you.

Now that you've identified what is important to you, it's time to review the notes you took during your networking, informational interviews, and shadowing. Compare what you learned to the criteria in Table 6.2. Then decide which positions or careers are good fits for you.

Using Your Street Smarts: Practical Intuition

There's more to the evaluation process than evaluating facts; you also must use your **street smarts.** Street smarts are a kind of practical intuition that tells you what to do, where to go, to whom to talk, and how to talk. Originally, the term *street smarts* referred to the resourcefulness that someone who lived on the street had to use to stay warm, hide, and find food. In this book we use the term to mean a gut sense of what's going on around you and the right way to get things done. Street smarts depend on:

- Quiet observation, rather than direct inquiry
- Gut feelings, rather than thinking
- An unwritten code of conduct, rather than well-known behavior guidelines

Street smarts come in handy when evaluating the information you gathered during your informational interviews. For example, it's possible that after talking to three contacts, the facts you

Street smarts, *noun*

practical knowledge of how things work or how to get something done; a capacity to be creative in the face of obstacles

Table 6.2 **What Are You Looking For?**	
Criteria	**Description**
Chain or independent company	Chains usually have well-organized workforces; established rules about conduct, duties, and employee treatment; and consistent and reliable pay systems. However, some employees may feel less important in a chain, or as if management doesn't value them as individuals with particular talents. Independent companies tend to offer more flexibility with less rigid rules, a looser atmosphere, and more personal management. Which do you prefer, a chain or an independent company?
Large or small company	A large company may have more financial strength, hiring power, job opportunities, and locations. The jobs available at a large company may cover a greater range of possibilities. However, even large companies have layoffs. Working at a small company offers you a more personal, comfortable environment with fewer employees. Your work may have less structure, and your duties may be more flexible. Even work time and schedules may be more flexible. Benefits packages will usually be smaller. Which do you prefer, a large or small company?
Regular or flexible schedule	Some people like a rigid, regular schedule to help them keep their lives organized. Others like a more flexible schedule due to personal preference or lifestyle. For example, do you want to work out of your home? Do you need to be home at odd hours to accommodate your children? Do you need flexibility because of your school schedule? Jobs with flexible hours do exist; however, you may lose out in job security or salary. Some employers will pay more for a full-time, steady employee than for a part-time one. Think about what is important to you.
Location	Do you want to work near your home? Are you willing to relocate? Do you like commuting or do you prefer walking or biking to work? These are all questions to ask yourself when it comes to a company's location.
Benefits	Some jobs offer benefits (for example, health insurance and vacation) and some don't. Decide whether benefits are crucial to you. If they are, decide which benefits are a must, and only pursue jobs at companies that offer those benefits. If benefits aren't necessary, you can probably pursue a wider variety of jobs. Later in this book you will learn how to negotiate benefits when you are offered a job.
Wages	Wages vary by geographic area, profession, and experience, so do your research and come up with a salary range that is both realistic and acceptable. For example, if you're just starting out in the business world, it's unrealistic to expect that you will immediately be making the "big bucks." You should, however, have an idea of the minimum wage you're willing to accept that will meet your basic financial needs and allow you to get your foot in the door. Having a general idea of what you're worth and what you'll settle for is wise before pursuing a job.
Skills	Make a list of your skills and competencies that you enjoy using on the job. You'll want to make sure that jobs you pursue require them.
Culture	Culture comprises a set of values, standards of conduct, and beliefs that guide behavior in an organization. If you plan to spend eight hours a day in a company, you need to know that the culture will be a good fit for you. Do you like a well-defined hierarchy and rules? Do you prefer a more "go with the flow" environment? Do you like ideas to flow from management down or from workers up? How do you feel about dress codes? Do you need an office or is a cubicle okay?

gathered are all very similar. Perhaps the positions involve similar types of tasks, a similar environment, and similar salaries. This is where your ability to observe and use your intuition comes into play.

During your informational interview at one company, you noticed that the person you talked to treated the secretary poorly. You noticed that most people within the company dressed formally. You observed that many of the people that worked at the company seemed unfriendly, hurried, stuck-up, and you therefore made some assumptions about the kinds of qualities the company values. As a result, your intuition tells you that the company would probably not be a good fit for your laid back, friendly, open personality.

Listen when your intuition speaks to you. It usually does so through feelings that you get, which often center in your solar plexus—the spot just below the center of your chest and above your diaphragm. Beware of feelings of anxiety, concern, or discomfort; they probably mean the situation is not right for you. Pay attention to positive feelings of anticipation, safety, or excitement; they probably mean the situation is a good fit. However, don't let a little anxiety after an informational interview stop you from pursuing a particular job. Anxiety is often nothing more than normal nervousness because you are in a situation that is new to you. However, if you feel strongly that you would be unhappy in a particular job after doing an informational interview, trust your intuition and keep looking. Something even better will come along.

The more you observe people around you and listen to your intuition, the more successful you will be at evaluating job leads. Let your street smarts guide you away from situations that would make you unhappy or would not suit your personality and talents. If you have taken a look at a trade, job, or company that for any reason turned you off, think it over before you put energy into applying and interviewing. Don't waste your time pursuing work that wouldn't be right for you.

Now You Try It: Using Your Street Smarts

Suppose you tell your friend Chandra that you just finished conducting an informational interview at a company where she used to work. She responds, "You'll dig your own grave if you take a job there. The employees will make your life a nightmare. I worked there for three months and couldn't take it. The manager was always checking on my progress and asking for status reports—it made me too nervous. I got out as soon as I could."

You are surprised at Chandra's words because you actually enjoyed talking with the person you interviewed and loved hearing about the work she did. You felt you would be good at that type of work. You also liked the fact that she seemed very organized and so did the company. You felt a well-structured company would be a good fit for you.

Using your intuition, interpret Chandra's comments in each of the following situations and decide how you might proceed:

1. You and Chandra are good friends and she really cares about you. However, she tends to have a very laid-back personality and you are very methodical and organized.

2. You are good friends with Chandra and her family. The family mentions that Chandra used to be engaged to a man who worked at the company, and when they broke up she was very upset and quit.

3. You and Chandra have not known one another very long, and she has always been jealous of your job successes.

Knowing your own personality and Chandra's, as well as your history with Chandra and her history with the company, can affect how you interpret her words and whether you use her input to come to a decision about the company. Only your intuition can help you.

Tracking Your Progress

As you build your network and conduct your informational interviews, it's a good idea to keep track of your progress. Do this by keeping a file that lists the following:

- People in your network
- People you have contacted or plan to contact
- Informational interviews you set up and notes from those interviews

- Companies or jobs you have ruled out (after conducting informational interviews)
- Companies to which you have applied or sent resumes

You can record information in a specific notebook or on index cards. Include names, addresses, and phone numbers that you need to know. It's also a wise idea to document the dates you held your interviews. Even if a contact or an informational interview doesn't pan out right away, you never know what may happen; sometimes a person you talked to will think about you months later when a job comes available and contact you. If you store your contact information electronically, be sure to print it out periodically in case something happens to the electronic copy.

Moving into the Job World

Now you know how to combine the following skills to effectively prepare yourself for the job search: interpersonal skills for networking and informational interviewing, information skills and street smarts for evaluating job information, basic skills (listening, writing, speaking, reading) for gathering advice, and thinking skills for making smart decisions.

After talking to a lot of contacts, you probably have a good idea of the type of job you want and where to find it. The next step will be to actually start applying for jobs. These can be jobs you found in the hidden market during your informational interviews (the jobs may not even exist yet, but you've identified a need for them); others may be jobs you found in the open market through newspaper or magazine ads or online job posting websites.

In the next chapter we will focus on the job application process—specifically, how to polish your resume and craft cover letters that make you stand out among all applicants.

Your Tool Kit at Work

6.1 Start Your Networking Engines

You probably know more people than you think. However, even if your circle of acquaintances is small, you can easily expand it once you start talking to people and they start giving you names of more people. Remember, being a good networker is like being a good detective—you follow your leads no matter where they take you.

Ultimately, you want to contact people who work in your field of interest or know people who work in that field. You can find these people by working through your networking list.

1. Start your networking list by using the following table to jot down at least one person in each category (if possible) who might be a potential contact.
2. Identify what you would like from that person. For example, you might want to ask the person to do any of the following: think of other possible contacts, give advice, provide information about your field of interest, or act as a reference.

Category	Person's name	What I need
Former employers		
Former coworkers		
Present employer		
Present coworkers		
Friends		
Relatives		
Religious group members		

Category	Person's name	What I need
Union members		
Counselors		
Teachers		
Clergy		
Neighbors		
Classmates		
Attorneys		
Members of the community (police, small business owners, service providers)		

3. Now that you have your list, consider what you might be able to do for your contacts in return. Remember, what goes around comes around! Write down a list of ways you can help others. For example, maybe you have connections at school or at work, or maybe your own research has turned up some information others could benefit from.

_____

_____

_____

_____

6.2 What Are You Going to Say?

Now that you have a list of potential networking contacts, it's time to come up with your elevator pitch. What are you going to say to these people? Your pitch may vary from person to person, but it's a good idea to have an all-purpose pitch that you can customize.

- Fill in your pitch below. Refer back to Figure 6.3 for sample templates.

_____

_____

_____

- Next, pick one person from your list of networking contacts and decide what type of help you will seek from that person. Different people can help you in different ways. What can this person do to help your job search? Check one or more.

  _____ Provide information about a job or career

  _____ Relay their connections to other people who may have jobs available or know more about a career

  _____ Give advice on job-hunting strategies, resumes, and/or interviews

  _____ Provide moral support and life-planning help

- Adjust your elevator pitch accordingly. Make sure it ends with a specific request.

_____

_____

_____

- Now make the phone call. If the person doesn't know you, be sure to introduce yourself by stating your name and how you heard about the person. Then give your elevator pitch, ending with your request. If your request is to learn more about a career or what the individual does on the job, this is the perfect time to set up an informational interview. See Activity 6.4 for details.

6.3 Career Priorities

Before you hold the informational interview, it's a good idea to get your priorities straight. Define what is and isn't important to you in a job so you can ask intelligent questions. Decide which of the following conditions and responsibilities you prefer. Your intelligence, experience, and intuition will help you; they will lead you toward the environment in which you feel the most comfortable, and that is the place where you can do your best and most productive work.

Answer the following questions to define your job priorities. These will guide you toward discovering your most ideal working conditions and atmosphere.

1. What size workplace do I prefer?

   _____ Small (under 25 employees)   _____ Parent company (many locations)

   _____ Medium (up to 100 employees)   _____ Multinational

   _____ Large (over 100 employees in one location)

2. What environment is my favorite?

   _____ Working indoors   _____ Working in my home

   _____ Working outdoors   _____ A combination of environments

   _____ Traveling/field work

3. What schedules fit my lifestyle?

   _____ 9:00 to 5:00/conventional   _____ Evening shift

   _____ Flex-time   _____ Early morning start

   _____ Part-time   _____ Independent contract (set own hours)

   _____ Rotating shifts

4. What kind of job structure do I prefer?

   _____ Permanent position   _____ Self-employment/entrepreneur

   _____ Temporary position   _____ Seasonal work

5. What are my favorite courses in school?

   _____

   a. What skills am I learning in these courses?

   _____

   b. What are my least favorite courses?

   _____

   c. What about these courses do I dislike?

   _____

   d. What are my favorite responsibilities in the jobs I've had?

   _____

e. Based on my answers to a through e, what skills would I like to use the most in my career/job?

_____

f. What responsibilities would I like to be given?

_____

6. I prefer my work to center around:

_____ A few tasks I perform well

_____ Responsibilities that change from day to day

_____ Meeting customers and clients

_____ Very little personal contact

_____ New duties for which I'll receive training

7. I would like my workplace to have (check all that apply):

_____ Convenient location/less than 30 minutes from home

_____ Location accessible by public transportation

_____ Covered parking

_____ Nearby parking

_____ Attractive offices, well-decorated with pleasing colors

_____ Individual workstations

_____ Individual offices

_____ Windows/natural light

_____ Up-to-date equipment

_____ State-of-the-art equipment

_____ Environmental safety

_____ Friendly, compatible coworkers

_____ Cafeteria

_____ Fitness center

_____ Childcare facilities

_____ Orderly, professional atmosphere

_____ Casual, laid-back atmosphere

_____ Other (specify) _____

8. How do I want to be paid?

_____ Hourly wage (may be higher but might involve fewer benefits)

_____ Yearly salary

_____ Weekly

_____ Biweekly

_____ Bimonthly

9. What benefits do I need and want? (Larger companies usually can afford to offer better benefits.)

_____ Educational/training opportunities

_____ Medical/dental insurance

_____ Life/disability insurance

_____ Paid vacation/holidays

_____ Maternity/paternity leave

_____ Personal day(s)

_____ Overtime pay

_____ Retirement plan

_____ Savings plan

No job will have every one of your preferred conditions. As with planning your to-do list or your budget, you need to set priorities. Go over your choices and give them an A, B, or C priority.

- A is for the essentials you must have to be productive and successful.
- B is for the conditions that aren't quite as crucial but will make your job a special experience.
- C is for the extras that will be great if they are offered but aren't necessary for your job satisfaction.

As you prioritize, let your self-knowledge be your guide. Now when you hold an informational interview you will have a better idea of what to ask and how to evaluate what you learn.

6.4 Informational Interview Time

This is your opportunity to plan and conduct a real informational interview. Based on the networking you've done, pick the person you want to interview. If you feel a bit shy, choose someone you know fairly well, even if they do not work at a job you are that interested in, just to get the hang of conducting an interview.

1. Create your phone script to ask for the interview. Don't forget to explain the purpose of the interview. If you plan to meet in person, be sure to describe your physical appearance and ask for a description of your interview subject if you have never met.

_____

_____

_____

_____

_____

_____

2. Identify the logistics for the interview.

   - Person you plan to interview:

   _____

   - Contact information:

   _____

   - Appearance (if you've never seen them before):

   _____

   - Date and time:

   _____

   - Location:

   _____

3. Write down your interview questions in a notebook. Feel free to refer to Figure 6.8 for ideas. These should be questions that help you learn more about the type of work the person does, as well as address the job priorities you identified in the earlier activity.

4. Practice your introduction so you know what you will say to the person when you meet him or her. Explain the purpose of the informational interview and how long it will take. On the day of the interview, remember to arrive a few minutes early.

5. On the day of the interview, don't forget a pen and the notebook with your questions. Leave plenty of space to take notes.

6. Remember to send a handwritten thank you note within 24 hours of the informational interview.

6.5 Evaluate Your Options

The informational interview is over and you've sent the thank you note. Now it's time to look over your interview notes and decide what to do next.

1. Transcribe the notes you took during the informational interview.

2. Compare what you learned with your list of career priorities.

3. What issues do you see? What benefits do you see?

_____

_____

_____

_____

4. What are some of the most important things you learned about the work your interviewee does?

_____

_____

_____

_____

5. Whom do you plan on talking to next? Why?

_____

_____

_____

_____

6.6 Plug Your Knowledge into Real Life

Throughout this chapter you've been exposed to a number of ideas that can help you in your job hunt. Building a network of contacts and mentors can greatly assist you as you look for work. Street smarts, based on your experience and intuition, can help you evaluate situations and effectively react to them as you network. The skills you've learned in prior chapters, such as the ability to listen, communicate, and make decisions, come in handy as you research possible jobs and careers. However, not everyone has the knowledge that you do. See if you can use what you've learned to help Rosie get back on track with her job hunt.

Rosie enrolled in the two-year electronics program at Taylor Tech. The first month she attended every day and earned mostly As on her assignments and quizzes. But Rosie and her husband had been having problems for a while, and he decided to move out. Without her husband's income to help pay the bills, Rosie had to find a job. Her attendance and her grades dropped. She didn't tell her family about her predicament. Her friends weren't aware of the situation or her troubled state of mind. She didn't talk with her teachers at Taylor. After three months of trying to help her through offers of tutoring and counseling, Rosie's advisor at Taylor asked her to leave. Rosie became angry and yelled at the administrators.

When she went out to look for a job in the electronics field, Rosie discovered that she wasn't qualified. She wants to go back to Taylor Tech, but she is afraid to call because of the scene she created.

1. What advice do you have for Rosie? How can she balance her life and get back in good graces at Taylor? As you think about your answer, consider how Rosie might use the following tools:

- Understanding social and organizational (school and company) systems
- Communicating thoughts effectively
- Problem solving and decision making
- Integrity and honesty
- Responsibility and commitment

• Self-knowledge and self-esteem

_____

_____

_____

_____

Employers hire people who are flexible, responsible, have excellent attendance and good grades, learn technical knowledge in school, and communicate well with colleagues at all levels of authority. Although Rosie didn't exhibit these qualities at first, her advisor and the administrators would certainly consider improvement, so it's not too late.

2. Based on some of the ideas you explored for Rosie, what advice can you take away for yourself? You are in a good position: You are still a student and have the opportunity to make immediate improvements in a supportive atmosphere.

_____

_____

_____

_____

6.7 Technology Exercise

There are a number of websites that can help you become a better networker. LinkedIn is one such site. In this exercise you will create a profile that you can use if you choose to join LinkedIn. If you are already a member of LinkedIn, you may choose to update the profile you already have.

You may want to review the sample LinkedIn profile information in Figure 6.2 or the online learning materials on the LinkedIn Learning Center found at http://learn.linkedin.com.

1. Fill in the information for the following sections of your LinkedIn profile:

Executive Summary

_____

_____

Specialties

_____

_____

Experience

_____

_____

_____

2. When you are ready, go to www.linkedin.com.

• Enter your first and last name, then click **Join**.

• Fill in your profile.

• If you are already a member, log in and edit your profile accordingly.

Build Your Personal Brand

Put Your Tools to Good Use

By the work one knows the workman.

Jean de la Fontaine

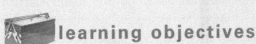learning objectives

- What is the primary purpose of a resume, and what are three common types?
- What are the components of a successful cover letter?
- Whom should you choose as your references?
- What is the purpose of a portfolio and how do you create one?
- Why are business cards a good idea?
- What should you remember when filling out an application?

myth

"I don't need a resume. I just need to fill out job applications."

reality

A resume is a key tool to help market yourself for that job you seek. A typical human resources recruiter will spend roughly 20 to 30 seconds scanning a resume to determine if it should be passed on for further review. As a result, think about how you can streamline your resume and improve its attractiveness with more relevant experiences, skills, and examples of achievement that will capture and not distract the recruiter's attention. If your resume catches the reader's eye, you're more likely to get an interview.

Dominic spent 10 years working for various construction crews, operating heavy equipment such as bulldozers, backhoes, and dump trucks. But when the housing industry went bust, the general contractor he worked for laid off the entire crew. Luckily, Dominic had a friend who needed help with his moving company. Dominic had a strong back and started working part-time right away. He also decided to go back to school, and chose to study clean energy technology at the local community college. He figured that was the wave of the future.

Because of his construction experience, Dominic volunteered to help build a small recycling center on campus, and then volunteered more time to operate the center. However, he soon realized that his part-time moving job was barely paying the bills, and he needed to find something better. One of his cousins mentioned that she'd heard about an opening at the local university for a part-time truck driver to collect and sort materials for recycling on campus. The pay was supposed to be good and the job had actual benefits—healthcare and vacation time!

Dominic immediately asked his cousin for the name of someone he could contact at the university to learn more about the job. One short phone call later, Dominic was convinced the job was right for him and picked up an application. However, he wondered if he really had the right experience for the job. Plus, he'd heard rumors that getting an interview at the university was almost impossible because of the large number of applicants.

Undaunted, Dominic paid a visit to the career counseling center at the community college for a quick review of resumes and cover letters. The counselor helped him create his own personal "brand" in the form of a professional resume and cover letter. With the counselor's help, Dominic identified a wide variety of skills he'd picked up over the years that would be perfect for the university job. The counselor suggested putting together a "hybrid" resume that would play up his relevant skills and experience. The counselor also helped Dominic craft a cover letter that would really get someone's attention.

Finally, Dominic requested letters of recommendation from his former construction boss, one of his satisfied moving customers, and a favorite instructor at the community college. As he worked on the resume and cover letter and read his letters of recommendation, Dominic started feeling pretty good about himself.

After he sent in his resume, cover letter, and application by email, he followed up with a phone call. When he didn't hear back, he mailed a hard copy of his application materials to the university, as a reminder. His diligence paid off, because two weeks later he got a phone call—the university wanted to schedule an interview with him!

You may not be in the same position as Dominic—recently laid off or recently returned to school. However, you have explored your inner self and your outside world, looking for the options that fit you best. You have networked like a pro and located the companies you think you want to work for and the positions you're interested in. Now it's time to get out there and apply for those positions. Like Dominic, you will need to prepare your own personal brand—materials that show who you are and what you can do. Armed with these materials, you will be able to present yourself on paper as professionally as possible so you can land that sought-after interview.

This chapter focuses on creating your personal brand with a neat, complete, and professional-looking resume, cover letter, and portfolio. It also delves into establishing reliable references, designing a business card, and filling out applications.

By following the steps in this chapter, as illustrated in Figure 7.1, you come across as a professional and capable individual before your potential employer ever meets you in person. The goal of this process is to get you an interview (more about that in Chapter 8).

Your Brand

In today's world, *brand* often refers to a trademark, label, design, or symbol associated with a product—for example, the Nike swoosh, the Coke name, or a particular type of coffee. However, **brand** also refers to unique characteristics that identify any product, and that product can include you!

In this chapter we will focus on the marketing collateral you must develop to define your brand and promote yourself. These materials include:

Brand, *noun*

a particular product or a characteristic that serves to identify a particular product

- **Resume.** A one- or two-page document that summarizes your career goal, experience, and skills.
- **Cover letter.** A brief letter that introduces you to a potential employer and explains why you are interested in a particular position and what you have to offer.
- **References.** A list of individuals who can vouch for your character and your abilities.
- **Portfolio.** Samples of work you have done that demonstrate your skills and talents.
- **Business card.** A small calling card that serves as a way to introduce who you are and what you do.
- **Elevator speech.** A short piece of marketing material that you say out loud when you meet someone for the first time. (Refer back to Chapter 6 for the discussion of elevator speeches.)

Let's dive into your marketing material by starting with the resume.

Resumes

The purpose of a resume is to get an interview. Your resume is usually the first impression your potential employer has of you, so it's important that the resume is both complete and professional. When you submit the resume, the employer will examine what you have to offer and decide if you're a match for the company's needs. Generally, the people assigned

Figure 7.1 **Getting that interview**

to screen resumes within a company spend only 30 seconds scanning each resume. That's why it is so important that your resume is attractive, easy to read, and not too long. In fact, a one- or two-page resume is usually best.

Trying to condense your work history into your resume is not always an easy task. However, taking time to think about your job objective, skills, and past experience before you create the resume can make the task easier. Remember, creating a resume is a process. Don't expect to sit down and pound out a resume in a few minutes. It requires preparation, writing, and formatting.

Collect Your Resume Information

Before you develop a resume, it's important to think about what you want to do, the position you are applying for, and what you've done in the past. Too many people jump right into the resume

writing process without taking the time to collect their thoughts or their employment history information. To help you in the collection process, we have listed items that will eventually end up on your resume. As you collect your information, feel free to write down as much as you want. Don't worry about typing a nicely formatted resume at this point. You can streamline things when you actually create the resume later in the chapter.

Contact Information

Make sure you have a phone number, email address, and physical address a potential employer can use to contact you. Your email address, in particular, should be a professional email, not a silly nickname or something worse.

Examples

- Unprofessional email: HotMama@yahoo.com
- Professional email: mtesla@gmail.com

This may mean that you have to get a new email account for business correspondence. Consider getting a Gmail account. The account is free and all email you send or receive is automatically archived.

Career Objective

A career objective is your goal—what you want to do. This objective helps anyone scanning your resume to identify the type of job you're looking for and decide who should receive your resume. If the job you are applying for has a particular title, you can use it as your job objective.

Examples

- Apply my machining and welding experience as a Journeyman Machinist in a union shop.
- Use my word-processing skills as an entry-level Technical Writer I.

If you are not applying for a specific advertised job, you can create an objective that describes your career goal and skill set. It's best to make the objective narrow enough to help the resume reader categorize your talent and ambitions, but not so narrow that you're excluded from possible opportunities. A good approach is to specify: (1) your background, (2) your skill set, and (3) the type of work you want to do.

Examples

- Full-time employment blending my GIS studies with my existing computer science skills.
- Use my creative and analytical skills, along with my experience in electromechanical devices, with a team of professionals who design and test new products.

Some people prefer to use a professional profile instead of an objective. This is usually for professionals with a great deal of experience who want to highlight their background experience rather than identify a specific type of work.

Examples

- Results-oriented quality assurance professional with proven 12-year track record using manual and automated software testing on multiple platforms. Skilled in wide range of software development environments with strong technical, communication, and management skills.

- Over 20 years experience as an innovative, hands-on senior executive, working in diverse industries such as manufacturing and emergency medical response. Proven track record dealing with unstable environments, quickly identifying pain points, and providing innovative solutions that remove impediments to success.

Hard and Soft Skills

This is your chance to think of all the things you do well or like to do that could help an employer. These skills may come from experiences at home, at school, volunteering, or on the job. These skills can be hard skills or soft skills. *Hard skills* deal with things you can *do*; *soft skills* deal with who you *are* (your characteristics). Table 7.1 shows you some sample skills in both categories.

As you consider your skills, think back to the SCANS list of skills in Chapter 1. These are the skills most crucial to your success. Looking at the categories and their specific items can help you define how your skills are marketable. Choose skills that you feel would have value in the workplace.

Paid and Unpaid Experience

Collect your old employment history so you can document the jobs you've held over the past 10 years. For professionals, this is not difficult. A word of warning, though—there is no need to go back more than 10 years. An exception to this rule is when you are switching careers and want to highlight something you did more than 10 years ago that demonstrates aptitude for your new career. If you have had too many to include on your resume, list only the ones that gave you the most responsibility and the ones that relate to your current career path. A very important job at which you held a respectable position, even if it doesn't seem to fit the kind of job you now want, shows personal qualities that apply to any line of work.

For students or people who have been out of the workforce for some time, it may be difficult to compile 10 years of work experience. However, it becomes easier when you consider non-paid work as well. Experience is experience—skills develop even when you don't receive a paycheck. Think about informal or volunteer positions you held at school, in church, in the community, or at home. Following are some examples.

Table 7.1 Examples of Hard and Soft Skills	
Soft Skills	**Hard Skills**
• Accurate	• Type 75 words per minute
• Adaptable	• Write technical manuals
• Cooperative	• Repair cars and trucks
• Detail oriented	• Test printed circuit boards
• Efficient	• Repair bad haircuts and color
• Energetic	• Coach soccer
• Empathetic	• Edit textbooks
• Goal oriented	• Install sprinkler systems
• Hardworking	• Operate heavy equipment
• Innovative	• Frame houses
• Organized	• Schedule appointments
• Practical	• Use Microsoft Word and PowerPoint
• Problem solver	• Promote products and events
• Results oriented	• Design promotional materials
• Thoughtful	• Write web content
• Thorough	• Install solar panels

Working at a friend or family's business without pay. This shows dedication and loyalty.

- Did you take phone calls? You communicate well and have good telephone skills.
- Did you help to re-sort and clean up files or equipment? You may be skilled at organizing data and company assets.
- Did you help to take in money, count it, or keep the books? You might be a whiz at money management, records, and accounts.

Taking on special responsibilities at school or at home. This shows responsibility, dedication, dependability, and energy.

- Were you a representative for your class at any school, administration, or alumni meetings? You show leadership qualities and skill in working with others.
- Did you help with budgeting and financial planning at home? You may know a lot about organizing and evaluating information as well as budget maintenance.
- Were you a teacher's aide? You may be good at taking initiative, cooperating, and listening.

Volunteer work. This shows caring, values, and good time management skills.

- Did you help out at a center for children with emotional disabilities? You may have a talent for creative thinking and decision making because you never knew what might happen next.
- Did you spend time socializing with residents at a home for the elderly? You may have a solid command of social systems, communication, and listening.
- Did you help to rebuild and repaint a dilapidated school? You show command of the equipment and technology you used as well as a good sense of cooperation and self-management.

Childcare duties at home. This shows responsibility, flexibility, and a caring nature.

- Did you care for children who have schedules full of school, sports practices, play dates, and other appointments? You have good time-management skills.

Like athletic accomplishments, action verbs demonstrate what you can do and what you are capable of.

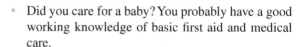

- Did you care for a baby? You probably have a good working knowledge of basic first aid and medical care.
- Did you care for more than one child at a time? You may be especially efficient and capable of handling multiple tasks.

Now develop your list of jobs. This includes the job title, employer or organization where you volunteered, location (city and state), and dates of employment or volunteering. For each job, write a brief summary describing the purpose of the job. Then list your primary tasks and accomplishments. Figures 7.2 and 7.3 provide some good examples.

Notice that the tasks and accomplishments in Figures 7.2 and 7.3 always begin with action verbs. These are words that convey *doing* something. If you're

Figure 7.2 Job title and experience example (paid job)

Design Consultant, Everest Associates, Savannah, GA, 2009–2012

Responsible for increasing client base and managing client design projects.

- Acted as team leader for ongoing work for a large regional client.
- Coordinated design work and client relations.
- Developed training materials for new employees.
- Planned and participated in Savannah's annual Design Awards dinner.
- Brought in 10 new clients during 2010 and increased department revenue by 15%.

Figure 7.3 Job title and experience example (unpaid job)

Caretaker of Elderly Parent, Nashville, TN, 2005 to 2010

Responsible for all aspects of home care for my elderly mother.

- Accompanied my mother to all medical appointments to ensure that the doctor was respectful and explained things clearly.
- Monitored my mother's blood pressure, blood sugar, diet, and activity level.
- Administered daily medications and cooked all meals according to the nutritionist's guidelines.
- Helped my mother locate social activities in town to keep her entertained and engaged.

not sure what action verbs to use, review the following partial list (there are plenty more words you could use):

Sample Action Verbs for Job Tasks and Accomplishments

Assess	Generate	Prioritize
Build	Handle	Repair
Collaborate	Instruct	Solve
Communicate	Lead	Teach
Document	Manage	Train
Evaluate	Perform	

Certificates

List any professional certificates you have and the dates you received them. Some may not seem applicable to the line of work you want to do, but this is the place to identify them.

Examples

- Drafter Certification, American Drafter Association, 2008
- Certified First Aid and CPR, American Red Cross, 2005–present

Education

Identify degrees that you obtained or toward which you are working. If you did not actually get a degree but spent a certain amount of time working toward it (or received so many credits), identify that as well.

Examples

- Institute of Business and Medical Careers, Pharmacy Technician Certificate, 2010
- University of California–Davis, B.S. Environmental Science, 2000

- Humboldt State University, California, 100 credits toward B.A. in Child Development, 2008–present

Professional Development

If you have taken courses on the job that enhance your marketable skill set, write them down, along with the dates (if you know them).

Examples

- Attended professional training courses through American Society of Training and Development (ASTD): Teaching Adult Learners, Computer-Based Training, On-line Learning
- Completed The Institute of Learning and Teaching (TILT) workshops on study skills, presentations, and written communication

Awards and Honors

Have you ever been recognized for any superior talent or achievement? If so, write it down. Include the date if possible. Even if an award doesn't seem to directly relate to your skills, it may say something about your reliability, your honesty, or other valuable personal qualities.

Examples

- Employee of the month, Elecktra Manufacturing, 2010
- Volunteer of the month, Kiwanis Club, 2009
- Honor Society member, 2009–present

Now let's see how all that information fits into an actual resume.

Select Your Resume Format

Once you've gathered your information, it's time to figure out what belongs on your resume and what resume format to use. There are several standard formats to choose from: chronological, functional, and hybrid. Let's take a look at each type of resume and decide which might work best for you.

Chronological Resume

This is the most common type of resume. It focuses on the jobs you've had and lists them in reverse chronological order. Each job description includes important tasks you performed and skills you demonstrated, along with your accomplishments. This type of resume is good for people who have a steady job history with few gaps or job changes. It allows readers to quickly see how your career has progressed over time and the skills you've gained. Figures 7.4 and 7.5 show chronological resumes for Thomas Zetlmeisel and Morgan Ashley.

Functional Resume

This resume focuses on your skill sets, rather than your job history. Skills and accomplishments from your entire career, including volunteer work and internships, are featured prominently, rather than the actual jobs you've held. This type of resume is excellent for people who have changed jobs frequently or have gaps in their job history. It focuses on what skills they have, not whom they have worked for or when. This type of resume is also good for people who have worked at a variety of jobs, but performed the same types of tasks at each.

Figure 7.4 Sample chronological resume for Thomas Zetlmeisel

THOMAS M. ZETLMEISEL

4757 Cragsmoor Court #9E	602-555-8055
Tucson, AZ 85719	tzetlmeisel@earthlink.net

OBJECTIVE

Seeking a position that uses my new and updated skills as a data processor

SKILLS

Word, WordPerfect, Excel, Lotus, Access, dBase, Windows, Typing (certified at 60 wpm)

EXPERIENCE

Wolfe Industries, Tucson, AZ

Inventory Control Clerk   Feb. 2005 to present

- Enter inventory data into computer system
- Enter new items into warehouse locations; enter locations into database
- Update database and eliminate out-of-date items
- Receive returned items and put them back in inventory

TGIFriday's Restaurant, Tucson, AZ

Manager   Sept. 2003 to Jan. 2005

- Interviewed, hired, and evaluated employees
- Managed activity on the restaurant floor
- Coordinated employee scheduling

TUSD Summer High School

Assistant Secretary   Summer 2003

- Entered student and class data into database
- Provided class lists and schedule from database
- Maintained and updated class schedules

TUSD Summer High School

Intern   Summer 2002

- Organized and made photocopies
- Assisted the secretary with telephone and distribution of materials to teachers

EDUCATION

Killingworth Business School, Tuscon, AZ

- Information Technology Program, due to graduate November 2005

HONORS

- Killingworth Business School Dean's List, Perfect Attendance Certificates

REFERENCES AVAILABLE UPON REQUEST

Figure 7.5 Sample chronological resume for Morgan Ashley

MORGAN L. ASHLEY

237 Smith St., Fort Collins, CO 80527   (970) 555-3975
                                                         morganash@mailto.com

OBJECTIVE

Seeking challenging employment that combines my skills in graphic design, user interface design, and software development, with opportunities for future advancement.

SKILLS

- **3D Design:** AutoCAD, Strata Studio Pro
- **Graphics and Animation:** Photoshop, Illustrator, GIF Animation
- **Programming Languages:** Java, HTML
- **Desktop Publishing:** Quark

EXPERIENCE

Neotech, Fort Collins, CO

Lead Designer & Project Manager   September 2007 to December 2010

- Directed software and website projects involving teams of 3 to 5 people
- Designed user interfaces for collaboration software
- Developed corporate websites using Java, HTML, graphics, and animation
- Designed site architecture

World Design, Austin, TX

Web Designer   July 2005 to August 2007

- Worked with clients to develop graphic design and information architecture for corporate Internet websites
- Used HTML, Photoshop, Illustrator, Java, and image mapping

Office Max, Fort Collins, CO

Electronics Sales Manager   May 2004 to June 2005

- Managed activity in electronics department
- Assisted customers with personal computer purchases
- Answered questions and supplied information about computers

EDUCATION

Colorado State University, Fort Collins, CO

- Bachelor of Arts, Graphic Design, May 2004
- Course concentration in Computer Science, Graphics Art, Mathematics, Technical Writing

HONORS

- Dean's Recognition of Outstanding Students, April 2004
- WebAward for most advanced website design, December 2003

REFERENCES AVAILABLE ON REQUEST

Figure 7.6 shows a functional resume for Thomas Zetlmeisel that focuses on his skill sets.

Hybrid Resume

A hybrid resume includes the skill set information found in a functional resume, along with the job history information (tasks and accomplishments) found in a chronological resume. This type of resume is great for people who are reentering the job market after a long period of absence or for people looking for a job in a different field than what they've worked in before.

Figure 7.7 shows a final hybrid resume for Thomas Zetlmeisel that still shows his skill sets, but also includes more job experience information.

References

As you write your resume, it's important to consider three to five people who might serve as references for you. Today's employers are cautious and want to know that you are the person you say you are.

Like a symphony, a hybrid resume is a unique composition.

Think of People Who Will Describe You Favorably

These are people who are aware of your personality and abilities, have seen you in action, and know how you operate and what you're capable of. These might be teachers, friends, managers, employees, or community leaders. They don't have to be the highest-ranking folks you know. Perhaps the people with the most impressive titles at your former jobs—manager, director— don't know you well enough to talk about you. If they do, great! Include them. If not, someone who knows you better will do you more good than a person with a big title who has no opinion of you. Just make sure that the person you choose as a reference really knows your qualifications and any other special abilities that make you marketable.

Ask People for Permission to Use Them as References

Contact each person and ask if he or she would be willing to serve as a reference. No one likes receiving a surprise phone call asking about your qualifications if you haven't contacted him or her first. If you are applying for a specific job, tell your reference what the job entails so the individual has a better idea of what to talk about if he or she is contacted. You might even share skills or accomplishments that you would like your references to emphasize with your potential employer.

Double-Check the Contact Information for Each Reference

Once someone agrees to be a reference, write down the name, title, phone number, email, and address for each person. Check that the spelling is correct and the information accurate. When all references have been contacted, create a nicely formatted list of your references. Most prospective employers will

---

Did You Know? LinkedIn is a great social media site for job hunting. It is solely career-based and is the site most frequently used by recruiters and hiring managers to find talent. Post a copy of your resume as well as your career information in the **History** section. It is important to include both because the link to your actual resume cannot be searched like the information on your profile. Make sure your email address is visible so potential hiring managers can reach you. Use the **Status** section to let people know what kind of opportunities you are interested in. Then, join groups that are associated with your industry so you can be notified of posted jobs.

Figure 7.6 Sample functional resume for Thomas Zetlmeisel

THOMAS M. ZETLMEISEL

4757 Cragsmoor Court #9E	602-555-8055
Tucson, AZ 85719	tzetlmeisel@earthlink.net

OBJECTIVE

Seeking a position that uses my new and updated skills as a data processor.

SKILLS

Technology	Management
■ Word and WordPerfect ■ Excel and Lotus ■ Access and Dbase ■ Windows ■ Typing (certified at 60 wpm)	■ Interviewed, hired, and evaluated employees ■ Handled operations on restaurant floor
Information Processing	**Organization and Communication**
■ Entered warehouse locations into database and inventory items into locations ■ Updated database and eliminated out-of-date items ■ Entered student and class data into school database ■ Maintained and updated class schedules	■ Kept files and made photocopies ■ Organized and distributed materials to teachers ■ Coordinated employee schedules ■ Handled incoming and outgoing telephone calls ■ Reported to teachers as student representative to school administration

EXPERIENCE

■ **Wolfe Industries, Tucson, AZ**

Inventory Control Clerk	Feb. 2005 to present

■ **TGIFriday's Restaurant, Tucson, AZ**

Manager	Sept. 2003 to Jan. 2005

■ **TUSD Summer High School**

Assistant Secretary	Summer 2003

■ **TUSD Summer High School**

Intern	Summer 2002

EDUCATION

Killingworth Business School, Tuscon, AZ

■ Information Technology Program, due to graduate November 2005

HONORS

■ Killingworth Business School: Dean's List, Perfect Attendance Certificates, Student Representative

REFERENCES AVAILABLE ON REQUEST

Figure 7.7 Sample hybrid resume for Thomas Zetlmeisel

THOMAS M. ZETLMEISEL

4757 Cragsmoor Court #9E	602-555-8055
Tucson, AZ 85719	tzetlmeisel@earthlink.net

PROFESSIONAL PROFILE

Skilled and accurate information processor. Proven effectiveness working with databases. Comfortable working with a wide variety of professionals and communicating in writing or in person.

Key Skills

Technology	Management	Information Processing	Organization & Communication
■ Word ■ Excel ■ Access ■ Windows	■ Interview and evaluate employees ■ Coordinate work schedules	■ Enter and update data ■ Generate database reports	■ Organize and distribute materials ■ Handle incoming and outgoing phone calls

EXPERIENCE

Wolfe Industries, Tucson, AZ

Inventory Control Clerk	Feb. 2005 to present

- Enter inventory data into computer system, including warehouse locations
- Update database and eliminate out-of-date items
- Receive returned items and return them to inventory

TGIFriday's Restaurant, Tucson, AZ

Manager	Sept. 2003 to Jan. 2005

- Interviewed, hired, and evaluated employees
- Managed activity on the restaurant floor
- Coordinated employee scheduling

TUSD Summer High School

Assistant Secretary	Summer 2003
Intern	Summer 2002

- Entered and updated student and class schedule data into database
- Generated class lists and schedules from database
- Answered phones and distributed materials to teachers

EDUCATION

Killingworth Business School, Tuscon, AZ

- Information Technology Program, due to graduate November 2005

HONORS

- Killingworth Business School: Dean's List, Perfect Attendance Certificates, Student Representative

REFERENCES AVAILABLE ON REQUEST

Figure 7.8 Reference list for Thomas Zetlmeisel

LIST OF REFERENCES FOR THOMAS M. ZETLMEISEL

4757 Cragsmoor Court #9E   602-555-8055
Tucson, AZ 85719   tzetlmeisel@earthlink.net

- Dr. Leslie Scott, CIS Professor, Killingworth Business School, Tucson, AZ, 602-555-0101 x25, LScott@killingworthbus.edu
- Ms. Deanna Moldova, Career Counselor, Killingworth Business School, Tucson, AZ, 602-555-0101 x89, DMoldova@killingworthbus.edu
- Mr. Ian Petrosky, Director of Data Processing, Wolfe Industries, Tucson, AZ, 602-444-7500 x1211, ian.petrosky@wolfeind.com
- Ms. Pamela Turnbow, Sr. Data Processor, Wolfe Industries, Tucson, AZ, 602-444-7500 x1233, pam.turnbow@wolfeind.com

contact your references, in the interest of their company. Employers don't want to make hiring mistakes. To stay on the safe side, assume that anyone you list or discuss will be contacted. Figure 7.8 shows a sample reference list.

Ask for a Letter of Recommendation

Consider asking a few of the references to write you a letter of recommendation. Not all people are writers, so make it easier for them by providing a list of points you would like them to address in their letters. This helps them craft a more directed reference letter.

 Now You Try It: Collecting the Facts

It's never too early to start collecting the information you need for a resume. You will have a chance to work on your resume at the end of the chapter, but in the meantime, start compiling the following information:

1. Ideas for a career objective
2. List of your hard and soft skills
3. List of jobs, volunteer positions, or internships you've had (titles, dates, tasks)
4. List of references

Review and Polish Your Resume

Now that you have a rough draft of your resume, take the time to polish it. Here are guidelines that you can use to review your resume.

1. Be Neat, Clean, and Concise

Resumes must be typed. Make sure the resume is in a legible font that is large enough to read. Table 7.2 lists some standard font types and sizes. Although you might want to use other fonts for headings, stick with the standard fonts for the body text.

Try to fit everything onto one page if possible, or two at most. If the resume is two pages, make sure to print it two-sided so it still remains on one physical piece of paper (put a *continued on back* note on the bottom). This prevents your pages from becoming separated. If you have too much information, evaluate it and prioritize. If your resume is two pages, make sure the most important information is on the first page, just in case the reader never gets to the second. Knock off the least important pieces. Reduce the print size a bit (but not to the point that it is difficult to read). Economize! Say only what you really need to say related to the job for which you are applying.

Table 7.2 Standard Fonts and Sizes for Resumes	
Font	**Size**
Times Roman	12 point and larger
Georgia	11 point and larger
Verdana	11 point and larger
Arial	11 point and larger
Tahoma	11 point and larger

2. Check for Standard Formatting

Make sure your resume follows one of the standard formats shown earlier. Regardless of format, ensure that it contains the information you learned about in the "Collect Your Resume Information" section of this chapter. It's likely that you will customize the Objective and Skills sections for a specific job you are seeking. It's generally too time consuming to customize the other sections.

Folllowing is a checklist for last minute changes to your resume details.

Contact Information. Put your full legal name, address, phone number, and email address at the top. Try to make your name stand out—make it bold, put in capital letters, use a different font, or make it larger than everything else.

Career Objective. Make sure the objective is one sentence long and fits on no more than two lines. Ensure that the objective you specify relates to the job for which you are applying. This is one part of the resume that you should customize for the job!

Applicable Work Skills. List your skills that are relevant to the job. If possible, use similar words to those you read in the job description, and make sure they are action words (refer to the list earlier in this chapter for examples). This is a good place to showcase technologies you are familiar with that were mentioned in the job description. To save space, consider listing the skills in multiple columns and bulleting them so they are easy to scan. You might also group them into categories to make them easier to read.

Work Experience. List work experience in reverse chronological order with the most recent job first. For each position, write your official title (if you had one), the name of the company, its location (city and state), and the dates you worked there. This information should be bolded or in a font that stands out. Then list your most important duties and accomplishments using action verbs (if you forgot what action verbs were, refer back to the list in this chapter). Be sure what you list demonstrates your ability to perform the job for which you are applying. This helps limit the list so your resume fits on one physical page (one- or two-sided).

Education. Make sure your educational background is listed just like your work experience—in reverse chronological order, most recent first. Recent college graduates can include high school, but it is not necessary. Include the name of the school, the degree or certification, and the year you finished or graduated.

Awards or Honors. List any that portray you in a positive light that might make you more attractive to a potential employer. Include the name and date of the award, as well as who awarded it.

References. Lastly, include *References available on request*. This way, your references don't take up space on your resume, and you won't automatically be giving out other people's personal information to all who receive your resume. If someone asks for your references, provide that person with your list of references. Ensure that the actual reference list contains the most up-to-date contact information.

3. Use Quality Paper

You don't need fancy paper, just clean, neat paper with a little weight to it, in white, off-white, or light gray. Photocopying service centers or printers will tell you which papers work well for resumes. Remember, appearances count, even for resumes. The appearance of your marketing collateral says something about you. You want your resume to make a good impression because it represents your personal brand.

4. Be Accurate

Pay attention to accuracy as you compile your resume. Check your educational facts and dates. Make sure you have the right years and months for when you held different jobs. Accurately report your duties and accomplishments at those jobs and schools.

Any untruths or inaccuracies can surface and cause you trouble. If your prospective employer calls a former supervisor of yours, you want that former supervisor to confirm everything that you wrote. Besides, why lie about your experience? If you say you performed certain duties but really didn't, and then get a job where you're asked to perform them, the truth will soon come out.

Take a break from your resume, then come back to it and proofread it with a fresh perspective.

5. Proofread

After you have finished and feel comfortable with the accuracy of your resume, activate your proofreading skills. Check carefully for mistakes, spelling problems, inconsistent spacing, or strange sentences. Also look for inconsistencies in formatting (for example, using different fonts or bolding throughout), phrasing, capitalization, or indentation. A picture-perfect resume shows that you care about how you present yourself, that you take time to do the job right, and that you take pride in your work. Conversely, a misspelled word on a resume can eliminate you from consideration. To be safe, have someone else proofread your resume as well.

6. Save in a Readable Format

When you use special fonts, margins, or layout for your resume, be sure to save the resume in a format that everyone can read if you plan to send it electronically. For example, suppose you create a resume in Microsoft Word using special fonts that you downloaded. If you send the resume to someone who does not use Word, he or she will not be able to open your resume. And even if the individual can open the resume, the fonts won't look right. Consider the following formats.

PDF. This stands for Print Document Format. When you convert a file to PDF it's almost like taking a picture of the document so you can share it with everyone. It will look exactly the same to the person reading it as it does to you. Free PDF converters are available online if you don't already have one. Once your resume is in PDF format, anyone can download Adobe Reader for free to read the PDF file.

RTF. This stands for Rich Text Format. If someone opens an RTF resume with any type of word processing software, he or she will be able to read the file. However, the only type of formatting that RTF supports is bolding, italics, numbered and bulleted lists, and indentation. It does not support special layouts or fonts.

Plain Text. This is a file that has no special formatting or fonts. Typically, job-posting sites such as Monster.com or Dice.com require you to provide this type of resume. It's wise to have a plain text version of your resume if you plan to use such sites. When you create this type of resume, you cannot use bold, italics, fonts, lists, or indentation. In fact, you should use a plain text tool like Notepad to create a plain text resume.

Figure 7.9 shows partial resumes in each format. You will notice that the PDF example has the best formatting. The RTF example maintains the bolding, but not the special fonts and layout. The plain text example has no special formatting at all and uses dashes and equal signs to help break up the resume.

Your finished resume presents the best of your employment record, but it is still only part of how you sell your brand. You have other ways of emphasizing your marketability, such as a cover letter.

Cover Letter

Although your resume describes you, it doesn't directly address the person who will read it. That's why you need to accompany it with a cover letter. In the past, a job seeker typically mailed his or her resume to a potential employer with a letter on top. The letter "covered" the resume, so it was called a *cover letter*. Today, most job seekers send their resumes by email, so the content of their cover letters is either in the body of the email or in an attachment.

If the purpose of a resume is to get the reader to invite you in for an interview, then the purpose of a cover letter is to get the reader to look over your resume. A cover letter gives you the chance to introduce yourself more personally and to warm up the cold facts of the resume. The person reading your cover letter probably has to scan dozens of letters each day, so it's important that your letter be short and to the point, but still manage to stand out.

You accomplish this by composing a letter that consists of these four paragraphs.

technology *at work*

Companies increasingly use computers to help find the best employees. They scan traditional paper resumes into a resume database, as well as ask for resumes in electronic form. The resumes are analyzed by a computer, which assigns points to each resume based on key words and phrases. Take care in choosing the words and phrases you use on a resume. If the resume is submitted only in electronic form, slightly longer resumes with more key words and phrases can be scored higher and have a higher probability for selection for further review.

- **First paragraph.** This is your opening paragraph. Identify the job you are applying for and how you heard about it (newspaper listing, website, personal reference, school referral).

- **Second paragraph.** Talk about why you want the job and what you have to offer (specific skills and experiences). It can be hard to decide exactly what to talk about, since you need to be brief. Consider the fact that your reader needs to quickly determine whether your abilities are a match for the company's needs. Focus on the skills and qualities that seem to fit best with the requirements of the specific job. Choose facts that will encourage the recipient to read your resume. This is where you can supplement information that's in your resume. For example, if you are switching careers or are new to the workforce, you might draw attention to skills gained from other positions or experiences that you feel will make you successful at this job.

- **Third paragraph.** Explain why you want to work for the employer—what you like about the company. This is where you can show you've done your homework and know a little about the company. Don't go overboard with the praise, just be honest.

- **Fourth paragraph.** This is your closing paragraph. Mention any enclosure (such as your resume), express your desire for an interview, and politely request a response.

Figures 7.10 and 7.11 provide good examples of professional cover letters.

As you write your letter, keep these guidelines in mind:

- Use the same heading as you used for your resume (consider it your brand).

- Use a legible font.

- Correctly spell the name of the person who will receive the letter. It is always best to address him or her as "Mr." or "Ms.," unless you are on a first name basis with the individual.

- Be friendly and professional—not too casual, but not too formal.

Figure 7.9 Different formats for your resume: (a) PDF, (b) RTF, and (c) plain text

(a) Partial PDF example

MORGAN L. ASHLEY

237 Smith St., Fort Collins, CO 80527   (970) 555-3975
morganash@mailto.com

OBJECTIVE

Seek challenging employment that combines my skills in graphic design, user interface design, and software development, with opportunities for future advancement.

SKILLS

- **3D Design:** AutoCAD, Strata Studio Pro
- **Graphics and Animation:** Photoshop, Illustrator, GIF Animation
- **Programming Languages:** Java, HTML
- **Desktop Publishing:** Quark

EXPERIENCE

Neotech, Fort Collins, CO

Lead Designer & Project Manager   September 2007 to December 2010

- Directed software and website projects involving teams of 3–5 people
- Designed user interfaces for collaboration software
- Developed corporate websites using Java, HTML, graphics, and animation
- Designed site architecture

World Design, Austin, TX

Web Designer   July 2005 to August 2007

- Worked with clients to develop graphic design and information architecture for corporate Internet websites
- Used HTML, Photoshop, Illustrator, Java, and image mapping

(b) Partial RTF example

MORGAN L. ASHLEY
237 Smith St., Fort Collins, CO 80527
(970) 555-3975
morganash@mailto.com

Objective

Seek challenging employment that combines my skills in graphic design, user interface design, and software development, with opportunities for future advancement.

(continued)

Figure 7.9 (Continued)

Skills

- **3D Design:** AutoCAD, Strata Studio Pro
- **Graphics and Animation:** Photoshop, Illustrator, GIF Animation
- **Programming Languages:** Java, HTML
- **Desktop Publishing:** Quark

Experience

Neotech, Fort Collins, CO
Lead Designer & Project Manager, September 2007 to December 2010
- Directed software and website projects involving teams of 3–5 people
- Designed user interfaces for collaboration software
- Developed corporate websites using Java, HTML, graphics, and animation
- Designed site architecture

World Design, Austin, TX
Web Designer, July 2005 to August 2007
- Worked with clients to develop graphic design and information architecture for corporate Internet websites
- Used HTML, Photoshop, Illustrator, Java, and image mapping

(c) Partial Plain Text Example

```
=============================================
MORGAN L. ASHLEY
=============================================

237 Smith St., Fort Collins, CO 80527
(970) 555-3975
morganash@mailto.com

Objective
=============================================

Seeking challenging employment that combines my
skills in graphic design, user interface design,
and software development, with opportunities for
future advancement.

Skills
=============================================

* 3D Design: AutoCAD, Strata Studio Pro

* Graphics and Animation: Photoshop, Illustrator,
GIF Animation

* Programming Languages: Java, HTML

* Desktop Publishing: Quark
```

(continued)

Figure 7.9 (Continued)

```
Experience
=======================================

Neotech, Fort Collins, CO
Lead Designer & Project Manager, September 2007 to
                                        December 2010
---------------------------------------------------------

* Directed software and website projects involving
teams of 3-5 people
* Designed user interfaces for collaboration software
* Developed corporate websites using Java, HTML,
graphics, and animation
* Designed site architecture

World Design, Austin, TX
Web Designer, July 2005 to August 2007
------------------------------------------------------

* Worked with clients to develop graphic design
and information architecture for corporate
Internet websites
* Used HTML, Photoshop, Illustrator, Java, and
image mapping
```

Did You Know? It's a wise idea to customize your cover letter to your reader, company, and job. Let's say you worked as an auto technician and an electrician in the past. Put both on your resume, but adjust your cover letter depending on the kind of job you're applying for. If you apply for a job in the electrical field, mention your employment as an electrician in the cover letter. If you seek something in auto repair, emphasize the assistant mechanic job you held. Your prospective employer wants to see immediately what qualifications you have that will make you the right person for the job. Help out by making the most important items perfectly clear in your cover letter.

- Use short sentences and bulleted items to make your letter easy to scan.
- Check your spelling and grammar.
- Do not handwrite the letter.
- If you are submitting printed materials, use the same paper you used for your resume.

 ## Now You Try It: Generic Cover Letter

Cover letters should always be customized to the person and company to which they are going. However, it's a good idea to have a generic letter with which to start.

1. Identify the types of companies to which you would like to apply.
2. Create a rough draft of a generic cover letter you can adjust based on the four-paragraph structure you learned about. You will get to customize it later.

Figure 7.10 Sample cover letter for Thomas Zetlmeisel

THOMAS M. ZETLMEISEL

4757 Cragsmoor Court #9E   602-555-8055
Tucson, AZ 85719   tzetlmeisel@earthlink.net

5 October 2010

Ms. Melinda Mayotte
Personnel Director
Tessian Communication, Inc.
93 Avery Drive, Suite #800
Tuscon, AZ 85719

Dear Ms. Mayotte:

I am an Information Technology student at the Killingworth
Business School and will be graduating next month. I made the
decision some time ago to pursue a career in computers and am
looking forward to a full-time position in this field. I found out
about your job opening from a posted notice here at the school's
placement office.

I am interested in speaking with you about this job because I
spent the past two years perfecting the skills that the job description specifies. During that time I attended school at Killingworth Business School, studying Information Technology, while
working part-time as a computer operator at Wolfe Industries.
At Wolfe, I have received valuable hands-on experience in data
processing, giving me a chance to apply what I've been studying
in school.

Graduation is soon approaching and I am ready for a full-time
position. I have a particular interest in your company because
a neighbor of mine is one of your employees. He has given me
consistently good reviews about both the atmosphere and the
personnel at Tessian Communication, Inc.

Enclosed is my resume detailing my work experience and education. If you would like to interview me in person, I can be
reached at 602-555-8055. If I don't hear from you by the end of
the month, I will call you. Thank you for your kind consideration,
and I look forward to hearing from you soon.

Best regards,

Thomas M. Zetlmeisel

Encl: Resume

Figure 7.11 Sample cover letter for Ashley Morgan

MORGAN L. ASHLEY

237 Smith St., Fort Collins, CO 80527 (970) 555-3975
morganash@mailto.com
9 December 2012

Ms. Leslie Boudreaux
Personnel Director
Southtech, Inc.
1189 Canal St., Suite #300
New Orleans, LA 76935

Dear Ms. Boudreaux,

I am a graphic designer who has been designing websites and software interfaces for the last 5 years. I am currently seeking a full-time position in a career that will combine my skills in graphic design, website construction, and software development. I found out about your Lead Design job opening after conducting an informational interview with a member of your technical staff who shared the job description with me.

I am interested in speaking with you because I have the technical, artistic, and people skills that the job requires, according to your job description. During my time at Neotech, I have worked with teams of three to five people, managing website and software projects with tight deadlines and complex functionality. As project manager and technical lead, I have developed the skills necessary to successfully design and develop high-quality websites and software applications, while keeping teams running effectively.

I am interested in your company because the individual I spoke with at your company said Southtech is a new and promising establishment, open to growth and development.

Enclosed is my resume with my professional and educational history. I also have a portfolio of sample projects I have worked on that are available for your review. If you would like to interview me in person, I can be contacted at (970) 555-3975. I will follow up at the end of the week to make sure you have received my materials. Thank you for your consideration and I look forward to hearing from you soon.

Best regards,

Morgan L. Ashley

Encl: Resume

Note: Later, in "Target Your Efforts," you will learn what to do if you do not know who should receive the letter.

If you follow the guidelines, you'll have a winning cover letter that ensures your resume gets read!

Portfolio

Cover letters and resumes are great for introducing your talents to potential employers, but portfolios actually demonstrate what you've written about in your letter and resume. Portfolios display samples of your best work, providing proof of your accomplishments. Portfolios are not just for artists; they are for any job seeker who wants to provide concrete evidence of his or her accomplishments.

Although certain professions, such as graphics design or website development, demand a portfolio, you can create a profile no matter what profession you are in. A portfolio is a great way to remind yourself of the things you've accomplished, as well as share those accomplishments with potential employers.

A portfolio typically exists in both hard copy and electronic formats. A hard copy portfolio might be a binder or folio filled with physical examples of your best work. This type of portfolio is handy because you can share it with anyone, anywhere, anytime, without a computer. An electronic portfolio is usually a set of files stored on your computer, on a website, or on a CD, DVD, or thumb drive. You can email or mail these files to potential employers, or allow employers to download the files to view at their leisure.

You may be wondering what to put in your portfolio. Those of you who have been in the workforce for a long time might think you have too much to put in the portfolio, and those fresh out of school may think you have too little. Following is a process to help you figure out what belongs in your portfolio.

1. **Collect Possible Portfolio Items.** These typically include samples demonstrating your activities, education, training, work projects, or community service. Here are a few examples to get you thinking:

   - Awards
   - Certificates of completion for personal development workshops
   - Transcripts (for new college graduates)
   - Diplomas
   - Examples of computer skills
   - Examples of writing activities
   - Photos of projects you've worked on
   - Performance reviews
   - Letters of recommendation
   - Screenshots of websites you worked on
   - List of accomplishments on or off the job
   - Presentations
   - Thank you notes from clients, customers, vendors, or volunteer organizations
   - Newsletters or bulletins you've worked on

2. **Determine the Categories.** Look through all the material you've collected and see if you can come up with some categories. This is particularly helpful if you have a lot of materials. For example, your categories might be:

   - Work projects
   - School projects
   - Community and volunteer projects
   - Letters (received or written)

   You may decide to further break down the project categories.

Making People Look and Feel Good

Estaben Hernandez
Hairdresser

After ten years of renting "stations" at various hair salons, my dream was to open my own hair salon, and I'd finally built up a large enough clientele to do it. I located a great space in the older section of my city and gave the landlord the first and last month's rent. With the help of friends and family, I completely refurnished the space.

All my clients followed me to my new shop and things were great. I was my own boss, my shop was in a great location, and business was booming. I carried local and unusual hair products. My clients were happy and so was I. And then, two years later, the bottom fell out—the landlord tripled the rent. It seems he needed the space for one of his own endeavors. I couldn't come up with that kind of money and had to pack it in. I could barely think about looking for another job. The city already had too many hairdressers. How was I going to compete? What could I do to distinguish myself?

Lucky for me, one of my former clients was a writer. She said she'd be happy to help me come up with a resume and cover letter that would really "pop." I was worried that salons wouldn't want someone who was used to being his own boss, but my friend said my experience showed real leadership, salesmanship, and problem-solving abilities. What salon wouldn't need that?

She suggested I make a list of salons I was interested in and we'd both visit them to see what we thought—she, as a potential client, and me, as a potential employee. I felt like an undercover detective, but I learned a lot about the environment of different shops, and discovered that only a few of them were places that I would feel comfortable working.

The next step was to target my letters and resume to the top three salons I'd visited. My resume was certainly eye-catching—a bold black and white graphic across the top (left over from my own salon), a clean and modern layout, complete with objective, a professional profile, a list of my areas of expertise, and my employment history (including my self-employment). We even added a personal philosophy statement ("I like making people look and feel good.") and a couple of customer testimonials at the end to make my resume stand out.

I thought we were done, but my friend reminded me that a cover letter was a must. I had no idea where to start, so she suggested I think about myself in the "third person." I was supposed to imagine I was writing the cover letter for another person. Well, it worked. With a little editing, I had a nice short, four-paragraph cover letter. I made sure it was addressed to each salon owner (good thing I'd visited the salons and gotten the names). I also made sure to mention that I would follow up by phone.

At the end of the week, I called all three salons to make sure they had received my resume. The first salon had not only received my resume, but was interested in having me come in for an interview. I came in, and after a short conversation with the owner, I was hired on the spot! I still dream about being my own boss again and opening another salon. In the meantime, though, I'm enjoying my new job, attracting more clients, and so glad that I got help with my resume and cover letter!

3. **Select and Assemble Your Portfolio.** Pick your best work from each category. As you do, imagine you are the potential employer looking at the portfolio and determine work that will be relevant to the employer. Would this work demonstrate that you are capable and can assist the employer? You may end up creating a "master" portfolio, and then selecting items from it and assembling different portfolios for different industries or employers.

* If you decide to create a hard copy portfolio, use a clean 3-ring binder so you can add and delete items as necessary. Consider using clear protector sheets for each example. Use tabs to divide your portfolio into categories and make it easy to find things. Add a table of contents to make it easy for the reader to navigate, and include a clean cover with a clear title.

* If you decide to create an electronic portfolio, consider using PDF or HTML format for all materials that will be viewed or printed. This ensures that the formatting remains correct, regardless of what operating system or software your reader is using. Store the files in a folder on your computer system where you will remember their location. Make sure you have a summary file that lists the names of the individual files and what they represent. If you plan

to email a portfolio to someone, you may need to "zip" all the files into a compressed file and attach that zipped file to your email. Be aware, though, that some email filters prevent recipients from opening zipped attachments, since they so often contain viruses.

- If your portfolio is too large to email, you might consider storing your portfolio files on your own website and then directing employers to that site so they can download the files themselves.

- Another option is to store the portfolio files on a physical medium, such as a CD, DVD, or thumb drive. You can mail or deliver these to the potential employer.

4. **Present Your Portfolio.** You should never send or share a portfolio with a potential employer unless you are asked to do so. When you send a cover letter or resume, it's fine to mention that you have a portfolio you would be happy to share. Then, wait until the recipient asks you for it. As you'll learn in the next chapter, you should always bring your portfolio to an interview in case you are asked to share it.

 ## Now You Try It: Digging for Treasure

Finding the information you want in your portfolio is like digging for treasure—you're never sure where you'll find it. This mini-activity will help you locate the information to make it easier for you to create a portfolio.

1. Identify the types of information you believe you'd like in your portfolio and jot down where they are currently located at your home, office, or elsewhere. Refer to "Collect Possible Portfolio Items" in the preceding list for ideas.

2. You will use Table 7.3 to create your portfolio at the end of the chapter.

Table 7.3 **Location of Portfolio Materials**			
Type	**Location**	**Hard Copy**	**Electronic**

Business Cards

If your resume is your most important piece of marketing collateral and your portfolio is your biggest, then a business card is the smallest but handiest component of your brand. You can hand out your business card to people as you network, include it with your cover letter and resume, or drop it off at an interview. It is truly an all-purpose piece of marketing collateral.

Even if you are a student or unemployed, a business card is an essential item in your job hunt. In fact, think of your business card as a personal introduction card, similar to the calling cards that people used in Victorian days to introduce themselves to one another.

There are several options for acquiring a business card: (1) have a professional designer create the card and get it printed by a print shop; (2) design it yourself on your computer and print it on your own printer (or have a print shop print it); and (3) order a card through an online card design website that provides professional templates and prints the cards for you.

If you decide on option 1, the cost will be higher, but the look will be highly professional and unique. If you decide on option 2, the process will require more effort, the look may be less professional (unless you have a graphics background), and the quality of paper may be less than optimal. However, the cost will be minimal. If you go with option 3, the look will be professional, but may look the same as someone else's card. The quality of paper will be similar to that of a print shop, but it will cost less. Regardless of which option you choose, following are some guidelines for a professional business card:

- **Content.** Do not include jargon or slang. Ensure the information is accurate.
- **Layout and design.** Keep the design simple and not crowded. Make sure your name is featured in a prominent position. Avoid color combinations that look amateurish or make it difficult for people to read the text.
- **Fonts.** Be sure the text is large enough to be legible. A 10-point font should be the smallest you use. Use standard fonts that are easy to read. Make sure the text is dark and the background is light, otherwise people will have difficulty reading the card.
- **Contact information.** Include your full name, phone, and email so people can reach you. As you learned with resumes, make sure the email address is a professional one. An address is also useful to let people know where you are located.
- **Tagline.** Create a short phrase that sums up who you are or what you do.
- **Skills.** If you opt for a two-sided card, you might consider providing a short bulleted list of your skills.

Your business card is small and cannot say everything about you. It simply needs to say enough to jog people's memory or get them interested in you. Figure 7.12 provides a few examples of business cards for people who are employed and unemployed. Notice how the student and volunteer promote their services, even though they do not yet work for any company. Also, notice how the machinist indicates his skills to encourage potential employers.

Applications

You can create a resume, reference list, cover letter, portfolio, and business card before you actually apply for a job. However, some things must be done at the time you apply for job, such as filling out an application. An application provides factual information about you that will help employers determine whether you fit their needs. Not all employers require an application, but if your potential employer does, ask the employer to mail or email you one. If you live or work nearby, pick up an application. Following is some advice for filling out your application.

1. **Make it Legible.** Whether you type your application or write it, your prospective employer must be able to read it. No one can begin to consider you for a job if your application is unclear. Make sure you print clearly and neatly. Printing is usually easier to read than cursive. If your prospective employer emails you a "writeable" PDF application, you will be able to enter your information directly into the PDF file, and won't have to worry about legibility.

2. **Be Complete.** An application may be long and involved. Carefully fill it in and then to go back and proofread your work. Ensure that every part has been completed. If you're not sure how to complete a particular section, ask for help. You can contact someone at the company for clarification, or ask a teacher or counselor for help.

technology at work

Some companies pay specialists to do social network checks. These specialists use custom software that systematically trolls social networking sites for evidence of bad character. This helps companies decide if they really want to hire you for a particular position. The custom software looks through Facebook, Twitter, Flickr, YouTube, LinkedIn, blogs, and other sources to develop a report on the "real you," not the carefully crafted you in your resume.[1]

[1]Egan, Mike. "Ore-crime comes to the HR dept." *Datamation*, September 29, 2010. Accessed on December 8, 2010, from http://itmanagement.earthweb.com/features/article.php/3905931/Pre-crime-Comes-to-the-HR-Dept.htm

Figure 7.12   **Sample business cards for: (a) student, (b) unemployed machinist, (c) volunteer, (d) currently employed cleanroom technician**

(a)

(b)

(c)

(d)

3. **Be Honest.** Applications may ask questions about your landlord, credit status, and previous employment; many ask if you have ever been convicted of a crime. Honesty is definitely the best policy. Employers can verify any information you give them, and they often do so for their own protection. They want to make sure they're hiring a person of integrity. They may contact your teachers, landlords, or previous employers; examine your credit history by contacting a credit bureau; or check with the police department to make sure you have no file there.

   Even if something in your past wouldn't look good on an application, an employer would rather hear it from you than from an outside source. Lying on an application can disqualify you from a hiring pool immediately. Honesty just might keep you there, despite any questionable history.

4. **Be Quick.** Sometimes so many people apply for a job that the ones who return their applications promptly have a better chance of getting an interview. Make completing the application a priority. The more quickly you complete and return your application, the sooner the employer can consider it and give you an answer. If you do get an interview, your speed may have put you ahead of a number of other applicants. If you don't get an interview, you can move on to other job applications without wasting any more time. See Figure 7.13 for a sample application.

Targeting Your Efforts

Let's assume you spent a lot of time and effort on your professional marketing materials and now they're ready for the world to see. Don't waste them on the wrong people. If you did your networking, you probably already have names of the right people. If you're responding to a

Figure 7.13 Sample application for employment

FORMER EMPLOYERS (List below last four employers, starting with last one first).

Date Month & Year	Name and Address of Employer	Salary	Position	Reason for Leaving
From				
To				
From				
To				
From				
To				
From				
To				

REFERENCES Give the names of three persons not related to you, whom you have known at least one year.

	Name	Address	Business	Years Acquainted
1				
2				
3				

PHYSICAL RECORD
Do you have any physical limitations that preclude you from performing any work for which you are being considered? ☐ Yes ☐ No

Please Describe _____

In Case Of
Emergency Notify _____
           Name   Address   Phone No.

"I certify that the facts contained in this application are true and complete to the best of my knowledge and understand that, if employed, falsified statements on this application shall be grounds for dismissal.

I authorize investigation of all statements contained herein and the references listed above to give you any and all information concerning my previous employment and any pertinent information they may have, personal or otherwise, and release all parties from all liability for any damage that may result from furnishing same to you.

I understand and agree that, if hired, my employment is for no definite period and may, regardless of the date of payment of my wages and salary, be terminated at any time without prior notice."

Date _____ Signature _____

Do Not Write Below This Line

_____ Date _____

Hired: ☐ Yes ☐ No _____ Position _____ Dept. _____

Salary/Wage _____ Date reporting to work _____

Approved: 1. _____ 2. _____ 3. _____
       Employment Manager   Dept. Head   General Manager

This form has been designed to strictly comply with State and Federal fair employment practice laws prohibiting employment discrimination. This Application for Employment Form is sold for general use throughout the United States. Gussco assumes no responsibility for the inclusion and said form of any questions which, when asked by the Employer of the Job Applicant, may violate State and/or Federal Law.

77 105

posted job description, you may have a name, but not always. More and more, online job listings only provide a generic email address.

Letters addressed to a real person always get more attention, so this is where your networking skills come in handy. Try calling the company and doing some investigating to discover the name and contact information of the person who should receive your materials. You might call your friends or contacts within the company. You may also be able to find the name of the proper individual on the company's website. It's best to get the name of an actual decision maker so your cover letter and resume wind up in the right hands. Sometimes you may be unable to get a name, no matter how hard you try. In this case, address the letter to human resources or to the department doing the hiring. For example:

- Dear Human Resources Staff:
- Dear Marketing Department:

When you don't have a name and must send your cover letter and resume to a department, be sure to mention anyone you have spoken with in the company. This way, the individual who reads your material will know you took the time to do some investigating. For example:

- I recently spoke with Marci in Marketing, and she suggested I submit my resume to your department.
- My friend Estaben, in Facilities, recommended I submit my resume to your department.

It's also wise to follow up by phone to make sure your cover letter and resume were received. Always mention when you submitted your materials. In fact, you might even consider sending a hard copy of your cover letter and resume a week or two later. In this case, you can adjust your cover letter to mention that you are following up on a letter and resume you submitted electronically (indicate the date), and would like to provide a hard copy for reference. This is an excellent way to get people to notice or remember you.

The Interview Will Happen

Maybe you will get an interview right away, or maybe you will have to go through several months of applications, customized cover letters, updated resumes, and lots of follow-up calls. Either way, you will gain valuable experience and a self-esteem boost in the process. Your resume will remind you of what you have to offer to the world. Your portfolio will provide tangible evidence of your accomplishments. Your cover letters will show you the progress you're making in your job hunt.

If you've followed the guidelines in this chapter and followed up, you *will* get that interview. This is where Chapter 8 will come in handy, ensuring that all goes well with the interview so you get the job!

Your Tool Kit at Work

This section offers a special set of activities to help you prepare your professional marketing collateral: a resume, portfolio, and cover letter for your real-life job hunt. Take time to go through every activity and make the most of it.

To make things easier for you, you may want to pull up the information you wrote down for the earlier mini-activity, "Now You Try It: Collecting the Facts."

7.1 Assess Your Skills

It's a good idea to know your skill set before you create your resume. Refer back to Table 7.1 for ideas.

My Skill Set

Hard Skills	Soft Skills

Knowing your skill set helps you write a better resume and cover letter that accurately portray who you are and what you can do.

7.2 Compile Your Employment Information

Sometimes getting started is the hardest part. Before you become overwhelmed by the idea of writing your resume or compiling a portfolio, fill out this form. It will help you organize the information that eventually belongs in your resume.

You already got a head start on this collection process during the mini-activity "Now You Try It: Collecting the Facts." Now's your chance to consolidate all the information in one place.

1. Personal information

Name: _____

Address: _____

Phone: _____

Email: _____

2. Education

a. Schools

	Name	Graduation (Month/Year)
High school		
GED		
College (2 or 4 year)		
Technical/ vocational school		

Fill in b–d if you are a recent graduate; otherwise, skip to Step 3.

b. Skills learned at school

_____

_____

c. Extracurricular activities

_____

_____

d. Honors/awards

_____

_____

3. Work experience (paid, informal, or volunteer) (start with the most recent and work backward)

a. Job Title: _____

   Company or Organization: _____

   Location (city/state): _____

   Dates of employment or volunteering: _____

   Supervisor: _____

   Responsibilities:

   _____

   _____

   Skills (used to perform your responsibilities):

   _____

   _____

b. Job Title: _____

   Company or Organization: _____

   Location (city/state): _____

   Dates of employment or volunteering: _____

   Supervisor: _____

   Responsibilities:

   _____

   _____

   Skills (used to perform your responsibilities):

   _____

   _____

c. Job Title: _____

   Company or Organization: _____

   Location (city/state): _____

   Dates of employment or volunteering: _____

Supervisor: _____

Responsibilities:

_____

_____

Skills (used to perform your responsibilities):

_____

_____

d. Job Title: _____

Company or Organization: _____

Location (city/state): _____

Dates of employment or volunteering: _____

Supervisor: _____

Responsibilities:

_____

_____

Skills (used to perform your responsibilities):

_____

_____

4. Military information

Rank: _____

Branch: _____

Date of discharge: _____

Skills learned:

_____

_____

5. Specific skills I have/equipment I can use

_____

_____

6. Hobbies/interests (list these only if they indicate skills related to your chosen field and would enhance your employability)

_____

_____

7. Licenses and certificates of proficiency

Type	Name on License	Exp. Date or Date Received	Level of Proficiency
Driver's license			

8. Memberships

Type	Title	Dates
Union		
Professional		
Community		
Club		

Now you have a comprehensive list of your vital information. You will need this information when you create your resume or fill out an application.

7.3 Develop a Professional Resume

Choose the best type of resume: chronological, functional, or hybrid. Refer to the examples in Figures 7.4 through 7.7.

1. Come up with a good career objective. For examples, refer to the earlier section "Collect Your Resume Information."
2. Transfer your collected information to the resume. Be sure to use action verbs for all tasks you performed. For examples, refer to the list earlier in this chapter.
3. Limit the resume to one page (either single- or double-sided).
4. Use the checklist under "Check for Standard Formatting" to finalize the resume.
5. Convert your finished resume to PDF format.
6. Print the resume on quality paper.

7.4 Line Up Your References

It's never too early to compile your list of references and contact the individuals for letters of recommendation.

1. Find the list of references you created in the mini-activity "Now You Try It: Collecting the Facts."
2. Contact each reference and make sure you have his or her most up-to-date contact information. Also, find out which references would be willing to write you a letter of recommendation.
3. Create a one-page, professionally formatted list of references. Be sure to include the name, title, organization, city, state, phone, and email for each reference.

7.5 Craft the Ideal Cover Letter

Review your networking notes from Chapter 6 to identify companies to which you would like to apply.

1. List the people to whom you plan to send your cover letter and resume at each company. If you don't know who they are, do your research and find out.
2. Customize the generic cover letter you created earlier in the chapter for each company and job.
3. Be sure to use the four-paragraph structure. For assistance, refer to Figures 7.10 and 7.11.

7.6 Produce Your Professional Portfolio

This activity might take awhile, so plan to complete it over several settings.

1. Refer to Table 7.3 in the mini-activity "Now You Try It: Digging for Treasure." This lists the types of samples you would like to put in the portfolio and where they are currently located.

2. Start going through hard copy materials and electronic files you listed to identify your best work.

3. Make sure that all the electronic files that make up your portfolio are safely stored in one or more well-organized folders on your computer.

4. If necessary, write the files to a CD, DVD, or thumb drive and put the media in a safe place.

5. Print the examples that you would like in a hard copy portfolio.

6. Organize your hard copy portfolio in a clean binder. Include a cover and table of contents.

7.7 Create Your Own Calling Card

Here's a chance to brainstorm ideas for a business card in case you do not already have one.

1. Fill in the outlines below with general ideas. Be sure to include the important information mentioned in the previous section on business cards for ideas.

2. Do a search of "business card" on the Internet to locate sites where you can design your own cards. Visit them to see if any of them might suit your needs.

3. Check your printed or online phone book for local print shops that do business card design and printing. Find out their prices. The more design work you do up front, the less the cost will be.

8

Select Your Tools for the Interview

Winning Strategies to Seal the Deal

It's the first impression and will either open the door or close it.
It's that important, so don't mess it up.

Nicholas Sparks, author

 learning objectives

- What should you know about a phone interview?
- How do you research a company prior to an interview?
- What are some guidelines for dressing for an interview?
- What are some winning interview techniques?
- What kinds of questions should you ask?
- How should you deal with difficult questions, objections, or rejection?
- What are illegal questions and how should you handle them?
- How do you negotiate a job offer?

auren didn't like interviews. The truth was, she felt uncomfortable talking about herself and didn't like being asked questions. It reminded her too much of the crime dramas she watched on television, where the suspect was sitting in the interview room of a police department being interrogated by several detectives. Sadly, her feelings about being interviewed caused her many problems. She was typically nervous and defensive, and often complained about her prior employers to the interviewers. As a result, she rarely ended up getting the job she wanted.

After years of bad interviews and jobs she didn't like, Lauren decided to get some help. She talked with a job counselor at the local community college who suggested that Lauren go through some mock interviews. The counselor acted as the interviewer and Lauren was the interviewee. Afterward, the counselor evaluated everything about the interview, from Lauren's clothes and handshake, to her voice and mannerisms, to her answers and final closing.

Even though Lauren knew the interview wasn't a real one, she was just as nervous and defensive, getting upset when the counselor probed about prior jobs, and clamming up when the counselor asked her about her strengths and weaknesses. What a disaster!

Lauren learned that her difficulty with interviews wasn't unique—many people feel uncomfortable with interviews, and there was something she could do about it. For the next several weeks, she met with the counselor to go over good interview etiquette. She learned how to dress, shake hands, warm up her interviewers, handle difficult questions, overcome objections, and promote herself. She learned to highlight different parts of her resume to show how she had used her skills and talents at different jobs to make a difference. She even learned the fine art of salary negotiation, something she'd always been afraid to do.

The counselor urged Lauren to "quit worrying about getting the job and just enjoy the interview. Consider each interview as a chance to practice your new skills." As hard as that advice was to take, Lauren did what the interviewer said. At her next interview she focused on making the interviewer feel comfortable and stopped worrying about herself. At the interview after that, she actually looked forward to difficult questions, just so she could try out her newfound skills for handling objections. And when she went in for her third interview, with a company she really liked, everything came together like magic. Her interview practice paid off—she got an offer (which she negotiated), and started her new job feeling confident and excited!

Maybe you're like Lauren and fear the interview process, or maybe you don't. Either way, once you've applied for the

myth

"How I look or act during an interview doesn't really matter. What matters is my experience, skills, and talents—everything that's on my resume."

reality

No matter how good you look on paper, everything you do during an interview, from how you treat each member of the interview team, to what you're wearing, to what you say or don't say, is taken into account in the hiring decision. Sloppy dress may be interpreted as a lack of respect. Not acknowledging people with a smile and a handshake may be interpreted as arrogance. Not asking any questions may be interpreted as overconfidence. All of these behaviors could cost you the job.

job and have gotten the interview, you're only one step away from getting the job of your dreams. What next? Prepare for your interview so you're comfortable and relaxed. Become fluent in interview etiquette and learn the secrets of handling failure and success. Give yourself the best possible opportunity to succeed by using all the skills you have mastered.

Preparing for an Interview

Although your resume can attract the attention of your potential employer, the interview really gives you the chance to open the door to career success. All jobs will require an interview. If you've been offered an interview, the company already knows you are qualified based on your resume. However, an interview allows the company to determine whether you are a good fit for a position and for the company's culture. It also lets you see if the company is a fit for you. Even if you are being considered for a promotion or a different job within the same company, you will have to interview with your prospective supervisor.

To do well in your interview, you must be prepared. This section deals with different preparation activities that can help you get ready for the interview.

Schedule the Interview

Once you are invited for an interview, be sure to follow these tips when you schedule the interview:

1. Ask the person who calls for the name and position of the interviewer, the exact address and office location, and the expected duration of the interview.
2. Schedule the interview when you know that you can make it on time comfortably (and stay for a while) without throwing the rest of your life into a tailspin.
3. Ask the caller for detailed directions to the interview location if you have never been there. Ask for public transportation information if you need it.
4. Write the date and time where you will notice it—in your appointment book, on a bulletin board, on a note pasted to your bathroom mirror—whatever works. If you tend to track appointments online, make a hard copy reminder as well. Write the name of your contact person and the phone number next to the time and date, in case you need to reach that person for any reason.

Research the Employer

It's smart to know about the company before you interview. If you have done your research and can ask knowledgeable questions about people, structure, activities, money, and your role in the company, your interviewer will take notice. Your effort will display intelligence, resourcefulness, and diligence. Plus, you will benefit more from the interview because you know the basics and will be able to go into more depth.

Here are some excellent pre-interview questions you might consider researching to help you understand the company and the position:

1. What's the business climate like in the industry?
2. What changes are occurring in the industry and how do they impact the company?
3. How large is the company?
4. How old is the company?
5. What exactly does the company do (products and services)?
6. Who are the major competitors?
7. Is this a new position? If so, why was it created?
8. What is the impact of this position on the company as a whole?

You can find answers to these questions from a variety of resources. See Table 8.1 for ideas on how to find this information.

You might also consider some "undercover" research, for which you visit the company in person and hang out so you can see what people look like and how they act. This kind of research

Table 8.1   **Resources for Pre-Interview Research**

Resource	Description
The personnel department of the company	People who supervise interviewing and hiring know that potential employees will be looking for information. They may be able to answer your questions regarding company structure, activity, size, and scope.
People you know who work there	Talk to any friends, family, or alumni you know who are currently employed by the company. They will have more "insider" information regarding salary potential, how people get along at the company, power hierarchy, and rules and regulations.
Annual reports	You can request these from any publicly held company (any company traded on the stock exchange). They contain the basic facts about the company and offer details about their financial performance.
Library	Annual reports can be found here. Your library may also have access to articles about the company in newspapers or periodicals. Check the business directories such as Standard & Poor's for basic data including address, size, income, and profit.
Your school	Your placement directors and instructors may know about the company from placing others there. They may be able to put you in touch with alumni who interviewed there or worked there in the past.
The Better Business Bureau (BBB)	The BBB can tell you the company's legal track record and inform you of any violations, investigations, or claims of bad business practice.
Company website	The company's website tends to have good information about its products, services, and clients (although the information may be a bit biased). It may also include more information about the job description. Even the appearance of the website can give you clues about the company's personality. The website address is typically found on the company business card. If you don't have the business card, use a search engine to locate the company or call and ask for the website address.

is usually possible when you know someone at the company. But even if you don't, you can always sit outside and watch people as they arrive and leave the company building.

Every career field has its individual requirements, style of operation, and particular personality. Individual businesses or firms within each field may differ. One plant may require uniforms, whereas another will only require that clothing fit the safety standards without regard to color or style. Different offices may have different rules about hours, coffee breaks, and office etiquette. Every situation is unique. The following is a list of things to look for when conducting your undercover research or participating in an actual interview:

- **Dress.** How people dress on the job—uniforms? suits? jeans? shorts and flip flops?
- **Behavior.** Behavior toward one another (formal or informal, first names or titles).
- **Power structure.** Who is at the top of the pile, who is next in importance, and who is important to please.
- **Operational structure.** Who answers to whom, who takes orders from whom, and who reports to whom.
- **Manners.** Big or small emphasis.
- **Credentials.** What kind of experience, schooling, degrees, or certificates you need.
- **Skills.** Which are necessary and which are icing on the cake.

Pay Attention to Your Appearance

The job market can be quite competitive, so it's wise to look as professional as possible for your interview. During your interview, you'll be evaluated on qualities that are not even listed in the job description, such as your clothing, voice, and mannerisms. These qualities may seem superficial, but they tend to form the first impression your interviewer has of you.

Based on your appearance, people may draw conclusions about your trustworthiness, sophistication, social position, economic status, educational level, and moral characteristics. Although it doesn't seem fair, people often judge each other instantly, with little to no information. Consider your own experience. What happens when you meet someone for the first time? Within a few seconds, you have formed an opinion about that person based on dress, speech patterns, degree of eye contact, body language, and grooming. If the opinion is good, you are probably more open to what the person has to say. If the opinion is bad, you are probably more closed to that individual.

Although first impressions take only a few seconds to make, they tend to last forever, so make your first impression a good one. Your best defense is to dress for success. This does not necessarily mean spending a fortune on a wardrobe. It means dressing nicely, in clothes that you feel comfortable in and look good in. It also means dressing just a bit more formally than the normal dress at the company where you are interviewing. Why? Because your interviewers typically assume that the way you look for the interview is the best you'll ever look. After you're hired, you can always start dressing like the rest of the employees. If you're not sure what the standard style of dress is, visit the company some time before your interview and observe what people are wearing.

Undercover research can help you check out the culture of a company that you are considering as a potential employer.

A neat, clean, healthy appearance tells an employer or interviewer that you care about yourself. It also shows you understand that your appearance subtly tells customers and clients that you care about their needs as much as you care about your own.

Make sure your clothes are clean and neat (not necessarily new—just in good shape). Stick with something relatively neutral in color and style that you feel comfortable wearing. In fact, try wearing the outfit at least once before your interview. You want your interviewer to focus on the real you, not the outfit you are wearing.

Even if the job you're applying for requires that you dress in a uniform and get dirty on the job, it's still important to wear something nice for the interview to make a good impression. Styles and degrees of formality tend to differ in different parts of the country, so do a little research to find out how people dress. For example, something that is proper in Chicago, Illinois, might make you seem overdressed in Boise, Idaho. Play the game and wear what they want to see!

If you're still not sure what to wear, Table 8.2 provides tips for your interview appearance. The main idea is this: You do not want your appearance to get in the way of someone hiring you, nor do you want your appearance to be the only thing your interviewers remember about you. You want your interviewers to focus on you, not on what you look like.

With appearance under control, what else should you think about as you get ready for your interview? How about your handshake?

Did You Know?

Appearances do count. Consider the candidate who applied for an Account Executive position in an organization and didn't get the job. When the president of the company was asked why he turned down the candidate, he replied, "His shirt was so wrinkled that it looked like he'd worn it the day before, balled it up in a corner of his room, put it back on the next morning and wore it to the interview. He didn't even bother to try and cover it up by putting a jacket over it. My thought was that if he couldn't even take the time to impress me at our first meeting, what was he going to be like with our customers?"[1]

---

[1]Ferguson, Cheryl. "A second look at first impressions." *The Recruiter's Studio.* Accessed on December 29, 2010, from http://jobsearch.about.com/od/interviewsnetworking/a/interviewimpres.htm

Table 8.2	**Professional Appearance Tips**	
Dress Point	**Men**	**Women**
Hygiene	Always shower or bathe before an interview.	Always shower or bathe before an interview.
Hair	Get a haircut a few days before the interview. Pull back longer hair with a ponytail holder.	Wear your hair pulled away from face or in a simple style.
	Dry your hair completely and avoid excessive hair products.	Dry your hair completely and avoid excessive hair products.
Cologne	Use scent sparingly, or not at all. Do not smell like smoke.	Use scent sparingly, or not at all. Do not smell like smoke.
Nails	Make sure your nails are clean.	Make sure your nails are clean. Avoid excessively long or colored nails.
Facial hair or makeup	Men should be neatly shaven or facial hair (beard, mustache) should be well groomed.	Keep makeup to a minimum.
Jewelry	Remove obvious piercings, and keep chains and rings to a minimum.	Keep jewelry to a minimum and remove obvious facial piercings. Wear understated rather than large jewelry.
Tattoos	Cover tattoos for an interview.	Cover tattoos for an interview.
Belts	If you have belt loops, wear a belt. Always tuck your shirt in for an interview.	If you have belt loops, wear a belt. Always tuck your shirt in for an interview.
Pants	Choose a dark color. Make sure the pants are not wrinkled.	Choose a dark color. Make sure the pants are not wrinkled.
Suits	Dry cleaned or pressed; not wrinkled. Make sure the suit is not too tight or too loose.	Dry cleaned or pressed; not wrinkled. Make sure your skirt hem does not rise above the knee, and the suit is not too tight.
Skirt or dress	N/A	Dry cleaned or pressed; not wrinkled. Make sure your hem does not rise above the knee, and the skirt or dress is not too tight.
Shirt	Always wear a tie when interviewing unless the office is very informal. In that case, wear a sport coat. Choose a color that does not wash out your face and make you look pale. Make sure the shirt is not wrinkled.	Do not wear a low-cut shirt. Choose a color that does not wash out your face and make you look pale. Make sure the shirt is not wrinkled.
Shoes	Polished dress shoes or loafers for an informal interview. Matching socks. Do not wear athletic shoes.	Polished, closed-toe shoes are advised for interviews. Avoid stiletto heels or excessively pointed shoes. Hosiery is required in formal offices.

Practice Your Handshake

Although you might not have thought about it, in the business world your handshake says a lot about you: Are you confident? Are you fearful? Are you friendly? Are you aggressive? Those qualities actually come through in a handshake.

When you meet someone for the first time, the best way to make a good impression is with a good handshake. This should be a nice firm handshake, not a limp-wristed extension of your arm or a bone-crushing grip that leaves the recipient wincing. One way to find out how your handshake comes across is to try it on your friends. If they tell you it's too soft, try tensing your lower arm a bit as you grasp someone's hand, rather than squeezing harder. If your friends tell you your handshake is too rough, focus on embracing the other person's hand instead of squeezing it. And don't forget to smile as you shake hands—you will come across as friendly and professional.

Now You Try It: Looking Good

Imagine that you have an interview for the job of your dreams. Based on what you've read about a professional appearance and the importance of a handshake, do the following:

1. Go through your closet and dresser to identify all the components of an interview outfit that you believe you will be comfortable in.
2. Try on your clothes, shoes, and hairstyle. Check out your appearance in the mirror. How do you look and feel? Overdressed? Underdressed? Comfortable? Uncomfortable?
3. Get someone else's opinion about your interview look—perhaps a coworker, friend, or family member who has a sense of what looks professional.
4. Besides getting feedback on your interview look, try out your handshake on friends.
5. What feedback do you get about your clothing? Your handshake?
6. Consider the advice and work on improving your look and your handshake.

Remember, the images you've seen of professionals on various television shows or in different magazines rarely reflect real people and how they dress on the job. It's always best to visit the place where you might interview and observe how people are dressed.

Conduct a Practice Interview

With your professional appearance and handshake ready, there's only one thing left to do—conduct a practice interview. This typically reduces stress and helps you anticipate what to expect during the actual interview. You can practice by yourself if you like. Think about the questions you might be asked and answer them aloud in front of a mirror. Evaluate your answers and delivery. Are you using the information on your resume, in your cover letter, and from your job research?

Role-play is one of the most effective ways to prepare for an interview. You can practice with a friend or family member who agrees to play the role of interviewer. You dress the part, meet the person, shake hands, and introduce yourself just like you would in a real interview situation. The other person asks questions that you have provided and you answer them to the best of your ability. Your mock interviewer then shares any observations with you at the end of the interview regarding your appearance, voice, body language, and the content of your answers. Based on the input, you may need to write down answers to possible questions and study them, change your clothes or mannerisms, and hold the practice interview again. As the saying goes, "practice makes perfect."

Following are some questions you might think about prior to your actual interview.

Background and Interest Questions

These are questions that someone asks to try to get to know you. They tend to focus on your professional and personal background and interests. Answering these questions lets you talk about what you know best—you.

1. How did you choose your major?
2. What inspired your change in majors?
3. Tell me about your college experience?
4. What brought you out to this city or state?
5. What made you decide to do this type of work?
6. What types of companies have you worked for in the past?
7. What made you change careers?
8. What are you looking for in a position?
9. What do you do in your free time?

Behavioral Questions

These are questions that someone might ask you about your past experiences and behaviors to try to predict your future behavior in the company.

1. Have you ever had a conflict with coworkers? How did you resolve it?
2. What was your greatest challenge on your last job? How did you overcome it?
3. Have you ever had to deal with an unhappy client? What did you do?
4. What is your greatest success? How did you achieve it?
5. What is the most difficult situation you ever found yourself in? How did you handle it?
6. Walk me through one of your previous projects from start to finish.
7. Share a time when you failed to reach your goal. What happened?
8. Discuss a time you felt overwhelmed. How did you handle the stress?
9. Have you ever worked on a team project? What role did you play?
10. Have you ever had difficulty with a manager's decision? How did you handle it?

Situational Questions

These are questions that pose hypothetical situations so that interviewers can see how you think. These questions usually revolve around situations that you might encounter on the job. For example, here are some sample situational questions that would be appropriate for someone considering a position as a dental hygienist:

1. What would you do if one of your patients were consistently late for appointments?
2. What would you do if you realized the office manager booked two people for teeth cleanings at the same time?
3. How would you handle a dentist who consistently criticized your work, even though your patients praised you?
4. How would you deal with a frightened patient who had not seen a dentist in years because of a very painful experience in the past?
5. What would you do if you saw a coworker stealing from the company?

Difficult Questions

These are questions that interviewers use to see how you respond under pressure, to dig a little deeper into your background, or to simply learn more about you.

1. Why did you change majors so often?
2. It appears you weren't a very serious student. Why did you receive such poor grades?
3. Why should I hire you, when I have three candidates more qualified?
4. Why would a person interested in this career major in English?
5. Why are there gaps in your employment?
6. Why weren't you more involved in academic or community activities?
7. How can someone with no experience relate to our customers?

The best way to deal with these questions is to: (a) not get defensive, (b) answer honestly, and (c) put a positive spin on your response by indicating what you learned from the experience. For example, suppose someone asks you, "Why were you at Storm Research for only three months?" You could answer this way:

> "I had been unemployed for six months when I got the position at Storm Research. I guess you can say I was so happy to be employed again that I didn't look too deeply at the company or the job. It turns out I wasn't a fit for Storm Research and they weren't a fit for me. They wanted a highly analytical, process-oriented person who could work alone, analyzing computer-based weather data all day. I was more of a big picture person who wanted to be involved with people and planning. It was a mutual decision that I leave, and I left on good terms. Since then, I've learned to do a lot more research into any position I'm interested in, and make sure it allows me to interact with others and get involved in upfront planning."

By answering in this way, you play up your positive traits (big picture person who likes people and planning), which will be useful to your potential employer as they look at possible fit. Your answers also show that you learn from experience. Plus, you didn't bad-mouth your former employer, which shows respect and maturity.

It's unlikely that you will ever be asked *all* of these questions during your interview. However, by thinking about them ahead of time, you will be much more prepared and confident than the average interviewee.

 ## Now You Try It: Collecting Your Questions and Your Thoughts

Whether you've been invited to interview or not, it's never too early to start thinking about the questions you might be asked during an interview.

1. Recall a previous interview experience. What went well? What could you have done better? For which questions were you unprepared?

2. Review the sample background, behavior, situational, and difficult questions you read in this chapter. Answer each question in your own words. You can refine your answers as time goes on, but having some idea of how you might answer them can be very helpful.

3. Think about other questions you might be asked, even questions you are uncomfortable with—ones you may have been asked in a prior interview. Then come up with some possible answers.

4. Now stand in front of a mirror and answer some of those uncomfortable questions you've thought about. How do you look? Practice looking calm, confident, and happy.

Asking yourself questions, especially difficult ones, and preparing answers is a great way to take the worry out of future interviews.

The Night Before the Interview

Even with plenty of preparation, it's natural to feel nervous the night before your interview. Here are some things you can do to calm down, prepare for the next day, and feel good about yourself.

1. **Verify your instructions.** Make sure you have the interview date and time right, as well as directions for getting to the interview location.

2. **Make sure your car has gas.** If you have to drive to the interview, get gas now instead of the morning of your interview. It will be one less thing to do. If you are taking public transportation, be sure you know the schedule. If you are walking or biking, make sure you know how long it will take and what route to follow.

3. **Gather your materials.** Make sure you have all necessary materials for your interview: copies of your resume and application, your list of references, your portfolio, a notepad and pen to take notes, and a briefcase or business purse to hold the materials. You might also consider bringing a water bottle, since you will be doing a lot of talking. It doesn't hurt to have a list of a few extra references, just in case. If you get called in for a second interview, your interviewers may ask for some additional references.

4. **Lay out your clothes.** There's something comforting about having everything laid out and ready to go the night before so you don't have to worry about it when you wake up in the morning.

5. **Set your alarm.** Make sure you have given yourself enough time to dress, eat, and get to the interview on time. Be sure to consider traffic and weather conditions.

6. **Get enough sleep.** This is not the time to stay up until the crack of dawn. Try to get at least eight hours of sleep before your interview. If you have trouble sleeping, try visualizing yourself shaking the interviewer's hand at the end of the interview, with a big smile on your face, feeling satisfied with your performance.

7. **Eat breakfast.** Even if you're nervous, make sure to put something in your stomach to prepare you for the day. A little protein and some carbohydrates can go a long way to keeping your blood sugar stable so your brain can do the thinking it needs to do. Try to avoid too much sugar or caffeine, though. No one wants to get jittery or sleepy during an interview.

8. **Review your accomplishments.** On the way to the interview, take time to think about all the things you've accomplished (you may want to refer to your own resume). This will boost your self-esteem and remind you of stories you might want to share with your interviewers.

Surviving the Interview

You have worked hard to develop your skills and to get this interview. Your primary goal on the day of your interview is to be there! Strangely enough, people often neglect to show up for interview appointments. Keep in mind that this is your chance to show off, move ahead in your career, and start a new life. You can't even begin to take advantage of a job opportunity unless you appear in person to show that you deserve it. So be there, and let your interviewer know that you mean to make something of your life.

Handling a Phone Interview

Some companies like to screen potential candidates on the phone before they call them in for an in-person interview. If this is the case with you, take some time before the interview to have a friend listen to your voice on the phone and tell you how you come across. Strive to sound as clear, upbeat, and energetic as possible, without talking too fast or too slow.

Before the phone rings, prepare yourself as follows:

Dress and behave for a phone interview exactly as you would for an in-person meeting.

1. **Gather all your materials** (cover letter, resume, portfolio). You never know what the interviewer might ask you.

2. **Charge your phone.** If you plan to take the call on a cell phone, make sure the batteries don't die and you will have good reception.

3. **Dress professionally.** Answering the phone in your work clothes makes you feel and sound much more professional than answering in your underwear or pajamas. In addition, some phone interviews may be conducted as a phone conference using a webcam, in which case people will actually see you.

When the phone rings, take the call in a quiet space, using a high-quality phone. Your interviewer is not interested in hearing a lot of background noise when he or she asks you questions. It's a good idea to stand and smile during the phone

interview. Why? Because your voice carries better and you are likely to sound more positive.

The difficult part of a phone interview is that you cannot depend on visual cues from the interviewer to see how you are doing. You'll have to rely on your listening skills to pick up other cues. In fact, when interviewing on the phone, it's particularly important not to interrupt. Let the interviewer finish speaking before you answer. Don't worry about taking your time to come up with an answer—a little silence never hurt anyone.

If you pass the phone interview, you'll be invited for an in-person interview, and the interviewer will set up a time and date that are mutually convenient. Make sure to write down that information, including the name of the person (or persons) who will be interviewing you and directions for how to get to the company. Then follow the rest of the suggestions in this section.

Conduct a Last Minute Check

Before you walk out the door to your in-person interview, it doesn't hurt to perform a last minute check to make sure you have everything you need:

1. **Review your instructions.** Do you know how to get to the company and who to talk to? Are you clear on the time?

2. **Collect your materials.** Do you have your resume, portfolio, references, and other marketing collateral? (Hopefully you laid these out the night before.)

3. **Check the mirror.** Is your hair okay? Are tags sticking out of your clothes? For men: Is there any shaving cream or tissue on your face? For women: Is your lipstick smudged or are there any runs in your stockings?

Give yourself a quick pep talk in the mirror, take a deep breath, and walk out the door. You're on your way!

Arrive Early

Allow more than enough time to get where you need to go. You never know what may happen—traffic, train behind schedule, or a car breakdown. Unexpected delays can take up valuable time. If you plan ahead and give yourself extra time, you will be ready to handle whatever difficulties may come your way.

The Interview

You look nice (having followed the tips in Table 8.2 and walked through your checklist), you arrived comfortably early, and you have pen and paper with you to take notes. You have a copy of your cover letter and resume so that you can review the key points you want to make in the interview. You even have something fun to read just in case you have to wait for a while. But now it's time—the interviewer has arrived. Here are some guidelines for the interview itself.

1. Greet Your Interviewers

Stand tall, smile, and shake hands using the firm handshake you learned about earlier in this chapter. Make sure to say your own name and look directly at the person who greets you, and repeat his or her name. This will help you remember names. Make some small talk; you can always comment on the weather or some neutral topic, or share something pleasant. This will help ease the tension and make your interviewers feel comfortable. Interviewers feel nervous, too.

2. Understand the Interview Process

Interviews vary from company to company. Some companies like to schedule a whole day for an interview, including lunch, and you will meet with everyone involved in the hiring process. Other companies schedule a half-day interview and you will meet only with the hiring manager and different people on his or her team. Finally, other companies schedule only an hour or so with one or two people.

In general, you will be meeting with only one person at a time. Each individual may be responsible for asking you specific questions, or they may all ask similar questions. In these situations, remember that most of the people who talk to you are not professional interviewers. They are as uncomfortable as you are. If you go out of the way to make them feel comfortable, you will feel less nervous yourself.

Occasionally, you may be involved in a group interview. This is where several people interview you at the same time. Although you may feel nervous sitting across from a panel of interviewers, it's not as bad as you think. Treat the interview as a conversation with multiple people. When one person asks you a question, turn to that individual and answer as if the two of you were having a conversation. Then let your eyes move around the room to the other people in the group, so they feel you are addressing them as well.

3. Remember, They Want to Like You

It's true! If a company takes the time to advertise for a job, read resumes, and interview candidates, they want to fill the position as soon as they can with the best candidate for the job. The quicker a company finds a qualified person, the sooner they can get on with integrating that person into the company. When you come in, it makes sense that your interviewer hopes you are the person the company needs. Keep a confident attitude by reminding yourself that you are what the company wants. Refer to Figure 8.1 for some positive statements that can help boost your confidence.

Finally, as you answer questions, weave the following statements into your answers to show you're a "can do" type of person:

- "Here's what I can do for you. . . ."
- "I am willing to. . . ."
- "I am able to. . . ."
- "I look forward to. . . ."
- "I enjoy. . . ."

4. Relax and Be Yourself

Don't feel badly if you find yourself nervous—you're not alone. Lots of people have a case of the nerves when it comes to interviews. Do your best to relax. Look around and read something to take your mind off your nervousness. Take some deep breaths and remind yourself of your skills and talents. Visualize yourself walking out of the interview with a big smile on your face!

Once you start your interview, remember that your interviewer knows about your skills and qualifications from reading the material you sent. Now the interviewer wants to get to know the real

Figure 8.1   **Interview attitude**

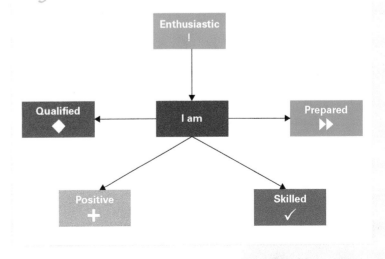

Relax and visualize your successful interview.

you—your personality, your ability to react to a new situation, and your thoughts on your goals and skills. Don't disappoint anyone by clamming up or trying to be someone else. You are the best at being yourself.

Interviewers typically have a general idea of the skills and qualities they are looking for in a potential employee. During the interview process, they are waiting for that someone to come in and clarify the image for them, to embody the perfect person for the job. You might be that person. The more you share the unique qualities that are "you," the more clearly the interviewer will see the image you create, and the easier it will be for the interviewer to determine if that image is the answer for their hiring dilemma.

For example, suppose Dr. Cusato needs to fill a dental assistant position. He knows that he doesn't want to waste his time interviewing candidates who don't have adequate skills and experience, so he weeds out those candidates by scrutinizing their resumes. Then he sets up seven interviews. All seven of these people have met the skills qualifications equally. What will be the deciding factor? Dr. Cusato doesn't really know for sure. He simply wants to see everyone and determine where to go from there. Of course he wants someone who has important personal qualities such as self-management, courtesy, integrity, and responsibility. He also wants someone with good interpersonal skills. But that is the extent of the requirements he has determined.

As it turns out, the second candidate who interviews has an energy and a freshness that seem to be missing from the office. Dr. Cusato didn't even realize the energy was missing until he saw this candidate and thought about how pleasant it would be to have that person around. He still saw the other candidates and liked them fine, but the second candidate defined and clarified his image of what he most wanted in the position. How did the candidate do this? By simply being herself.

5. Pay Attention to Verbal and Nonverbal Cues

Keep in mind that many interviewers are not comfortable with their role. In most companies, the people who interview you are not professional interviewers; they are simply people "from the ranks" who have been asked to talk to you. In fact, if you are interviewing for a technical position, your interviewers may be very analytical or introverted by nature, and quite uncomfortable in the role of interviewer. The more you do to make your interviewer feel comfortable, the more your interviewer will see you in a positive light and the more comfortable you will become.

To improve the comfort level of your interviewers (and you), pay attention to your voice and body language, as well as that of your interviewers. Table 8.3 lists things to think about regarding your verbal and nonverbal behavior.

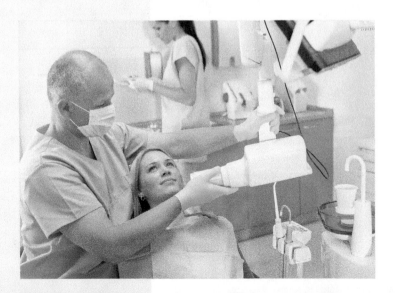

6. Listen

Listening closely to what your interviewer says will make you a better interviewee. For one thing, you can answer questions completely only if you've heard the whole question clearly. Listen, let the question sink in, and give yourself time to answer. If you don't understand a question, ask for clarification; you can even rephrase the question for the interviewer to see if you have the right idea.

Here are some standard interview questions, and some notes on answering them. As you read them, consider how you might answer each in an interview for a job in your chosen field.

• **What experience qualifies you for this kind of work?** This is a specific question. Your interviewer wants you to discuss specific experience, education, and training that make you qualified for the kind of work you would do if you got the job. Do

Table 8.3	**Professional Behavior Tips**
Category	**Behavior**
Greeting	• DO arrive early (about 15 minutes). Greet your interviewer by name and shake hands. • DON'T arrive late.
Voice	• DO establish a positive tone of voice as soon as possible. Avoid a monotone voice—let your voice go up and down. • DON'T speak too fast, too slowly, too loudly, or too softly.
Posture	• DO keep your arms open as you stand or sit. • DON'T cross your arms and look defensive. Avoid putting your hands in your pockets and jingling your change.
Eye contact	• DO look at the person speaking to you and address him or her directly. • DON'T stare intently (this can feel threatening) or look so briefly that you appear to be avoiding the interviewer.
Listen	• DO listen to your interviewers and answer when they stop speaking. • DON'T interrupt.
Attention	• DO make sure you still have your interviewer's attention. If he or she is shuffling papers or looking away, do something to draw the person back in. Try smiling and asking a question. • DON'T ignore your interviewers.
Body language	• DO try to subtly mimic your interviewer's body language. For example, if he or she leans forward to speak to you, you might do the same. This can often put your interviewer at ease. • DON'T fidget, lean away from the interviewer, or appear bored. • DON'T chew gum, or smoke.
Technology	• DO turn off your cell phone during the interview. • DON'T text or take other calls.
Questions and comments	• DO speak honestly and confidently about your work experience. • DON'T exaggerate your experience or lie about it. • DON'T speak negatively about prior employers. • DO ask questions if you don't understand something. • DON'T ask questions about information you should have researched before the interview (such as the company's size, products, services, etc.). • DO say you are interested in the job if you are. • DON'T say you are interested in the job if you are not sure or know you are not.

not go into a general listing of your training (schools, degrees) or a rundown of all the jobs you have held. The interviewer can find that information on your resume, and has probably already read it. Be specific about courses, jobs, or projects you have worked on that have prepared you to do *this* job.

• **Tell me about yourself.** This is a general question. The interviewer wants to hear about the aspects of your life that relate to your ability to succeed on the job. Give a brief overview of your training and your experience: the schools you attended, your focus in those schools, any related jobs you have held, any awards or commendations you have received, and any other facts about you that convey your fitness for the job.

• **What are your strengths and weaknesses?** This is not a trick question. The interviewer wants to know how you perceive yourself, so share at least three to five strengths that are relevant to the position. For example, suppose you are applying for a job that involves writing reports and you happen to be a very detail-oriented person. You might explain how your attention to detail and your analytical nature make you good at researching and producing quality reports.

As for weaknesses, the interviewer wants to know if you are self-aware. Select a weakness that is not directly related to the job and turn it upside down. For example, suppose you are applying for the same job mentioned earlier. You might mention that you tend to be a perfectionist. You know that it sometimes drives people crazy, but you are the kind of person who always wants to make sure the job is done right the first time, and you never let your perfectionism get in the way of a deadline. Your interviewer might see your "weakness" as a hidden strength for a job that requires you produce well-written reports for the public.

- **I see you just came out of (X) program.** This is your chance to talk about how your program has prepared you for work. For students just out of school, this is a chance to emphasize how fresh the knowledge is in your mind and how ready you are to put it all to work, especially if you have little or no job experience. This is not a time to bring up any negative impressions of the program or the people there. Instead, stick with the positives.

- **Talk to me about what you did at your last job.** If your last job required you to perform tasks and use technologies similar to what the employer requires for this job, talk about those. If the duties you performed and skills you used at your last job were completely different from the job for which you are interviewing, discuss personal qualities you possess that will serve you well on the job: promptness, attitude, willingness to learn, dependability, flexibility, and ability to work well with others. You can also bring up skills you learned outside the job that would be relevant to the current position. These might be skills gained while volunteering with schools, community organizations, or churches. Or they might be skills gained at home, such as managing money and schedules.

- **What did you like most/least about your previous job?** The potential employer wants to get a sense of what you like doing and what you dislike. After all, the more you like what you do, the better you will do it. When it comes to what you liked most, state factors that are relevant to the job you are interviewing for. Help your potential employer understand how what you liked in the past relates to what you plan to do in the new job.

  When it comes to what you like least, try mentioning something that is not too relevant to the job you are interviewing for. However, if there is something that you absolutely cannot tolerate on the job, this is the time to be honest about it. It's better for an employer to find out now that you can't stand being continually interrupted than to hire you and have you quit a month later because you have to constantly switch back and forth between four different projects and attend so many meetings that you never get the chance to focus on your work.

- **What interests you about this job or our company?** Your answer shows just how informed you are about the company. If you speak in general terms, "I heard you were very successful" or "I think you put out a great product," it will seem as though you weren't interested enough in the company to do your research. Instead, combine your research with a discussion of your needs and interests. For example, "I always wanted to work with X type of equipment, and I understand that is your specialty. Plus, I recently moved to an apartment that is near your new office."

- **How would a previous employer describe you?** Good question! This is your chance to confirm any information that your interviewer may have received, or will receive, from a previous employer, while emphasizing your useful qualities. Be honest because the interviewer may already have information about you, but stick with the positives. Think about praise you received from a previous employer. If that is hard to do, try to remember a specific work success that your employer recognized. What did you do well?

- **Where do you see yourself in 3, 5, or 10 years?** *OR* **What are your career goals?** Your interviewer wants to know three things: (1) Have you thought through your long-term goals? (2) What are those goals? and (3) How do they fit in with the company's needs? You will answer all three of these questions at the same time if you answer completely and honestly. Being able to answer shows you have the vision to plan ahead.

  Talk about the goals you have that you feel you could achieve with the company; don't mention goals you know would not be satisfied at the company. For example, if your goal is to work in a city but you are interviewing at a suburban company with the idea that you will eventually work in the city, avoid mentioning your city plans. The interviewer may think you only plan to treat this job as a stepping-stone to something that you really want. It's also fine to discuss goals that you are not sure the company can fulfill, such as a certain job title, lifestyle, level of employment, security, or stability.

Table 8.4	**Answering Diplomatically**
Wrong Way	**Right Way (Diplomatic)**
"My boss was a tyrant."	"I felt creatively stifled; I was not able to try out new ideas."
"I hated my supervisor."	"My supervisor and I had trouble meshing our workstyles."
"They fired me when I put my kids first."	"The company didn't share my value of family."

When you talk about where you see yourself in the future, be honest; if you go against your true desires and only say what you think the interviewer wants to hear, you may come across as insincere. Worse, if your interviewer believes your dishonest answer and you take the job, you may become unhappy when you realize that working at this company gets in the way of your long-term goals. On the other hand, what you want may fit in perfectly with what the company needs, in which case everyone wins!

• **Why did you leave your last job?** Your interviewer wants to find out the circumstances of your leaving, which will give further information about you. If the circumstances were positive—you left to go to school, found a better job, or moved—just say so. If they were negative—you quit because of trouble on the job or you were fired—explain the situation in the most positive terms possible. Stay honest because the interviewer could ask former employers for their version of the story. Avoid talking about the job problems specifically; for example, say "I found that the work environment no longer suited me." If asked to elaborate, be diplomatic. Assess the situation and decide on a smart way to phrase your statement. Table 8.4 shows some wrong and right (diplomatic) ways to answer this question.

• **Why do you feel you would be an asset to our company?** This is your chance to outline your skills and qualities that would best fulfill the company's needs. To organize your thoughts quickly, you could answer in a way that pairs up the company's needs with the skills you have to fulfill them. For example: "You require someone with experience, and I've held two long-term jobs in this field. You need someone who is flexible and dedicated, and I currently have no other commitments in my life. I am ready to devote myself to the job." Emphasize your interpersonal skills and tell them why they would benefit from having you on their team.

• **What are your most important values?** This is a fact-finding question to discover if your values mesh with those of the company. There are no right or wrong answers; there is only one answer, the honest answer. Don't worry about trying to figure out what your interviewer wants to hear. Talk about what you value in your life. Most likely you interviewer will appreciate your sincerity and admire what you think is important.

7. Handle Objections

During your interview, you may face some objections from your interviewers. They might disagree with you or challenge the answers you provide. That's why it's a good idea to be prepared. Part of being prepared means understanding where the interviewers are coming from when they voice an objection. Maybe they are worried that you can't handle the job and need more details from you. Maybe they want to see how you handle confrontation, since it's bound to happen on the job at some time or another.

When an objection arises, follows these steps to keep you calm and centered:

1. Take a deep breath and do not respond immediately.

2. When you respond, avoid being defensive. Instead, address the interviewer's underlying concern, not the visible emotion you might detect. Filter out the emotion from the interviewer's voice to get at the heart of the matter.

3. As you answer, restate the interviewer's objection. If you are unclear about the objection, ask some clarifying questions. For example, suppose the interviewer says, "It doesn't sound like you have the right experience for the job." You might respond, "Can you be more explicit? What part

of my experience doesn't seem to meet your needs?" The interviewer might then say something like, "Well, every medical assistant we've hired in the past has worked in a doctor's office for at least two years. You're fresh out of school, and I'm not sure you'll be able to keep up."

4. Once you have enough information to understand the objection, you can address it in a positive manner. For example, you might answer the interviewer's concern by stating, "For two years, while I attended the Institute of Business and Medical Careers, I worked in the registrar's office. I filed documents, filled out forms, answered phones, located students' records, and processed tuition payments. I believe that with my Medical Assistant Certificate and registrar's office experience, I should have no problem handling office duties in your medical office."

Objections are part of the normal interview process and should not be taken personally. Do your best to calm your interviewers' concerns and you'll do fine.

8. Ask Questions

An interview is not just a chance for an interviewer to learn about you; it's a chance for you to learn about a company. Just as the interviewer needs to decide whether you are right for the job, you need to decide if the company is right for you. By asking questions and listening well, you will have a clear picture of what awaits you at this job so you can make an informed decision.

Often, after an interviewer has asked several questions, he or she will say, "Do you have any questions for me?" Even if you don't receive that obvious invitation to ask questions, make sure to ask them—you have the right to do so.

Prepare some questions ahead of time. Your interviewer may answer them during the interview; otherwise, you can address whatever doesn't come up at the end of the interview. Always ask questions politely and sincerely. What do you want to know?

- Hours
- Dress style/uniforms
- Opportunities for moving up
- Duties
- Company policies or history
- Other requirements
- Work environment
- Company communication style
- Salary and benefits (Typically, you will *not* ask questions about this during your first interview. However, you can broach the subject in certain situations: (a) The interviewer brings it up, (b) you have a feeling that your chances of a job offer are pretty good, or (c) you have actually received an offer. You will learn more about this under "Delay Salary Discussions.")

Additional questions may come to mind. Ask whatever you want to know, within reason. Make sure you leave the interview with all the important information you need to help make your decision.

9. Be Wary of Illegal Questions

There are quite a few questions a potential employer cannot legally require you to answer because they are designated as unfair questions by law. These questions are not permitted because they request information that should not be part of the hiring decision. Of course, that doesn't keep everyone from asking them. Review the list of illegal questions below to become familiar with them. Note that this is a general list. Some minor differences may occur from state to state. If you want to know your state's specific laws, check with your school or write to your state's human rights organization. Such an agency will be able to send you a copy of the human rights law rulings related to race, creed, color, national origin, sex, age, disability, marital status, and arrest records.

Illegal Questions   We have listed illegal questions by topic. Some topics are not completely off limits. For these topics, we list only the kind of questions that are *not* permitted. For topics that are completely off limits, we specify that all questions are off limits.

- **Age:** How old are you? What is your date of birth? Can I see your birth certificate?
- **Criminal record:** Have you ever been arrested?

- **Birth control:** Questions about birth control or family planning (children that you have, plan to have, whether you are pregnant).
- **Disability:** Questions about whether you have a disability, the nature of a disability, whether you have a disease, or the treatment of any disease.
- **Marital status:** All questions are off limits.
- **Nationality:** All questions are off limits.
- **Race/color:** All questions are off limits.
- **Religion:** All questions are off limits.
- **Organizations:** Any question about your membership in organizations that you have not mentioned or listed on your resume as relevant to your ability to perform the job.
- **Sex/gender:** All questions are off limits.
- **Birthplace:** All questions are off limits.
- **Citizenship:** Are you a naturalized or native-born citizen? Of what country are you a citizen? Can I see naturalization papers? Are your parents naturalized or native-born citizens?
- **Military service:** Any question regarding your service in militia other than that of the United States.
- **Education:** During what years did you attend? What was your graduation date? (These questions are illegal only if you did not put the information on your resume.)
- **Language:** What is your native language? How did you learn to speak (any) language?
- **Names:** What is your original name (if name has been changed by court order, marriage, or otherwise)? Have you worked under another name?
- **Photograph:** Any request for a photograph before hiring.
- **Relatives:** Any request for names, addresses, numbers, and ages of relatives not employed by the company that is hiring.

Some employers may require certain kinds of information that fall within these categories. For example, if you are interviewing to be a bartender, you must be of legal drinking age. Even if the interviewer cannot ask how old you are, he or she can certainly ask if you are 21 years or older. Asking about arrests is illegal because you may not have committed a crime for which you were arrested; however, asking about convictions is legal because your involvement in the crime is much more certain. The following questions can legally be asked in an interview.

Legal Questions

- **Age:** Are you over the age of 18/21?
- **Criminal record:** Have you ever been convicted of a crime?
- **Disability:** Any question that inquires only about your basic physical ability to perform a job without directly referring to disability, pregnancy, or plans for a family. For example: A deaf person interviewing for an office position might be asked about his ability to read the lips of other employees who may not know sign language. Someone in a wheelchair interviewing for a job that requires field visits may be asked about her ability to get around quickly and efficiently in a car.
- **Citizenship and residence:** Are you a citizen of the United States? If not, do you intend to become a citizen? If not, do you have the legal right to remain permanently in the United States? Do you intend to remain permanently in the United States? What is your place of residence? How long have you been a resident of this state or city?
- **Organizations:** Questions about memberships in organizations that you have indicated are relevant to job skills.
- **Military service:** Questions about your service in any branch of the armed forces.
- **Education:** Questions about what schools you have attended and the education received.
- **Language:** What languages do you speak or write? Are you fluent?

- **Name:** Have you ever worked for this company under a different name? Do we need to have information regarding a change of name to check into your work history?
- **Relatives:** Names of relatives already employed by the company.

10. Be Realistic

Most employers know they are not supposed to ask illegal questions, and they follow the rules. But some employers ask illegal questions even though they know they cannot do so by law. Then there are poorly informed people who just don't realize they have asked an illegal question. During an interview, you may run up against some questions you are not legally required to answer. If you object to a question and tell the interviewer "That's illegal, I refuse to answer," you may offend the interviewer. If you answer the question, you are encouraging the interviewer to continue on a discriminatory path. So, what should you do?

First, do not assume the interviewer is a terrible person for asking an inappropriate question. Instead, give him or her the benefit of the doubt and assume no harm was intended. Next, go through the following steps to decide whether you want to answer the question:

1. **Think about what this job may mean to you.** If you don't have a good feeling about the job anyway, it may not hurt to politely and courteously refuse to answer a question. If this job is important to you, you may make some concessions to stay in the running.

2. **Quickly size up the interviewer.** Do you think the interviewer has deliberately asked an illegal question to entrap you, or does the person just seem ignorant of the laws? You might be more likely to answer if you feel that an honest mistake has been made.

3. **Consider the question itself.** Do you care if the interviewer knows this information? You may feel very strongly about withholding certain pieces of information. But you may decide you'd rather answer than cause a stir if giving the information doesn't upset you in any way.

4. **Think about how you might feel later.** You might regret answering an illegal question, feeling as though you had sacrificed your integrity. You might feel you wouldn't want to work for a company that would ask you that kind of question anyway. Conversely, you may regret not answering if you think your refusal ruined an otherwise dynamite interview. Try to make a decision that won't keep you up nights thinking about what you could have done differently.

If you decide *not* to answer the question, you might tactfully remind the interviewer that the question is illegal. You could say: "I'm sorry, but I believe you asked me a question that I am not legally bound to answer during an interview. I'd rather cover other points." Or, "I'd prefer to discuss my qualifications for this job, which are. . . ." By responding in a calm and professional way, you demonstrate your assertiveness and knowledge of the law. It's unlikely you'll be asked another improper question.

If you *do* decide to answer the question, you might try either of the following responses:

- If you feel the question is harmless and the answer is of little consequence to getting the job, answer it without indicating you're offended. Assume the interviewer was simply curious and unaware you might be put off by the question.

- If you feel the question is important to getting the job, address the underlying concern of the interviewer rather than his or her specific question. For example, if the interviewer asks, "Do you have any children?" the underlying concern might be whether you're likely to miss work to care for a sick child. Your response could be, "I have three children in school, and they have excellent, full-time childcare." Or perhaps you might answer, "Yes, my wife and I have two children. We feel our commitment to raising our children in loving, supportive household shows our dedication to the future." Either answer shows you are a committed, dedicated person—someone an employer would like to have on board.

Every situation is unique. It's tough to do, but try to balance your ideals with your realism.

11. Avoid Negativity

When you list a job on your resume or application, you are telling your interviewer that you are prepared to talk about your experience on that job, even if that experience was less than stellar. If you were fired, be honest about it; explain the situation clearly. If you feel you made mistakes, talk about what you learned from them. If you feel you were wrongly dismissed, take a moment to calmly justify your side of the story.

Most importantly, never bad-mouth a former employer, fellow employee, or place of employment. If you have negative feelings, don't go into detail about them. If you spend time in an interview talking about what a nightmare you had at that other job, your interviewer might wonder what you would say about this job in the future. Plus, you never know whether your interviewer has a close and friendly connection with someone you dislike! Play it safe—if you can't say something nice, hold back.

12. Delay Salary Discussions

Some people want to get salary discussions out of the way as soon as possible, but this is never a good idea. Salary discussions typically occur during the second interview or *after* you are offered the job. The main purpose of the first interview is to see if you can meet the employer's needs. Salary and benefits are not the employer's needs, they are your needs. If the employer does bring up salary during the interview, do *not* be the first person to state a dollar amount. According to Kate Wendleton, president of the Five O'Clock Club (a career counseling and outplacement organization), "The person who brings up a number first loses the game."[2] It's important to talk about the job before you ever discuss salary. Once you have negotiated the job and have an offer in hand, that's when you should start salary negotiations.

If you are asked about your prior salary, either mention a number that is what you are actually looking for, or make sure to include any bonuses or perks you may have had in a prior job. If you are pushed to make some statement about the salary you want before you receive an offer, try changing the topic or ask to discuss it later. If necessary, you can say, "I'm sure my needs are in the range you're offering, and I'll be happy to discuss them later if we pursue a formal offer." Or, if you feel you know enough about the job to consider it and the interviewer asks "How much do you want?" you can always answer, "How much are you offering?"

The most important thing to remember is this: You need to learn as much about the position as possible before you commit yourself to a specific salary. You'll have a chance to look at negotiating an offer later in this chapter.

Checklist for a Successful Interview

1. **Make eye contact.** It shows that you are direct, sincere, honest, and that you mean business.

2. **Use a firm handshake** and introduce yourself using your first and last names.

3. **Bring a spare copy of your resume**. That way you can refer to it as you speak, and you will also be able to point items out to the interviewer if the copy you sent isn't at hand.

4. **Speak clearly and distinctly,** in full sentences. Use proper grammar. Don't chew gum or smoke!

5. **Avoid discussing salary unless you have been offered the job.** Be realistic about how much to expect and honest about how much you need. However, respect the salary range and limit that the interviewer may convey to you.

6. **Emphasize the positive.** Discuss your good points and put a positive spin on your weaknesses instead of apologizing for them. Express how willing you are to learn and improve.

7. **Focus on action.** The company wants to know what you can do for it more than anything else. Emphasize your qualifications and experience in terms of what you have done and what you now are able to do that will help the company.

8. **Know the interviewer's name and use it in the interview.** It will make you seem prepared and warmly conversational. Ask the secretary's name too; use it when you arrive or when you talk to the secretary on the phone. Sometimes a good impression made on a secretary will give you a boost with the manager.

---

[2]Rangwala, Sakina. "How to . . . negotiate salary: Tips from the pros." *Washington Post,* November 23, 2010. Accessed on December 29, 2010, from www.washingtonpost.com/wp-srv/jobs/how-to/negotiate_salary_guidance.html

9. **Don't speak badly of others.** We said it before and we'll say it again: Don't ever speak badly about a former employer or coworker. It shows a poor attitude and an inclination to speak ill about the interviewer and the interviewing company in the future.

10. **Use your pen and paper after the interview.** This is the time to write everything you remember. If you write during the interview, it may disturb your concentration and it will break the eye contact you make with the interviewer.

11. **Thank the interviewer.** When you shake hands, thank the interviewer for taking time to speak with you.

 Now You Try It: Imagining the Worst

You've read a lot about what to expect during the interview process; now is your chance to see how you handle uncomfortable situations that might arise. For this activity, ask another student, friend, or family member to role-play with you. That person will become your interviewer. Make sure you have a resume and an imaginary (or real) job description that you can share with your interviewer. You can also do this activity on your own, but you will have to play both roles and evaluate yourself. You might even want to practice in front of a mirror so you can see how you look when you respond to uncomfortable questions.

1. Give your interviewer a list of what you think are your weaknesses. Then ask the interviewer to confront you with some negative information about one of these weaknesses. Practice responding positively.

2. Show your interviewer the list of illegal questions presented earlier in this chapter. Ask the interviewer to ask you a few of them as part of the interview. Figure out whether to answer the questions. If you decide not to, practice tactfully declining.

3. Ask your interviewer to object to some aspect of your experience or lack of experience for the job. Practice responding calmly.

4. When you finish, ask the interviewer what he or she noticed about how you responded to objections and confrontation. Did you blush? Get nervous? Get angry? Get shaky?

Imagining the worst, and then practicing your responses in a safe environment, is a good way to prepare yourself for and desensitize yourself to negative emotions and responses from interviewers. This allows you to respond more calmly in real-life situations.

After the Interview

Whew! You survived the interview, but you're not done yet. When you arrive home, write the interviewer a courteous note on good paper or a simple note card (handwritten is better, but if your handwriting is not very legible, feel free to type) to thank him or her for taking the time to see you. If you have a sincere interest in working there, you can add a note of hope, such as: "I look forward to hearing from you." If you don't want to pursue the job, just say thank you. Keeping in touch will remind the company of you and, if they are having trouble making a decision, it could give you an edge.

Handling Failure and Success

Now comes the hard part—the wait. Did you or did you not get the job? In job hunting, as in most things, there are no guarantees. A lucky few may get their dream job right away. But for most, it takes time to find a situation that makes you happy. You need to prepare yourself for whatever comes your way. As Figure 8.2 notes, many different possibilities exist.

Figure 8.2 **Your job will happen**

Finding a job takes effort . . .
Plan and work your plan.

It will take time . . .
Perhaps weeks or months?

You will have emotional highs . . .
You get an interview.

You will have emotional lows . . .
You get turned down for the job.

Learn to deal with success and rejection . . .
Constructively channel your emotions.

First, let's take a look at receiving bad news—a job rejection. Then we'll end the chapter on a good note—a job offer.

Dealing with Failure: The Job Rejection

Perhaps the awaited phone call never comes; instead, a rejection letter arrives in the mail. Failure can take many forms! But it all depends on how you define it. What you consider a failure may seem like a step in the right direction to someone else. Maybe you get some job offers, but not your favorite one. Maybe you get none. Maybe you only apply for one job and don't get it. Maybe it takes you three months to get a job offer. How do you deal with your version of failure? Try some of these responses.

Remember That You Are Capable

It's vital to remind yourself that you are a capable, valuable person. Dig down to those tools from the earlier chapters—your self-knowledge, positive attitude, motivation, commitment, and patience. If you believe in yourself, you will persevere through the emotional rollercoaster of the job hunt. You will be able to accept the way the process unfolds for you, and you will be able to stay confident that the job you were meant to have will eventually arrive.

Talk to the Interviewer

You don't always know exactly why you did not receive an offer. Maybe someone at the company wanted to move up and the company went with a sure thing. Maybe economic difficulties forced the company to downsize. When that happens, jobs may be merged or filled with other employees. Maybe the interviewer had a bad day or didn't feel well when meeting you, and ended up hiring someone that came in on a better day. You cannot assume that you did not have enough talent and skill for the job.

If you are curious as to why you did not get the position, try talking to one of the interviewers. The interviewer may not be able to tell you everything, but his or her input will be valuable and help you with future interviews. For example, you might call or email an interviewer and say something like this:

> "Thanks for considering me for the Night Shift Manager position. I am always looking for ways to improve my qualifications and would greatly appreciate your honesty in sharing any reasons you had for choosing another candidate. I am very impressed with your company, and would like to better prepare myself for the next opening. I welcome your candid feedback."

This is an opportunity for you to receive some honest, constructive criticism. It's your job to listen to everything the interviewer has to say and ask for suggestions. Always thank the individual for his or her assistance and honesty.

Talk to Other Job Hunters

When you talk to other job hunters, you will discover that failing to secure the perfect job right away happens to all sorts of people, all the time. You are not alone. Trading stories with others who know what you are going through can bring you peace and comfort. We tend to hold back our disappointments because they embarrass us—we feel we are the only ones who have ever failed. But when we finally do talk about the experience, we discover that many other people have had the same experience and they are eager to exchange stories because they're so relieved that someone else has failed too. More importantly, by talking to others who have "tried and failed, and tried again," you learn how to move ahead, improve, and gain the confidence you need to succeed.

Improve Yourself

If the interviewer feedback you received indicates a limitation on your part, set out to improve yourself. Maybe you already realized that you lacked punch in some important area. Perhaps you sensed that your answers to some questions weren't what the interviewer wanted to hear. Don't waste your time moaning over your shortcomings; instead, take action. Should you look for a different kind of job? Should you improve your skills, interviewing techniques, or even your interview outfit? Take a close look, and give yourself the best possible chance by making the improvements you think you need.

Always look on the bright side to learn as much as you can from a failed interview.

Look on the Bright Side

When you can manage to do it, look on the bright side. If you didn't get an offer for your first choice but received other offers, at least you weren't turned down everywhere—companies want you. Would you consider those other offers? Think about it. If your search seems to be dragging out, at least you have time to really concentrate on what kind of job you want.

Sometimes taking the first offer too hastily, without thinking it through, can be dangerous. And maybe, if you stay in touch with companies that turned you down initially, something else will come up and they may call you. Sometimes a company offers a position to its first choice candidate and that candidate turns it down. In this case, the company almost always offers the position to the second choice. If you were that second choice, you're in.

We learn our lessons best when we learn them the hard way. Everyone **fails**—failure is part of the human experience. Failure simply means that a situation did not work out to your desired expectation. Failure does not mean that there is something wrong with you. People who are afraid of failure are afraid to try. Failure actually has some benefits: (1) It can point out mistakes clearly, whereas success can mask them, and (2) it gives you the awareness you need to learn and avoid the mistake next time. If you can learn from your failure and use that knowledge to move ahead, then you have made a success of the failure. That next job interview will be a winner!

Fail, *verb*

to fall short of success or achievement in something expected, attempted, desired, or approved

Dealing with Success: The Job Offer

Instead of receiving a rejection letter, what if the phone finally rings and you have a job offer. Now what? As much as you probably want to jump at the offer, it's a good idea to take time to carefully evaluate it.

Evaluate the Offer

Evaluating a job offer typically takes several steps.

1. Research. First, make sure you know your own cost-of-living expenses—the minimum amount of money you need to pay for rent or mortgage, utilities, groceries, and other necessities. Next, research what you are worth. Many people believe that skills, experience, and education are the only things that impact their worth in terms of salary. However, there are several other factors: geographic location, industry, and company size. Websites such as Salary.com are a good place to start. If the job offer requires that you move to another part of the country, find out how your living costs would differ in the new location. For example, living in San Francisco, California, is far more expensive than living in Omaha, Nebraska. You can use a website such as PayScale.com to help evaluate living costs.

2. Prioritize. Once you know what you need to survive (money-wise), think about *all* the factors that are important to you in a job and prioritize them. Here are some factors you should consider; however, you'll probably think of other factors on your own:

- Salary
- Healthcare benefits
- Potential for advancement
- Level of responsibility
- Opportunity to use and expand your skills
- Work–life balance
- Type of people you work with
- Travel requirements
- Commuting distance

Put the factors in order, based on their importance. For example, suppose you list your priorities as (1) salary, (2) healthcare benefits, (3) easy commute, (4) nice people to work with, and (5) chance to occasionally work at home. Chances are, you would probably accept a job with pretty good wages and a long commute, but probably reject a job that has nice people, a short commute, and poor wages. Prioritizing helps you balance your options.

3. Look at trade-offs. Not many people find a job that meets *all* their priorities, at least not right away. You will probably find a position that will match with some of them, but you need to know when to make a compromise. Even though a job does not fulfill an important priority, you may have to make a few sacrifices.

Suppose you find a job that fits your two top priorities, but it scores zero on your third and fourth. What should you do? You might want to compromise and take the job anyway. Trade the lesser priorities for the privilege of having the most important ones. Or, you can keep looking. You might even take a job that requires you to perform duties that you don't really like because it has everything else that you want!

Trade-offs such as these happen all the time. You take a job with a good location and trade flexible time, or you take a job with flexible time and nice people, and trade a higher wage—there are many possibilities. Your unique situation will bring its own.

4. Consider your personality. People often forget about their special talents and needs when they've been searching for a job for months and months and finally get an offer. The job hunt can sometimes make you feel stressed, tired, insecure, and desperate. Keep who you are in the forefront of your mind. Remember, if a job suits your personality, it will make you happy, and a happy person is a more efficient and successful employee. If the job you're offered doesn't seem like a fit for your personality, chances are you won't stick with it.

By following steps 1 through 4, you should be able to make a decision about whether to accept the offer. However, there may be times where you want to accept the offer, but feel that certain aspects of it are not quite right for you. In this situation, you might choose to negotiate.

Job negotiations are a normal part of doing business.

Negotiate the Offer

Just because you decide the job is the right one for you doesn't mean you have to accept the offer exactly as it's presented. It is acceptable to ask for what you want if the job offer is not exactly what you expected. If you don't ask, how will you get it? Few people are comfortable with negotiation situations. If you are uncomfortable asking for what you really deserve, this information is for you.

Did You Know?

If you are female, it definitely pays to negotiate salary. Otherwise, you are likely to make less money than you deserve. Just look at these statistics:

1. Women, on average, ask for 30% less money than men.
   - Men are eight times more likely than women to negotiate their starting salary and benefits.
   - Women ask for raises or promotions 85% less often than their male counterparts.
2. In 2007, women who were full-time wage and salary workers earned 80% of their male counterparts' salaries.[3]

[3]McCarty, Maureen. "Salary stats: Men vs. women." *Washington Post,* November 7, 2008. Accessed on December 29, 2010. from www.washingtonpost.com/wp-dyn/content/article/2008/11/06/AR2008110602982.html

Before you enter into a job offer negotiation, get clear on what you're willing to negotiate—salary, benefits, hours, vacations, training, or retirement plans. For example, what if the initial salary offer is unacceptable? This often happens when you first enter the workforce or are switching careers. If the employer originally indicated a certain salary range and the amount you need is somewhere within the range, it is appropriate to negotiate. Too many employees make the mistake of accepting a low starting salary because they assume they will eventually get raises. But raises may not happen every year, depending on the economic climate, and they may be small. That's why it's best to be assertive and state the salary you want before you accept the job offer.[4]

Your future employer will not be upset with you for asking for what you want. However, you need to be tactful, patient, and persistent during negotiations. Focus on creating a "win–win" outcome for you and the employer. Below are some salary negotiation tips to help you feel more comfortable in a negotiation situation.

Negotiating Your Starting Salary

1. Use "we" statements so the person offering you the position feels you are thinking about the company, not just yourself.

2. Mention the salary range you desire, rather than a specific number. This gives you room for negotiation. Often, a potential employer is trying to see if the company can afford you. By providing a range, you don't immediately price yourself out of the running if the employer cannot afford your higher number, nor do you come across as too inexperienced because the salary number is too low.

3. Mention any concerns about the offer and offer your insights about a more appropriate salary.

4. Make sure to tell the individual you're talking to that you don't want money to be an obstacle to accepting the position. This shows that you do care about the job and not just the money. If the money offered is too low, you might consider discussing how to upgrade the job so that a higher salary would be appropriate for the duties.

5. Show your enthusiasm for the job and your desire to work for the company. Reinforce the reasons why you want to work with the company.

It is possible that the company simply doesn't have the funds to offer you the exact salary you want. If this is the case, perhaps the company could still offer you a bit more without breaking the bank. Or maybe it could offer something else instead—for example, additional vacation days or the opportunity to work one day a week from home.

Ultimately, it is up to you to decide whether to accept the offer. Even if you don't negotiate, you may decide that even though the salary is not what you want, you've been out of work too long and need the job. There is no crime in taking it. Or maybe the negotiations didn't quite go the way you'd hoped, and the company cannot pay you more. You may still decide to take the job because you really like the people and the company environment. You can always suggest a performance review in the next three months to revisit the salary issue.

Decline the Offer

If you have been made an offer but the job or the salary is simply not what you want (even after negotiation), do not feel badly about declining. It is better to find another job that will make you happy than to accept one that will make you miserable. When you decline, do so politely, either in person, by phone, or by letter (not by text or email). Be frank but tactful when you state your reasons for declining. These reasons may be logistical, financial, or professional. If you are interested in the job and the company really wants you, the company may decide to put together a different job offer that pays special attention to the points you mentioned in your letter.

Whether you are interested or not, it is always a good idea to keep the doors of communication open. Even though you decline the job, you may want to network with the company in the future. Or you may even decide to apply for a different job with them. By declining professionally and politely, you are not burning any bridges. Figure 8.3 shows a good example of a letter declining a job offer.

---

[4]Joslyn, Heather. "Closing the Gap: Tips for negotiating a robust starting salary." *The Chronicle of Philanthropy,* March 20, 2003. Accessed on April 14, 2010, from http://philanthropy.com/article/Closing-the-Gap-Tips-for/50036

Figure 8.3 Declining a job offer

26305 Jackson Ave.
San Leandro, CA 94577

December 27, 2010

Ms. Latisha Jordan
Office Manager, The Smile Doctor
516 A Street
Hayward, CA 94545

Dear Ms. Jordan:

Thank you for your kind offer to work at The Smile Doctor as a dental technician. As we discussed on the phone, I made the difficult decision to work internationally for Dentists without Borders. By doing so, I hope to help a large number of impoverished children and adults, and return to the States with even more dental experience.

I do hope that an opportunity presents itself for future employment at The Smile Doctor. I would be honored to work for such a wonderful team. Please accept my gratitude and best wishes for your office.

Sincerely,

Amanda Mosconi

Accept the Offer

Whether you've negotiated or not, once you receive an offer in writing that you can live with, accept it. You will typically accept the offer in person or on the phone, and your future employer will then confirm the agreement in writing and specify your start date.

This big moment is only the beginning! Your future employer has indicated confidence that you have what it takes. The company has given you a vote of confidence as well. Remember this point as you begin working and show them that their confidence was well founded. You have only just begun the route to success on the job.

Stay sensitive to others around you who may not enjoy success right away. You probably know other people who have joined you in the job hunt. Try to remain supportive of them as they continue looking for work. No one knows what the future brings. Remember that you may encounter a disappointing time down the road when you will need to turn to them for help. If you have been kind to them, they will be there for you as well. Support is a two-way street.

Celebrate, and then get to work! You definitely owe yourself a little pat on the back. Go out, have a little party, treat yourself to something special, and then start your job with a clear head.

 Now You Try It: The Fine Art of Negotiation

Negotiation is often the most uncomfortable task that people face with a job offer. However, it is not as difficult as you think when you are prepared. This mini-activity gives you a chance to think about what you really want and how to ask for it.

1. Imagine that you have a particular salary in mind for a particular job. Now imagine that you have been offered $5,000 less per year than you expected. Come up with a short script you might use to ask for more. As you do so, consider:

    *   Salary range
    *   Job tasks
    *   Enthusiasm for the company
    *   Experience
    *   Desire for a win–win situation

2. Follow the earlier negotiation tips as you write your script.

3. Practice saying your script out loud. Ask a friend to listen and tell you how you sound.

The more comfortable you get with asking for what you want, without feeling resentful or afraid, the more confident you will come across, and the more likely you will get what you want.

Learning from Experience
A Perspective from the Working World

Putting Your Best Foot Forward

Krayton Walker
Technical Assistant and Electronic Engineering Student

I worked for 10 years as a truck driver for a large freight company. Then I was involved in a serious accident on the job. I had to be hospitalized and undergo lengthy rehabilitation. The trucking company helped me pay the bills, but in the end, injuries to my hips and legs made it difficult for me to return to work. And even if I could have, I never wanted to drive a truck again.

I received a small settlement from the freight company and, with the help of my disability insurance, was able to afford go back to school. Because I've always been good with vehicles, I thought about attending a local technical institute and getting involved in the diesel and industrial technology training program. But then I realized I no longer wanted to be around trucks and with my disability, I'd never be able to be a mechanic. So what should I do? When I met with a guidance counselor, he helped me by asking three simple questions: What do you like to do? What are you good at? What are you interested in?

It turns out that I always liked working with my hands, I was good at troubleshooting (just think of all the years I had to troubleshoot problems with trucks), and I was very interested in electronics (probably from all the hours I spent pouring over *Popular Electronics* magazines when I was in the hospital). So I enrolled in the Electronics Engineering Technology Program. My wife got a part-time job at a local retail store to help with the bills, and my parents helped watch my son when I was at school or my wife was at work.

About a year ago, Bennett Diagnostics came to our school to interview potential candidates for a summer internship as a quality assurance technician. Bennett is a family-run company that makes a heart-monitoring device for veterinarians to use when performing surgery on animals.

I was certainly the oldest candidate to apply for the position, but after surviving my accident and going back to school at the age of 40, getting interviewed didn't sound too scary. When the interviewer asked me why I received a B– in one of my engineering courses, I told him I was proud of that grade because I started off failing the class. I explained how I formed a study group and invited other students to attend at my home. I told him how my wife started quizzing me to help me prepare for exams, and how my son bought me a personalized soldering iron to inspire me to keep at it. I shared that attending school had become a collaborative affair involving other students and my family—we were all motivating one another, and in the end, we all benefited with better grades and self-esteem.

My honest answer must have scored points with the interviewer because I got the job. It turns out that in similar interviews, students often made excuses for their grades and blamed the instructors. And few students were willing to reach out for help or get others involved in improving their knowledge.

I also learned a valuable lesson from that interview—how important it is to find common ground with the interviewer. Even though I spent a lot of time on the road alone when I was driving a truck, I always enjoyed talking to people whenever I could; it helped me connect. When I met the interviewer, I started a short conversation so I would feel less nervous. I asked him about some of the models he had on his shelves and he shared that he had been a car enthusiast for years, but decided to make models because he wasn't a very good mechanic. That was the perfect opening for me to talk about my truck-driving days, including some funny stories about engine and electrical problems I had solved on the road.

I think one of the main reasons I landed that job was because the interviewer felt comfortable with me and also felt confident that I would be a good team player and a good troubleshooter—just what they needed in the quality assurance department!

The Job Will Happen

Maybe you get a job right away, or maybe you have to go through several months of applications and interviews. Either way, you will achieve your goal. Finding a job is an end and a beginning. The end of one particular job search is the beginning of your experience as a working person in a new environment. You may undergo a few more job searches in your life, or you may stick with one job for a long time, but that's the future. For now, this is your new beginning.

As an employed person, you have cleared one of your biggest hurdles—entering (or getting back into) the working world. You will probably stay there, in one capacity or another, for a long time! Do what you can to make your stay pleasant and beneficial for both you and those with whom you work.

Your Tool Kit at Work

8.1 Your PAL

Interviewing is time consuming for employers. When you interview, the employer hopes that you will be the one with the qualities that fit the bill. If you are, then everyone, including you, can get back to work. Your job is to send the message that you are the most qualified candidate. Knowing the traits that employers want will help you do just that.

1. The following are some key traits that employers seek. Check the ones you possess. If you possess every one of these traits, you are the kind of employable person companies want to hire. If you are missing a few, write them at the end of the list, in the space provided. Work on developing them before you interview.

_____ **Accepts responsibility.** Commits to duties and completes them promptly and efficiently.

_____ **Takes direction.** Carries out directives without a fuss.

_____ **Technical skills.** Shows and uses competent skill with technology.

_____ **Integrity/honesty.** Works and speaks honestly, can be trusted.

_____ **Takes initiative.** Comes up with ideas and performs extra duties without always needing direction.

_____ **Understands how to work with others.** Cooperates consistently as a team member.

_____ **Dependable.** Can be counted on to work hard and to be flexible and efficient.

_____ **Energetic.** Stays upbeat and on schedule.

_____ **Speaks and listens well.** Is a good communicator.

I will develop my abilities to:

_____

_____

2. File or post what you wrote with your other attitude cards. Of course, you always need your positive attitude. That's what PAL stands for.

8.2 Do Your Company Research

Whether you've been invited to interview or not, it's a good idea to research the company you are interested in.

1. Complete the following table by putting a checkmark in the **Done** column if you have already gathered this information about the company.

2. If you do not yet have the information, indicate *when* you will get it in the **To Do by** column.

Company Information

Research Information	Done	To Do by (Date)
I will get information about the company from:		
Its product or service is:		
Its market is:		
The approximate number of employees is:		
The number of locations is:		
It has been in business for:		
Other information about the company is:		

8.3 Be Prepared

When you are offered an interview, it's because your resume or application is interesting and shows you have the required skills. During that interview, you will have the opportunity to demonstrate that you also have the required qualities. Preparation is the key to a winning interview. The more prepared you are, the less nervous you will be and the more confident you will feel. This exercise helps you review things you learned in the chapter to make sure you are well-prepared for any interview.

Appearance

1. Go through the following Appearance Evaluation table and determine whether each item is:

   - Okay as is
   - Needs improvement
   - Missing (you need to get it)

   If you're not sure what condition the item should be in, revisit Table 8.2 earlier in the chapter.

2. If the item needs improvement or is missing, indicate what you plan to do.

Appearance Evaluation

Item	Condition	What Will I Do About It?
Hair		
Makeup or Facial Hair		
Nails		
Jewelry		
Tattoos		
Belt		

Item	Condition	What Will I Do About It?
Pants		
Suit		
Skirt or Dress		
Shoes		

Professional Materials and Questions

1. Go through the following Professional Materials and Questions form and fill in the information you have in the **Comments** column.
2. If you do not yet have the information, indicate **when** you plan to have it and start collecting it.

Professional Materials and Questions

Item	Comments
Date, time, and location of interview	
Directions to the interview	
Name of interviewer (spelling and how to pronounce)	
Resume	
Cover letter	
Portfolio	
Letters of recommendation	
List of references	
Pen and notebook	
Answers to at least three interview questions (write the questions and answers)	
At least three questions to ask the interviewer (write the questions)	

8.4 Role Play

This exercise gives you a chance to put everything you've learned in this chapter into practice. It involves pairing up with a classmate for a mock interview.

1. If possible, schedule the mock interview ahead of time so you can prepare for it: (a) dress the part, (b) bring the job description, (c) bring your resume, portfolio, and list of references, and (d) bring a set of sample interview questions. Otherwise, bring your interview questions and simply describe to your classmate what you would be wearing and what materials you would bring with you.
2. Feel free to revisit any sections in the chapter that will help you prepare for your role-play.
3. Take turns playing the role of the candidate and the interviewer using the following Interview Practice Form.
4. If time permits, when you and your partner have each had a chance to play both interviewer and interviewee, conduct the interview in front of the class. Let the class use the same form to evaluate you.

Interview Practice Form

First Impression
Was the candidate dressed appropriately?
Did the candidate make eye contact well?
Did the candidate introduce him- or herself and shake hands?
Did the candidate seem at ease?
Did the candidate come prepared with the necessary materials?
Additional comments:

Candidate Skill Set
Did the candidate have the necessary experience for the position? Explain.
Did the candidate provide examples of his or her past successes that were relevant to the job?
How well did the candidate demonstrate his or her knowledge of the company's objectives and challenges?

Candidate Interaction
How did the candidate respond to tough questions? How well did the candidate maintain his or her composure?
How well did the candidate respond to your objections and concerns?
Additional comments:

Don't be hard on yourself if you did not do well in certain areas. No one has a perfect interview, and you may have done better than you think.

8.5   Plug Your Knowledge into Real Life

You don't need a crystal ball to see the future. You can shape your own future with a positive self-image. Too often people focus on their failures instead of thinking about their successes. Here's an example of how one person focused on his successes to prepare for an interview.

Sam's Preparation

Sam prepared for his interview with MBS Heating and Refrigeration. Two days before, he rehearsed the questions he wanted to ask, made a test run to the company location during rush hour, and picked up his jacket from the cleaners.

The night before the interview, Sam sat in his living room and took the last important step of his preparation: He thought about the times in the past when he remained calm and achieved his goals. He remembered the homecoming game in his senior year when he carried the ball for the winning touchdown; the A he earned at Columbia Tech in English, his most difficult subject; and the time he rescued his two-year-old cousin from drowning at the community pool. He let himself relive the feelings of accomplishment and exhilaration he experienced after each success, and he thought about the state of mind and the specific actions that brought him those successes. He didn't spoil his positive thinking with thoughts of the games where he sat on the bench, the low English grades he got in high school, or the company that laid him off. As he visualized his successes, Sam wrote the following comments in the notebook he'd carry to the interview:

- I am a team player.
- I am a star.
- I am a good student.
- I think and act quickly.
- I make good decisions.

Then Sam took another step. He imagined how he would feel and behave if he were offered the job. He visualized happily shaking his interviewer's hand, imagined the excitement he would feel on the drive home, and pictured the look his wife would have on her face when he told her the news.

Your Preparation

Give yourself the same opportunity. Think quietly for a few minutes and then write down three of your past successes and how you felt about each. List the skills you used in each situation and write affirmations that fit your accomplishments. Finally, imagine the hour after a successful job interview. What will it be like?

I was successful when I:

1. _____

_____

2. _____

_____

3. _____

_____

After each success I felt:

1. _____

_____

2. _____

_____

3. _____

_____

I used the following skills and took the following actions to achieve my successes:

1. _____

_____

2. _____

_____

3. _____

_____

After thinking about my successes, I affirm that I have the following positive qualities and abilities:

1. _____

_____

2. _____

_____

3. _____

_____

After these skills lead me through a successful interview, I will do the following:

1. _____

_____

2. _____

_____

3. _____

_____

8.6 Technology Exercise

In this exercise, you'll do some online research to assist you with all aspects of the interviewing process.

1. Find websites you can use to check salaries for several different jobs of interest in different geographic areas where you might want to live. Write down what you learn below.

Website	Job Title	Geographic Area	Salary Range

2. Find websites that contain some interview and negotiation tips (including sites that might show videos of mock interviews). Jot down any tips that you did not encounter in this chapter.

Website	Additional Tips

Diversity in the Workplace
Today's World

"Give me your tired, your poor,
Your huddled masses yearning to breathe free,
The wretched refuse of your teeming shore,
Send these, the homeless, tempest-tossed to me,
I lift my lamp beside the golden door."

Emma Lazarus, Inscription beneath the Statue of Liberty

 learning objectives

- As you make your transition to a new job, what adjustments might be necessary?
- What should you be aware of on the job when it comes to working with people from different generations, life circumstances, abilities, and values?
- What 10 factors define a culture and impact communication?
- What is the difference between prejudice and discrimination?
- What is the difference between tolerance and acceptance?
- What is the best way to communicate with someone whose native language is not English or who may not be fluent in English?
- What are the five greatest barriers to communication in a multicultural workplace?

Sanjay came to the United States from India as a junior in college. He was lucky enough to get a scholarship to attend school in Ohio and planned to live on campus in student housing. It was his first time in the United States, but he wasn't too worried about the language. After all, he had spoken English from the time he was six years old. Because there were so many dialects spoken throughout India, English was the common language that helped bridge the communication gap.

However, once he was living in the United States, Sanjay found that people had difficulty understanding his accent and he had trouble understanding their slang. He also had a hard time getting used to keeping his shoes on when he entered someone's dorm room or home; he was so used to taking them off as a sign of respect. People seemed to feel very comfortable disagreeing with one another, even arguing or raising their voices to make a point, something that would be considered very discourteous in India. One of the biggest mistakes he made was assuming that gestures meant the same thing in India as in the United States. In India, people shook their heads from side to side to say "Yes, I understand." But in the United States that gesture meant "no." When he went to open his first bank account and the teller asked him if he had money to put in his account, he shook his head the Indian way. It took a little explaining and some laughter to convince her that he really did have some money to deposit.

Sanjay found that college was a great way to get introduced to a new culture. Everyone was from somewhere else—another state or another country—so diversity was the norm. Everyone talked, studied, and socialized together, learning a lot about each other's cultures—from food preferences, to family and religion, to dating practices. Whenever possible, Sanjay took road trips to visit other parts of the state and the country. He always took special care to work on his accent so people could understand him no matter where he traveled. His travels really helped him correct his own stereotypes about Americans (that they were all materialistic, didn't care about family, and would do anything to make money) and helped him adjust to life in the United States.

By the time he graduated, he had networked with teachers and alumni and attended many job fairs. As a result, he was able to find a job as a software developer with one of the larger software companies in the area. He felt very lucky, because several other foreign students had given up and gone home without jobs.

Once he started working, he met a few Indian engineers on the job, and was so thankful his school and travel experience had allowed him to assimilate as well as he had. Sure, he still had to explain that he didn't eat meat because he was Hindu. But he was so happy to have achieved the job he always wanted, straight out of school, and in the United States. Life was good!

You did it! Just like Sanjay, you landed the job of your dreams. And even if it isn't your dream job, it's still a new start for you, whether it's your first job out of school, or the tenth job in your profession. Part of this new start is getting to know your workplace—especially its diversity. Diversity comes in many forms—cultural and ethnic groups, nationalities, age groups, life circumstances, the differently abled (sometimes referred to as people with disabilities or physical challenges), and value systems (such as religious affiliation and sexual orientation).

In this chapter, we look at diversity and how it may affect you. We discuss how to handle any prejudice and discrimination that you may encounter, and introduce qualities that will serve you well in this ever-diversifying world—your skills with languages, your ethnic and cultural identity, and your tolerance and acceptance. Like Sanjay, it's your job to learn how to get along with people inside and outside the workplace, regardless of culture, age, or other differences.

Making the Transition to the Workplace

You may not think that starting a job after being in school is a big deal. Many of you may have held jobs in the past and have a good idea of what to expect. But you still might need to get used to working again. Don't expect to make an instant transformation from student or unemployed professional to working person. Give yourself some time to adjust to the changes in independence and responsibility.

Gaining Your Independence

While you're a student, you don't make all the decisions about how you spend your days. Your class schedule dictates when you attend class, when you to study, and when you meet with a counselor. When a teacher has students work on an exercise, everyone does it at a certain time, and together. Much of your daily schedule is laid out for you to follow. You generally don't have the opportunity to say "It would be better for me if this class took place later." You take the schedule as written and plan your other activities around it.

When you move into the working world, you are suddenly in charge of your time, although others may tell you when you need to arrive at work and when you can leave. Even when you have to follow schedules and meet deadlines, you must structure your own time so you can meet your deadlines. No one will monitor your every move the way an instructor might. You will have to make decisions on your own about what you need to do and when.

If you've been unemployed for a while, you may have the opposite problem. While you were unemployed you were completely in charge of your schedule. You decided when to get up, when to eat, when to work on your resume, when to network, and when to follow up. When you re-enter the workplace, you may feel constrained because you have to arrive at a certain time and leave at a certain time. That's only natural. Even though your start and end

times are defined, you can rest easy knowing that you pretty much get to create the rest of the schedule for your day.

It can be tough to use your independence wisely, so put into action the time management skills you learned earlier in Chapter 3. When you accomplish a lot, you get the credit and the satisfaction. When you make mistakes, you take responsibility for them. It can take some getting used to, even if you've been there before. Take time to think your schedules through and make efficient decisions. Don't worry about miscalculations—they will happen. Try to remember the lessons they teach. You have the power to schedule your time so make it a positive power.

Taking Responsibility

When you are in school, you turn in homework, read articles or books, and work on specific projects, all assigned by a teacher. You are responsible for completing those tasks to the satisfaction of that teacher, but you don't have to create, choose, or structure your tasks.

As a working person you win back your responsibility, with all its pros and cons. You are responsible for completing tasks at work, and you take more of a role in deciding how to approach those tasks. Now you receive money in exchange for hard work, but if you miss work or don't work efficiently, you risk losing your job.

The working environment demands a different state of mind than you have in school or at home. As you assert your independence and take responsibility for your actions, you will gradually make the adjustment. You'll take things more seriously when a salary, or maybe supporting a family, depends on your actions. You'll carefully consider when to take time off. You'll learn to take the needs of the business, and those who work there, into consideration.

 ## Now You Try It: New Job, New Responsibilities

Imagine that you just landed the job of your dreams. Whether you were a student before, working at a different job, or unemployed, your life will now be a bit different. Write down several things that you think will be different now and how you plan to deal with them (for example, your schedule, budget, appearance, etc.).

_____

_____

_____

_____

_____

A Mosaic of People

With the advent of high-tech communication devices, such as the Internet, Skype, video conferencing, cell phones, and web cams, the workplace may not even be a single "place" any more. Some companies consist of employees in different cities, states, or countries who work remotely from their homes, communicating by email and instant message or online meetings. Other companies have offices in different parts of the nation or world, requiring employees to travel or communicate frequently by phone, email, or teleconference. Still others have only one small office where people meet regularly, in person.

Multicultural Aspects

Regardless of the structure and location of your workplace, it's highly likely that you will encounter people of different cultures. After all, the United States is a land of many people who come from many different traditions. Except for Native Americans, everyone else (or their ancestors) has come from another part of the world. We are a jumble of cultures that do not necessarily melt together. We are a mosaic of nationalities that sometimes mix and sometimes remain distinct. You are a piece of that mosaic and it's your job in the workplace to figure out how to communicate with everyone!

Multigenerational Aspects

In addition, the U.S. workforce consists of people of all ages. In fact, for the first time in history, four generations of people are sharing the workplace. Figure 9.1 identifies them.

As you might imagine, each generation has its own experiences and its own way of doing things, and somehow they must all work together. You'll learn more about these different generations later in the chapter.

To be able to better fit into today's multicultural working world, you need a sense of the big picture. The biggest of the big pictures is what we call a *world view*. Ease of travel and communication, coupled with the growth and intensity of global business, have caused the world to "shrink." Just think, a mechanical design drawing traveling by email can go from Quebec, Canada, to Beijing, China, on the Internet in a few seconds. The television news network tells us what is currently happening all over the world, 24 hours a day. Businesspeople in three different countries can all meet by teleconference without ever leaving their offices. We are all so accessible to each other that the world seems quite small. Figure 9.2 shows how we now have more frequent, better, and quicker access to our neighbors throughout the world.

Certain factors result from this rapidly shrinking world, such as

- The prosperity and welfare of countries across the globe are increasingly intertwined.
- We encounter people of other cultures more often.
- People are more aware of different ways of doing things.

Figure 9.1   Generation timeline

1922–1945	1946–1964	1965–1980	1981–2000
Veterans	Baby Boomers	Gen X	Gen Y
Traditionalists		Generation X	Generation Y
Silent Generation		Xers	Millennial
			Echo Boomers

Figure 9.2   Today's world—the diversity of the workplace

We live in a diverse world, made smaller by global business, ease of travel, and high-tech communication.

- Nations and people are more interdependent.
- We work with a greater variety of people with new and different ideas of how to work and act.
- We encounter people of different cultures more often.
- We socialize, date, and marry people of cultures different than our own.
- We see that what happens elsewhere in the world affects us in our own nation.
- We live in communities that look different—different stores and goods for diverse populations.

You may think these factors are terrific, or you may have concerns. Regardless of your opinion, these factors are real. You need to know how to deal with them and how they can help us in our working lives.

As we progress through the 21st century, the United States will only become culturally diverse. Recent studies tell us that U.S. demographics—the "map" of cultures and races that comprise our population—are shifting. The people now referred to as *minority* will soon make up at least half of the U.S. population. Instead of the historical process by which immigrants adjusted to the culture and behavior of the native majority, we are moving into an era in which we will all have to adjust to each other, more or less equally. There won't be one standard anymore—every situation will be unique.

It makes sense to deal with these issues now so we are all prepared for the future. Remember, we *are* the future—the career success of every one of us will determine the future of the world economy.

The working world reflects this mix of cultures and generations. It is important for you to understand the multicultural environment where you work so you can tailor your behavior to fit smoothly into the mix. When you start a job, you typically learn about the physical environment of the business, but you should also learn about the human and cultural environment. It will make just as big an impact.

Cultural Diversity

Culture, *noun*

all socially transmitted behavior patterns of a particular society; the region of the world where a person lives and everything that goes with it

The mix of people in this country will affect you in many ways, no matter where you work or what you do. Sometimes that mix of **cultures** brings positive energy and new perspectives to the workplace. Other times it results in conflict.

Recognizing Differences

As you enter the multicultural workforce, consider the different cultural factors you need to take into account to effectively communicate and collaborate. Figure 9.3 identifies the 10 most important factors. Consider these factors as you interact with coworkers who come from different cultures than you. These factors are particularly important when you work in an international business or in one for which you may work or travel in other countries. People who don't consider these factors often end up offending or alienating the people they work with.

 ## Now You Try It: Multicultural Lunch

Imagine that four new employees from the United States, Mexico, India, and Japan have been hired by the same company. They decide to meet for lunch to get to know one another and talk about their new jobs.

Review Figure 9.3 and consider the different cultures of the employees. Then describe an imaginary scenario, explaining what might occur at the luncheon and how each employee might behave. To get you started, consider these factors:

* When to meet
* How to greet
* What to eat
* What to talk about

_____

_____

_____

_____

_____

_____

_____

Figure 9.3 Multicultural communication factors

Language Fluency. Are you working with native English speakers? If not, how much English do they know? Did they learn it in school or on the job? Are they fluent?

Non-native English speakers might not understand you if you talk too fast or use slang. Carefully consider your words to make sure they will not confuse or offend your listeners. For example, "off-the-wall" or "hanging out" might have very different meanings to non-English speakers who take the words literally.

Age. Are you older or younger than the people you work with? How does this impact their perception of you?

Some cultures are more respectful of older people than Americans are and expect you to address them by their title (Mr., Miss, Mrs., Dr.) when you first meet them.

Gender. Are gender roles strongly defined in the cultures of your coworkers?

In many cultures of the world, men and women dress and interact according to strongly defined roles. For example, in some cultures in the Middle East, men and women are forbidden to interact in public and social situations without a third party present.

Family. How important is the family to your coworkers? How does this impact their lives?

In many cultures, including India, Mexico, and Saudi Arabia, a person's family is the most important aspect of his or her life. In cultures such as these, asking personal questions about someone's family before discussing business is not only welcome, it's almost required.

Religion. How important is religion to your coworkers, and how does it affect people's lives?

In many cultures, religion permeates all aspects of life, both at home and at work. For example, it affects when you can do business (holidays and time of day), how you dress, and what you eat when dining with others. Some foods are even forbidden in certain cultures.

Eating Behavior. How do your coworkers eat? With a particular hand? With utensils?

This affects what and how you eat to avoid embarrassing yourself or offending others. When it comes to business functions, especially holiday functions, you need to take into account differences in people's tastes in foods, as well as religious practices. This may mean providing Kosher food for Jews, serving nonalcoholic beverages for Muslims, or providing nonmeat alternatives for vegetarians. Accommodating others in this way shows respect and consideration.

Greeting Behavior. How do people greet one another in your coworkers' cultures? Do people shake hands? Hug? Bow?

Good greeting behavior is important because it creates a good first impression. Regardless of the culture, people often make up their minds about you in less than 30 seconds—just about the time that's required to greet one another.

Business and Public Behavior. How do you address your coworkers when you first meet at work? By first name or last name? Should you make small talk before discussing business?

Some business cultures, such as the Japanese business culture, are more formal than others and adhere to a strict hierarchy; other business cultures, such as the U.S. business culture, are informal and collaborative. Some cultures view the often time-consuming negotiation process as an enjoyable part of business. In other cultures, people just want to make a decision as quickly as possible.

Personal Space. How close can you stand next to someone without invading his or her space? Can you make direct eye contact without offending the person?

In some cultures, such as Indian and Southeast Asian, people are comfortable standing close together. In other cultures this is taboo. In some cultures, such as the United States and Western Europe, people expect you to look at them when you speak. In other cultures, such as Japan, direct eye contact is considered rude.

Perception of Time. How important is punctuality?

Some cultures are more rigid about time than others. For example, people in the United States and Western Europe adhere pretty rigidly to deadlines and times—give or take 10 minutes. However, in Latin American countries, time is fluid. It's common for people to show up an hour late and no offense is taken.

Dealing with Prejudice and Discrimination

Considering the different factors associated with multicultural communication, it's easy to see how some actions might be misunderstood or misinterpreted. However, you may have seen or experienced incidents in which you or others were mistreated, denied work, or simply disrespected because of someone else's perception. It's hard to forgive and forget. Situations such as

Prejudice, *noun*

a judgment or opinion formed before the facts are known, usually unreasonable and/or unfavorable, often marked by suspicion or fear

Discrimination, *noun*

a showing of partiality or prejudice in treatment, specifically action or policies directed against the welfare of minority groups or people with social, physical, or behavioral differences

these stick with you for a long time. We have come a long way since the civil rights movement of the 1960s, but prejudice and discrimination are still part of our world. What is the difference between the two?

Prejudice is the feeling about or judgment of another person, which is typically unreasonable. **Discrimination** is the action taken by a prejudiced person. Federal laws regarding discrimination are important and serve a valuable purpose. It is unlawful for you to be denied work—or the chance to apply for work—based on your race, gender, ethnic origin, religion, or sexual preference. The laws reduce the number of incidents that occur, but they don't eliminate them. Occasionally things go unreported, unnoticed, or people aren't willing to make waves by fighting back. Human beings still have some evolving to do when it comes to treating each other equally and respectfully.

Sadly, prejudice and discrimination still exist in many businesses. For example, here is a scenario that is not too far-fetched. Imagine that you are a recent immigrant from Southeast Asia. You are having difficulty explaining what you need to a salesperson at a local hardware store, and you hear someone in the background mimicking your accent. How does that make you feel? Or, suppose you are Hispanic. You are hosting a group of important customers at one of the best restaurants in town. Yet after you order a nice bottle of wine, the server pours the first taste of wine in the glass of one of your Caucasian guests for approval, rather than in your glass. How would you feel? Although seemingly small, these types of incidents happen every day and they hurt. Let's appreciate and be sensitive to our differences, and do our part to diplomatically educate those who unconsciously are not.

What can you do about prejudice and discrimination? Your best tool is your own conscience. If each of us takes responsibility for living a prejudice-free life, if we pay attention to our own thoughts and actions to make sure they are not discriminatory, we will change the world person by person. You may not be able to change what someone else thinks, feels, or does, but you can control your own thoughts and actions. Keep an open mind when meeting new people. Catch yourself when you think prejudicial thoughts and turn those thoughts around. Treat people with equal respect at work. Make an effort to include those who are different from you in your life. As you get to know them, you will be able to see their common human qualities, rather than their superficial differences.

Another way to improve the situation is to avoid jumping to conclusions and assuming you have been discriminated against. Although prejudice and discriminatory behavior can surface in the workplace, if you actively seek it out and focus on it (when it may or may not exist), you only serve to continue it. For example, if you suffer a work setback, control the immediate impulse to assume that you were discriminated against. Look first for the truth and assess yourself honestly: Did you slip up? Is there something you could have improved? Was your supervisor accurate in the assessment of your performance? If the answer to these questions is yes, then you will realize that the situation has gone according to the rules and you can make your own improvements from there. Conversely, if you honestly feel you did nothing wrong, then you need to meet with your supervisor to discuss your concerns about what happened.

Once you have taken the time to think through the incident, you may decide that you or someone else has been the victim of discrimination. If this is the case, carefully consider how to address the issue. Each situation is unique and requires its own plan of action. The following are examples of three situations that might arise:

1. Your coworkers tell racially offensive jokes around you, often at your expense. You feel so uncomfortable that you're having trouble concentrating on your daily work.

2. A coworker or friend makes a prejudicial comment about someone else in front of you, and the comment offends you even though it was directed at someone else.

3. You are extremely qualified for a job, but in the interview you felt quickly dismissed; you're having trouble attributing it to anything but the fact that your race is different from most everyone that you met at the company.

Here are some ideas about how you might handle these situations.

Incident at Work. Write down exactly what happened and when. Schedule a meeting with your supervisor (if a coworker created the problem) and discuss what happened and how it is affecting your position or performance. Ask the supervisor to observe the person's behavior or even intervene if you feel comfortable doing so. If the supervisor is the problem, see if you can go farther up in the hierarchy and ask someone to help you. The company is legally bound to fight prejudice in its ranks; you may elect to take legal action if you aren't satisfied with how the company reacts.

Personal Incident with a Friend or Acquaintance. If you feel that someone has behaved in a prejudicial manner toward you or insulted you in some way, talk to that person in private after your feelings have calmed a bit. Let the person know what he or she said and why it caused you pain. As diplomatically as possible, help the individual understand why the behavior was harmful and what he or she could do to change it and to make amends. In many situations, the person may have been unaware of his or her actions, and did not intend to offend you or someone else.

Incident While Applying for Work. If you feel that you lost a job opportunity due to prejudicial practices, you have the right to investigate the situation. Employers have broken a law if they refuse to hire you because of your race, your intent to have children, or the fact that you have a disability. Contact your local equal opportunity office and ask for recommendations about how to address the situation. It may take time and even money (if you end up going to court) to right the wrong, but if the job or the principle means enough to you, you should give it a shot.

It is important to handle upsetting situations involving discrimination, rather than pretending they did not happen.

Reality Check

We realize that not every situation can be logically and calmly fixed. In fact, some people don't even feel comfortable addressing the issue. Every situation is unique, and every person handles things differently. At times people may feel that if they put up a fuss about prejudice in their workplace they may put their jobs in jeopardy, so they keep their feelings under wraps. At times people may overreact to prejudice and lose a job or a chance at a job because they go overboard. Sticking up for your principles may cost you some friendships, and not sticking up for them may cost you some inner peace. Ultimately, you are in control of your life. Look at each situation and make the decision that best suits your needs without sacrificing your integrity. Just make sure you examine all your options and their consequences before you act.

Your Differences Are Useful Tools

Realize that your differences are actually unique qualities that can help you in your working life. Your specific differences are sought after by a large number of employers. Companies are striving to diversify, due in part to federal legislation and new rules from upper management. They want to attract a diverse workforce and offer them a pleasant work environment that accepts their differences. In fact, there are laws that reward and require employment of a diverse staff and laws that prohibit discrimination, imposing strict penalties on those who do discriminate.

Handling Language Differences

With different ethnic groups come different languages. Although English is the "official" language of the United States, many people still use the language that they grew up speaking. In fact, so many people use their native language that many communities are multilingual, meaning

Learning from Experience
A Perspective from the Working World

Finding Common Ground

Chai Boonmee
Nail technician and cosmetology student

Even though I grew up near a large city, I didn't have much interaction with people from other cultures. My high school, for example, was predominantly Asian. My parents were from Thailand and so were many of my friends' families. Now I'm attending a cosmetology school where most of the students are Hispanic. When I started the program, it was a little intimidating. Everyone seemed to be speaking Spanish between classes and sometimes during classes. I wondered if I was going to be accepted.

Over time, I began to make friends at school. The students made me feel welcome, and I soon realized we had a lot more in common than our differences. Many people had parents who were immigrants, just like mine, and everyone seemed to have families who were constantly worried about them or trying to fix them up with potential spouses. It was nice to learn that despite outward appearances, we were all very similar. I realized that even though people may like different foods, music, or clothes, we all want to be treated with respect. Anyway, I think it would be boring if we were all alike. Maybe we focus too much on what makes us different instead of what we have in common.

At school, we are all working toward the same goal: earning a license. I hope to one day open my own nail salon and feel pretty excited about the possibility of being my own boss. But sometimes cosmetology school can get pretty monotonous—we're here eight hours a day, four or five days a week—and sometimes I want to quit. However, my friends at school are helping me get through this, and I hope I'm helping them, too.

I really like the environment at the beauty school. When someone graduates, we throw a nice luncheon to congratulate her. We are there for one another, and we see the best in each other. I think getting along with people is one of the most important parts of life. Building relationships with others can make a big difference in your life. In fact, when I helped out at my parents' restaurant as waitress during high school, the way I greeted people made a big difference in my tips.

After high school, I really didn't really know what I wanted to do. My parents wanted me to go to college, but I had no idea what major to choose. So I went to junior college instead, taking general education courses. I managed to get an A.A. (Associates in Arts) degree, but I still didn't have a clue what to do with my life. That's when my best friend took me to the Nails Plus salon for a super deluxe manicure, pedicure, exfoliation, and foot massage to celebrate my graduation. The atmosphere in the salon was terrific: I felt pampered and special. When I left, I couldn't believe how good I felt and how great my nails looked. That visit really had an impact on me. I wanted to work in that kind of atmosphere. I wanted to make people feel that good.

I went back a couple of weeks later for another appointment and talked to one of the salon specialists. She told me how she had gotten into the business. Then I talked to another and heard a similar story. I decided then and there to become a nail technician and eventually own my own business.

My goal right now is to finish beauty school and establish my own clientele as a nail technician. I'm also working part-time at Nails Plus to gain some experience. I'm drawn to the creativity of my future career, and I look forward to learning more about how to do nail extensions and nail art. And along the way, I plan to make a few good friends from a variety of cultures.

many languages are used. If you speak more than one language, you have a very important and marketable skill. Languages such as Spanish, Chinese, and Japanese have become so widely used that businesses are taking note. Company growth depends on building a client base. Businesses that want to appeal to more diverse people need to be able to serve them, and one way to do so is to hire workers who speak their languages. On the job, you can use your language skills with customers, distributors, and coworkers. You will broaden your base of communication and therefore increase business.

Today, most Americans are still monolingual (only speak one language), but they often expect people from other cultures to know English. Many non-native English speakers know English quite well, while others might not be as fluent or may not understand all regional dialects. Whether you speak one language or many, consider the following tips to improve your communication with others who may be non-native English speakers.

- **Avoid using too much slang.** Slang is typically unique to your culture and your age group. It's wiser to use standard English so everyone can understand you.

- **Speak slowly and clearly.** Speaking too quickly can cause confusion for someone who is not as proficient in English as you. Also note that speaking loudly does *not* help the other person understand you.

- **Don't speak down.** Just because someone has an accent doesn't mean he or she is not as intelligent as you. Speak to that person as an equal.

If you speak multiple languages, your native language can be a useful tool rather than a barrier. Of course you need a working knowledge of English and you should always work to improve your English if it is not your first language. But your other language(s) can create opportunities for you wherever you work.

Valuing Your Ethnic and Cultural Identity

The U.S. workforce will continue to diversify. U.S. business today is being forced to accept a culturally diverse workforce for two reasons:

1. First, when a business needs to hire someone, chances are increasing that the person they find will be of some non-European ethnic origin.

2. Second, to sell a product or service, a company wants to do business with all kinds of people. One way to do that is to employ all kinds of workers. That is where your ethnic identity comes into play. If you can relate to a certain ethnic group and they can relate to you, that quality itself is valuable to a business.

On the downside, if you are not of northern European ethnic origin, you or people close to you may have had experiences when they were denied work because of their heritage or their appearance. Of course, women and people with disabilities also face this discrimination. This has been a problem for a long time and continues to be a struggle. What can you do? Certainly anger and violence won't change anyone's mind. You can fight it by working hard to prove yourself and your abilities. You can bring your battle into the legal system, although that is an expensive and time-consuming solution. Or, as we said before, you can realize that your identity is a plus and find an employer who agrees with you and has values that match your own.

For example, what if you were from the Dominican Republic, spoke Spanish and English, and saw a job opening for a tax preparer at an accounting firm in a mainly Hispanic area of your town? The firm would be wise to hire you because you would help make the business accessible to a large section of the population. Without a Spanish-speaking employee, the firm would only appeal to a limited number of people. As a bilingual employee, you would be able to greet, recruit, and serve any client whose main language was Spanish, while communicating effectively in English with the other customers, employees, and managers at the firm. Even your appearance might contribute to helping Hispanic clients feel comfortable; people often feel more at home around others who resemble them in appearance. Your ethnic heritage would be a marketable quality.

Avoiding Barriers to Successful Communication

You've read a lot about how to successfully work and communicate in a diverse workplace. Now it's time to look at barriers to success. Consider the following behaviors to be the five big "no-nos" when working with people of different cultures. Avoid them at all costs!

Ethnocentrism. This term means believing your culture is superior to all others and your way of doing things is the only way. Some people call this "my way or the highway." An ethnocentric attitude makes communication difficult because others feel defensive and unvalued. This kind of attitude only serves to divide a business and make it less successful.

Did You Know? A widespread study by the National Institute of Health found there was no correlation between perceived cultural characteristics and the actual traits observed in real people.[1] In other words, stereotypes have nothing to do with reality!

Assumptions. Assumptions are beliefs, not facts. If you fall back on assumptions about people because of their appearance, culture, age, or another factor, you are likely to misjudge them. These assumptions are typically based on stereotypes that narrow your perspective, limit your ideas, and have little to do with reality. In business, this may cause you to make poor decisions that hurt others and the company.

Closed-Mindedness. This is similar to ethnocentrism, but not identical. If you are closed-minded, you might not think your culture is the best in the world, but you have no interest in learning about any other cultures. With this attitude, you are likely to miss out on a lot of interesting things in life: people, activities, and food, to name a few. You probably won't be able to think outside the box, which means you may be less able to come up with creative solutions to business problems.

Ignorance. Being ignorant is not the same as being stupid. When you are ignorant, you are uninformed or lack personal experience with a culture. Stupidity means you have no interest in learning. Ignorance can be cured with education. Ignorance has a downside when it comes to interacting with people from another culture and can certainly get in the way of communication. When you have no knowledge of another culture it is very easy to offend or anger someone, something you certainly don't want to do in the workplace or anywhere. That's why it's so important to get to know people from other cultures and expose yourself to their traditions and ideas.

Fear. Of all the attitudes you might have, fear is the most dangerous. It is a huge barrier to intercultural communication. When you are afraid of people from another culture, you feel uncomfortable around them and you probably don't spend time getting to know or understand them. When you don't understand someone, fear can develop into hatred. This attitude has no place in the workplace. It is up to you to examine your fears and face them head-on. When you make the effort to really get to know someone from another culture, you will probably find that your fears are completely unfounded.

Recognizing and overcoming these barriers will put you well on your way to success in any business.

 Now You Try It: Uncovering Your Stereotypes

It is time to think about your own views and challenge any stereotypes that you hold.

1. Look at the following types of people and write down your *first* thoughts about the characteristics of each.

Mexican	
Arab	
Man	
Woman	
Teenager	
Senior citizen	
Asian	

[1]Merali, Zeeya. "Exploding the myth of cultural stereotypes." *New Scientist,* October 6, 2006. Accessed September 6, 2009, from www.newscientist.com/article/dn8111-exploding-the-myth-of-cultural-stereotypes.html

2. Examine what you have written.

   a. Which characteristics are negative?

   _____

   _____

   b. Which are based on movies, television, or the Internet?

   _____

   _____

   c. Which are based on what other people have told you?

   _____

   _____

   d. Did you write down anything based on real people that you actually know?

   _____

   _____

3. Based on your answers and what you've read so far about barriers to successful communication, identify any issues you have and how you might address them.

   _____

   _____

   _____

Ages, Stages, Abilities, and Values

We have to remember the growing diversity in the working world does not only involve ethnic groups. It also involves a growing variety of people of different age groups and life circumstances, as well as people with disabilities and people with different value systems. Accepting this diversity and treating people of all ages and life stages equally carries as much weight as tolerating and respecting different ethnicities.

Working with Multiple Age Groups

Many years ago, you might have had an easier time putting age groups into job categories. Young people had entry-level jobs. People in their 30s to 50s had established careers. People over 60 retired and lived on pensions. But all that has changed. The economic upheaval has made a mish-mash of those definitions and categories.

Today, there are more people between the ages of 50 and 85 in the workplace than ever before. Many older people have gone back to work because they cannot survive on only a pension or social security. Younger people with special abilities or connections rise up more quickly than they used to. Middle-aged people often encounter one of two kinds of situations: They become dissatisfied with their careers and want to switch gears, or they fall victim to company layoffs and lose their jobs in the prime of their lives. Many reach a career plateau or have to start over.

The result is that you will find a great diversity of ages in the workforce today—in many cases, all four generations are sharing the workplace. That diversity creates a different environment, one to which everyone needs to adjust. Table 9.1 shows some general personal and lifestyle differences between generations. The differences in personal and lifestyle characteristics lead to differences in workplace behaviors. Table 9.2 summarizes some key behaviors of each generation in a work environment.

Table 9.1 — Personal and Lifestyle Changes by Generation

Characteristics	Veterans (1922–1945)	Baby Boomers (1946–1964)	Gen X (1965–1980)	Gen Y (1981–2000)
Core Values	Respect for authority Conformity Discipline	Optimism Involvement	Skepticism Fun Informality	Realism Confidence Extreme fun Social
Family	Traditional	Disintegrating	Latchkey kids	Merged families
Education	A dream	A birthright	A way to get there	An incredible expense
Communication Tool	Rotary phone One-on-one Memo	Touch-tone phone Call anytime	Cell phone Call me at work Email	Smart phones Email Text message
Money Approach	Save Pay cash	Buy now, pay later	Conservative Save, save, save	Earn to spend

Table 9.2 — Workplace Characteristics by Generation

Characteristics	Veterans (1922–1945)	Baby Boomers (1946–1964)	Gen X (1965–1980)	Gen Y (1981–2000)
Communication Style	Formal Memos	Informal Meetings	Immediate Email Voicemail	Immediate Text messages Social media
Interaction Style	Individual	Team player	Entrepreneur	Participative
Leadership Style	Directive Command-and-control Hierarchical	Consensual Collaborative	Everyone is the same Challenge others Ask why	To be determined*
Messages That Motivate	Your experience is respected.	You are valued and needed.	Do it your own way. Forget the rules.	You will work with other creative people.
Preferred Reward	Satisfaction in a job well done	Title Recognition Money	Freedom	Meaningful work
Work Ethic	Hard work Respect authority Duty before fun Adhere to rules	Workaholic Desire quality Crusade causes Question authority	Eliminate the task Need structure and direction Skeptical	Goal oriented Multitasking Entrepreneurial Tolerant
Work Is . . .	An obligation	An exciting adventure	A difficult challenge	A means to an end

When working with someone from a particular generation, do not assume that he or she will exhibit every characteristic of that generation. The most important thing is to find out how people around you prefer to communicate, regardless of age, and then let them know your preferences as well.

Another thing to consider is high-tech etiquette between generations. Most students have grown up with technology and are comfortable multitasking with different devices and switching their attention back and forth between equipment and people. For example, you might text on the phone while talking to a friend sitting next to you. In fact, you might not even look at your friend as you speak. However, if you were talking to an older person while texting, he or she would probably consider you rude because eye contact and focused attention indicate respect, and you would not be giving either to that individual.

With the possibility of four generations in the workplace, you will probably end up communicating in a variety of ways to make sure that everyone understands one another. Regardless of how you communicate, working with people of different ages has both benefits and drawbacks.

The Positive Side. If you are younger, you can learn much from the experience and wisdom of older people. If you are older, you can benefit from the energy and fresh ideas of younger people. As more diverse ideas emerge from different people and blend, better solutions will come to mind.

The Tough Parts. An older person new to a job may have trouble taking orders from a young (but more experienced) supervisor. Older people may feel that younger supervisors don't respect their wisdom and experience. In turn, sometimes younger people may feel that older people who report to them deny them respect because of their age. Sometimes older people may believe that younger people feel entitled to more than they actually deserve, simply because they are ignorant of what it really takes to get ahead—and older people who have worked hard to gain their experience can resent this.

Whatever your age, as you become sensitive to the emotions and feelings of others and better understand where they are coming from, you can more quickly reach an understanding of one another's needs and positions. Through mutual respect and honest communications you can learn from others in the workplace.

Not everyone wants to communicate by email or texting. Make an effort to communicate in person as well.

technology *at work*

With the increasing use of text messages and instant messages, many workers have begun using texting language in their conversations, emails, and written correspondence. Be careful of this trend. Not everyone texts, especially older workers, and not everyone uses or understands acronyms such as LOL, BFF, or OMG. It is best to use standard English terms so everyone knows what you are talking about, regardless of age or culture in the workplace. This is especially important when writing formal reports or requests, where texting language may cause you to be perceived as immature or unprofessional.

 Now You Try It: Communicating with People of All Ages

People of different generations may have different ways of communicating. However, for a business to function properly, those differences must be taken into consideration and accommodated.

1. Write down the ways you feel most comfortable communicating with others in your personal and business life.

_____

_____

_____

2. Describe an instance in your own life when you had difficulty communicating with someone of a different age. How did you resolve the problem?

_____

_____

_____

3. If you are working with someone older than you and need to communicate effectively, what might you have to do differently? What if that person was younger than you?

_____

_____

_____

_____

_____

Handling Different Life Circumstances

Diversity comprises more than just differences in ethnicity and age; it also includes difference in life circumstances. You may end up working with other employees who have any of the following circumstances:

- Starting a new job fresh out of school
- An established employee in a semipermanent career
- Married, with no children
- Beginning again after a divorce
- A new parent
- A single parent
- Working part time in between careers
- Getting a job after being unemployed for awhile
- Embarking on a second career late in life
- Working to supplement social security benefits

People in different circumstances have different needs. For example, a single parent may need to leave work earlier than others to pick up a child. An older person may have limited hours due to other obligations or health problems. Someone who works part time as a fill-in between careers may not have the same level of commitment as a young person who has chosen and trained for a particular profession. Someone who has taken years to climb the corporate ladder may not tolerate others who are unwilling to put in the same number of long hours at work. No matter what the situation, working with people in different life circumstances has both benefits and drawbacks.

The Positive Side. Workers can learn to appreciate the different perspectives of coworkers. The mix of different circumstances often requires a higher level of cooperation in terms of scheduling and task assignment, and with more cooperation, a group of employees becomes a true team.

In today's constantly shifting marketplace, there are many jobs for people who don't want to, or cannot, make full-time or long-term commitments. Often, when companies lay off full-time employees during an economic downturn, those companies still need help. In this situation, they often turn to contract or part-time workers who don't want to make a long-term commitment and don't mind being let go when a project is over. A person switching careers or an older person re-entering the workforce might be perfect for this sort of position.

The Tough Parts. People with different life circumstances have different needs. It can be hard to adjust to those needs when the adjustment creates a hardship for you. Perhaps your coworker is a parent with children who are frequently ill, so she often takes off early to get them to a pediatrician. You end up staying late to finish work that she could not complete. You may become resentful, but there are ways to solve the situation that take both of your circumstances into account. Simply sitting down and honestly communicating your feelings with each other goes a long way toward relaxing your resentment. If you are aware of particular circumstances of people around you, you will learn to accept their needs and to treat them with compassion… and they will do the same for you.

Working with Individuals with Disabilities

Individuals with physical, mental, or emotional differences are becoming a larger part of the workforce. More and more companies are starting to benefit from their unique abilities and to accommodate their special needs. Certain organizations work to place people with disabilities in jobs that suit their individual talents and requirements. You may find yourself working alongside a person whose behavior differs radically from your own, or whose situation demands special procedures or privileges. But no matter what their ability, working with people with disabilities has both benefits and drawbacks.

The Positive Side. People are people. Those who have disabilities, whether from birth or due to an accident or injury, have equal value. They also have the ability to make valuable contributions at work, despite their unique challenges. It benefits us to recognize that fact. It expands our sense of justice to accept those who differ from us, and it gives people with disabilities a much-deserved opportunity to find fulfillment in a challenging career.

If you work to accept and tolerate differences, you will be open to the new perspectives offered by a coworker who has a disability. You may find yourself incredibly inspired to see how people overcome obstacles to make the most of their potential. If you can learn to appreciate each other, you will gain a greater appreciation of the strength and range of power of humanity.

The Tough Parts. Just like adjusting to the needs of coworkers of different ages or with different circumstances, it can take time to adapt to someone with special needs. Their needs may seem to infringe on yours if they need more workspace or time to complete a task. Your workload may change, or you may have to work in a different way to accommodate how they work. For example, if you have a deaf coworker, you may have to write more or learn some rudimentary sign language.

Once you understand and accept someone's particular situation, you will be able to cooperate and learn from him or her. Everyone's contribution is equally valuable. Free your mind!

Looking at Different Value Systems

As our world becomes more tolerant of visible differences such as age, ethnicity, and disabilities, we learn that other differences exist that are not as obvious. These differences have to do with our **values**—what we think is important, proper, and standard respectable behavior.

Value systems vary widely from person to person, and even within cultures and families. For example, consider how parents who believe in living together only after marriage may struggle against their young daughter who plans to move in with her boyfriend. Or imagine a young man who endures the disapproval of his family because he decides to marry someone from a different background than his own. In each case, one member of a family has a different value system than the other members, and those ideas collide against each other despite the close family ties.

We tend to build our value systems partly from ideas gathered from our families and friends, and partly from our own inclinations. It's important to spend time thinking about your own values; it will give you great insight into who you are and it will help you set personal goals.

Some specific ideas that make up our value systems include: (1) our lifestyles, (2) the way we treat family and friends, (3) how we prioritize family, peers, work, and other activities,

Values, *noun*

the social principles, goals, or standards held or accepted by an individual, class, group, or society

(4) our sexual orientation, and (5) our attitudes about childrearing. You will encounter a wide range of value systems as you make your way through your career; some you will understand, some may seem foreign to you, and some may upset or disturb you. It's important to remember this: To each his own. There are, however, both benefits and drawbacks in the workplace.

The Positive Side. Just as you can learn from other differences, you can learn from observing and trying to understand different value systems. Trying to understand why different values work for different people will stretch your tolerance and your knowledge. For example, it may seem easy to judge a coworker who sends her child to school and after-school care five days per week when your own values tell you it's important to spend a lot of time with a child. However, you don't know the background behind this person's values. Perhaps a bitter divorce or even the death of a spouse prompted the mother to shift her values so she could survive. She decided that making a decent salary and leaving her child with a capable caretaker was better than staying home and drawing welfare. As you get to know people, you will learn to hold back judgments and to respect different values.

You will also learn that each person's value system is personal and, if it doesn't interfere with the day-to-day operation of the business, no one should take issue with it. Someone at work may be initially uncomfortable working with a homosexual coworker, but if that person's sexual orientation has no effect on the high quality of his or her work, then no one should take offense to it in the workplace. There is only so much time and energy in a given workday. Try to stick to what directly affects the work and let the rest ride.

The Tough Parts. It can be difficult to let it ride when you have a strong disagreement with a coworker's values and lifestyle. We all like to feel that we have the right answers, and often we have the urge to "show someone the light" so he or she can see the "true path in life." Keep in mind that this may be *your* true path, but it certainly isn't everyone's. Think about how different we all are. It would be a strange world if everyone agreed on one standard value system. Not only would it be boring, but it would also be very competitive because we would all be fighting for the same important things.

As hard as it is, try to resist imposing your own values on other people. You may not agree with their personal choices, but as long as those choices don't affect work or hurt anyone, you need to be tolerant of other people's values.

If you feel that someone's choices or values are causing a work-related problem, address it by focusing on the work problem, *not* that person's value system. If someone's lifestyle affects his or her schedule to the point where you find you are doing extra work, talk about fixing the schedule rather than criticizing the lifestyle. If customers or clients have made unfavorable comments about an employee's appearance, discuss the appearance and how it affects business, rather than the values that may cause the employee to dress that way. You'll be more effective if you work cooperatively to solve the problem and avoid assaulting someone else's values. Plus, you will display strong integrity. Values run deep and strong and people will fight hard to defend them, but cooperation and change can happen in the workplace fairly easily with a little diplomatic discussion.

Practicing Tolerance and Acceptance

Tolerance, *noun*

the ability to recognize and respect others' beliefs, practices, and so on that differ from one's own

With this growing diversity, it is less likely that you will work in a homogenous environment where everyone has the same ethnic background, the same abilities, and the same values. You will probably work with people whose origin and ideas are different from your own. **Tolerance** and **acceptance**—essential tools for any job—will help you function efficiently and happily in this new environment. Without them we have little chance of comfortably cooperating with others in the workplace.

The phrase "If you are not part of the solution, you are part of the problem" definitely applies to the diverse workplace. If you are intolerant of differences and look down on others who live differently or have a different physical appearance, you are holding negative feelings that will come out while you work. Your attitude may hurt your performance and make it difficult for others to effectively work with you. If you expect others to be tolerant of you, make sure you return the favor. Tolerance means live and let live, no matter what differences exist.

Tolerance must exist before acceptance takes place. Tolerance is a passive attitude, whereas acceptance is an action. When you tolerate people, you recognize their existence. You understand that they deserve to be valued and must be allowed to live their unique lifestyle. When you show acceptance, you receive people positively, freely interact with them when the opportunity arises, and show them respect. If you tolerate but ignore those who differ from you, you can hinder cooperation in the workplace. When everyone accepts each other's differences, cooperation can thrive. Don't let everyone else do the accepting—be part of the solution and actively work to build acceptance and unbiased cooperation in the workplace.

Besides improving the interaction among ethnic groups, our tolerance and acceptance can bridge the gender gap in the workplace. Women still have trouble reaching certain management levels within organizations or holding certain occupations, and sometimes they receive lower salaries than men for identical work. As employers learn to tolerate the different needs of men and women and to accept the fact that proficiency on the job is based on skills and talent, rather than on gender, the situation is gradually improving.

Tolerance and acceptance are powerful tools in the quest to solve the conflicts that often arise in an increasingly diverse world. Different groups often prefer different work styles, values, and communication patterns. It is very human to think "My (or our) way is the best way" or "We've always done it that way!" Just think about conflict on the very smallest scale—within your household. People who live together can disagree about all kinds of things, such as how to do the cleaning and cooking, how much television to watch, and how to raise a child. It's a miracle that anyone gets along at all! If

> **Acceptance,** *noun*
>
> an approving reception; the act of receiving willingly and favorably

An attitude of tolerance and acceptance goes a long way in a diverse workplace.

Did You Know? As of 2010, women, on average, earned only 77 cents to a man's dollar, and the disparity is greater for women of color. While the pay gap has been slowly closing over the last 40 years (women earned 59 cents to a man's dollar in 1963), we're still not there.[2] What's particularly troubling is that women now make up 50% of U.S. workers and two-thirds of U.S. families with children now rely on a woman's earnings for a significant portion of their family's income. The gender pay gap has taken on added importance because, as of 2010, more families rely on the woman's paycheck as men lose their jobs during the economic downturn.[3]

Numerous reasons for this pay discrepancy abound, from women taking maternity leave, to women's discomfort with negotiating salaries, to lower pay in female-dominated occupations. But whatever the reason, women with equal ambition and equal education to men, in the same professions and same geographic regions, still make less.

---

[2]Ludden, Jennifer. "Despite new law, gender salary gap persists." National Public Radio, April 10, 2010. Accessed January 12, 2011, from www.npr.org/templates/story/story.php?storyId=125998232

[3]Boushey, Heather, Jessica Arons, and Lauren Smith. "Families can't afford the gender gap." Center for American Progress, April 20, 2010. Accessed January 14, 2011, from www.americanprogress.org/issues/2010/04/equal_pay.html

It's best to resolve problems calmly, instead of blowing up in anger.

conflict can arise even with the people closest to you, it's easy to see how it can easily arise in the workplace, where you are often dealing with people from entirely different backgrounds.

When conflict does arise due to different ways of working and relating, it's important to discuss the issues in a calm and respectful manner. When both sides listen and take each other's opinions into account, they can better understand each other and come up with new ideas that they might never have thought of alone. Resolving the conflict in this way improves the atmosphere and function of the workplace.

It is not always easy to resolve a problem calmly. We often feel it's easier to get angry and let it all out, or get quiet and hold it all in. Both methods are harmful. When you yell at someone else you may feel better, but you have harmed that person and damaged your relationship with him or her. When you don't say anything and hold in your anger you hurt yourself, as stress hormones course through your body, increasing your blood pressure and harming your immune system.[4] That's why it's so important to give yourself time to think things through and then honestly and calmly share how you feel.

Becoming more tolerant and accepting of differences is one way to avoid conflict before it starts. Many conflicts arise because people lash out when their needs aren't met, rather than trying to figure out the real problem. If a supervisor is annoyed when an employee does not complete a project on schedule, that supervisor has two choices: (1) create conflict by stewing in silence or blowing up at the employee, or (2) investigate the situation to find out why the employee did not complete the project on time. Suppose the supervisor investigates the situation and learns the employee had an emergency at home—an elderly parent fell and had to be taken to the hospital. The employee was so upset that she had difficulty focusing on the project. The supervisor understands there is nothing the employee could do differently to change the situation (except maybe apprise her supervisor of the situation) and accepts that the project will be late. Instead of yelling at the employee and berating her for not completing the project, the supervisor talks to the employee about ways to finish the project and still visit her parent in the hospital. This type of behavior brings increased knowledge about the situation, which allows the people involved to resolve the problem in a calmer and wiser fashion, instead of blindly clashing with each other.

Being tolerant and accepting is the best way to build a better working and living environment.

Figure 9.4 Embracing diversity

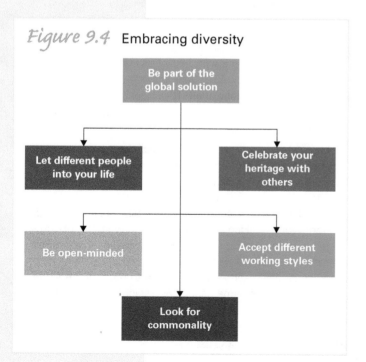

Your Corner of the World: Be Part of the Solution

How can you put your new tools to use? Figure 9.4 illustrates how we might use them.

- Be open-minded about the kinds of people you encounter, both on and off the job. Restrain yourself from making snap judgments based on external factors such as skin color, body type, or gender.
- Allow yourself to learn about other cultures, ages, and life circumstances by getting to know people who represent them. When you encounter these people, let them into your life.

---

[4]Mayo Clinic Staff. "Stress: Constant stress puts your health at risk." MayoClinic Website, September 11, 2010. Accessed January 11, 2011, from www.mayoclinic.com/health/stress/SR00001

- Accept different working styles at your job, as long as the people who practice them don't break rules.

- Explore and be proud of your own heritage, whether your ancestors were from Africa, Scotland, or any other region in the world.

- Share your heritage and situation with others. Give your family, friends, and coworkers the chance to learn about you and to understand your version of the world, as you work to understand their version. Celebrate the unique you and your special way of living and being.

- Look for what you *do* have in common. Do you like the same food for lunch? Do you both have young children? Are you both disorganized? Beyond the cultural and behavioral differences you may find many similarities. You might just build a friendship on them, or at least a mutual respect. When you get to know someone as an individual, it's hard to dislike his or her entire culture.

- Know that underneath the skin we really are all quite similar. We all love, hurt, think, like, dislike, hope, fear, and plan. Although we may express ourselves differently, we are essentially human.

The Diverse World and Your Job

How does this all relate to your success on the job? Your school, workplace, and your neighborhood are all microcosms of the world. The more you understand our diverse and changing world, the more you will understand your small part of it. As the world changes, so does your workplace and the people in it. Being part of the solution will help you to make where you work a more efficient and accepting place, as well as a more successful one!

Your Tool Kit at Work

9.1 Another World of Work

Expand your horizons by interviewing someone from another culture about the work habits common to that culture or country of origin.

1. Use the list that follows to guide you as you think of questions you might want to ask.
   a. What are your normal working hours?
   b. How long is the break for lunch?
   c. What kinds of jobs are traditionally held by women? By men?
   d. At what age do most people start work?
   e. Where do people get training for their careers?
   f. What office or technical equipment is used by most companies?
   g. How are medical care, maternity leave, and childcare handled?
   h. What differences and similarities have you noticed between your native country and the United States?
   i. If English was not your first language, how did you learn it?
   j. How did you find a job?
   k. What culturally related challenges did you face in the workplace?
   l. Who helped you feel comfortable in the workplace?

2. Write a short, two-part essay about your findings. In the first part, describe what you discovered about the work habits of the other culture. In the second, discuss how those work habits differ from your own. You can even use your findings to kick off a discussion about which work habits are the most efficient in various work situations.

9.2 Put Yourself into Another World of Work

After you complete the interview, imagine yourself moving to a country with the culture you just researched. Think about how you would adjust to the work customs. Write another short essay about your plans for adjustment, incorporating answers to the following questions. Compare your answers with those of the person you interviewed.

1. You know only a few words of the language. How will you learn how to speak it?
2. You need a job. How will you find one?
3. What kind of job do you think you will be able to get?
4. What challenges are you likely to face in the following areas?

   a. Adjusting to the job
   b. Being successful in the job
   c. Getting promoted

5. What do you need to do to feel comfortable in your new country?
6. What do you want the people to do that would help you adjust?
7. What new positive work customs could you bring from the United States?
8. What customs could you adopt in this country—customs that you would want to introduce to workers in the United States when you return?

9.3 A Multicultural Workforce

Countries stay strong when new, positive ideas are introduced. One reason the United States became a world leader was its ability to accept different views and incorporate them into the culture. Today's multicultural workplace and world community demand more new ideas and understanding, even as they continue to use traditional work customs.

Almost all U.S. families or their ancestors have come from other countries; the only non-immigrants are Native Americans. Chances are, your ancestors lived and worked in another country. Take some time to research your own ancestral heritage by answering the following questions. One interesting way to find the answers to these questions is to talk with older relatives in your family. They often have a wealth of information, history, and stories that will enrich your sense of who you are as a member of a family and a culture.

1. My family came from (name the country and region or city, if you know it):

   _____

2. In their country of origin, they worked as:

   _____

3. They arrived in the United States in (year):

   _____

4. In the United States, they worked as:

   _____

5. What hardships did they encounter when they first arrived?

   _____

6. How did they overcome them?

   _____

9.4 Reject the Rejection

If people in your work environment reject you on the basis of differences, they are showing their own weaknesses, not yours. Work hard and maintain a good attitude—reject the rejection. You will come out ahead.

Our unique qualities and differences bring positives to the workplace, as well as challenges that require us to modify our work style or behavior. It is important to pay attention to your unique qualities in two ways: (1) recognize their value in the workplace and (2) explore any modifications you may need to make in your behavior to make the most of your qualities.

For example, consider Jenny, who is hearing impaired. She wants to be a graphic designer. Jenny brings good concentration and visual awareness (her unique qualities) to a graphic design program and career. However, she has some difficulty keeping up with her classes (the challenge). Learning to lip read or using an interpreter (some modifications) will help her become more successful.

To remember your importance in the diverse workplace, complete the following sentences.

- A unique quality I bring to the diverse workplace is:

  _____

- This quality will help my career because:

  a.

  _____

  b.

  _____

- To allow this quality to contribute positively to the workplace, I may need to make the following modifications:

  a.

  _____

  b.

  _____

9.5 Your Diversity Quotient: A Check of Your Global and Cultural Awareness

Indicate whether the following statements are true or false.

_____ Carnation Ice Cream is owned by a Swiss company.

_____ You are comfortable working for a younger female manager.

_____ Many Toyota models are classified as American-made cars.

_____ Dim Sum is a Chinese food.

_____ You want to learn a foreign language in anticipation of future opportunities.

_____ Kwanzaa is an African celebration.

_____ Squid is part of Italian and Japanese cuisines.

_____ Bic Pens is owned by a French company.

_____ Cinco de Mayo is not considered the Independence Day of Mexico.

_____ You enjoy trying different ethnic foods.

If you answered true to:

- **7–10 questions:** Congratulations! You are sensitive to your global and diverse environment.
- **4–6 questions:** You are aware. Consider deepening your use of global and cultural awareness.
- **0–3 questions:** You might consider setting a goal of increasing your global and cultural awareness.

9.6 Getting in Touch with Our Prejudices

We often hold prejudices of which we are not even aware. Discuss with a classmate or a friend how you would feel in the following situations.

1. You are ready to cross a busy street when you notice a blind person waiting to cross the street. This blind person doesn't have a Seeing Eye dog or any other assistance. What do you do? Do you ignore this situation? Do you help? Do you feel uncomfortable and don't know what to do?

2. You are on your way to work and find yourself driving behind a senior citizen. The senior citizen is driving the speed limit, which is slower than most other drivers on the highway. Do you view this driver differently than other drivers? Are you frustrated or patient?

3. You see an interracial couple walking down the street and then notice that the woman is your sister. What is your reaction? How do you feel about this?

4. You are treated rudely and receive poor service at a coffee shop, and then notice the customers who are similar in appearance to the employees seem to be getting respect and good service. How do you feel? What might you do?

5. You think your younger, male boss is asking you to meet more requirements than other employees just so you can make a small change in your work schedule. What do you do? How do you feel?

9.7 Your Positive Attitude List—Your PAL

The attitudes listed below are important in the workplace today. Circle the attitudes you already have and put an X next to the ones you want to improve.

Adaptable	Adjusts well to new situations.
Tolerant	Allows others to be themselves.
Trustworthy	Is dependable and loyal.
Insightful	Finds ways to understand unfamiliar work practices and people.
Thoughtful	Takes time to think things through before acting or passing judgment.
Unprejudiced	Accepts everyone for who they are.
Down-to-earth	Can go with the flow; is realistic and practical.
Empathetic	Can put oneself in another's shoes and see a situation from that perspective.
Supportive	Helps others affirm their identity and encourages individuality.

1. Write each circled attitude as a positive affirmation and put it on a card or note where you will see it. Repeat the affirmation daily. For example:

I Am Dependable

I Am Unprejudiced

2. Write the attitudes that you want to improve below:

I will develop my ability to be:

_____

_____

_____

9.8 Technology Exercises

Here's your chance to get some "in-the-trenches" information about diversity in today's workplace.

1. Visit the Diversity Inc website located at www.diversityinc.com.

   a. Click the **Diversity Management: Best Practices** menu item. From the resulting web page, select and read two or three featured articles. Notice that you can click the numbered buttons at the bottom of the web page to move to other pages and find more articles.

   b. Hover over the **Diversity Management: Best Practices** menu item again to view the drop-down menu. Select **Mentoring** to learn more about formal and informal mentoring. Then select two or three articles to read.

   c. Summarize your observations in writing.

2. Visit the PBS website "Faces of America" at www.pbs.org/wnet/facesofamerica.

   a. Click the photo of any of the famous Americans listed to watch a video clip and learn more about his or her family background.

   b. Write a brief paragraph about what you learned from one of the programs, focusing on something that surprised you or of which you were unaware.

3. Visit the NPR website "Beyond Black and White" at www.npr.org/series/120652135/beyond-black-and-white.

   a. Click any of the titles to listen to a program from this series.

   b. Write a brief paragraph about what you learned from one of the programs, focusing on something that surprised you or of which you were unaware.

4. Visit the Equal Opportunity website at www.eop.com.

   a. Click any of the magazines shown at the bottom (for example, *Equal Opportunity, Minority Engineer, Careers and the disABLED)* and read some of the featured articles.

   b. Based on an article you read, write one to two short paragraphs about what you learned, focusing on something that surprised you or of which you were unaware.

10

Get the Job Done with Communication

Stay Ahead of the Curve

*Communication — the human connection —
is the key to personal and career success.*

Paul J. Meyer

 learning objectives

- What part do personality types and work styles play in building and maintaining relationships in the workplace?

- What are some useful tips for getting along with managers, coworkers, clients, as well as friends and family?

- Why are teams important to a business and how can you deal with "toxic" team members and "difficult" employees?

- What is a virtual team and what communication practices make it more effective?

- What are the six common communication styles?

- What are three techniques for effective communication, and why are "I" statements more effective than "you" statements?

- How can you effectively communicate in person (verbally and nonverbally), over the phone, and in writing?

- What are some effective techniques for dealing with conflict?

- What is the difference between passive, aggressive, and assertive behavior?

- What are five steps to better public speaking?

Amy landed the job of her dreams, or so she thought. She was now the office manager at Clean Pressed, a local uniform laundry service. When she took the job, she knew there would be some stress involved—after all, she would be responsible for keeping things running smoothly in a busy office and interacting with customers, truck drivers, sales reps, and laundry personnel. She also knew the salary and benefits were great, plus, she was promised a raise in six months.

What she didn't know was the dream job involved nightmare employees and clients. Amy constantly fielded calls from customers who were upset about late deliveries. When Amy talked to the truck drivers about it, they were rude and short-tempered with her. The sales reps never remembered to tell her when they would be out of the office or who they were visiting, and they never turned in their expense reports on time. As for the laundry personnel, they rarely said a thing.

The office seemed full of people who had short fuses, cared little about details, or had real difficulty talking to one another. In fact, some employees would only communicate by email, and never talk face-to-face. It all seemed very strange to Amy.

The job was taking its toll on Amy, so she finally shared her frustrations with the owner, who suggested weekly status meetings. During the meetings, Amy noticed that the truck drivers just wanted to complain about traffic, and yell at anyone who disagreed with them. The schedulers constantly discussed current routes, alternative routes, and estimated times, without ever coming to any conclusions. The sales reps wanted to tell everyone about the customers they'd visited, and the laundry personnel were usually very quiet, asking only a few questions. Although everyone in the office said something, nothing ever got resolved or accomplished.

Amy was at her wits' end. Even though it wasn't really her job, what could she do to get people to sit down, listen to one another, and really communicate?

myth

"My manager should know what I am thinking."

reality

Frustrations can develop at work when we assume our manager should know what we like and don't like, what our goals are, or what we do or don't want to do. Managers are people. They don't read minds. Even though it might not always be easy or pleasant, be sure to communicate your thoughts with your supervisor. Let him or her know what you need, what obstacles are getting in the way, or what issues are arising. You'll be surprised at the results you get when you communicate honestly.

As you learned in Amy's story, landing a great job is just the beginning for any job seeker. Once you have the job, you need to learn how to communicate and get along with your coworkers. In the previous chapter you learned to become more comfortable in a diverse workplace. In this chapter you will gain tools to help you operate effectively in that workplace with coworkers, superiors, contractors, clients, and customers—no matter what their communication style. Too bad Amy didn't have those tools!

In addition, this chapter provides the tools you need to build constructive, ongoing relationships in and out of the workplace. It shows you how to work effectively with teams and to communicate clearly—verbally, nonverbally, and in writing. Finally, the chapter discusses a topic that people often struggle with: how to deal with criticism and conflict. Good communication skills are central to being effective at work and at school.

Building Relationships

The ability to build relationships and communicate well makes you extremely valuable to your employer. The smartest people in the world cannot function in a working environment if they cannot ask others about what has been done, what needs to be done, or how things should be done. The most talented employees will create problems at work if they keep to themselves, refuse to collaborate, and criticize or sabotage the efforts of others. A healthy, productive workplace is a collaborative one, not a competitive, mean-spirited place.

Why is building good relationships so important? When people get along on the job, work progresses more quickly and efficiently. When people clash on the job, work suffers. People cannot work together to accomplish tasks unless they put their personal issues and egos aside. When they do so and make an effort to build relationships with their coworkers, they accomplish more than they imagined.

Your Personality at Work

It's important to think about your personality as you work on building and maintaining your workplace relationships. Your Myers-Briggs personality type, which you learned about in Chapter 2, has a strong impact on these relationships. This helps determine who you get along with easily and who you don't.

For example, an ENFP—an extroverted, intuitive, feeling, perceptive person—may get along well with an ISFP—an introverted, sensing, feeling, perceptive person. These two share a perceptive "look at the big picture" nature and tend to focus on emotions and feelings. The difference between E and I can be complementary, because often an extrovert doesn't like to share attention, and an introvert doesn't want it. This could be a great working relationship.

On the other hand, an ENFP might have a harder time with an ESTJ because two extroverts may compete for attention. Also, the ESTJ's attention to fact and detail may bother the ENFP, and the free-spirited ENFP's random and unplanned thought process may make no sense to the orderly ESTJ. This relationship may call for more effort and adjustment on both sides.

The fact is, you rarely choose your coworkers. Instead of using your personality type to decide who you will or won't like, use it to determine who might be easy to work with and who might be more of a challenge. If you have trouble with someone, let your personality styles provide clues about how to understand each other and get along. For example, the ENFP and the ESTJ could decide that the ESTJ should handle all the money and detail work, the ENFP could be the "idea person," and both could share the leadership duties that appeal to extroverts. Most often, you will find a way to work it out if you make the effort.

Figure 10.1 shows a way of looking at your personality in terms of your working style. It is a grid that divides people into four general work styles. Each quadrant of the grid represents a combination of two of the four listed qualities: task oriented or people oriented, and passive or assertive. For example, a task-oriented, passive person would be an analyst.

The descriptions below help you understand the qualities of people in each quadrant. Think about where you fit in.

Figure 10.1   Personality and working style are interrelated

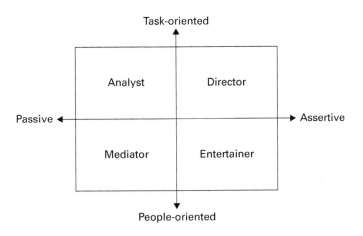

ANALYST	DIRECTOR
Priority: Be the expert	**Priority:** Be in control
• Acquires and evaluates information	• Interprets and processes information
• Gathers and examines facts, weighs the evidence	• Acts and produces results
• Makes decisions slowly	• Makes decisions easily
• Works carefully	• Works hard
• Loves stability and does not take risks	• Takes risks and challenges stability
• Dislikes conflict	• Thrives on conflict
• Speaks quietly, but firmly	• Speaks forcefully
MEDIATOR	ENTERTAINER
Priority: Be needed	**Priority:** Be recognized
• Organizes and maintains information	• Communicates information
• Harmonizes the workplace	• Energizes the workplace
• Makes decisions reluctantly	• Makes spur-of-the-moment decisions
• Works thoroughly	• Works fast
• Likes stability and is rarely bored	• Loves risks and is easily bored
• Can't stand conflict	• Accepts conflict
• Speaks supportively	• Speaks spontaneously and well

Use this grid as a way to evaluate yourself and others. You may find you have characteristics from several quadrants, but it's likely that you will feel most comfortable in one because it expresses more of your natural work style. However, everyone can operate in the other quadrants with a little more thought and effort. Your evaluation will help you understand how different people work, and why you get along or clash. Understanding is the bridge to improvement. Once you clearly recognize the differences, you can decide together what adjustments might be necessary. No one's personality can change over night, but understanding differences makes it easier to work on your approach to working with one another.

Suppose you look at the grid and decide that you are an analyst because more of your characteristics fall into that quadrant than any other: You like to work carefully in a stable, constant environment; you dislike and avoid conflict; and you work well with information and facts. Then, suppose you deal daily with two particular coworkers. You work well with one, but have trouble communicating with the other, which results in occasional clashes. How do you determine the reason?

Think about both coworkers in terms of the qualities in the grid. The first coworker doesn't like conflict either, and is always the one to defuse conflicts that arise among others. He likes to work with people more than you, and tries hard to support them in their work. He's clearly a mediator. You get along because you both dislike conflict and enjoy a stable work environment.

Mediators are good at preventing and resolving conflicts.

You also have similar talents with information organization and evaluation. The second coworker, on the other hand, seems to seek conflict and even create it where it didn't really exist. She works hard and processes information well, but when she develops new ideas and takes risks it can disrupt the stability that you and the other coworker enjoy. She's a director. Her aggressive style can clash with your passive, methodical way of working. You resist her control when she wants to make a change that you don't like.

What can you do? If you can work more often with your more compatible mediator co-worker, do so. When you deal with the director co-worker, make sure you communicate your needs clearly and pleasantly. Use your other communication skills to overcome the differences in your styles. For example, you may need to be more assertive, focus on results, and be willing to disagree and stand up for yourself.

Getting Along with Different People at Work and at Home

Getting along with people in the workplace means you can consistently complete tasks, which provides the stability and security necessary to keep your job. In addition to your knowledge about personality styles, you may need to use some different techniques and behaviors with different categories of people. We've named four groups of people to consider.

People in Charge

The relationships you have with those who have some control over what you do—your teachers, manager, higher management, or owner of the business or company—should be built on a foundation of mutual respect. People relate to their superiors in many different ways: friendly, buddy-buddy, strictly business, strained, or almost no contact. Regardless of the type of the relationship, both people must show respect for one another. You will have much less trouble taking orders from people when you respect them, even if you don't happen to want to spend your free time with them.

Here are some personal qualities, basic skills, and interpersonal skills that can help you relate to a superior:

- **Listen.** Review the section on listening in Chapter 4.
- **Behave in a respectful manner.** Treat others the way you want to be treated.
- **Follow directives pleasantly.** Trust that the person has good reasons for deciding what you should do. Realize that when you help your manager succeed, you succeed as well.
- **Deal directly with the issues.** If you have a problem or complaint, make an appointment and address the person directly and calmly in private, instead of blowing up or talking behind the person's back.
- **Show your appreciation.** Show your appreciation when your manager compliments you or does something nice for you.
- **Take time.** When you can, get to know your manager as a person and not just as a your "boss."

If your manager doesn't seem to want to be "one of the gang" and resists your attempts to become better acquainted, respect that too. Some managers find it easier to give orders to people when they don't become personally involved.

If you don't relate well with your manager's personality or communication style and the two of you don't seem to get along, don't give up right away. Schedule a meeting and talk it over. Express yourself calmly and use "I" statements such as these to describe your concerns:

- "I don't understand what you mean when. . . ."
- "I have taken it the wrong way when. . . ."
- "I feel like you don't approve of. . . ."

Avoid "you" statements that accuse, such as the following:

- "You don't respect me. . . . "
- "You take things the wrong way. . . ."
- "You don't approve. . . ."

As you speak, communicate pride in your skills and achievements. Make eye contact and listen well. Use the conflict-resolution techniques discussed later in this chapter. If the two of you can reach a comfortable understanding (or even a friendly agreement), it will make life much easier for both of you on the job!

Coworkers

You and your coworkers operate on about the same level. Some people may have been with the company longer and some may have more advanced positions, but you all work together to keep the whole "machine" running smoothly.

Some of the skills that help you get along with coworkers are the same skills for getting along with superiors, and some are different.

- **Listen.** Don't interrupt and make sure you understand what your coworker has said.
- **Show respect for one another.** Discuss issues calmly with coworkers. Compliment them when they succeed and don't criticize or gossip about their failures.
- **Get familiar with the company system.** Learn its policies and procedures. That way, when changes occur, you can help your coworkers smoothly transition to the new system by adapting quickly and congenially.
- **Respect territories.** Don't step into anyone else's territory—actual physical space or assigned work—without asking that person first.
- **Get to know people.** If it's important to you, make an effort to spend time together with coworkers outside of work to get to know each other—lunches, working out, or Friday nights at the end of the work week.
- **Privately deal with personal issues.** Address any problems, bad feelings, or complaints in private with the person involved; don't gossip about the problems with other people.
- **Give credit where credit is due.** Always acknowledge your coworkers' successes and efforts.

Working with someone who shares your views and supports your ideas can be one of life's most rewarding experiences. If you find a coworker with whom you click in that way, cultivate the relationship. It makes work more fun and more productive.

On the other hand, working with a difficult coworker can make your job unbearable. If you're having problems with a coworker, talk to the person in private first. See if the two of you can work out your differences on your own. If that does not work, speak privately to your manager. Explain why this coworker's behavior makes it difficult for you to do your work efficiently. Ask if the manager can intervene to improve the situation—perhaps the three of you can meet together. The next step might be to stay at your job but change your duties or location so that you no longer have to work directly with that coworker.

Leaving your job is a last resort, although on occasion it makes the most sense for everyone concerned. However, don't let a disagreement drive you out of a job that suits you in every other way. Evaluate the situation and decide which solution is the most beneficial.

Note: The tips about relationships with coworkers also apply to your peers at school. Read them again, replacing the words coworker, manager, and work with peer, teacher, and school. You are generally on equal footing with your fellow students at school, and can use the same principles to develop healthy relationships with them and to repair not-so-healthy ones.

Customers and Clients

Treating customers and clients well keeps your business alive. Customers are the most important people in any business. Selling products or services to customers supports the existence of the company and pays the salaries of all its employees.

The customer deserves courtesy and attention at all times. Arguments or power struggles with a customer should be avoided at all cost. Any customer deserves the same treatment you would give to a friend: consideration, positive attitude, interest, generosity, friendliness, patience, and alert assistance.

Some companies believe that "the customer is always right." This premise may make customers happy, but it can make life difficult for employees who have to swallow their words (and maybe even cough up a refund) when a customer has clearly made the mistake. Find out at the start how your particular employer wants you to handle customer disagreements. Often a customer's loyalty can be retained, despite any disputes, with a little kindness and a reasonable compromise.

Following are some ideas for getting along with customers.

- **Listen.** The only way to fulfill a customer's needs is to hear exactly what those needs are. If you didn't hear everything clearly, ask the person to repeat. Too often, employees jump to conclusions and begin providing answers before the customer has clearly described the problem.

- **Behave in a respectful manner.** Do not talk down to customers and act as if they are stupid. Do not get angry with them because they have problems.

- **Acknowledge the customer's feelings.** A little empathy goes a long way. Try to imagine what the customer is feeling and what he or she is going through. It may help you respond in a more helpful manner.

- **Focus on one person at a time.** Each customer deserves your full attention. Listen to the customer carefully and avoid doing other work at the same time.

- **Follow up.** Thank the customer verbally or in a note (depending on what your job requires) for their business.

- **Go the extra mile.** If you can improve your service to a customer in any way, big or small, do so.

- **Deal with customers in a pleasant manner.** Leave your bad mood at the door when you go to work.

Customers and clients come in all personality types and states of mind. Your job is to hold steady through the highs and the lows of customer moods and demands. Don't take any customer's anger or annoyance personally, but simply work through it so you can do your job. As you learned earlier in Chapter 4, try to listen for the real issue under all the emotion and address that issue without reacting to the emotion.

Family and Friends

What do your relationships with your family and friends have to do with getting along with others in school and at work? The state of your personal relationships has a strong effect on your mood, attitude, self-image, and energy. You need a positive personal support system so you can work well with the people in your professional life. If your personal life drags you down, your working life will suffer as well.

Your two best strategies for making sure your personal life supports your job stability are:

- **Make your personal relationships a priority and keep them in balance.** That balance forms the core of your strength. Put it above all else. Go out of your way to maintain or repair relationships with family or close friends.

- **Leave personal problems and moods at home.** When you do have personal problems that occupy your mind, make you feel unsettled, or put you in a bad mood, try to leave them at home.

The many relationships in your life—family, friends, classmates, coworkers, managers—are intertwined; what happens with one can easily affect your situation with another.

 ## Now You Try It: How Is Your Communication?

Think about work style and the people you work with every day.

1. In the following table, list one person in each category and identify whether you think the individual is a director, analyst, mediator, or entertainer.
2. Jot down how you typically communicate with each type of person.
3. Indicate any frustrations you have and how you might be able to communicate better.

Name of Person	Notes about Communication and Any Issues
Manager or teacher: Communication style:	
Coworker or fellow student: Communication style:	
Customer: Communication style:	
Friend or family member: Communication style:	

Teamwork

All employees are part of a team, whether it's a department, an office, or a project team. As a member of a work team, you are much like a member of a sports team in which all the players work together to win. If they don't work together, they lose. Just imagine a basketball or volleyball team in which every player tried to score as many points as possible. You would not expect the team to achieve its potential or be successful.

Teamwork can be as simple as sharing resources, information, or customers, and it is critical to the success of a business. Yet, you often find employees in many companies so busy with their own day-to-day challenges that they lose sight of company goals. It's easy to get wrapped up in your own challenges, particularly with the number of demands on your time. But remember, it is the success of the business that counts, and teamwork is the key to business success.

Working with Other Team Members

When working with a team, always consider the personality types involved (as shown earlier in Figure 10.1) and communicate appropriately.

- **Analysts.** Be sure to provide accurate facts and figures. Analysts feel most comfortable with plenty of data to help them make decisions. Give them time to make decisions; don't rush them.
- **Directors.** Allow the person to feel in control, but be prepared to stand up for what you believe if the individual disagrees. Don't take the conflict personally— just present your case in a well-organized, direct manner, as quickly as possible.
- **Mediators.** Realize that constant conflicts and distractions make life difficult for mediators. Provide stories and personal experiences to illustrate your ideas, and present them in positive ways that show how they can benefit the whole team. Don't force them to make decisions.
- **Entertainers.** Be prepared for some spur-of-the-moment decisions and unusual ideas. Do not immediately reject the ideas; they are likely to change quickly. Instead, be open and encourage the individual to think things through.

No matter who your team members are, your team meetings will be much more effective when you follow agendas and practice good meeting etiquette, as discussed earlier in Chapter 4.

 ## Now You Try It: The Cast of Characters

Every team is made up of its own unique cast of characters. Think back to a time you worked with a team on a particular project and consider the types of people you might have interacted with: directors, analysts, mediators, and entertainers.

1. How many people were on the team and what was the team working on?
2. Was there a "director" on the team? What was the person like?
3. How did you deal with him or her?
4. Was there an "analyst" on the team? What was the person like?
5. How did you deal with him or her?
6. Was there a "mediator" on the team? What was the person like?
7. How did you deal with him or her?
8. Was there an "entertainer" on the team? What was the person like?
9. How did you deal with him or her?
10. Who was easiest to work with and why?

High-Tech Assistance

Many teams today are not actually physical teams, they are virtual teams. This means they do not meet in person in a physical location; rather, they meet by phone, online, or through some other electronic medium. Here are some basic relationship-building tips that can help a team work well over long distances.

- **Make a personal connection.** Take the time to get to know your virtual team members. This may mean making small talk before a meeting begins or adding some personal information about your life when you send an email. Since you cannot see your remote team and they cannot see you, you might even send a digital photo of yourself.
- **Speak clearly.** When you attend a virtual meeting, always say your name clearly and introduce yourself. Speak loud enough so others on the phone can hear you. You may need to say "This is [name]" each time you share an idea until people get used to your voice. If you are part of an international team, speak a little more slowly than usual so that those who are non-native English speakers can follow your conversation.

- **Pick up the phone.** If you can't get the results you want with email, instant messages, texts, or virtual meetings, try calling and talking to someone directly. A single phone call is worth 10 emails!

Ultimately, your ability to work well with others has a profound effect on your personal success and your team's success.

Communication Styles

Inside or outside your team, it's vital that you recognize there are as many different styles of communication as there are people in the world! Some people come right out and talk about feelings; some hide them. Some people speak quietly and carefully; some let all kinds of thoughts pour right out without censoring them. Some get to the point immediately, while others take awhile to get to the central idea of the conversation. As you become aware of your own communication style and the styles of those with whom you work, you can avoid communication clashes and misunderstandings.

To give you an idea of how different communication styles work in real life, consider the following scenario and then read about how people with different communication styles might handle the situation. As you work to understand these different styles, think about what kind of style you use and how you might change it when necessary. Do people often misunderstand you? Do others at work ever become confused about what you want or what you say? Your style may make your meaning unclear. Examine your style and make any necessary changes.

THE SCENARIO

You participated in a project at work that involved two major tasks—we'll call them X and Y. Y was new to you, but you had a lot of experience with X. You want to know what your manager thinks of your performance, and you leave her a note asking her about it. Here are different responses you might receive based on your manager's communication style.

Direct Style. This person is honest about both compliments and criticism, and rarely dwells on unimportant chatter. "Your idea about X was great, and I'm glad you followed through on it, because it worked. You need to improve your technique with Y; I see it cost you some extra time. Talk to Sherry about how you can work on it—she's done it before." **Lesson:** Keep things short with this person and do not waste his or her time.

Indirect Style. Someone like this has a hard time getting to the point. This person will meander around the question, and maybe never really answer it. "Everything seemed fine, I guess. I don't know whether Y could have happened faster or not, but, oh well, it seemed okay. By the way, did you have problems with Y?" **Lesson:** Be patient with this person. If necessary, restate the question and guide the person to an answer.

Noncommunicative. This kind of person will almost always choose to say nothing at all. You probably won't get a response to your note or email, leaving you to assume that nothing is wrong, even if something is. If you ask again, maybe in person, you probably will get a brief response. **Lesson:** Realize that this person shies away from communication, so you have to make an extra effort to speak to the individual in person.

Confrontational. This kind of person has no fear of an argument and will usually express opinions in no uncertain terms—in other words, confront you, focusing too much on the negative. You'll hear directly from this person without even asking. "You need to fix the problem with Y. Find a way to take care of it." **Lesson:** Avoid getting defensive and don't take the confrontation personally. Think of it this way—the individual is simply questioning you in a loud voice. Instead, adopt a sense of humor and ask a few questions to get clarity.

Nonconfrontational. This person will avoid confrontation at all costs and dislikes conflict. You may have to dig to get any kind of helpful criticism. You will probably get an answer if you ask directly. "Oh, yeah, sure, I approved of everything that you did. It was fine." **Lesson:** Learn to read this person's body language and probe a bit to find out what he or she is really thinking. Give the person permission to disagree with you.

Unexamined. This person rarely thinks before speaking. You might have to weed through jumbled, off-the-cuff words to pick out the important information. "Wow, I'm late—what?

Oh, yeah, X was terrific, did you have anything to do with that? Have you seen Sherry around? I'm supposed to go to a meeting with her. I heard Y was a nightmare; you all need to get your heads on straight." **Lesson:** Dealing with the individual is similar to dealing with the indirect person. Be very clear with your question, continue to remind the person what you are asking, and keep the person focused when he or she goes off on a tangent.

You may know of even more styles of communication used by people around you. It's a wonder we get the message across to each other at all! You're bound to feel more comfortable with some of these styles than others, because they are closer to your own style of communication. When you begin to understand the styles, you can find the real message underneath. It's easy to feel confused, unsupported, uninformed, or offended if you don't understand the communication style and take every word at face value.

The more you get to know the people you work with, the better you will become at interpreting what they say. The next time you feel something doesn't come across quite right, take a moment to think about it. Should you take the words literally or does the meaning change if you consider the person's communication style? It's amazing how words can change. When a non-confrontational person says "It's okay," that can mean "What a disaster!" But when an unexamined person says "What a disaster!" it can mean "No big deal, we can fix this." Remember—it's the way you communicate, not just the words you say.

Effective Communication Techniques

With so many communication styles, you need techniques to help you listen, analyze, and solve problems during communication. First, remember that communication involves giving and receiving ideas and information. It takes thought and effort to communicate efficiently. Figure 10.2 illustrates this.

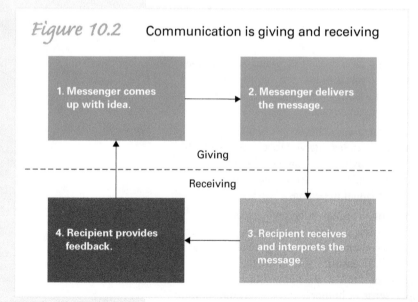

Figure 10.2   Communication is giving and receiving

1. Messenger comes up with idea.

2. Messenger delivers the message.

Giving

Receiving

4. Recipient provides feedback.

3. Recipient receives and interprets the message.

As you might guess, lots of things can go wrong. You might have a great idea, but have difficulty communicating it. You might communicate it just right, but the listener may not understand it. Or the listener may understand it, but give poor feedback so you don't know whether you said the right thing. It's so easy to make a mistake.

Consider times in your life when a mistake in communication cost you time, money, or happiness. Did you ever wait for a long time at a specified pick-up location only to find out that your friend or spouse was waiting somewhere else? Someone heard incorrectly or spoke unclearly, and it cost time, caused anger, and may have made someone late for an important appointment. Have you ever fought with someone only to discover later that you misunderstood something the person said? It may have made you so upset you couldn't stop to hear the person trying to clear up the misunderstanding. It saves a lot of trouble if you try to get it right the first time.

To make sure problems do not occur, here are three tips to help ensure the message is accurately communicated and received.

1. Alternately play the role of sender and receiver. You need to fully engage in your role of sender or receiver. You cannot simultaneously be a sender and a receiver; you will be unable to accurately convey your message or understand someone else's message. For example, consider these examples:

- One person is talking to another person who is talking to a third person on the telephone.
- One person is addressing a group in which one person is chatting with a friend.
- One person is talking to a friend and that person is texting or surfing the Internet.

In each situation, the first person is playing sender only. The second person, however, is trying to receive information from the first person while corresponding with another person. The second person will be unable to receive information clearly or send it efficiently if he or she tries to do both at once.

When you communicate, choose your role and play it to the hilt. If someone talks to you, be a good receiver: Stop what you are doing and focus your full attention on that person to clearly receive his or her message. If you want to communicate to another person, be a good sender: Make sure you have that person's full attention before you begin; otherwise, he or she will not be able to listen and remember what you are saying. Remember to take turns being sender and receiver; no one should do all the talking or all the listening in a conversation.

2. Support your ideas by reasoning. Some ideas can be difficult to explain to people. You may need to clarify your idea through explanation. Link your idea to solid and simple examples of how something works or what could result from it. Compare your idea to something that already exists to help your listener understand. You might even tell a story to illustrate your idea. Think of the idea as a large ship, with reasons and examples as anchors.

3. Speak in terms of your own needs rather than focusing on what you think someone else needs. Communication can involve tension, especially when it concerns conflict or a touchy subject. Anger, fear, or other emotions may hamper your ability to speak clearly about what you need. To communicate effectively, try using "I" statements instead of "you" statements. "You"

"You" statements only put people on the defensive and make them angrier.

statements point the finger at the other person, attacking, accusing, or blaming the individual (often unfairly and prematurely) for the problem at hand. As a result, the other person feels wronged and launches a corresponding set of "you" statements right back. This only creates anger and resentment, with two people feeling unjustly blamed and no reasonable and fair solution at hand.

"I" statements, on the other hand, promote conversation and resolution because they keep people focused on their own needs and problems, instead of on someone else's mistakes. When you turn your statements toward yourself, the other person will feel more comfortable, more willing to help, and may even acknowledge where mistakes were made.

Table 10.1 illustrates accusatory "you" statements that have been rephrased to more appropriate "I" statements. If you were the receiver, which would you rather hear? In the table, the "I" statements leave room for the other person to offer an explanation. They express feelings rather than harsh judgments. What if the other person wasn't the one who left the door unlocked? The "you" statement would have created anger. You might be glad you stayed neutral if you hear this response: "I agree, and I talked to Andrew about it this morning. He's really sorry; he was the last one to leave yesterday and he was in a rush to get to the hospital. His wife just had a baby boy."

Give yourself some time to adjust to this kind of communication. Most of us aren't used to it. Jumping into "you" statements is often easier and feels more natural; however, your efforts to stay calm and use "I" statements will pay off. When you feel angry about something at work or at home, before you lash out, think first about why you are angry. Translate your anger into an

Table 10.1 **"You" versus "I" Statements**	
"You" Statement	**"I" Statement**
"You didn't lock the door!"	"I felt uneasy when I came into work this morning and found the door unlocked."
"You never called when you said you would!"	"I was worried about you when you didn't call."
"You always leave me out of the deal!"	"I felt disappointed and left out when I realized the deal had gone through without my input."

"I" statement about your feelings. After you express how you feel, invite conversation by saying "Can we talk about how to improve this situation together?" Ask the other person, "How do you feel about what happened?" Slowly but surely, the "I" statement will seem more natural—and it will bring results.

 Now You Try It: Clash of Communication Styles

We're often so used to our own communication style that we never think about it.

1. Based on what you read earlier, what do you think your communication style is (direct, indirect, confrontational, etc.)?
2. Have you ever worked with someone with a different communication style? What was his or her style?
3. What problems did the different styles create?
4. How did you resolve the problems?

Verbal and Nonverbal Communication

People communicate in two different ways: verbally (speaking) and nonverbally (body language—the way you walk, sit, gesture, twist your facial features, or move your eyes). People often communicate verbally and nonverbally at the same time, and may end up sending conflicting messages. You can't imagine how much time and energy go into correcting mistakes made in the workplace when miscommunication occurs. If you learn to properly use both verbal and nonverbal communication, you will greatly increase your work efficiency.

Verbal Communication

It seems that people commonly mangle the spoken word. We frequently speak unclearly, use words that convey a meaning that we don't intend, or leave out important words or thoughts. But when we say what we want to say and the person hears it as we mean it, it makes all the difference. What follows are some ideas to consider for improving your verbal communication skills.

1. Choose to communicate. You cannot change or improve anything if you don't say anything. No one can help you if you don't ask for help. If you have something to say, choose to say it. You have the right to speak your mind, stand up for your needs, and express your suggestions and opinions.

2. Think before you speak. Give yourself a chance to figure out what you mean to say before you actually say it. If the message is important, take time to rehearse it. If it comes out too fast it may not reflect your true thoughts. Later you may be forced to admit, "I didn't mean it that way!" Then you will have to spend time and energy apologizing, explaining, and trying again if you want the person to come away with the right impression.

3. Don't put it off. When you have something to say, say it as soon as you possibly can. If you want to express a compliment or a positive feeling, why hold back? We don't talk enough about positive things on the job. If you need to discuss a problem, that problem will only grow while you wait to bring it up. We have all seen what happens when problems, concerns, or complaints are not discussed. They pile up and then tumble out in a huge angry heap when least expected.

It's not just what your words say; it's what your body says as well.

4. Assess listening conditions. What would happen if you went to your manager with a problem when she was pulling on a coat and rushing home? How about if you met a friend in a crowded, noisy lunch area to talk about something serious? Or tried to talk to someone who was in the middle of finishing a project with a tight deadline? In any of these cases, you wouldn't get your message across. The conditions don't lend themselves to clear communication. Instead, ask people what time is good for them—whether you are speaking with them in person or calling on the phone. Avoid noisy or distracting places. Don't initiate an important talk when other work needs completing or other activities interfere. Try to avoid conversation when someone is under time pressure to be somewhere else. Make sure you have chosen the right time and the right place, and that the person you need to talk to is ready to listen and that you have his or her full attention.

5. Speak clearly. Speak directly to the person in words he or she understands, focusing on your message and not on other topics. If you mumble, speak too fast, or don't get to the point, you might not communicate your message clearly.

> Suppose you want to say, "We need to order 12 more cartons of cardboard boxes." What is your listener going to do if you say something like this?
>
> "Um, you know, like, when we were in the supply room the other day, and we were talking about stuff, and then you said something about boxes, and I went, like, what boxes? Well, I think, like, we need to get some more. I don't know, maybe 12?"

Who knows what that person is going to do? You never asked him or her to actually order anything and you were unclear about the number of boxes, and worse, you took forever to get to the point. With all those "ums" and "likes," it would be amazing if the person had a clue what you were trying to say.

6. Be brief and precise. As for the actual words you use, don't include too many extras. Say exactly what you need to say. The more quickly you get to the point and the fewer words you use, the more efficiently you will communicate. Let's look at a person talking with her boss about a problem, before and after a little communication improvement.

> Before: "I need to talk to you because I'm having this problem. You see, yesterday it happened again, and I don't think that I can take much more of it. I went over to the mailboxes and someone had left all of the mail out again, and they didn't put it in anyone's box, and it spills all over the place when people come in and put their coats and stuff near there. I was expecting a letter that's really important and now I'm not sure if I haven't gotten it yet or if maybe it is just ripped up somewhere on the floor, and I'm really sick of it."
>
> After: "The mail was left out again and someone spilled it all over the floor. I'm expecting an important letter and now I don't know whether it arrived. Can we assign someone to distribute the mail right when it arrives? I think it would save a lot of trouble."

Do you see the improvement? The "after" message got right to the point, explained the problem, didn't waste time complaining, and offered a quick solution. The "before" message didn't get

technology at work

Technology is making communications easier and faster—texting, instant messages, email, voicemail, faxes, cell phones, and the list goes on. Yet technology is also making communications less personal—email can be very sterile and cold. People are losing their ability to "read" others through their voices and body language. Maintaining interpersonal communication in relationships is crucial in life and careers.

Consider periodically meeting face-to-face to keep your verbal and nonverbal skills sharp, or pick up the telephone to call instead of using a less personal form of communications such as email, instant messages, or texting. Having personal relationships with others and being viewed as a good person can make the difference in receiving a timely response to a critical question or getting a very late email, or having one of your recommendations approved rather than ignored. Balancing high-tech forms of communication, like email and texting, with personal forms of communication, like a phone call or a visit, is important for maintaining healthy relationships.

to the problem until the third sentence. If you have a problem, it goes without saying that you are upset and want a change, so don't waste time talking about how upset you are. Instead, save your time for more important things. When you speak your mind quickly and precisely, your listeners will be relieved and pleased.

7. Be honest. This tip will also help you to be brief. It takes more time to make up stories and avoid saying what you really mean than it does to be honest and direct. Sometimes honesty can be tough when you have to say something that won't make the other person happy, but it usually makes sense in the long run. People cannot begin to solve problems until they know the truth about what's happening. When you supply the truth, you will get results.

If you are consistently gentle but honest in your communications, you will develop a reputation as a person of integrity. People will begin to trust you and to count on you for an honest answer. Honesty and integrity promote more communication from others. When people sense your integrity, they're more likely to come talk to you because they feel comfortable expressing their ideas and feelings. You will build strong bridges of communication to all who know you.

8. Watch your tone. It's not just the words you use, it's the way your voice sounds when you say them. People pick up 38%[1] of your message from your tone of voice. It's important to stay aware of your tone and to make sure it communicates what you intend to say. There are several tones to avoid because they often prevent people from properly understanding your message. Table 10.2 provides descriptions and examples or each inappropriate tone.

Table 10.2 **Beware of These Tones!**	
Tone	**Example**
Parental tone scolds or tells listeners what to do.	"Don't make the copies that way. They are supposed to be two-sided, not one-sided. You waste too much paper that way. Can't you do anything right?"
Arrogant tone is condescending and patronizing, communicating you are better than everyone else. This quickly alienates your listener.	"I don't know why you seem incapable of making two-sided copies. Everyone knows that one-sided copies waste too much paper."
Questioning tone makes you sound as if you don't know what you're talking about.	"Are you sure the copies are supposed to be one-sided? I thought they were supposed to be two-sided. But I'm not sure, maybe I'm wrong?"
Overly cheerful tone makes your message seem less serious than it is, and belies its importance.	"I'm so glad you made those copies. It was really nice of you. It's no big deal, but maybe next time you should make them two-sided."
Instead, use the appropriate tone that sends the right message: Thanks for making the copies. I appreciate it. Next time though, please make two-sided copies. The office is trying to be more environmentally sensitive and that will really make a difference!	

---

[1]Barbour, Alton. *Louder than words: nonverbal communication.* Columbus, Ohio: Merrill, 1976.

Nonverbal Communication

All of us say things with our bodies, often without thinking about it. People pick up on our nonverbal signals even when we don't want them to. In turn, we read the body language of others. Our thoughts and feelings affect the way we stand, the gestures we make, and the tone of the words we speak—all of which reinforce or interfere with our actual message. First impressions are based on a combination of elements: nonverbal signals, tone of voice, and actual words spoken. The nonverbal element makes up 55% of a first impression, the tone makes up 38%, and the actual words make up only 7%![2]

This makes sense when you consider that when you first meet someone, you have a visual impression of that individual before anyone speaks a word. You make assumptions based on posture, degree of eye contact, and speed of movement. Even when someone makes an introductory remark such as "Hello, nice to meet you," that remark won't tell you much about the person inside. You find out more from the tone the person uses when greeting you—bright or apprehensive, bored or interested, cheerful or sullen.

Deciding what someone is saying without words takes practice. Understanding nonverbal communication gives you important insights into your own feelings as well as those of others. What's more, it gives you a real advantage in conversations because you are better able to "read" people. Here are three suggestions for improving your nonverbal communication.

1. Become aware. Look at what people say to you with their bodies. It will help you understand more about their true thoughts. If a coworker compliments you while making eye contact, standing up straight, and smiling, you can be fairly sure that the person means what he or she says. If that same person says the same words but doesn't look you in the eye, hunches over with arms crossed, and doesn't have a happy expression, that person has left something unsaid.

It's up to you to decide when you need to deal with what is left unsaid. Ultimately, you are not responsible for how another person feels—those feelings belong to him or her. However, you are responsible for getting the individual to clarify those feelings and the reasons behind them. Paying attention to body language will help you do so.

2. Use it, but don't confuse with it. As you learn to look at the nonverbal language of others, start noticing your own as well. You can use body language to help clarify your thoughts for others. For example, if you have a meeting with your manager and want to make a case for your salary raise, express confidence with your body—sit up straight, look the person in the eye, relax your shoulders, and don't cross your arms.

Avoid body language that conflicts with what you say. Body language comes through more clearly than you might think. If your nonverbal message goes against your verbal one, you will confuse the receiver. Nonverbal messages come across before verbal ones. Suppose your manager didn't give you the raise and you told her that was fine (when it really wasn't). Your body language—sagging posture or a defiant expression—would show your true feelings and your words would sound like lies. Both of you would suffer—your manager would be confused, and you would have to carry the hurt inside that comes from not expressing your true feelings. There is nothing wrong with communicating your disappointment in words, as long as you do so honestly, calmly, and without accusation.

Did You Know? Nonverbal communication styles differ from one culture to another. As you learned in Chapter 9, some cultures avoid eye contact and consider it disrespectful. Europeans and Americans tend to encourage it and wonder what's wrong if someone looks away. People in some cultures feel comfortable standing very close to each other (within six to seven inches). People in other cultures maintain what they consider a respectful distance and feel invaded if casual acquaintances come too close.

Consider those differences as you encounter different communication styles, and don't be too quick to judge. If you get a "message" that you find negative, look again. You may simply have misinterpreted a gesture that is meant positively and respectfully in another person's culture. (Remember Sanjay's misinterpreted head gesture in the story at the beginning of Chapter 9?) Don't ever assume that someone is avoiding you; that person may simply be observing other customs. Be sure to talk about it and try to come to a mutual understanding.

[2]*Ibid*

Figure 10.3 **Quick checklist for verbal and nonverbal communication**

- Is your tone positive and upbeat?
- Do you sound focused or distracted?
- Do your gestures and body language communicate the same message?
- Do you exude confidence?
- Do you convey genuine enthusiasm?

If you think you might convey something nonverbally that you don't feel comfortable saying, make a choice. Either face up to talking about what you really feel, or make a major effort to turn off the body language. Otherwise, people will view you as someone who hides information and consider you untrustworthy.

Figure 10.3 provides a quick checklist to review before giving voice to your message, to be sure that you come across the way you want to, both verbally and nonverbally.

 ## Now You Try It: Do You Speak Body Language?

Some people read body language better than others. Some people seem oblivious to it. Try writing down the different gestures you've seen people exhibit during conversations and what you think those gestures mean. We've even provided a few to get you started. If you can't think of any body language gestures, start watching people. You're sure to start noticing their body language.

Body Language	Meaning
Arms crossed on chest	Defensive
No eye contact	Embarrassed, shy, angry
Tapping fingers on the desk	Nervous, worried about time, bored

Telephone Techniques

Talking on the phone is a type of verbal communication, but it's different enough to deserve its own section. Because the telephone eliminates the opportunity to see a person and make eye contact, phone communication depends on tone of voice and words. When you use the phone, pay special attention to *what* you say and *how* you say it. Telephone etiquette is crucial in the workplace because you project an image of your company through your conversation.

The following techniques will help you adequately assist the person on the other line while creating the most favorable image possible.

1. Answer promptly. Pick up the phone as soon as you hear it ring and, if possible, no later than the third ring. Callers tend to hang up shortly after that, especially if they are calling a business.

2. Speak clearly. Identify yourself and your company. Enunciate your words, and don't speak too quickly or too slowly. Keep the receiver near your mouth so the caller can hear you.

3. Use a positive, alert, "smiling" tone of voice. The caller will pick up on your tone. If you sound tired or annoyed, callers may be turned off and concerned that they will not receive adequate assistance. You don't have to sound ecstatic, just pleasant and ready to help. Keep a mirror nearby so you can look at yourself and make sure you are smiling. The smile comes through in your voice, and it will improve your customer's reactions to what you say., Callers decide within the first minute of the call whether they feel good about doing business with you.

4. Find out who is calling and ask how you might assist. Identification saves time and trouble. First, jot down the person's name and use it in your conversation with him or her. Be sure to listen to the person's question or concern before you offer suggestions or transfer the person to someone else.

5. Be courteous when putting someone on hold. If a call is on hold for more than 45 seconds, pick up the call again and ask the caller if he or she wants to continue holding or leave a message. Be sure to wait for a response—do not simply say the words and automatically put the person on hold. Remember, time passes very slowly for someone on hold; it can feel like an eternity.

6. Transfer carefully. Before transferring a call, give the extension number so the caller can dial it directly in case the call is disconnected during the transfer.

L e a r n i n g   f r o m   E x p e r i e n c e
A Perspective from the Working World

Keep It Simple

Kai Mahaulu,
Security officer

I work as a security officer in Hawaii for an agency that provides security guards and patrol agents to banks, high-tech firms, and busy ports. To get this job, I had to pass a six-month training program. During training, it was drilled into all potential recruits that the primary goal of any security officer is to protect the employees, customers, and assets of the company where you are placed.

During the training program, we had to learn to use a number of communication tools, including surveillance cameras, radios, telephones, email, and GPS systems. We also worked on improving our own personal communication skills so we could effectively communicate with people in writing and in person. Our trainers reminded us that those communication skills could help prevent or diffuse a potential conflict situation.

Everyone in the training program would read the training manual on their own and then meet as a group to discuss the material. Sometimes we talked about how we would respond in different conflict situations and sometimes we did role-playing. I was really surprised by how different our perspectives were from one another. I liked studying in a group because I learned so much by listening to how other people thought.

When I graduated I was placed at a local high-tech firm that produces satellite communication software for the government. It's a secure facility with very strict rules. One area of potential conflict in my job is dealing with visitors who arrive. Some are vendors, some are friends of employees, and some are interviewees. They are often in a hurry and do not understand why they have to fill out the visitor paperwork, provide a photo ID, get a visitor's badge, and walk through a security check. They often become annoyed with the process and can even get hostile.

I've learned that simply being polite can help take the edge off angry visitors. It also seems to help when I agree with them that going through a security check is a hassle. However, I don't take any shortcuts because security must come first. Unfortunately, I've seen some of my fellow security guards go on a power trip. They provoke the visitors by demanding their cooperation and dictating what they do. I do things differently; I try to make it a habit of showing respect to everyone I meet.

Communication is also involved when I first report to my post. Before I take over, I have to find out what went on earlier in the day. If I don't talk to the security guard I'm relieving, I end up having to call supervisors about the alarm system, missing visitor badges, or other problems, instead of taking care of them myself. When it's time for a break, all security guards report to the message center. That's where we receive and send emails, or call other guards or company employees to ask or answer questions. The message center keeps us in touch.

For me, the tricky part about communication is picking out the key points you want to make. Even when we communicate well, there are still barriers to overcome. All kinds of things can distort a message: the words we use, our upbringing, our culture, even the kind of day we're having. To really say what you mean, you have to stop and think first. You can use a lot of words, but people still may not understand what you're talking about. That's why my motto on the job is: Keep it simple.

7. Take complete and legible messages. Write clearly so someone else (or you) can read the message later. Include the following information:

- Date
- Time
- Caller's full name and company (if applicable)
- Caller's phone number (including area code and extension)
- Caller's message and desired action (for example: return the call, caller will call back later, no need to call, call if you cannot make it, call at 4 p.m.)
- Your name

Even if the person receiving the call knows the person who is calling, always write down a phone number and first and last names. For example, suppose Larry calls to talk to your manager. What if your manager knows two Larrys and you forgot to write down a last name? What if your manager can't remember Larry's number and has to take time to look it up because you forgot to write it down? What if Larry is not at his regular office and you neglected to write down the phone number where he can be reached? Make it easy—take down all the information, all the time.

Written Communication

So far we've looked at in-person communication (both verbal and nonverbal), as well as phone communication. But what about written communication? We already discussed good writing skills in Chapter 4, so let's look at when to write your messages versus when to speak them, examine different mechanisms for sending written messages, and identify the different purposes of written messages.

There are times when it's best to deliver a message in person or over the phone. There are other times when an email, memo, or letter is the best way to communicate. How do you know what is best? Table 10.3 can help you decide.

If you decide to write a message, make sure you are clear about the purpose of your message. For example, do you need an answer to a question? Are you sharing information? Are you asking for something? Are you thanking someone for a job well done?

Next, be sure you are clear on who your audience is. Ultimately, your audience determines the tone and style of your written communication. If you are writing to your manager, you may want to be more formal than if you are writing to a coworker. If you are writing to a customer, you may want to avoid using company jargon because the customer will be unfamiliar with the terms.

Now you can write your message. Regardless of audience or purpose, there are typically several parts to the message. The organization of the parts depends on whether you are delivering neutral or positive news or delivering negative news. Negative news is simply information that you believe someone will not want to hear. Standard organization for both positive and negative written messages appears in Table 10.4.

As you can see, the main difference between the organization of good new and bad news is this: When you have to deliver bad news, you do not want to get to the point immediately. Instead, you want to cushion the news with a neutral buffer and then work into the news by providing background information first. Finally, it's always important to finish your negative message with a positive closing, to keep the doors of communication open. Figures 10.4 and 10.5 provide examples of correctly organized positive and negative messages.

 Now You Try It: Email Miscommunication

Everyone, at some time or another, has sent or received an email that did not make sense or seemed cold and angry. Think back to an instance when you sent or received an email that was misinterpreted, and answer the following questions:

1. What was the subject of the email?
2. Why do you think it came across badly?
3. What could have been done to improve it?
4. Do you think the message should have been delivered by email in the first place? Why or why not?

Table 10.3	**When to Use Written versus Spoken Communication**
Type	**When to Use**
Written Communication	
Letter	This paper communication is best for formal messages that must be documented and delivered widely throughout the company or to clients. For example: a letter indicating company-wide reorganization or layoffs (Something this serious would probably be accompanied by in-person meetings.)
Memo	This paper communication is best for formal messages that must be delivered quickly throughout a department. For example: a reminder of a monthly meeting
Email	This electronic communication is printable and is best for general purpose communication between coworkers, managers, and clients. For example: a question about a meeting time, a request to discuss an issue, or an explanation of a procedure
Spoken Communication	
Phone	This is best for messages that must be delivered immediately, for asking essential questions and getting clarification, and for delivery of serious or bad news when you cannot meet with the individual in person. For example: calling a customer about a later delivery or calling a coworker in another city to discuss a misunderstanding
In person	This is best for resolving conflict, discussing issues, and for delivering serious or bad news. For example: reviewing an employee's performance or reprimanding an employee for inappropriate behavior

Table 10.4	**Organization of Written Messages**

Positive News	Negative News
• **Main objective.** Be clear about your main idea. Are you asking a question? Voicing a concern? Requesting feedback? Get right to the point. • **Explanation.** Briefly provide any background information that further explains or justifies your message. • **Call for action.** Always end with the action that you want your reader to take.	• **Buffer.** Provide a neutral, nonconfrontational message that engages your reader before you get to the meat of the problem. You don't want to scare off your reader! • **Reason.** Outline the facts behind the bad news, but don't give the news yet. • **News.** Position the bad news near the middle of the message. Keep your tone noninflammatory and factual, not cold. You may even want to show some concern. • **Call for action.** Identify the action you want the person to take, based on the news you delivered. • **Close.** Always end with something positive.

At this point, you've been exposed to the various ways to communicate: verbally, nonverbally, over the phone, and in writing. Now let's look at two topics that come up no matter how you communicate: criticism and conflict.

Now that you have a sense of how to communicate with others on a one-on-one basis, even in conflict situations, let's look at what's involved in speaking to groups.

Figure 10.4   **Positive message**

To:	RandDStaff; AdminStaff; SupportStaff; MktgStaff
Cc:	svanderlinden@starstreams.com
Subject:	First Offsite Staff Meeting

Dear Team,   — Main objective

Please plan to attend our first offsite staff meeting on Friday, March 25, from 9:00 am to 4:00 pm. We will be meeting at the Atrium Conference Center in the Sunrise Room. Lunch and snacks will be provided. For address and directions, click here.   — Explanation

This meeting will give us a chance to celebrate our successes, analyze our failures, and brainstorm ideas for the future. In particular, we'll be looking at last year's high point the Andromeda Project, and our ill-fated Solaris Project. Then we'll share some "outside-of-the-box" ideas for next year's projects. The more people who attend, the more ideas we'll have!   — Call to action

Please respond by March 1, so we can let the Atrium staff know the number of people to expect.

NOTE: If you cannot attend, we will provide comprehensive notes after the meeting, and can even meet with you one-on-one, if necessary.

Regards,

Soroya Vanderlinden
Director of Innovation
Starstreams Enterprises
www.starstreams.com

Figure 10.5   **Negative message**

To:	Manual.ruiz@contactpoint.com
Cc:	Ramona.Delgado@contactpoint.com
Subject:	Teleconference setup

Dear Manuel,

Thanks for your hard work setting up the conference room and all electronic equipment for last Friday's teleconference.   — Buffer (praise)

We realize we gave you little advance warning, since the teleconference was proposed at the last minute. And we know that you had your regular duties to attend to while you worked on setting up the teleconference.   — Reasons

That said, it's perfectly understandable that something might go wrong. As it turned out, we had a lot of difficulty with the phone connection and website. Many attendees could not call in or access the website successfully.   — Bad news

In the future, we'd appreciate it if you could test the teleconference connections with one person from each time zone – that should prevent the problems we experienced. In fact, we will make sure to give you the names and phone numbers of those people, as well as give you adequate time for planning.   — Call to action

We look forward to holding more teleconferences in the future with you as our "go-to-guy" and appreciate your assistance.   — Positive close

Sincerely,

Ramona Delgado

Effective Public Speaking

The term *public speaking* refers to the most public form of communication—making presentations in front of groups. The ideas about good communication that we already discussed apply to any type of speaking. Speaking at length in front of others also involves some special techniques.

Some of you may have jobs that never require you to speak formally in front of others; however, the principles of effective speaking also apply to situations such as interviews, meetings with your manager, or group planning sessions. In school, you may need to present a project or demonstrate something you built or learned. Some people feel just as nervous about a discussion or evaluation meeting with a manager as they feel about standing before a large group of people and talking.

Don't worry if you're uncomfortable speaking in front of others. You are not alone. You may think that others don't seem afraid, but often they conceal their fears. No one wants other people to think that they are afraid. If speaking makes you nervous, you are in good company with most of the world. The truth is, most people get anxious whenever they have to present ideas in front of others. A little nervousness isn't a bad thing; it can help you focus and pay attention, and it is common in everyone who gets ready to make a presentation.

Excessive nervousness and fear can get in the way of being clear and persuasive. One of the best ways to conquer your fear is to remember that what you say in a speech or at a meeting is no different from what you would say in a conversation with one friend—you simply say it to more people. Think of a presentation as a conversation with a group of people. Since you're probably fairly comfortable having a conversation, this should help take the edge off your nervousness.

To get comfortable making a presentation, it's wise to go through these five stages:

- Prepare mentally
- Develop your speech
- Add visual aids

 **Did You Know?** "If speaking in public scares you, you aren't alone," says Paul L. Witt, PhD, assistant professor of communication studies at Texas Christian University, Fort Worth. "It is even scarier than rattlesnakes. The idea of making a presentation in public is the No. 1 fear reported by people in the U.S."[3]

---

[3]DeNoon, Daniel J. "Fear of public speaking hardwired: Speech anxiety worse for some, but most can overcome it." WebMD, April 20, 2006. Accessed on January 25, 2011, from www.webmd.com/anxiety-panic/guide/20061101/fear-public-speaking

- Fine-tune and practice
- Make your presentation

We will now provide advice for each stage so you can prepare and present your ideas clearly and thoughtfully.

Prepare Mentally

Before you actually give a presentation, you need to sit down and think about the purpose, audience, and outcome of your talk.

1. The first question to ask yourself is: "Why do I need to speak and what do I gain by speaking? Will I inform, persuade, or motivate?" You might need to present some facts and figures to your department. You might want to present a case to your manager for a pay raise. You might need to motivate a group of new employees. Whatever you need to accomplish, establish that goal for yourself before you do anything. Your audience won't get the point unless you have a strongly established purpose.

2. The next question to ask yourself is: "Who needs to hear what I have to say and why would they listen?" Unless you plan to talk to yourself in the mirror, some other person is your audience. By understanding what motivates your audience, you will be better able to present your information in a way that your audience will accept. This will also prevent you from presenting too much information; you will only share what will interest your audience.

3. A final question to ask yourself is: "What do I want the outcome to be?" No one makes a presentation for no reason. Get clear on what you hope will happen when you finish. Will people go out and do something? Will they behave differently? Will they think differently?

Once you decide on a presentation goal and outcome, make sure you believe in what you plan to talk about. If you don't believe in it, no one else will either. Then make the decision to give your presentation and commit to it, even if you're not sure how you are going to accomplish the task. Your commitment is what will drive you forward and help you figure out what to do. Without that commitment, you're likely to give up the first time you encounter any problems.

Develop Your Speech

Now that you've answered those three important questions and made the decision to give the presentation, it's time to figure out what you're going to say and how you're going to say it. Gather facts, evidence, examples, true stories, and other fuel for your fire, always keeping the goal of the presentation in mind. Stories and personal example in particular will help engage your audience and make your message stick. Don't worry about how to organize things yet, just collect the information you need.

For example, suppose you plan to ask the board of directors for a raise. Gather information that demonstrates how you have helped the company since you were hired. Did you increase production? Do other supervisors have good things to say about you? Did you boost sales? If you want to persuade, research your topic and know your audience. When you understand what motivates your audience, it's easier to select the points to make and decide what information will persuade.

Once you've collected your information, decide the best way to organize it. Some people like to write ideas on index cards and then move the cards around to arrange and rearrange ideas. Others like to handwrite or type an outline and add information to it as needed. Use whatever method with which you feel comfortable. As you think about different ways to organize your ideas, consider any of the schemes below that you think will work well for your subject:

- **Procedural.** Explain how to do something, step-by-step.
- **Chronological.** Present your topic along a timeline, from the past to the present.
- **Simple to complex.** Present a specific example, and then discuss how it relates to a broader topic.
- **General to specific.** Present general information first, and then show how it applies to a specific topic.

Regardless of the organization scheme you choose, you'll want to follow a simple 4-step approach to putting together your presentation:

1. Begin with a catchy fact, idea, or question.
2. Introduce the central concept(s) of your speech.
3. Plan how you will make your points in the middle.
4. Summarize at the end.

Work on the information until it flows comfortably and feels like "you."

Add Visual Aids

Even though we call it a *speech*, there's more to presenting ideas to people than talking. Visual aids are any type of visual material that helps illustrate your ideas and makes them more interesting and memorable to your audience. Such materials also help engage your audience. Table 10.5 lists common visual aids and when to use them.

Regardless of the type of visual aids you use, keep these tips in mind (especially if you use electronic slides).

Table 10.5 Common Types of Visual Aids	
Visual Aid	**Description**
Flip chart Large, portable pad of paper that you can write on. You can also save the pages of paper you've written on for later reference or post them on the wall.	**Best used for:** Interactive presentations with small groups where you want to capture ideas and keep them. **Benefits:** Lets you add or cross out points at any time, capture questions for later discussion or research, and invites participation. **Remember:** Make sure to write legibly, using a dark color in a large enough print for people to see. Stand to the side when you write and do not talk while your back is to your audience.
Whiteboard White, porcelain-on-steel board, similar to a blackboard. You use dry erase markers to write on the whiteboard, rather than chalk.	**Best used for:** Casual, interactive presentations where you want to capture thoughts, erase them, and then generate more ideas (brainstorming). **Benefits:** Easy to remove and add ideas, easy to see, usually comes with the room. **Remember:** Do not write at the very bottom (no one can see), do not talk while your back is turned (no one can hear), use dark colors that people can see, and make sure you are using dry erase markers, NOT permanent markers.

(continued)

Table 10.5 *(Continued)*

Visual Aid	Description
Overhead projector A large box with a very bright light, a lens, and a mirror. You place a transparency on the flat surface, the light travels through the transparency and the lens, and is then projected from the mirror onto a screen for all to see.	**Best used for:** Presentations where you need to do a lot of writing and commenting on screen. **Benefits:** Lets you write on a horizontal surface, adding or removing information as you go. Transparencies can be premade so that all you have to do is mark them up as you speak, or you can write as you go. **Remember:** Do not stay "glued" to the projector, droning on and on, and writing too much. The soft hum of the projector and your voice will put people to sleep.
Electronic projector High-tech version of an overhead projector. You connect the projector to your laptop or desktop computer and project the image from the computer monitor to a screen your audience can see.	**Best used for:** Small or large presentations where you want everyone to be able to see slides that have been made up ahead of time—slides that help punctuate and illustrate your talk. **Benefits:** Allows all audience members to clearly see illustrations, diagrams, photos, and text to help engage them and remind them of key points. Lets you share anything you can access on your computer, including audio and video files. **Remember:** Do not "slide" people to death. Too many slides with too many points make people restless and bored. They came to hear you, not read slides.
Handouts Sheets of paper you hand out containing additional information or illustrations to accompany your talk. These may also include questions or short notes so people will follow along more closely as you speak.	**Best used for:** Information you want people to take home with them as reference, especially if you are not planning to go into great detail during your presentation. **Benefits:** Lets people review information at home or at work, at their leisure. **Remember:** If you plan to use handouts with questions or brief notes, hand them out at the beginning of your presentation. People will pay more attention because they will be listening for the answers. If you plan to provide reference handouts for people to study later, hand them out at the end of the presentation. Otherwise, they will be distracted reading them and will not pay attention to you.
Demos, props, and questions Physical demonstrations involving people or props along with question sessions	**Best used for:** Large or small presentations where you want to demonstrate a procedure or action. **Benefits:** Demonstrations get people's attention, especially if they involve the audience. They are a great way to break up your presentation. **Remember:** Practice your demonstration BEFORE you give your presentation to make sure everything works.

1. **Use quality pictures.** If you are writing on a flipchart or whiteboard, you can sketch any type of simple images you want. If you are using electronic slides, use quality images from stock photo websites, such as istock.com. Use images to illustrate ideas and capture the audience's interest.

2. **Avoid wordiness and clutter.** Keep words to a minimum. Your visual aids are supposed to get your audience's attention and serve as a reminder of key topics; they are not supposed to contain every single word you say. Don't crowd your slides with too many images either. Keep as much white space as possible for a clean, professional look.

3. **Use consistent fonts and colors.** Make sure people can see the text. If you are writing on a flipchart or overhead, write legibly and large enough. If you are using a slide, pick a sans-serif font, such as Arial, Verdana, or Trebuchet in a size that everyone can read—14 pt text is the smallest you will want to go. Headings should be at least 4 points bigger and can be a different color than the body text to draw attention.

4. **Make things easy to scan and read.** People read from top to bottom, left to right. Make sure the information on your visual aid follows that pattern. Keep text left-aligned, rather than centered, so people can easily scan downward. Use a few bullet points instead of long paragraphs.

Figures 10.6 and 10.7 illustrate the tips you just learned by comparing a poor visual aid with a good one.

Fine-Tune and Practice

Once your information is organized and the visual aids are prepared, it's time to fine-tune your presentation and practice. Get rid of information that is not essential to producing the outcome you want. This is important because we often add information to a presentation because it's information we like, not because it matters to our audience. Then review the information and make sure it will engage the audience and "stick" with them. According to Chip and Dan Heath, coauthors of *Made to Stick: Why Some Ideas Survive and Others Die*,[4] a presentation that "sticks" is a presentation that makes an audience:

1. **Pay attention.** People want to hear something new and interesting.

2. **Understand and remember**. The message must be clear and concrete. Stick to the point and use words that your audience understands.

3. **Agree or believe.** The message must be credible. If you don't believe it, your audience won't either.

4. **Care**. You must touch your audience's emotions. People remember things when their emotions are involved.

5. **Act on the message.** Make sure your presentation motivates your audience to do what you want them to do.

To practice your speech, do the following:

1. **Eliminate overworked words and expressions.** Many of us pepper our casual conversation with filler words that serve very little purpose, such as "you know," "right," "like," "okay," "um," and "well." These take up time without adding substance to your speech. Using them is a habit that is tough to break. Ask someone to listen to you as you speak and tell you when you use those filler words.

2. **Although you want to know your talk well, do not memorize it.** A memorized speech can also sound robotic and less interesting to an audience. Memorizing will lock you into an exact speech, not allowing for the give-and-take that occurs with any conversation. The ability to speak in a spontaneous way, adjusting to audience response and ideas, is the mark of a talented speaker.

3. **Don't go in cold.** Practice alone first, standing and using your visual aids as if you had an audience. Some people like to practice in front of a mirror to help them look more confident. Practice makes perfect! The more you rehearse your speech aloud, the more freely and comfortably you will speak when it really counts. After practicing on your own, try out your talk in front of people who will give you a good honest critique. Ask for feedback on both your ideas and your delivery.

You've done all the hard work, so now let's look at how to stand up in front of others and make the best possible presentation you can.

Make Your Presentation

The tips in this section will help you feel calmer and more confident as you make your presentation. The tips will also ensure that your audience gets out of the presentation what you intended.

Anti-nervousness routine. Everyone feels a little nervous before speaking to a group. Come up with a simple anti-nervousness routine that works for you. Some people like to take a quick walk or do some deep breathing exercises. Others like to talk or sing to

---

[4]Heath, Chip and Dan Heath. *Made to Stick: Why Some Ideas Survive and Others Die*. New York: Random House, 2007.

Figure 10.6 Poor visual aid

Tips for Creating Good Visual Aids

- Use quality pictures. If you are writing on a flipchart or white board, you can sketch any type of simple images you want. If you are using electronic slides, please use quality images from stock photo webstites, such as istock.com. Use images to illustrate ideas and capture the audience's interest.

- Avoid wordiness and clutter. Keep words to a minimum. Your visual aids are supposed to get your audience's attention and serve as a reminder of key topics; they are not supposed to contain every single word you say. Don't crowd your slides with too many images either. Keep as much white space as possible for a clean, professional look.

- Use consistent fonts and colors, Make sure people can see the text. If you are writing on a flipchart or overhead, write clearly and large enough. If you are using a slide, pick a sans-serif font, such as Arial or Verdana, in a size that everyone can read—14 pt text is the smallest you will want to go. Headings should be at least 4 points bigger (probably 24 pt).

- Make things easy to scan and read. People read top to bottom, left to right. Make sure the information on your visual aid follows that pattern. Keep text left-aligned, rather than centered, so people can easily scan downward. Use a few bullet points instead of long paragraphs.

What's Wrong?

- Font is serif (Times Roman) and too small to easily see.

- Text is centered with bullets, making it hard to scan.

- There is too much text on the page.

- The picture is not very professional.

---

themselves in a mirror. Still others enjoy chatting with members of the audience as they come in. Find out what works for you.

A good entrance. When you walk into the room, stand tall and walk confidently. Before you speak, look around the room and take a deep breath.

Get their attention. Your opening lines should make your audience sit up and listen, engaging them enough that they want to hear the rest of what you have to say. Some people like asking an interesting question, others like to make an unusual or surprising comment, and some like to tell a brief story. For example, suppose you are planning to present an idea for a labor-saving process to a group of managers. You might start with the question: "Do you know how many hours the average employee works to get just one of our products to market?" or "How would you like to get our products out the door in half the time?"

Speak with sincerity and believe what you say. The person or people listening to you will quickly notice if you don't seem to believe in your own words, and consequently, they won't believe in them either. Only say aloud what you feel you can truthfully say silently, in your heart.

Speak clearly, audibly, and slowly. Do not rush what you have to say, but don't speak so slowly that you frustrate your audience. Make sure you are not speaking in a monotone voice, or you will put people to sleep. Think about it—if you have messy handwriting, no one can read your brilliant thoughts; likewise, it won't matter how wonderful your talk is if no one can hear or understand it. When you practice in front of others, ask them if they understood everything you said.

Figure 10.7 Good visual aid

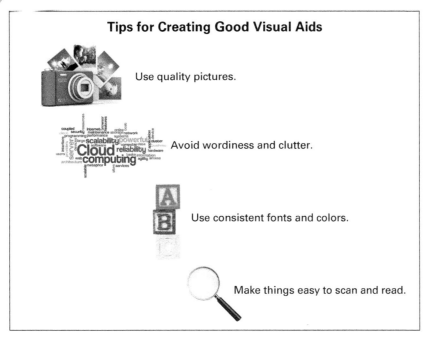

Tips for Creating Good Visual Aids

Use quality pictures.

Avoid wordiness and clutter.

Use consistent fonts and colors.

Make things easy to scan and read.

What's Right?

- Font is sans-serif and easy to read.
- Text flows easily from top to bottom, left to right, and is easy to scan.
- There is very little on the page, but enough to make key points.
- The pictures are all professional and help the audience remember the key points.

Maintain eye contact with your audience. People in an audience are more likely to pay attention when you catch their eyes. They feel as if you are addressing them directly, and they may take more of an interest. Of course, you can't look at them constantly because you will probably need to glance at your notes. If your audience consists of more than one person, you will have to shift your gaze from one audience member to another. Find some people in different areas of the room and move your gaze to those people. Be careful not to look so long that it seems like you're staring, or so briefly that it looks like your head is swiveling back and forth. If you feel shy about looking into peoples' eyes, glance above their foreheads for about three seconds—it will appear that you are looking at them.

Do not read your speech off the page. Like memorization, reading makes your talk seem too preset and dull. The audience may feel like they could have simply read a copy of your speech and gotten just as much benefit. Use the advantage of a live presentation to deliver your ideas with emphasis and individuality.

Do not read your slides word-for-word or rush through them. Just like you shouldn't read your speech word-for-word, you should not read your slides word-for-word. First, you will bore people, and second, they will wonder why you even have to be there, since they could simply read the slides and get the same information. Instead, keep your slides simple, and then embellish the information with your own words. No matter what you say, don't rush. People need time to absorb what you say and look at your slides. If you have to rush, you probably have too many slides.

Let a little humor into your talk! Humor relaxes people and draws their attention. Begin with something upbeat or funny, and then get to the more serious points. Be careful about telling jokes, however, because they can backfire. Use them only if you are comfortable telling jokes and, most importantly, if they are appropriate for the topic and the audience.

Stay aware of your audience, but don't let a audience reaction throw you. Use your body language skills to read your audience. If your audience seems bored, increase your energy and enthusiasm. If they seem puzzled, provide some more examples or try explaining things differently. If only a few faces seem unmoved, don't automatically assume the entire audience is not interested in what you are saying. People may be thinking hard, or they may not reveal their feelings immediately. If your audience reacts well to certain points, expand on them. The more you focus on your audience rather than on yourself, the more relaxed and in tune you will be.

Take periodic "breathers." Everyone gets tired of listening or looking at slides at some point, and finds his or her mind wandering. Keep in mind that the average adult has a 20-minute attention span. This means that if your talk is going to be more than 20 minutes in length, you better take some breaks. Breaks might include asking the audience for questions, telling a story, asking people to take a stretch break, or doing a demonstration—something to get your audience more involved.

Summarize. Make sure that when you close you summarize your talk by restating one or two major points and sharing your own conclusions. The summary gives you an opportunity to emphasize your most important ideas—the thoughts you want everyone to remember. Even if you lost a few people along the way, you have a chance at the end to rein them back in.

When you finish your presentation, it's always a good idea to review how things went. You can do this by yourself or with someone who heard you speak. Think about what went well and what could be improved. What you learn from each speaking engagement enables you to speak more effectively in the future. Reviewing is a chance to improve your skills and even your material.

A speech is an opportunity to communicate. Think of it as a chance to convince others of something that is important to you, rather than a frightening ordeal. The more you speak, the better speaker you will become.

 ## Now You Try It: A Presentation to Remember

If we're lucky, we get to attend a presentation that really makes us think—one we remember for a long time. Think back to a presentation you attended that you really liked.

1. What made it memorable?
2. Did the presenter use visual aids? What kind?
3. Did the presenter use humor? What kind?
4. How did the presenter keep you interested?

Communication is the lifeline of the workplace and the world.

Keep the Lines of Communication Open

Communication is the lifeline of the workplace—and of the world. Everything that happens does so because people communicate to others what must be done. When you know how to communicate well with different types of people in different situations, you will be a key link in that lifeline, one that your employer cannot do without. With good communication skills you will build lasting relationships at work, at school, and at home. The more you give and receive communication, the more marketable you become.

Your Tool Kit at Work

10.1 Words, Words, Words

Listen to yourself and others, and you'll hear these filler words and phrases: "You know, it's like, I mean, ummm, yeah, well, okay, right?" You may not even know how often you're filling sentences with words that say nothing and create an unprofessional impression.

Are you tired of these same old words? So are employers. They hear overworked slang and tired phrases during interviews, meetings, and presentations. When they are under stress, people tend to revert to old patterns, and you might find yourself using words that you thought you had eliminated from your vocabulary.

1. Put a check by your particular culprits. You know yourself—be honest. If you really aren't sure which ones you use, ask a close friend or family member what they hear you say.

   _____ a. You know

   _____ b. Like

   _____ c. Right?

   _____ d. Okay

   _____ e. Ummm

   _____ f. Yeah

   _____ g. What?

   _____ h. I mean. . . .

   _____ i. Well. . . .

   _____ j. Really?

   _____ k. Any other slang you overuse

   _____ l. Profanity you use

2. Write your problem words in a notebook, and carry it with you. For two days, put a check next to the words each time you catch yourself using them.

3. Take your top three "offenders" and used the rule of 21 against them. For the next 21 days, stop whenever you use an overworked word. If you don't know what to say in its place, try silence. Pauses make good, thoughtful impressions, but they're difficult to adjust to at first. Put a dime or a quarter into a jar each time you goof, and buy yourself something with your change at the end of 21 days. (Your biggest financial contribution will probably come during the early part of those 21 days.)

   You may need to repeat this exercise several times. These phrases took years to get into your speech patterns; give yourself time to get them out!

10.2 Are You Phonegenic?

When you answer the phone at work, you are often the only contact the caller has with your company. What you say and how you say it make a lasting impression. Naturally, employers expect you to be "phonegenic." Bad telephone manners and an unpleasant tone of voice are two main reasons employees are terminated.

1. Evaluate your telephone techniques by asking yourself the following questions. Circle the number that best fits your technique. If you don't answer the phone at work, use your home telephone style to test how "phonegenic" you are.

Questions	Sometimes	Often	Always
1. Do you answer the telephone with a smile in your voice?	1	2	3
2. Do you write messages completely and accurately?	1	2	3
3. Are you tactful and courteous on the telephone?	1	2	3
4. Do you use good speech habits?	1	2	3
5. Do you ask callers to spell their names if you aren't sure of the spelling?	1	2	3
6. Do you treat every call as important?	1	2	3
7. Do you apologize for errors or delays?	1	2	3
8. Do you speak at a moderate rate and enunciate clearly?	1	2	3
9. Do you use the caller's name when you respond?	1	2	3
10. Do you repeat the message, especially the telephone number?	1	2	3
11. Do you include the area code?	1	2	3
12. Do you recognize a voice after someone has called a few times?	1	2	3
13. When necessary, do you screen calls tactfully?	1	2	3
14. Do you respond "you're welcome" to the caller's "thank you"?	1	2	3
TOTALS			
GRAND TOTAL:			

- If you scored 35 points or more, your telephone techniques are excellent.
- If you scored 25–35 points, you're pretty good, but try to be more consistent on the telephone.
- If you scored below 25, you know what you need to do to become more phonegenic—turn your "sometimes" into "always" by practicing your telephone techniques.

2. Whatever you choose to say on the telephone should be phrased politely. Of course you should never lie, but you don't always have to tell everything. Reword the following sentences to reflect good telephone manners.

a. What do you want?

_____

_____

b. Who is this?

_____

_____

c. Just wait awhile.

_____

_____

d. What do you want to talk to Ms. Youngblood about?

_____

_____

e. Sorry. I don't know where Mr. Alder went. He's supposed to be at his desk.

_____

_____

f. Mrs. Grimsted is in a conference with the police.

_____

_____

g. Mr. Diego left word he isn't to be disturbed. Call back later.

_____

_____

h. I gave Ms. Sand your message twice. I don't know what the problem is.

_____

_____

10.3 Working Styles

As we discussed in the chapter, work styles fall into categories. We usually, but not always, exhibit the same characteristics at home.

1. To determine where your working personality style fits on the chart, read each line below and circle the words in each line that most closely resemble you. Remember to answer honestly based on who you are, not who you would like to be. None of the answers is negative—all are positive in different ways. The more honest you are, the more accurate a picture you will have of your working personality, and the more you will be able to use what you know to your benefit in the workplace.

Category A	Category B	Category C	Category D
Self-controlled	Quick tempered	Patient	Nervy
Tenacious	Leader	Responsible	Quick
Loyal	Persuasive	Supportive	Sociable
Considerate	Competitive	Empathetic	Convincing
Faithful	Forceful	Friendly	Animated
Scheduled	Efficient	Obliging	Playful
Determined	Strong willed	Sensitive	Spirited
Detailed	Effective	Adaptable	Spontaneous
Shy	Positive	Peaceful	Charming
Perfectionist	Doer	Team player	Promoter
Analytical	Resourceful	Considerate	Energetic
Realistic	Opportunistic	Idealistic	Optimistic
Planner	Decision maker	Listener	Storyteller
Consistent	Daring	Reliable	Creative

(continued)

Category A	Category B	Category C	Category D
Organized	Bold	Tolerant	Delightful
Persistent	Productive	Reasonable	Upbeat
Respectful	Frank	Thoughtful	Flexible
Expert	Problem solver	Helper	Inspiring
Careful	Headstrong	Responsive	Verbal
Deep thinker	Pragmatic	Compromiser	Demonstrative
Structured	Confident	Diplomatic	Imaginative
Introspective	Independent	Reserved	Mixes easily
Quiet	Strong opinions	Eager to please	Talkative
Hardworking	Mover and shaker	Negotiator	Popular
Dedicated	Sure of self	Sensitive	Fun
Polite	Adventurous	Join in fun	Lively
Skeptical	No-nonsense	Permissive	Restless
Critical	Argumentative	Hesitant	Forgetful
Worrier	Impatient	Submissive	Unorganized
Fact seeker	Solution seeker	Harmony seeker	Attention seeker
TOTAL:	**TOTAL:**	**TOTAL:**	**TOTAL:**

2. Count the words you circled in each column. Write the total at the bottom of each column. The column with the highest score indicates your primary work style.
   - **Category A:** Your work style is the Analyst.
   - **Category B:** Your work style is the Director.
   - **Category C:** Your work style is the Mediator.
   - **Category D:** Your work style is the Entertainer.

3. You now have an idea of your working personality. Like most of us, you probably have characteristics from a combination of work styles, although one tends to dominate. Now you can figure out the parts of your work style that hold you back. For instance, to be successful, people of *all* personality styles need to assert themselves, communicate their needs clearly, and ask other people what they want. By nature, the analyst and the mediator are often passive. If your personality falls on this side, you need to practice stating your own opinions and desires. If you're primarily the director or the entertainer, you can achieve balance by toning down your opinionated nature.

   Ask yourself what qualities you need to develop to balance your style and start practicing. How about beginning with 21 days?

10.4 Plug Your Knowledge into Real Life: It's Presentation Time

No matter where you work or what you do, you will probably have to give a presentation at some point in your career. Here's your chance to practice by using the tips you learned in this chapter. You will put together a short presentation (5–10 minutes) on a subject you are interested in.

Get Ready

1. What is the topic?

2. What is the purpose of your presentation?

3. Who is your audience for the presentation?

4. What do you want the outcome to be—what should the audience go away thinking, feeling, or doing as a result of the presentation?

Get Set

1. Identify the most important points you want to make during the presentation that will be relevant to your audience.

2. Organize the points in a logical order.

3. Gather information for each point. Make sure the information is essential to producing the desired outcome (not just information you are interested in).

4. Come up with a good introduction—an interesting question, quote, or fact to "hook" your audience so they want to listen to your presentation.

5. Come up with a good closing.

6. Decide if you want to use visual aids. If you do, create simple ones with minimal text.

7. Create a script for your presentation based on your introduction, information points, and closing.

Go

1. Practice delivering the presentation, complete with visual aids, if you have them.

2. Practice your own anti-nervousness routine.

3. Do some deep breathing, walk tall, and try giving the presentation to a small audience.

   - How do they react?

   - What did you do well?

   - What could you improve upon?

10.5 Your Communication PALs

The attitudes listed below are important in the workplace of today. Circle the attitudes you already have and put an X next to the ones you want to improve.

Assertive	Is upfront and direct in a polite way.
Truthful	Is honest and straightforward.
Thoughtful	Takes time to think things through before acting or passing judgment.
Interactive	Works well with others.
Tactful	Thinks things through; acts and speaks with politeness and awareness.
Understanding	Perceives the needs of and situations that affect self and others.
Discreet	Reveals only what is necessary for clear expression; keeps confidences.
Expressive	Communicates completely, promptly, openly, and freely.
Sincere	Says what is meant, means what is said.

1. Write each circled quality as a positive affirmation and put it on a card or note where you will see it. Repeat the affirmation daily. For example:

   I am assertive.

   I am sincere.

2. Write the qualities that you want to improve below (the ones with an X).
   I will develop my ability to be:

   _____

   _____

   _____

   Add these qualities to your collection of reinforcement cards or notes.

3. Take a moment to go back and look at your other cards and positive attitude lists to determine your progress. You're almost through the program. Is your list of positive attitudes growing and helping you?

10.6 Technology Exercise

We all use written communication to some extent in our daily lives. This is a chance to examine your professional communications and identify areas for improvement.

1. Go through professional emails (not to or from friends or family) that you sent or responded to over the last month.

2. Find at least three "good news" emails and three "bad news" emails.

3. Evaluate the emails against the criteria you learned about in this chapter.

4. What were the most common mistakes you found?

5. What did you do well? What did you do not so well?

6. Rewrite the emails according to the criteria.

Stand Out on the Job

Pack Up Your Tool Kit

Life grants nothing to us mortals without hard work.

Horace

learning objectives

- What can you do to make a fresh start at a new job?
- How do you give your best to a new job?
- What is the difference between formal and informal on-the-job training?
- What are seven effective work habits?
- What two skills make up critical thinking?
- What is "managing upward"?
- What is a leader, and what skills should you develop to become one?
- What are your rights as an employee?
- What steps can you take to get a promotion?
- What are reasons for leaving a job and how should you resign?
- Why is it important to embrace change and stay self-aware in the workplace?
- How does volunteer work contribute to your well-being and the well-being of the planet?

myth

"I found the perfect employer." OR "I found the perfect job."

reality

No employer or job is perfect. Employers and jobs are like people: We all have our good points, we all have weaknesses, and we all make mistakes. New employees can sometimes become disillusioned and unmotivated when they discover inefficiencies, awkward procedures, or poor communications in their new job. All employers and jobs have imperfections. But despite these imperfections, they can still be good, if not great. We need to understand that imperfections will exist. We need to have tolerance for these quirks and continue to strive to be better every day.

myth

"I will get that promotion if I just get my tasks done."

reality

Just getting our tasks done is not enough to get a promotion. In fact, just getting tasks done might not even be sufficient to keep a job. We need to do our best in our work and not just get by. Promotions are based on sustained, outstanding performance. Outstanding performance is defined as exceeding both what is required and what is expected, in terms of quality of work and responsibilities.

When Nick first went to work for Just Like New Computers, he was excited. He was getting in on the ground floor of a small, family-owned company that rebuilt and repaired computers using recycled and factory-refurbished parts. This was a chance to apply the computer and electronics knowledge he'd gained from a local vocational school, as well as pursue his personal interest in computers.

His first year was wonderful. His boss told him he was one of the best maintenance people the company had. He was great at quickly troubleshooting computers that customers brought in for repair. Plus, he often helped the rest of the repair people on the team. He had lots of good ideas for how to do things more efficiently and get the computers out to customers as soon as possible. He was happiest when he was helping others.

But during the second year, things changed. He got a new manager who knew less about computers than he did. Nick tried to help his manager by offering suggestions frequently, but the manager did not appreciate this and seemed to view Nick as a threat. When Nick tried to show the manager new repair procedures that could save the company money, the manager wasn't interested.

Nick felt like leaving the company because he wasn't appreciated. However, he decided that even though he didn't like his new manager, he liked everything else about the company. He also noticed that the manager treated everyone on his team in a similar fashion—Nick wasn't being singled out. And that's when Nick realized the manager was feeling insecure. This was his first management position and he felt that people were criticizing his every move.

Nick immediately stopped being so pushy with his manager. Instead of rushing over to his desk every day with ideas and suggestions, he simply sent the manager an occasional email with links to articles or websites that he thought the manager might find helpful. Nick also let the manager know he was available in case the manager had any questions about the department or concerns about the quality of Nick's work. Finally, he asked the manager to let him know if there were any ways he could help him.

By "leading from behind," Nick got the manager to open up to him. Soon the manager was asking Nick to brainstorm ideas with him. In addition, the manger found some new projects to stretch Nick's computer talents and help even more people. The manager was so impressed with Nick's willingness to help, that he promoted him a year later!

Nick's experience is not an unusual one. No job is perfect and not every manager is terrific. However, there are things you can do on the job that will make working an enjoyable experience and help you stand out and get ahead.

In this final chapter we will tie up some loose ends by showing you how to apply everything you've learned so far to move forward in your job. We will provide you with new tools to help you make a fresh start with your new job and acquire some new working habits. You will also learn what your rights are as an employee. We will talk about going for a promotion, changing jobs, and handling layoffs and firings. Finally, we will send you off with some ideas about staying aware in the workplace and expanding your sights to contribute to the health of your world.

The new tools you learn about in this chapter will help you whether you stick with your current career for a long time or decide to switch gears one or more times in the future. Whatever lies ahead, you have prepared yourself well.

It's a Fresh Start

Your experiences in life will always remain part of who you are. But that doesn't mean you can't make changes. You can close the door on some experiences and actively steer yourself toward others. You can even change the way you present yourself to the world.

Right now is the perfect time to make those kinds of changes. Your studies and your entry into the workplace give you the opportunity to approach your new working life with a positive state of mind. Figure 11.1 shows you a few ways to make lifelong learning and change positive parts of your life.

Figure 11.1 **Fresh start checklist**

- Change your attitude.
- Change your focus.
- Change your habits.
- Erase "common" knowledge.
- Change your appearance.

Change Your Attitude

There is nothing like a new environment to give your attitude a lift. Your search for a change may have led you back to school or to a new job. If you were bored with what you did before or disliked your work, your attitude probably suffered. But now you have a new environment, new coworkers, and new duties. You have every reason to move ahead with a positive attitude about your future.

Change Your Focus

Maybe in school or at your last job, you were pegged as someone who excelled at one specific ability or task, and that's all anyone ever asked you to do. Now that you are in a new job, you can switch your focus to something new and present yourself as proficient in a new area. Have you ever changed jobs or schools, or moved to a new town or state? Do you remember how you felt? It may have been difficult to make new friends, but it was probably a great opportunity to redefine yourself. Because no one really knew you yet, no one could judge or label you. At your new job you have a good chance to redefine yourself.

Change Your Habits

You know yourself fairly well by now, and you know which habits help you succeed and which weigh you down. It's difficult to adjust those habits, but sometimes a new job can give you the boost that you need. You will still need to use the rule of 21 to help you change your old habits, but it's easy to do when you are not surrounded by the same people and the same environment that helped create those habits.

Erase "Common" Knowledge

Many aspects of your past—your experiences and actions—influence how other people perceive you. Some of these perceptions can stick with you and act as roadblocks on the career path.

Perhaps a mistake on the job prevented a supervisor from asking you to take part in a particular activity. Perhaps someone else's idea of your talents and faults locked you into certain tasks that held little interest for you. Or maybe an unfounded rumor kept you from a promotion you deserved. With a new job, you have a clean slate. What preconceived opinions held by others would you like to change?

New coworkers come with a new job. These folks don't know your past, other than the skills and experiences listed on your resume or shared during an interview. Because they have no preconceived ideas about you, you can help steer their impressions in a positive direction. Ask to take part in projects that someone previously decided weren't in your area of expertise. Avoid situations or behaviors that started false rumors about you in the past. You now have a chance to draw a whole new picture of yourself.

 ## NowYou Try It: What WillYou Change?

Perhaps you just got a new job or are looking for one. Think about what you will be doing in your real or imagined job. Then look at each category below and identify an old aspect of yourself you want to change or get rid of, and a new aspect you want to take its place when you start your new job.

Category	Old	New
Attitude		
Focus		
Habits		
Common knowledge		
Appearance		

Giving Your Best for Yourself and Your Employer

When you have achieved the fresh start of a new job, you should give it your best. But remember, your best is your own—not someone else's. If your best isn't as developed as someone else's, that's okay—you progress at your own rate. If you make an improvement and it still doesn't equal the level of a coworker who is slacking off, you may still come out ahead. Why? Because you showed initiative and dedication, while the other person just kept on doing the same old thing and didn't put out any extra energy. Conversely, if your current best is better than everyone else's, you should still work to improve. You may complete a task better than someone else can, but not as well as *you* could—and that won't help you progress.

Every person has unique goals, talents, and weaknesses. If you compete with others, you trip yourself up by measuring yourself against their standards instead of your own. That's like trying to look good in clothing that doesn't fit you. You know yourself better than you know anyone else. You know the goals you have set and the rough spots you need to smooth. Keep striving to set new personal bests for yourself and you will continue to grow and succeed. Remember, success is a process—not the finish line. To give your best on the job, consider everything you have learned so far:

- Good attitude
- Positive self-image
- Motivation
- Commitment
- Good habits
- Patience
- Integrity and honesty
- Tolerance and acceptance
- Self-understanding
- Goal setting and prioritizing

- Resource management: time and money
- Reading, writing, listening, and other basic skills
- Teamwork
- Interpersonal skills: communication, dealing with conflict, handling criticism
- Speaking
- Handling stress
- Maintaining your mental and physical health

The workplace strategies we will address come from using these tools in combinations. They will help you to stand out on the job and make the most of your opportunities to succeed.

On-the-Job Training

Your education doesn't end when you leave school and accept your job, as illustrated in Figure 11.2. It continues with any initial training your company provides and with all the experience you gain as you perform your job.

On-the-job training concerns the specifics of a particular job, the ins and outs of different procedures, getting along with coworkers, and learning the ropes. The skills and attitudes in your career tool kit, along with your confidence in your abilities, come from your studies and past experience. When you bring these to a new job, on-the-job training shows you how to use them in a new environment.

Most companies provide some type of on-the-job training when you begin your employment, in either a formal or informal format. Your manager will determine which is necessary based on the situation. For example, a management position may require a one-week formal training session, whereas someone in a hands-on position may receive only informal advice and mentoring during the first few weeks.

Formal Training

Some larger businesses have a few days or even a week set aside for you to train when you first start. Others may have formal, structured training sessions that last even longer. Such training is standard for employees at certain levels performing certain jobs.

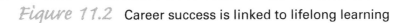

Figure 11.2 Career success is linked to lifelong learning

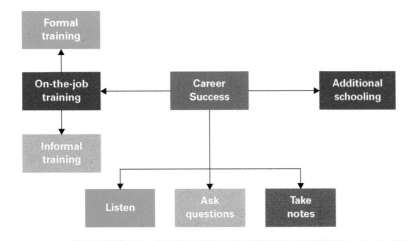

Did You Know? On-the-job training (OJT), not academic coursework, is the most significant source of preparation for most occupations.[1] It is considered one of the best training methods because it is planned, organized, and conducted at the employee's worksite. OJT is generally the primary method used to broaden employee skills and increase productivity. It is particularly appropriate for developing proficiency skills unique to an employee's job, especially for jobs that are relatively easy to learn and require locally owned equipment and facilities.[2]

This type of training helps you get used to your surroundings and figure out your duties. It requires the same attention, energy, and commitment that you are now giving to your studies. Avoid the temptation to slack off and think you are "home free." The more attentive and hard working you are during training, the better impression you will make from the start. What a great opportunity for you to make your employer think, "I made the right decision by hiring that person." This is your chance. Think promotion!

Informal Training

Many of you will go through an informal training process as you begin your new job. This type of training can take on many forms:

* Shadowing another more experienced employee by following that person around, watching what the employee does, and maybe helping him or her
* Getting a mentor who is available to answer questions or give you assistance when you run into problems
* A discussion of the particular rules and regulations of the company
* A tour of the facilities
* Lessons on any equipment you will have to operate
* Introductions to others working with you

Tips for On-the-Job Training

Whether you receive formal or informal training, here are some tips for getting the most out of it. These tips involve skills you've already learned, so none of them should come as a surprise.

* **Take notes when possible.** Bring a notebook and a pen with you during your first few days or when you receive training or any other information you need to know. Write everything you must know. That way you have it for a reference, instead of bothering your manager or coworkers with repetitive questions. Your notebook will become your homemade training manual. Even if it is only a sheet of important phone numbers, phone extensions, or prices, you will be glad you have it with you.
* **Listen, listen, listen.** Sometimes informal training is sandwiched in between lots of other work and it can go fast. The person talking to you has a lot to say and often little time to say it. Only by concentrated listening can you pick up everything you need to know.
* **Ask questions.** The only stupid question is the one you do not ask. Don't be afraid to ask anything that comes into your head. You are new here, so no one expects you to know how the place runs. Only by asking questions can you become informed and begin to feel comfortable in your new job. Speak up and listen carefully to the answers.

[1]Staff writer. "High-paying jobs requiring on-the-job training." *Occupational Outlook Quarterly,* Winter 2000–2001. Accessed on February 6, 2011, from www.bls.gov/opub/ooq/2000/winter/oochart.pdf

[2]Haselton, Erin. "Orange County Business Service Center Partners with PASTA MIA for On-the-Job Training." *Fullerton Chamber of Commerce* website. Accessed on September 14, 2012, from http://fullertonchamber.com/member-events-and-news/orange-county-business-service-center-partners-with-pasta-mia-for-on-the-job-training-3464

• **People are watching.** People will be evaluating you during training. They will be looking for signs that indicate how well you work with others and whether you are a team player, show initiative, or have a good attitude. Your nonverbal communication skills come in handy as you remember that your posture, eye contact, and facial expressions are a large part of the positive impression you will make.

Once you ease into your job, you'll need all the tools you've acquired so far to make your life easier and more productive. In particular, your managers and supervisors will look for specific skills that show how you can contribute to the success of a company or business. These skills appear in Figure 11.3.

If you master these skills, you increase your chances of job longevity and promotion within the company. The next several sections will describe these skills in detail.

Figure 11.3 Strategies for success

- Strive for Excellence
- Take the Lead
- Manage Upward
- Innovate
- Demonstrate Teamwork
- Enhance Critical Thinking
- Establish Effective Work Habits

Establish Effective Work Habits

This section looks at work habits that will keep you in your employer's good graces and bring simplicity, pleasure, and clarity to your working experience. Figure 11.4 provides a checklist of the habits you will be exploring.

Be Loyal and Dependable

These two qualities often carry more weight than skill level because it's easier to teach someone additional skills than to create loyalty and dependability where there none. Although the two qualities are related, they differ slightly. *Loyalty* refers to your faithfulness. A loyal employee is faithful to the ideals, rules, and integrity of the company, as well as to fellow employees. *Dependability* refers to how trustworthy you are. A dependable employee can always be relied on to complete assigned tasks, follow directives and rules, and remain committed to the company's needs and goals.

These two qualities must go together. If you are loyal without being dependable, your loyalty has no value. For example, if you believe in the company ideals and follow the rules, but have trouble completing your work adequately, your employer will perceive a problem despite your loyalty.

Figure 11.4 Effective work habits checklist

- Be loyal and dependable.
- Be pleasant.
- Be prompt.
- Be adaptable and flexible.
- Separate your work life from your personal life.
- Respect work privileges and resources.
- Respect company customs and practices.

Be Pleasant

A pleasant nature, tone, and attitude are jewels in the workplace. Problems are a given. You can't control what problems arise during the day, but you can control your attitude when handling them. A pleasant nature can make problems easier to work through and brighten the day in general. Best of all, a pleasant attitude can be contagious—one good-natured person can help others lighten up.

Be Prompt

You cannot begin to accomplish your tasks until you arrive at work. You don't necessarily need to be early, but you should arrive on time. Plan your travel to allow for the time you know your commute requires. Be smart—factor in daily obstacles such as

Being prompt shows respect for others.

the rush hour traffic or the time it takes to get your kids to the daycare, and add the extra time to your commute. If it means you have to leave your home a half-hour earlier than you had to in the past, do so. The impression you will make on your supervisors is worth the extra effort. It shows attention to detail, conscientiousness, and concern for your company. Then, when the unexpected does occur (a traffic jam, an emergency with a child, an illness), your tardy arrival will be forgiven without a second thought.

Be Adaptable and Flexible

No two days on the job are the same. If change upsets you, you may create more stress for your coworkers and manager. However, if you can roll with the punches and adapt your behavior, work schedule, and tasks to changes in situations as they occur, you will prove yourself a valuable asset to the company. **Adaptability** involves the ability to prioritize, a knowledge of your company's operations and social system, and the willingness to be flexible.

You need to shift gears efficiently as you learn which tasks take priority over others, and which people have the authority to make requests that take precedence over the daily routine of your work. Your state of mind also plays an important role. Realizing that nothing ever goes quite as planned and keeping a cool head will help you to rise above the turmoil of last-minute changes.

Adaptable, *adjective*

able to adjust readily to different conditions

Separate Your Work Life from Your Personal Life

These two sides of your existence can easily get in each other's way if you allow them to overlap. If your personal life issues show through at work, you may appear unprofessional and lacking in control. If you set boundaries and maintain the separation—addressing work issues at work and personal issues on personal time—you will impress those around you with your professionalism and maturity.

Respect Work Privileges and Resources

Don't take advantage of your workplace! Many jobs give you special privileges such as benefits and discounts on goods or services. You may have access to equipment and supplies to accomplish your work-related tasks. Use only what is rightfully given to you, and only for designated tasks. Any unauthorized use of supplies or discounts translates to theft.

There are gray areas, of course, so when in doubt you should ask. If you ask permission to print a quick private note on a computer printer during lunch hour, and your manager allows it, that's fine. But if you spend company time, paper supplies, and postage to mail invitations to a private party, you have gone over the line. Be honest with your requests, and be reasonable.

technology *at work*

The Internet is also a company resource, and one that can easily be exploited. While at work, do not surf the Internet. This means NO visiting social networking sites or chatrooms, playing online games, or checking out gossip sites. It also means NO sending or responding to personal emails. Your activity on the Internet should be related to your work projects only, as should your emails. Be aware that any emails written or sent from your work account are not private; they belong to the company and can be legally read at any time by anyone within the company. In addition, your Internet activity can easily be tracked if necessary—especially if porn sites are involved! Do not waste company time and jeopardize your job through Internet misuse.

Respect Company Practices and Customs

Every company has its own culture—its own method of operation, standard of behavior, value system, power structure, systems for completing tasks, dress code, physical surroundings, and customary ritual. As you become accustomed to a new job, trust your street smarts to help you recognize your workplace culture and fit into it.

Company culture comes in all shapes and sizes. Maybe your company has a casual day on Friday and everyone wears jeans. Perhaps there are certain tasks that you are not permitted to do even though you are capable. Maybe there are regularly scheduled meetings that you cannot miss, or little snack hours that serve as "pep rallies" to motivate employees for a big project. Perhaps there are unwritten codes of conduct and power structures among employees at the same level of management. Your ability to observe and work with these systems will help you to become an integral part of your company's staff.

NowYouTry It: How Good AreYour Work Habits?

Everyone needs to acquire and maintain good work habits to be successful. Look at the list of work habits below and do the following:

1. Rate how you are doing with each habit (**Excellent, Okay, Needs Improvement**).

2. Explain why you feel that way by describing a situation that involved those habits.

Habit	Rating	Explanation
Loyalty and dependability		
Pleasantness		
Promptness		
Adaptability and flexibility		
Ability to separate work and home life		
Respect for work privileges		
Respect for company culture		

Enhance Critical Thinking

Even if you master the previously mentioned work habits, you will not be successful until you become a skilled critical thinker. Critical thinking involves two specific skills: problem solving and decision making. Think about it: If you cannot solve a problem, you won't benefit from the skill development that comes from taking action to get past that problem. If you cannot make a decision, you won't even reach the point where you can use your skills.

Your success in the workplace depends on your ability to think through problems and make decisions wisely. Problems that require decisions occur every day in a business. Some problems are small and some are large—for example, deciding where to transfer a call, figuring out which size bit to use on a drill, prioritizing software bugs that need to be fixed, scheduling shifts on a hospital ward, or resolving a serious conflict among team members. Knowing how to efficiently deal with problems and decisions frees you to use and develop all the skills required for your particular job.

Problem Solving

This skill involves a rather simple sequence of steps: (1) analyze the problem, (2) brainstorm possible solutions, and (3) choose and execute the solution. The hardest part is taking the time and energy to think each one through. To illustrate these steps, let's look at the following situation.

Scenario: Emergency Decision

You are a computer repair person. You have a 2:15 p.m. system maintenance appointment scheduled at a business across town, but receive an emergency call on your beeper around 1:30 p.m. A hard drive went down at a business a mile away and they desperately need your help! Do you attend to the emergency, or the scheduled appointment?

Now let's walk through the steps and figure out what to do.

1. Analyze the problem. This step involves asking questions: What's the issue? What's at stake? Where in the dilemma lies the actual problem? In this situation, you do have a dilemma—you can't be in two places at once. You could try to find someone else to cover the 2:15 p.m. appointment, but no one else is currently on duty. Which situation is more important—the scheduled appointment or the emergency? You decide the emergency call needs your immediate attention. Conclusion: The problem is how to reschedule or cancel the 2:15 p.m. appointment.

2. Brainstorm. This step involves letting your mind roam and taking note of any ideas that arise, no matter how inappropriate or far-fetched they seem. Do not censor your thoughts and wait until you finish brainstorming before you begin evaluating. If you explore your ideas one by one as they arise, you may settle on an adequate choice but miss out on a better one just over the mental horizon. Also, ask others for their ideas. It's amazing how different each individual's perspective on a problem can be—you might hear some terrific advice.

In your situation, extensive brainstorming is not possible. Find a place where you can sit for five minutes without interruptions and contemplate the problem. Your possible solutions might include:

- Go immediately to the emergency call; when finished, make your way to the scheduled appointment.
- Reschedule the appointment for tomorrow, and then go to the emergency call.
- Call the scheduled company to see if you can set your appointment for later in the day, thereby making room for the emergency call.
- Attend the scheduled appointment on time; when finished, go to the emergency call.
- See if you can find another off-duty repair person who might handle the emergency call.
- Tell the company with the emergency that no one can make it until tomorrow.

3. Explore solutions. This step involves questions and decisions. What does each solution involve? What does each require of me? Try thinking backward from the solved problem through the solution process. Does it make sense? Is it workable? Finally, choose and execute the solution you believe is best for you and any others involved. Don't rush into the choice, but don't wait too long or you may lose your power or will to decide. Strike a balance and act when you feel ready.

In your current situation you don't have a lot of time to evaluate the possible solutions, but you can quickly think through the pros and cons of each of the following viable solutions.

- Arrive late to the scheduled appointment, at whatever time you finish with the emergency. This doesn't seem like a good idea. Your client deserves to know what's going on ahead of time, especially if there's a chance the schedule may change.
- Reschedule for tomorrow. This presents a problem because you're not working tomorrow. You know a lot more about that company's system than the other two programmers because you installed it. You don't think either one of them would feel confident working with it.
- Call the scheduled client to find out if that client could fit you in later in the day. This may work, depending on their schedule. This way you could handle the emergency first and still fulfill your prior commitment.
- Attend the scheduled appointment on time. This would please that particular company, but system maintenance doesn't seem as important as repairing a hard drive. The first company can still function without your visit; the second company's activity is at a standstill until you (or someone else) can fix the computer. The second company's problem is a priority.
- Try to find another repair person today. This is possible, but the phone calls you would have to make to find someone could be time consuming, and there's no guarantee you would succeed. You might disappoint both companies by the time you finish searching.
- Tell the second company their emergency will have to wait. This would be a mistake. Having to shut down their operations until tomorrow could cost them quite a bit of business. You would risk losing a customer with this solution.

4. Choose and execute the solution that seems best. Based on your analysis, the best bet is to call your scheduled client immediately and try to reschedule for later that day. You are told that you can come by at 4:30 p.m. You will have to extend your work hours to accommodate that request, but because the client didn't put up a fuss about rescheduling, you figure you can handle that small sacrifice.

Even if you follow these steps carefully, you won't always make perfect decisions. Take a lesson from each mishap to avoid repeating mistakes. Your mistakes are valuable teaching tools!

Innovate

Too many workers do just what their managers expect of them and no more. Following directives to the letter without going beyond won't cause you to lose your job, but you will probably reduce your chances of a promotion or developing your position to include more responsibility. You may end up feeling stuck in a holding pattern.

Innovation means coming up with new ideas, new ways of performing tasks, new structures, and new ways of cooperating. You have a lot of brain power—use it. If you see an existing problem (or anticipate one) and have an idea for a solution, share it. If you have ideas that you think will improve your personal efficiency or the efficiency of the workplace, tell someone. Make others around you aware of your thoughts, especially your managers.

Improvement comes in a variety of packages. Don't swallow your thoughts because you feel they won't make a difference or because you think they concern something insignificant. Even the smallest ideas create an atmosphere for change. What if you developed a new way to organize the schedule, or you installed a small refrigerator so employees could eat lunch nearby instead of taking extra time to go out? Those ideas could make people happier, and happier employees are more efficient. Every little bit counts.

Of course, some ideas work better than others. If after some consideration your manager doesn't think the idea will work, don't worry—there's always another idea you can share at a later date. Besides, you've already made a good impression by demonstrating that you care about the company and are willing to spend time and energy looking for innovative ways to improve things. That effort itself will impress those who observe you.

Manage Upward

Besides sharing innovative ideas, there is another way to help your company and improve your chances of advancement: learn to manage upward. *Managing upward* means looking for ways to empower your manager by helping him or her accomplish tasks and achieve goals.

Why do this? Because the success in your career is closely linked to the success of your manager. Your manager might have the organizational vision, but you are the one who does the work and has a deeper operational understanding of the detailed task requirements and challenges.

You are a reservoir of insights, energy, and suggestions. You have the potential to contribute value in many ways. While some managers might be afraid to let go and look to their employees for assistance, it never hurts to offer your help.

Look for Opportunities

Managing upward on your part may involve offering suggestions or taking action, resulting in small or large contributions. Managing upward on the part of managers involves creating an environment that encourages ideas and initiative, and providing support to employees as they take and make suggestions.

At this point you might think that managing upward could never work for you and your manager. Well, let's consider two situations.

Scenario: The Case of the Missing Agenda

You work for a telecommunications equipment firm that has grown rapidly. Staff meetings have recently been initiated to improve communications and coordination. The role of meeting facilitator rotates among the employees. However, frustration is building because nothing seems to get accomplished and the meetings are getting longer and longer. Issues and ideas are raised without resolution or closure, and the discussion has no focus, with people going off on all sorts of tangents.

You notice that no one uses an agenda and you believe an agenda would improve staff meeting efficiency. Why not share a simple draft agenda with your boss for the next meeting? Although your suggestion is unsolicited and may seem relatively small to you, the potential improvements are significant—especially when you consider the small investment in time required to create and implement the suggestion.

Scenario: The Case of the Looming Presentation

Your manager has been asked to create a special presentation on how your department supports other departments in your medical services company. Unfortunately, several weeks have passed and your manager has not been able to spend the necessary time to make significant progress on the presentation. The presentation date is fast approaching and your manager is getting stressed. Do you think your manager would welcome unsolicited, creative ideas and assistance, along with a thoughtful plan to get things done? You bet!

> Everything you learn on your job, any help you give others, moves you forward.

As these situations show, it's important to gain a better understanding of the objectives, challenges, and issues facing your manager. Then you can think about the ideas that could help your manager succeed. When in doubt, start with a relatively small, easy-to-implement suggestion, but start! Don't become one of the many people saying, "Could have, should have, but didn't."

Have Patience with Less-Experienced Managers

There may be times when you find yourself working with a manager who has less experience in a particular field than you do. The individual may be younger than you or have less time on the job than you do. Managers often find themselves in this position because they have good organization and people skills and the company desperately needs someone to fill the position; however, they may lack the technical or hands-on skills that you have.

Some employees choose to resent the less-experienced manager and think, "He isn't even as old as I am—how come he got promoted to manager?" or "No way does she have the experience I have. Why should I do what she says?" Instead of being resentful, consider the situation a learning experience, in which managing upward really becomes an art form.

Clearly, you need to be sensitive to when and how to make a suggestion to a less-experienced manager. You don't want to "tell" him or her what to do—you are not your manager's parent. Nor do you want to sit by and let the individual fail by withholding information that could help your manager succeed. What you need to do is be patient and find ways to "educate" your manager without appearing

Learning   from   Experience
A Perspective from the Working World

Hitting the Mark

Shilah Hunt,
Emergency medical technician

When I started my first job as an EMT, I had a lot of adjusting to do. Being new and meeting the demands of working in an emergency room put me under a lot of pressure. I soon realized that I needed to be patient with myself and with other people to make it on the job. Dealing with patients in crisis puts everyone on edge because you're frantically trying to save someone's life.

I had to get used to coworkers and medical staff using a sharp, demanding tone when they asked for my help. It used to really bug me because I felt they were treating me like some kind of dummy; but now I know they were just trying to take control of an awful situation and make sure the things that needed to get done, got done. I no longer take that kind of behavior personally.

Whenever you work with other people, you have to remember that everyone has their own individual personalities, and you have to accept people for who they are. In hospitals, some people want to take charge and be the heroes, and some want to support and assist others. As a new employee, I had to take the back seat so I wouldn't come across like a know-it-all.

Learning to view my coworkers as team members helped me stay focused on the needs at hand, like saving someone's life, instead of getting caught up in personality issues that didn't really matter. Now when I finish my work, I look around to see if another staff person needs my help. If someone's swamped, I offer to pitch in and help. I want my coworkers to know that I'm

not just concerned about myself—I care about every member of my team.

In any line of work, you have to be able to follow instructions under pressure, but in EMT work it's particularly important because not doing so can result in death. On the job, you constantly face the challenge of meeting deadlines and performance expectations. Sometimes you won't know if you're hitting the mark until your evaluation. But just like in class when you had to figure out what your instructor expected, the same rule applies to supervisors. Don't assume that you know what your boss considers important—ask. Shortly after you've been hired, set up a meeting with your supervisor to find out what's expected of you on the job. Maybe the two of you can put some specific goals on paper so you have something to refer to throughout the year.

As an EMT, I have to be able to prioritize very quickly because a patient's life may be at stake. My first code blue was an epileptic who had a seizure at work, fell and hit his head, and stopped breathing. Following instructions in that situation was essential. I learned that when someone in a position above you asks you to do something, make sure you understand their instructions. Listening well is crucial at these times. When in doubt, I ask questions.

Through my experiences, I've found out that school isn't the only place where intense learning occurs. When I started working at the hospital, I felt overwhelmed because there was so much to remember. It took time to settle into my new job. Now I'm a lot more comfortable. I've gotten to know my coworkers a little better and I understand what my role is at the hospital. My main message to graduates entering the workforce is: Don't be discouraged. Give yourself permission to fail and to learn from your mistakes. After you've been at your job a while, you'll get the hang of it.

superior or condescending. Most importantly, you need to remember that just as your manager can learn things from you, you can learn things from that manager.

Consider it an exchange of talents. You are sharing what you know about processes, equipment, and data with your manager, and your manager is sharing what he or she knows about people, organizations, and goals with you. By viewing your relationship this way, the two of you become collaborators, working together to improve the functioning of your department and the company.

Regardless of your manager's experience, when it comes to managing upward, please realize that your actions or inactions have an effect on your career success and job security. Employees need to move beyond seeing management as a one-way, downhill street. They need to take a deeper responsibility for themselves and the company. You can no longer afford to focus only on your assigned tasks and responsibilities. You need to identify those opportunities, small or large, when you can manage upward and add value to your organization.

Take the Lead

Leadership is an extension of teamwork and innovation. When you act as a leader in a team setting, you develop ideas and promote them. You also take charge of distributing tasks, setting schedules, and monitoring progress. Leaders take initiative and move ahead without direction from others.

What Is Leadership?

Leader, *noun*

an individual who significantly affects the thoughts, feelings, and behaviors of a significant number of individuals
—Dr. Howard Gardner, Professor of Cognition and Education, Harvard Graduate School of Education

Contrary to what you might think, being a **leader** is not about being famous, having a special title and a big salary, or having a lot of power. Being a leader is *not* about being a boss and driving people toward a goal like a herd of cattle. Being a leader *is* about presenting a vision that others can believe in. It's about motivating and inspiring others so they want to do the work required to achieve a goal. It's about guiding others toward a goal by example and creating an environment in which all team members feel actively involved in the entire process. When it comes to leadership, we cannot say it better than Lao Tzu, the Chinese philosopher: "When the best leader's work is done the people say, 'We did it ourselves.'"

How Can You Become an Effective Leader?

If you want to give leadership a try, there are a number of qualities you'll want to develop. These qualities will help you inspire others, keep a team working together, and get things done. Take a look at the list of qualities below and think about which ones you already have and which you need to develop.

Ability to influence. Leaders need to motivate others to embrace their vision. Always present a clear picture of your vision so that people get excited about it and believe it's possible. Use the communication skills you learned about in Chapter 10, especially those dealing with making your message stick.

Exceptional behavior. Leaders need to lead by example. People trust what you do more than what you say, so learn to walk your talk. Demonstrate how to do things instead of simply telling others what to do.

Follow-through skills. Leaders need to deliver on their promises. Strive to meet your deadlines and follow through on your commitments. When your team members know that you will come through when you say you will, they will work even harder.

Positive self-identity. Leaders need to be self-aware. You need to understand both your strengths and your weaknesses. You do not need to be superhuman. You just need to believe in yourself and strive to be the best you can. This means acknowledging when you've made a mistake (you're not perfect), or patting yourself (and your team) on the back when things go well.

Values. Leaders have a core set of values that reflect the team's best interests. Stay true to your values and let them drive your decisions and actions.

Vision. Leaders hold on to their vision of what is possible, even when obstacles arise. Continue to share your vision with the team—make it as real as possible. The belief in this vision will inspire the team to keep going, even when the going gets tough.

Being a leader means being visible, which means you often get more acknowledgment than the rest of the team. But it also means being responsible and accountable. When things go wrong, you need to accept responsibility and help your team get back on track. Whether you lead from up front, from behind, or prefer to work in the trenches, remember this: Focus on what you do best and realize that those merits will seem as valuable to your managers as those of a leader.

Your Rights as an Employee

In the United States, you are entitled to certain rights, privileges, and protections as an employee. Become aware of them so you know what you deserve and when your rights are being violated.

Right to a Contract

When you take a job, you are participating in an exchange: You trade your services for a combination of monetary compensation and benefits from the hiring company. The company must provide you a contract so that the details of the trade are clear to both parties. Read your contract thoroughly before signing, and be sure to keep a copy for yourself. You have a right to a contract that spells out your title, job duties, and responsibilities in general terms, as well as your salary and pay schedule, benefits you are to receive, and any perks such as free parking or reduced-price lunches in the cafeteria.

Right to Work without Discrimination

Your company is prohibited from discriminating in hiring, treatment, or promotion based on race, creed, color, national origin, age, gender, marital status, arrest records, potential or actual pregnancy, or potential or actual illness or disability (unless the illness or disability prevents you from performing the required tasks). If you feel that you have been denied a job or promotion for any of these reasons, then your rights may have been infringed. You can address the problem with your superiors, and if that doesn't settle the issue to your satisfaction, you may consult a lawyer. Legal procedures require patience, time, and often a great deal of money. Evaluate your options and decide if it's worthwhile before you proceed.

Right to Work without Sexual Harassment

You have a right to a workplace free of sexual harassment. Both men and women can be victims of sexual harassment, although the most common situation involves a woman subjected to harassment by a man. Sexual harassment covers a wide range of behavior that has been divided into two types.

Quid pro quo harassment. This refers to a request for some kind of sexual favor in exchange for something else. It is a type of bribe or threat. The employee is told something along these lines: "If you don't do X for me, then I will fire you, or refuse to promote you, or create problems for you at work."

Hostile environment harassment. This refers to any situation where sexually charged remarks, behavior, or items in the workplace cause discomfort for an employee. This type of harassment covers a wide range of complaints such as lewd conversation or jokes, inappropriate physical contact, or pornography in the office.

It is difficult to clearly define what constitutes sexual harassment. That definition is mainly up to the individual who suffers from it. If you take offense, feel degraded, or feel exploited by anything that goes on at your workplace, you are a victim of sexual harassment and have a right to speak up and address the problem. Solutions range from a simple discussion with colleagues to clarify standards of behavior, all the way to a trip to court. Start small to save yourself as much trouble as possible. If you feel comfortable doing so, talk directly to the person who harassed you. If you cannot speak directly to the individual involved due to fear or discomfort, approach your manager, or speak with another manager if your own manager is the problem. At best, the person who offended you has no idea how the behavior affected you, and needs to understand what behavior is offensive and off limits, and why. At worst, the person has dishonorable intentions toward you and needs to be reprimanded or fired.

As with responding to illegal questions during an interview, reporting sexual harassment at work is neither simple nor easy. Many people neglect to

Sound Bite

Don't let a situation go far. I had a male boss who continuously asked me out and even called me at home. I always said no to him, but one day he brushed up against me. I thought he did it on purpose and it made me feel uncomfortable. So I talked to someone above my boss. After that, he and another manager met with my boss to discuss the problem I was experiencing, and the problem stopped. Even though I was nervous, I am glad I reported my feelings of being sexually harassed. I am also glad that I work for an employer that will not tolerate this type of behavior.

—L. Mercado

address problems at work for fear they will lose their jobs or jeopardize their chances for advancement. Some feel that others will not believe them and that revealing what has occurred will cause them to lose respect. Unfortunately, victims of sexual harassment who do not report the event often damage their own self-respect, which can be extremely painful. Or, their unwillingness to speak up paves the way for others to suffer as they have.

All companies should have a zero-tolerance policy toward sexual harassment. This type of harassment is particularly insidious because it so seriously erodes self-esteem and damages the individual. If you have been sexually harassed, think over your situation before reporting the incident. Make sure you document the date(s) it occurred, who was involved, and what happened. Then ask yourself: How extensive was it? Do you have regular contact with this person at work? Is the individual putting you in danger? Armed with your information, report the incident. You may also need to talk to a counselor outside the company, someone who specializes in sexual harassment. This will allow you to work through your own feelings about it, and move from being a victim to being a survivor.

 ## Now You Try It: Tough Times on the Job

Think about the part-time and full-time jobs you've held over the years while you were in school or after you left school.

1. Did you ever have a job in which you felt discriminated against?

   a. What was the situation and why did you feel that way?

   b. What did you eventually do?

   c. Knowing what you know now, would you have handled anything differently?

2. Did you ever have a job in which you were sexually harassed?

   a. What was the situation and why did you feel that way?

   b. What did you eventually do?

   c. Knowing what you know now, would you have handled anything differently?

Going for the Promotion

When you know your rights as employee and strive for excellence, it's only natural to seek a promotion. There are a number of reasons for this. Perhaps you want to expand your responsibilities or be challenged by the duties a higher position offers. Maybe you desire the salary increase that usually accompanies a promotion. Perhaps you anticipate the feelings of progress and achievement that come from being promoted.

There are also a number of reasons why a company would want to promote you. Your company may decide that your skills and talents would be more useful in a higher position, that you are ready for more of a challenge, or the company structure may be changing—perhaps someone left a position above you, and promoting you will aid in the shift of jobs and responsibilities.

There are three parts to the formula of being worthy of promotion: (1) your seniority and education, (2) your ability to keep pace with your current job, and (3) your willingness to go beyond bottom-line requirements.

1. **Seniority and education.** At any moment, the fact exists that you have worked for the company for a certain period of time and have a certain type and level of education. These factors come into play for a promotion, but they cannot act alone. For example, even if you have been with a company for five years and you have a few impressive degrees, you won't automatically be promoted if your skills and thinking aren't up to par.

2. **Keeping pace.** You won't be considered for a higher, different, or more complex position until you perform well at your present duties. When you have shown that you are capable of handling your current responsibilities with ease and control, your superiors will consider advancing you.

3. **Willingness to go beyond.** No company considers you for a promotion unless you are willing to go beyond the bottom-line requirements of your job. Three qualities that can propel you through the ranks are dedication (willing to go the extra mile), **initiative** (being a self-starter), and creativity (coming up with new ideas).

However, no matter how hardworking, innovative, or creative you are, employers don't like to risk promoting someone who may leave the company on a moment's notice. They value loyalty as well. If you intend to work toward a promotion, make it clear to those around you that you are happy at your job and intend to continue your association with the company. If they see that you honestly mean to stick around for a while and they value your contributions, they will be more likely to make sure your happiness continues.

Be the person who asks for the promotion, not the one who waits for it.

Initiative, *noun*

the characteristic of originating new ideas or methods; the ability to think and act without being urged

 ## Now You Try It: Moving Up

Most people enjoy getting raises or promotions, but few actively pursue them. Consider the various jobs you have held. This mini-activity will help you think about what you might want to do differently (or the same) when seeking a raise or promotion in the future.

1. Did you ever feel that you deserved a raise or promotion?
2. If so, which of the following actions did you take to make yourself promotable?
   a. Took initiative
   b. Went the extra mile
   c. Was creative
   d. Was loyal and dedicated
3. Did you ask for the raise or promotion? Why or why not?
   a. If you did ask for it, what approach did you take?
   b. Did you receive the raise or promotion? Why or why not?
4. What might you do differently in the future?

Changing Jobs

Part of your career evolution involves endings as well as beginnings. Sometimes you have to end one job to move on to an even better one. In fact, more and more working people are changing jobs in the course of their careers. As of 2010, the average stay at one job was approximately three to five years.[3]

People change jobs for lots of reasons. The instability of the economy is one factor; the downsizing and merging of companies has resulted in shifting and reducing job opportunities. With many two-career households, parents change jobs as their financial needs and time commitments to their children change. Increased self-awareness leads many people to seek new jobs as their needs change and different desires and talents surface. People also change jobs to improve their working conditions (location, salary, staff, hours, opportunity for advancement, or benefits).

People also leave their jobs because they want to escape certain people, tasks, or surroundings. The desire to escape is probably the most dangerous reason for leaving. If you don't address issues at one job and instead try to run away from them, you may find yourself dealing with the very same issues at your next job. We will address this further later.

Think through all the options carefully if you are considering a job change. Apply your critical thinking skills. If you seek a better salary, are you willing to give up the great rapport you have with your current coworkers? Will the money you save by working closer to home offset a loss of benefits? Are you sure you have a better chance of being promoted elsewhere, or are you taking too big of a chance? Weigh all the factors before making your decision.

Resignations

You've decided to leave. Now what? A resignation is the most desirable way to go because you are in control. You have made the decision to leave based on the evaluation of your needs:

- Opportunity elsewhere
- Life change (impending parenthood, illness, or a move to a new location)
- Boredom or dissatisfaction with the job
- Trouble in the workplace (discrimination, conflict with supervisors or coworkers)

Obviously, it's much more pleasant to resign because you found a better opportunity at another company or have a positive life change on the horizon. Other times, it may become necessary to extricate yourself from a job due to some problem. If a problem at work is hindering your performance and you feel you may be fired, you can take the reins by resigning first. That way you have taken control of the situation and aren't subject to someone else's decision. With this strategy you can avoid having a firing on your record; a resignation always looks more favorable.

When you decide to resign, you have three important tasks:

1. Schedule a meeting with your manager. This is where you diplomatically lay out your reasons for wanting to leave. Be as calm and kind as possible. If you are leaving because of a problem at work, don't spend time ranting about what other people on the job did to make your life miserable. Concentrate on your feelings and the effect the problem has had on you. Who knows? Your manager might come up with a solution or will at least become aware of the problem and prevent it from happening to someone else.

2. Give adequate notice of your departure. A two-week notice is standard, but you may want to announce your leaving up to a month in advance if you can plan that far ahead. Giving notice allows your employer time to find a replacement for you before you leave. It is a courteous and proper gesture.

Depending on the situation, your manager may try to convince you to stay. Carefully consider any offers, and make sure that your needs are being addressed if you decide to stick around. For example, if you are leaving because you need to make more money, an offer of a salary increase may allow you to stay. On the other hand, if you want to transfer to another department to

---

[3]Germond, Nancy. "Risk management includes managing talent." *All Business,* June 25, 2010. Accessed on February 5, 2011, from www.allbusiness.com/company-activities-management/management-risk-management/14697997-1.html

Figure 11.5 Sample resignation letter

Jeremy Baker
179 Briarwood Dr.
Park City, KS 67219
jbaker@comcast.net (316) 744-1112
May 1, 2011

Dear Ms. Taylor,

I am writing to inform you that I will be leaving my position with LaRue's Groomers, effective June 1. I will be taking a grooming position at Plains Veterinary Services in Witchita.

I have appreciated being a part of the grooming team these last 2 years and enjoyed all the pets I worked with, as well as their "parents." You gave me a chance to learn how much I enjoy animals, and how much they like me.

I have put together a short training document for my replacement and will be happy to train him or her. Please let me know if there is anything else I can do to make this transition a smooth one.

Sincerely,

Jeremy Baker

get away from a problem coworker, but that isn't possible, you might want to resist pressure to stay. If the company values your contribution, they will do whatever they can to keep you. It's up to you to decide if the company's terms are acceptable to you.

3. Write your letter of resignation. Many companies may require your resignation in writing. However, even if they don't, it is polite to write a letter and give it to your manager or the human resources department (do not email it). This letter will be included in your employment file and could be shared with future employers. Be careful of what you write. Keep it short, positive, and professional, covering these main points:

1. The fact that you are leaving

2. When you are leaving

3. Thanks to your employer for the opportunity the company has given you

4. A positive closing

Try to avoid talking about why you are resigning, how you feel about it, or what you think about other employees.

A sample resignation letter appears in Figure 11.5. Notice how Jeremy offers to help train his replacement. This is not necessary, but some people offer because they genuinely want to help out their company.

Try to leave on the best possible terms. You never know when you will encounter your managers and coworkers again in your career. Do what you can to instill a positive impression, and it may help you in the future.

Embracing Change

Job changes are just part of the constant cycle of change that exists in life. In biology, there's a term called *dynamic equilibrium* that describes a living system in which everything appears stable, but in actuality everything is changing. It's just that the rate of loss equals the rate of gain, so things appear somewhat constant. As long as the changes continue the system is alive, but when the changes stop the system dies. We should all take a lesson from biology and realize that life equals change—nothing is constant in the world, nothing stays the same. Change is necessary for us to keep on living.

As you move through life you will find constant change in the outside world and within yourself. Some of the changes you will like; others may disturb you. One thing is certain: With change comes continued learning and greater wisdom.

The world is changing and we need to change with it. Just think of how the following changes affect employment and careers:

- Technology is changing the world. Even Microsoft, with dominant resources and market position, had to radically shift its strategy and is now competing fiercely with Google and others for success in the world of the Internet.

- Global competition is intensifying. Car companies like General Motors, Ford, and Chrysler are still learning their lessons that the world goes beyond the borders of the United States.

- Demographic shifts and fundamental changes in the ethnicity of our population pose opportunities and peril. Baby Boomers make up a large percentage of our population, yet mismanagement of mutual funds and stocks have cost them billions of dollars in potential retirement money. Instead of leaving the job market, many aging boomers now find themselves job hunting again because their retirement funds are dwindling. Still, many businesses have not recognized the change in demographics or the growing diversity of our population. Some businesses are struggling because they aren't taking advantage of the pool of older, experienced workers at their disposal. Others are struggling because their customers have changed, yet the companies have not adjusted their products or modified their services to meet the changing needs of their customers.

The forces of change, including technology, global competition, shifts in demographics, and ethnicity, make it difficult for businesses and employees to maintain their effectiveness and relevance in the workplace.

As an employee, you need to ask yourself: "How can I create or sustain success under these circumstances?" Although the answer to this question varies with the circumstances of the employee, here are some general ideas to consider as you formulate your game plan.

1. **Extend your antenna to identify the early signs of change.** Take an inward view and assess your performance and the condition of your company. Then look outside your organization to identify and monitor how technology, global competition, and shifts in demographics or ethnicity are likely to affect your position and your employer.

2. **Periodically take time to reflect on the forces of change.** It's important to understand the consequences of change on your circumstances. As you wade through constantly changing issues and deadlines at work, it's easy to forget to take time to simply sit and think about things—to assess, reflect, and plan. Yet, only by doing so will you become a proactive employee rather than someone who simply reacts to your environment.

3. **Be open to innovation and change.** Embrace change as good. View change as an opportunity for personal development and a chance to help your employer in new ways. Adjusting to change takes awareness and effort. Learning new skills and changing old habits requires time and commitment. Successful employees identify, embrace, and adapt to change. Mediocre employees wait until it's too late and then react badly to change, often putting their jobs at risk.

Stay open to change, in and out of the workplace. Look at each shift of gears and decide what you can learn from it. Even tough changes have valuable lessons inside, crystallized like diamonds inside black coal. Your priorities may adjust, work may become more crucial, or family time may take the lead. Your current goals may fade and new ones take their place. Your needs might flip-flop, and your life may take turns you never imagined. Anticipate change so that you can make the most of it in your own life.

Contributing to the Health of Your World

Your job is more than just dealing with change and getting a salary. The benefits of working go far beyond a paycheck. When you are doing something you enjoy, it stimulates your thoughts and interests. When you work to continually improve your skills and abilities, those good feelings carry over into your personal life. Conversely, when you are unhappy at work, that experience will spill over into other areas of your life. A work experience that fulfills you helps give your life meaning and provides a feeling of success.

However, success is not just about work. Although it sometimes feels like it, work does not make up your whole life. True success comes from a balance of your career, your personal life, and your social life.

Your personal life means your friends and family. Your social life, however, means something different than you might think. We don't mean parties and dating; we mean activities that benefit society as a whole. In these days of social troubles and a shrinking world, we see problems in our neighborhoods and in distant countries that affect our lives in a powerful way. When this happens, we want to understand why we're here on the earth and what we can do to make a difference. That's where volunteering comes into play—making a contribution to those in need.

Volunteering for a Better World

How can you make a contribution? Some people choose to give money, and that certainly helps. Writing a quick check to a charity seems like an easy way to contribute, but many of us don't have money to spare. Your time and effort are sometimes more appreciated than money. Though making financial donations to charities is certainly noble and helpful, sending money off in the mail (or over the Internet) prevents you from encountering the people you might be helping. You don't have the benefit of performing an action and seeing its effects, however small.

When you help someone in person, you donate time, which is your most valuable resource. When money goes, you can make more; when a minute goes, it is gone forever. The value of direct human contact is that people see that you care, and you see first hand how you have helped. When you make an effort to improve life for someone less fortunate, you derive a deep sense of satisfaction.

If giving your time and energy to others is a priority for your life, you can weave it into both your work and your personal life. Is there a group from your company that tutors at a school? Can your company designate a volunteer project in which employees can participate—such as visiting a nursing home or a children's hospital, cleaning up a neighborhood, or developing a community garden? Whoever organizes the activities can schedule them so they use work time, personal time, or a little of both. If you volunteer on your own personal time, you can later bring some of your coworkers in on the job.

Volunteering can be a very rewarding activity that brings joy and satisfaction into your life and the lives of others.

These days, companies are realizing that they have to pitch in and do their part to improve the world, whether that means donating money, energy, or time. Whether you contribute on your own or take part in company-sponsored volunteering, you help the company fulfill its goal of lending a helping hand or two. Believe it or not, many employers look for community involvement and a spirit of cooperation when they evaluate potential employees. A person who volunteers displays an understanding of how caring for and helping each other makes a difference. That may impress a potential employer.

What Can You Do, and When?

How can you go about putting your energy toward making the world a better place? Many efforts need your helping hands. Some are independent and some are affiliated with religious groups, hospitals, or other national organizations. You might find an opportunity to serve food in a homeless shelter or read to disadvantaged children. You might visit elderly patients in nursing homes or in their homes, or work with

individuals with disabilities of many ages. You might volunteer with organizations attempting to bring affordable healthcare to communities. You might even pitch in with cleaning, gardening, or building efforts in run-down or damaged neighborhoods.

One more question arises: How do you find the time to volunteer? It isn't always easy. So many things compete for your time; however, you can make volunteering one of your priorities, just like exercising, recreation, or family time. In fact, you can often combine more than one of these elements with volunteering. You might get great exercise from a community cleaning or painting project. You might take your whole family to a nursing home to sing songs and talk with some of the residents. It takes a little bit of thought, but you can successfully work the gift of your time into your other activities. For all that you give, you get the satisfaction of knowing you made someone else's life a little bit brighter.

 Now You Try It: Helping Out

We hope that most of you have tried volunteering at least once in your life, and hopefully more times than that. This mini-activity should help you better identify skills you could share with others and areas in which you might volunteer.

1. Please answer these three general questions:

   a. What do you feel are your greatest skills?
   b. What are you interested in outside of work?
   c. What are your concerns outside of work?

2. If you are already volunteering, please answer these questions; otherwise, skip to question #3.

   a. What types of organizations do you currently volunteer with?
   b. What do you do?
   c. How many hours per week or month do you volunteer? Would you like to increase or decrease your hours? Why?
   d. Do you like what you do and does it use your skills? If not, what would you rather do?

3. If you are not happy in your current volunteer capacity, or are not currently volunteering, please answer the following questions:

   a. What types of organizations address some of your interests and concerns?
   b. What do you think you could do for these organizations using your skills?
   c. How can you find out the names of specific organizations where you might want to volunteer? Who should you talk to?
   d. How many hours per week or month do you think you could realistically volunteer?

Your Career Tool Kit—Don't Leave Home Without It

Although this book is coming to an end, your learning doesn't stop with the last page. We hope it will never stop! If you take one lesson from this entire text, let it be that learning is a never-ending, lifelong process. Just as your career tools will serve you throughout your life, so will your greatest tool—your brain—if you continue to challenge it and present it with new information and questions to contemplate.

By now, you probably realize that the only real job security comes from being secure in yourself: your skills, talents, experience, and resourcefulness. Ultimately, your ability to remain employed comes from within. The more secure you are in yourself, the more secure you are in your job. *You* are your own employment security!

To help you realize just how marketable you are, let's look back at the list of universal work skill categories identified in Chapter 1. With continued work, you can show your future employers that you have a high level of proficiency and willingness to learn and progress in each category: interpersonal, information, systems, technology, basic skills, thinking skills, personal qualities, and resources. The successes of conscientious workers such as yourself will help strengthen the economy of the entire nation; your personal success will impact the nation's success.

You have a great collection of tools in your tool kit, but tools are only the means to an end. Use them to build, expand, and renovate your knowledge and skills. There is no limit to what you can do, learn, and know. School is not just a place where you stop learning when you walk out the door. School is also where you learn how to learn; it is a springboard to lifelong learning.

Think of life as a hallway with an infinite number of doors on both walls. Imagine yourself walking past door after door. You have the keys to open some doors and explore what lies beyond them, but you don't have the keys to open them all. As you continue to learn and grow, you gain the keys you need to open other doors that lead to fresh opportunities. With a changing and growing mind, you will know how to use old tools to access new areas of knowledge each time you open a new door.

You now have the most important and valuable gifts to offer the world, inside and outside the workplace: yourself and everything that you do. Remember how important you are. You are part of the whole, part of all of us working together to improve life on earth. So use your tool kit to build a successful, bright future for yourself and the world!

Your Tool Kit at Work

11.1 Knowing How to Work Productively

As you move into the workplace, take your how-to-learn skills with you. Workplace know-how makes it easy to perform effectively. The more you know how to learn, the more quickly and efficiently you can adapt to the changes you encounter at work each day. That adaptability is one of your most valuable tools.

1. Review your skills here and circle the number that most closely fits your present skill level. Total your score at the end.

Statement	Rarely	Sometimes	Often	Almost Always
1. I have a regular place to work and store my supplies.	1	2	3	4
2. I schedule my hardest tasks at work to correspond to when I am most alert.	1	2	3	4
3. I plan my work time and set priorities with a to-do list.	1	2	3	4
4. I read information about the company and my field.	1	2	3	4
5. I read directions carefully and follow them step-by-step.	1	2	3	4
6. When I read, I underline, highlight, or take notes.	1	2	3	4

(continued)

Statement	Rarely	Sometimes	Often	Almost Always
7. I ask myself questions on what I just read.	1	2	3	4
8. I look up unknown words in the dictionary.	1	2	3	4
9. I work when I am scheduled.	1	2	3	4
10. I come to work early.	1	2	3	4
11. I listen intently to my supervisor and coworkers.	1	2	3	4
12. I keep a notebook for work notes.	1	2	3	4
13. I take notes on my assignments, directions I'm given, and meetings I attend.	1	2	3	4
14. I know how to determine the key points made in a meeting or by my manager.	1	2	3	4
15. I take breaks and a lunch hour to relax.	1	2	3	4
16. I write assignments in my manager's exact words.	1	2	3	4
17. I review my notes as I work to make sure I understand.	1	2	3	4
18. I perform the priority items on my to-do list first.	1	2	3	4
19. During a meeting or discussion, I contribute with my ideas and suggestions.	1	2	3	4
20. I proofread.	1	2	3	4
21. My concentration is good; I am able to focus on my work.	1	2	3	4
22. I know and use methods to help my memory.	1	2	3	4
23. I review my work to make sure I'm up to date.	1	2	3	4
24. I ask questions if I don't understand.	1	2	3	4
25. I reward myself when I complete a difficult assignment.	1	2	3	4
26. I dress appropriately and present a well-groomed appearance.	1	2	3	4
27. I don't spend work time gossiping and complaining about the company, the supervisors, or the coworkers.	1	2	3	4

Statement	Rarely	Sometimes	Often	Almost Always
28. I check my work before I submit it.	1	2	3	4
29. I spend more time working than I do worrying about the work.	1	2	3	4
30. I know I am the only person responsible for how well I work.	1	2	3	4
TOTALS:				
GRAND TOTAL:				

- **110–120 points:** Congratulations! You have excellent work skills. Keep working on making your skills even better.
- **100–109 points:** You have good work skills. Look at the **Rarely** or **Sometimes** statements and try new hints to achieve excellence in those areas.
- **90–99 points:** You have average work skills. Search for similarities in the **Rarely** and **Sometimes** skills. Then make changes in the habits that hold you back in those areas. If you do so, you'll do better in school and feel more confident in your career.
- **Below 90:** Your skills have weaknesses that may cause you difficulty at work. Find your potential by reviewing and building these how-to-work skills.

11.2 The Bill of Rights and Responsibilities

You are currently a student and probably also an employee. As a student you listen to your teachers, and on the job you report to a manager. Your duties at work often include treating customers well and communicating clearly. What are your rights in different work circumstances? What are your responsibilities? What are the rights and responsibilities of your instructors, employers, and customers?

In every situation, all the people involved have both rights and responsibilities. The two Rs go hand in hand. When one person has a right, the same person or another person has a responsibility to uphold that right. To develop open, assertive relationships with others on the job, pay attention to the responsibility that correlates to each right. The following table contains a list of key rights and their related responsibilities.

	Rights		Responsibilities
1.	The right to be treated with respect.	1.	The responsibility to treat others with respect.
2.	The right to be treated with friendliness and a smile.	2.	The responsibility to treat others with friendliness and a smile.
3.	The right to be heard.	3.	The responsibility to listen.
4.	The right to express ideas.	4.	The responsibility to allow freedom of expression.
5.	The right to have your ideas considered.	5.	The responsibility to consider the ideas of others.
6.	The right to say no when something can't be done.	6.	The responsibility to say no when something can't be done.
7.	The right to not feel guilty about saying no.	7.	The responsibility to not let guilt get in the way of saying no.
8.	The right to make mistakes.	8.	The responsibility to learn from mistakes.
9.	The right to receive praise as well as criticism.	9.	The responsibility to praise as well as to criticize.
10.	The right to feel angry.	10.	The responsibility to handle anger and resolve conflicts appropriately.

Study the following situations. For each, decide who has what responsibility and who has what right. One person can have more than one right or responsibility.

- Enter the right and responsibility numbers in the spaces provided.
- Check with your instructor for possible answers.

Situation 1: Maggie and Elise

Maggie's supervisor, Elise, discovered an error that Maggie made in a report she turned in.

Rights

The right to _____ belongs to _____

The right to _____ belongs to _____

The right to _____ belongs to _____

The right to _____ belongs to _____

Responsibilities

The responsibility _____ to belongs to _____

The responsibility _____ to belongs to _____

The responsibility _____ to belongs to _____

The responsibility _____ to belongs to _____

Situation 2: Frank and Henley

Frank has a new idea about the repair procedure he and his coworker, Henley, have been following. If they implement it, it would require some shifting of duties between Frank and Henley.

Rights

The right to _____ belongs to _____

The right to _____ belongs to _____

The right to _____ belongs to _____

The right to _____ belongs to _____

Responsibilities

The responsibility _____ to belongs to _____

The responsibility _____ to belongs to _____

The responsibility _____ to belongs to _____

The responsibility _____ to belongs to _____

Situation 3: Claudia and Mark

Claudia left work early four times in the last two weeks. She asks Mark, her manager, if she can do so again today. He needs to reach a certain goal by the end of today, and the task assigned to Claudia is essential to that goal. She has not yet completed her task.

Rights

The right to _____ belongs to _____

The right to _____ belongs to _____

The right to _____ belongs to _____

The right to _____ belongs to _____

Responsibilities

The responsibility to _____ belongs to _____

The responsibility to _ _____ belongs to _____

The responsibility to _____ belongs to _____

The responsibility to _____ belongs to _____

11.3 Stylish Decisions

We all make decisions, but what's your decision-making style? Apply your intelligence, experience, and intuition to the following questions.

- Check the column that fits your style.
- Put a (+) by the ideas you'd like to develop.
- Put a (−) by those you plan to eliminate.

I Make Decisions:	Mostly	Sometimes	Rarely
1. After I look at alternatives.			
2. Quickly without looking at alternatives.			
3. By turning over the control to someone else.			
4. And blame others when the decision turns out badly.			
5. Easily.			
6. Slowly, while agonizing over them.			
7. Using my feelings and intuition.			
8. That are usually disastrous.			
9. And usually view them as correct.			
10. Myself, but I ask others their opinions before making the final decision.			
11. Without anyone else's input.			
12. While considering the needs of others.			
13. After a preliminary test of my decision.			
14. And take responsibility for the outcome.			
15. And try another plan if my decision doesn't work.			

No particular style is correct. What's right is what works for you, as long as you take responsibility for the decision, stay aware of alternatives, and change your plan if your decision doesn't work.

Here's an exercise to guide your decision making, no matter what your style. It will help everyone from the methodical planner to the quick and intuitive decision maker.

Take a career decision you have pending. The decision may involve which job to apply for, which job to accept, where you want to live, or what requirements you can compromise to get a job offer. If you're still in school, you may be wrestling with decisions dealing with switching majors, getting a part-time job, or perhaps moving back with your parents while you finish school.

1. State the issue that requires making a decision.

_____

_____

_____

2. The options are:

a.

_____

b.

_____

c.

_____

d.

_____

3. For each option, list the pros and cons. Number pros and cons in order of importance (1 = most important, 2 = somewhat important, 3 = not that important).

Option	Pro	Con
a.		
b.		
c.		
d.		

4. The result:

a. Which options have more positives than negatives?

_____

b. Which have more *important* positives than negatives?

_____

c. Which option is the best decision right now?

_____

5. Go ahead and act on the decision that you so carefully made. Commit to it and see how it goes. Remember, no decision has to be final, although every decision has its consequences. Life is full of choices and changes.

11.4 Plug Your Knowledge into Real Life

Volunteering is an excellent way to help others, make a difference in the world, get experience, and network. This exercise allows you to apply what you've learned about decision making to help another person make a wise decision, and to help you do the same.

1. Read this passage and decide how to best advise Gloria.

   Gloria is a graduate of Cutting Edge Cosmetology School. She works at Cut-Ups in the afternoons and evenings. Her husband, Gus, works the early shift as a medical assistant at Stuart Hospital, and Gloria has time to volunteer weekday mornings and any time on Monday, her day off.

   Gloria is trying to figure out how to use her volunteer time. Her husband, Gus, is a member of Alcoholics Anonymous (AA), as is Gloria's father. A homeless shelter just called her. Both the Rape Crisis Center and the Suicide Hotline could use help.

   Gloria is confused about where to volunteer and how much time to give. She is interested in assisting at AA, ACOA (Adult Children of Alcoholics), and the crisis center. She also thinks she may want to volunteer with immigrants who are learning English. Gloria's family is from Chile. She learned to read and speak English starting in the fifth grade through the ESL (English as a second language) program.

   Gloria has quite a bit of housework to do during her time off and knows she only has time for one activity per week. How can she make a decision?

   Using the decision-making skills you've learned in this chapter, apply the principle that we do our best volunteer work in areas where we have had personal experience.

   a. Where would you advise Gloria to volunteer?

   _____

   b. How can she arrive at the best decision?

   _____

   _____

   _____

2. Now let's think about volunteering activities for you.

   a. Where are you most interested in volunteering in your locale?

   _____

   b. Where would you be of greatest help?

   _____

   c. How much time can you devote to volunteering while still maintaining the rest of your responsibilities?

   _____

   d. If you don't currently have extra time, what are some other ways you can help others without endangering your commitments to school, work, and your personal life?

   _____

   _____

   _____

11.5 Technology Exercise

The Internet is full of good advice for getting promotions, job changes, and more. Some of that advice comes in the form of articles, and some comes in the form of YouTube videos. Watching a video is sometimes useful because you get to see and hear real people talking about their experiences, not just read words.

1. To get you interested in searching Youtube.com for helpful videos, here are a few you might be interested in.

   - How to ask for a raise: www.youtube.com/watch?v=nOYz_ZTKy0I

   - How to ask for a raise in a difficult economy: www.youtube.com/watch?v=3QfJUSX2mV0

   - How to know when to quit your job: www.youtube.com/watch?v=bd_Te7-ZMO8&feature=channel

   - How to find a job during a recession: www.youtube.com/watch?v=5kq7-47yz7Y

2. Now, use the search field in YouTube to search for videos on any of the topics we've covered in this chapter. Happy hunting!